DATE DUE

~~JUL 23~~			
DEC 8 '75	MAR 21 '90		
~~SEP 25 76~~	APR 18 '90		
~~AP 2 6 77~~			
~~NO 6 78~~	JAN 0 '93		
~~78~~	RTD DEC 14 92		
~~OC 8 79~~			
~~OC 22 79~~	DEC 27 '93		
~~NOV 8 79~~			
~~FE 1 2 79~~ RTD DEC 1 1 93			
~~FE 27 80~~			
~~MR 1 7 80~~			
~~MR 3 1 80~~			
~~AP 1 4 80~~			
~~80~~			
~~OC 1 2 '80~~			
~~OC 2 8 '80~~			
~~APR 2 1994~~			

| | |

Mainstream of America Series

EDITED BY LEWIS GANNETT

THE
ANGRY SCAR

THE
ANGRY SCAR

The Story of Reconstruction

HODDING CARTER

GREENWOOD PRESS, PUBLISHERS
WESTPORT, CONNECTICUT

Library of Congress Cataloging in Publication Data

Carter, Hodding, 1907-1972.
    The angry scar; the story of reconstruction.

    Reprint of ed. published by Doubleday, Garden
City, N. Y., in series: Mainstream of America series.
    Bibliography: p.
    1. Reconstruction. I. Title.
[E668.C3 1974]   973.8   73-10751
ISBN 0-8371-7022-2

Originally published in 1959 by Doubleday & Company, Inc.,
New York

Reprinted with the permission of Doubleday & Company

Reprinted in 1973 by Greenwood Press,
a division of Williamhouse-Regency Inc.

Library of Congress Catalogue Card Number 73-10751

ISBN 0-8371-7022-2

Printed in the United States of America

To

JANE *and* WILLIAM RANSOM HOGAN

for reasons lost to history

Acknowledgments

THIS work is essentially an interpretive synthesis of a considerable body of writing on the Reconstruction period. During its preparation I experienced eye trouble severe enough to have far longer postponed or even prevented its completion had it not been for four persons: my wife, Betty Werlein Carter, Josephine Davis Haxton, and Elizabeth Calvert, to whom I am indebted for the research that I was unable to complete personally, and my secretary, Ione Boudreaux Lundy, who mastered the unfamiliar task of transcribing from recording discs many of the notes and all three drafts of this book.

I am also happy to acknowledge the invaluable assistance of Dr. William Ransom Hogan, Chairman of the History Department of Tulane University; Lewis Gannett, the knowledgeable editor of the Mainstream of America Series, Ben Wasson of Greenville, and Arna Bontemps, librarian of Fisk University.

While I am reluctant to single out for especial recognition any of the scholars from whose works I have so freely borrowed, it seems only fitting that I should cite those who have been most valuable to me. They are: Dr. C. Vann Woodward, whose *The Strange Career of Jim Crow, Reunion and Reaction,* and *Origins of the New South* cast much light in dark corners; Dr. Benjamin Botkin, whose compilation of the old W.P.A. Writers' Project interviews with former slaves, *Lay My Burden Down,* was the source of the slave quotations appearing throughout this book; Dr. E. Merton Coulter, for his many-faceted *The South During Reconstruction;* Paul H. Buck, for the trail-blazing *The Road to Reunion;* Francis Butler Simkins, for his *The South Old and New;* George Fort Milton, for *The Age of Hate;* and Robert Selph Henry, for the encyclopedic *The Story of Reconstruction.* To these and many another go this unscholarly poacher's thanks.

Foreword

Reconstruction . . .

Spell the word one way, with a small *r*, and it has a good American purposefulness; for it means a putting together, a rebuilding, a rehabilitation. Spell it another way, with a capital *R*, and it becomes for many a malediction; and for others an almost forgotten, unreached, and needful goal; and for still others a vaguely unclean memory. And for some the word Reconstruction was once a high mountain from which they could see Jubilee's free, waiting valley that would turn into a desert's mirage.

Among those who ponder the diverse meanings, differing as to which is the true one, there is one point of agreement. The Reconstruction period—the decade that followed the Civil War—has left an angry scar upon the nation's body politic. Beneath the scar an old wound has not entirely healed.

Reconstruction was intended as a device by which the defeated states of the Southern Confederacy would be joined again to the Union, the more than three million black freedmen living within them absorbed politically and economically in a nation reunited by the force of arms, and safeguards provided against any possible renewal of rebellion. These ends were partially achieved; but Reconstruction also became in fact and in legend something else again.

For more than seventy-five years historians and laymen have disputed the reasons for Reconstruction's failure. They have quarreled over fact and their interpretations of fact. Those who participated in Reconstruction as its architects, those who profited, honestly or dishonestly, those who suffered and those who were remote from it have differed inevitably and profoundly in their accountings. Racial conflict, self-vindication, and passionate partisanship have combined to create and perpetuate the unending argument.

In making this appraisal of the Reconstruction period I have been less concerned with historical sequence than with historical consequence. The chapter content is, with few exceptions, topical rather than chronological.

I have tried to emphasize some aspects of Reconstruction in addition to those which are incorporated in sectional and, in lesser degree, national folklore. I have sought to treat Reconstruction and its immediate aftermath as a part of the American mainstream rather than as apart from it; and my overriding purposes have been to separate truth from myth and to link significant past events with the present legacies of those events. In attempting to do these things I have become convinced that it has been almost as unfortunate for our nation that the North has remembered so little of Reconstruction as that the South has remembered so much.

Contents

BOOK I

*INGREDIENTS
FOR TRAGEDY*

CHAPTER 1

The Mood of the Victor

On the thinly misted night of April 11, 1865, Abraham Lincoln, a lighted candle in his left hand and a prepared speech in his right, waited patiently on the balcony of the White House until the cheers of the serenading throngs and the blaring of the bands behind which they had marched died away. Then he began reading what was to be his last address to his fellow Americans.

Two days before, at Appomattox Court House, Robert E. Lee had surrendered the remnants of the Army of Northern Virginia to Ulysses S. Grant. Two nights hence the President, a posturing madman's bullet in his brain, would be borne unconscious from Ford's Theater to a lodginghouse across the street. His death the next morning would doom the already forlorn hope that the Union would respect the forgiving, realistic, and sometimes expedient border man's plea for a compassionate peace.

To Noah Brooks, the journalist and intimate friend of the Lincoln family, "there was something terrible in the enthusiasm with which the beloved chief magistrate was received. Cheers upon cheers, wave after wave of applause rolled up, the President patiently standing quiet until it was all over." But the later applause with which the serenaders only occasionally punctuated his message lacked the unrestrained quality of their initial greeting. And as he put aside the manuscript the acclaim of the celebrants was not for what he had said but for the nation's victory and for himself. This night the President had spelled out the appeal he had made a week earlier, in his second inaugural address, for malice toward none, for charity for all, for a binding of the nation's wounds. He had resumed, in so doing, the debate that had raged within the Republican party since the war's beginning: *what is to be done to and with and for the Confederate South?* Tonight the prevailing mood of the Union was not merciful. Too much had happened and for too long.

Not logic, not legislative or judicial decision, but the North's superior fire power and manpower and industrial power had answered the doctrines of nullification and secession. Now the eleven Southern states, which believed that these twin principles upon which they had rested their case for states' rights were constitutional, must again become one with the Union they had quitted. What penalties should be meted out? What political devices need be fashioned to re-establish the late Confederate states as part of an indissoluble body politic? Were they to be treated as equals who had not, in reality, left the Union, though they had tried, or as conquered territories which by secession had forfeited statehood? And what of the 3,500,000 freed Negroes whose new status created political and economic and social issues as inflammatory—and almost as basic—as had been the issue of slavery itself?

By candlelight Abraham Lincoln gives his answers. This, he says, is the situation:

"By these recent successes, the re-inauguration of national authority—reconstruction—which has had a large share of our thoughts from the first, is pressed much more closely upon our attention. It is fraught with great difficulty. Unlike a case of war between independent nations, there is no authorized organ for us to treat with—no one man has authority to give up the rebellion for any other man. We simply must begin with and mold from disorganized and discordant elements."

Now the President takes to the people the controversy which has plagued the Union. It is no small embarrassment, he tells the silent listeners, that loyal people differ as to the mode, manner, and measure of Reconstruction. He himself has been attacked. He has been censured for setting up and seeking to sustain the new state government of Louisiana.

The crowd knows about the Louisiana program. It is a much discussed and acrimonious subject. New Orleans and a number of Louisiana's parishes had been occupied by Union troops in 1862. Soon thereafter the President had begun searching for a formula for the reconstruction of a state government for Louisiana. He had subsequently appointed provisional military governors for Louisiana and for Arkansas and Tennessee, which had in turn been overrun. On December 8, 1863, he had announced in a proclamation his Reconstruction plan. Amnesty would be granted, with certain exceptions, to all Southerners who took a prescribed loyalty oath. Executive recognition would be given to civil governments in the Southern states where 10 per cent of the 1860 electorate took the oath of loyalty and where the states agreed to emancipation.

Such governments had been set up in Arkansas and Louisiana before the presidential election of 1864 and in Tennessee and Virginia soon afterward. In 1864 Louisiana and Arkansas had sent representatives to Congress; but a Senate and House of Representatives, hostile to so magnanimous a Reconstruction plan and to what they considered to be a usurpation of legislative function, refused to seat them. Nor were the presidential votes of these two states recognized by Congress in the election of 1864.

Well before then the temper of the congressional majority had become all too evident. Senator Benjamin Franklin Wade of Ohio and Representative Henry Winter Davis of Maryland, two of the most Cromwellian proponents of a hard peace, had sponsored a far more severe program of Reconstruction, notably including a requirement that a majority of the electorate in each Confederate state—rather than Lincoln's 10 per cent—take an oath as to past as well as future loyalty before that state could be restored to the Union. Their bill also made emancipation immediately compulsory, required the repudiation of all Southern war debts, and proscribed a vast number of Confederates. The President pocket-vetoed the bill on July 4, 1864, and its mutinous authors retaliated a month later with what was to be known as the Wade-Davis Manifesto, a scathing public attack in which they accused the President of "a studied outrage on the legislative authority of the people" and declared that in Reconstruction policy Congress was "paramount and must be respected."

In June the President had been renominated at the National Union Convention—a broader-based designation decided upon in the face of strong Democratic challenge—with Andrew Johnson, loyal Democrat of Tennessee, as his running mate. In late summer his political enemies plotted unsuccessfully to call a new convention to reconsider his nomination.

Lincoln himself had thought during the summer that he would be defeated for the presidency, so split were the Republicans and so powerful was the national spirit of pacifism and defeatism.

"It seems exceedingly probable that this administration will not be re-elected," he wrote on August 23. "Then it will be my duty to so co-operate with the president-elect as to save the Union between the election and the inauguration, as he will have secured his election on such ground that he cannot possibly save it afterwards."

On the twenty-ninth of August the Democratic National Convention adopted a resolution of utter defeatism, declaring that "after four years of failure to restore the Union by the experiment of war . . . justice, humanity, liberty, and the public welfare demand that immediate efforts be made for a cessation of hostilities . . . to the end that at the earliest practicable moment, peace may be restored on the basis of the Federal Union of the states."

General George B. McClellan accepted the Democratic nomination, though he repudiated the peace plank. Jefferson Davis haughtily answered a peace feeler with a message to Lincoln that he would receive proposals for peace only on the basis of Southern independence. And then, on September 2, General William Tecumseh Sherman captured Atlanta. The Republicans closed ranks, and on November 8, 1864, four million voters gave Lincoln a majority of 400,000 and 212 of 233 electoral college votes.

But, behind the scenes, the conflict over the reconstruction of the South went on unabated. And so, from the White House balcony two nights be-

fore his assassination, Abraham Lincoln restated his case to the citizens of
Washington, to the United States, and to the South:

"This plan [the Reconstruction proclamation of December 8, 1863] was
in advance submitted to the then cabinet, and distinctly approved by every
member of it. One of them suggested that I should then and in that connection apply the Emancipation Proclamation to theretofore excepted parts
of Virginia and Louisiana; that I should drop the suggestion about apprenticeship for freed people, and that I should omit the protests against my
own power in regard to the admission of members of Congress. But even
he [Salmon P. Chase, onetime Secretary of the Treasury in Lincoln's cabinet
and, during Reconstruction, Chief Justice of the Supreme Court, whom the
plotters had planned to substitute for Lincoln] approved every part and
parcel of the plan. . . . The new constitution of Louisiana, declaring
emancipation for the whole state, practically applies the proclamation to
the part previously excepted. It does not adopt apprenticeship for freed
people, and is silent, as it could not well be otherwise, about the admission
of members to Congress. So that, as it applied to Louisiana, every member
of the cabinet fully approved of the plan. . . .

"We all agree that the seceded states, so called, are out of their proper
practical relation with the Union, and that the sole object of the government,
civil and military, in regard to those states, is to again get them into that
proper practical relation. I believe that it is not only possible, but in fact
easier, to do this without deciding or even considering whether these states
have ever been out of the Union, than with it. Finding themselves safely at
home, it would be utterly immaterial whether they had ever been abroad.
Let us all join in doing the acts necessary to restoring the proper practical
relations between these states and the Union, and each forever after innocently indulge his own opinion whether in doing the acts he brought the
states from without into the Union, or only gave them proper assistance,
they never having been out of it. The amount of constituency, so to speak,
on which the new Louisiana government rests, would be more satisfactory
to all if it contained 40,000 or 30,000, or even 20,000, instead of only
about 12,000, as it does [this was the number of white citizens who had
taken the oath]. It is also unsatisfactory to some that the elective franchise
is not given to the colored man. I would myself prefer that it were now conferred on the very intelligent, and on those who serve our cause as soldiers.

"Still the question is not whether the Louisiana government, as it stands,
is quite all that is desirable. The question is, will it be wiser to take it as it is
and help to improve it, or to reject and disperse it? Can Louisiana be
brought into proper practical relation with the Union sooner by sustaining
or by discarding her new state government? Some 12,000 voters in the
heretofore slave state of Louisiana have sworn allegiance to the Union,
assumed to be the rightful political power of the state, held elections, or-

ganized a state government, adopted a free-state constitution, giving the benefit of public schools equally to black and white, and empowering the legislature to confer the elective franchise upon the colored man. Their legislature has already voted to ratify the constitutional amendment recently passed by Congress, abolishing slavery throughout the nation. These 12,000 persons are thus fully committed to the Union and to perpetual freedom in the state—committed to the very things and nearly all the things the nation wants—and they ask the nation's recognition and its assistance to make good their committal.

"If we reject and spurn them, we do our utmost to disorganize and disperse them. We, in effect, say to the white man: You are worthless or worse; we will neither help you, nor be helped by you. To the blacks, we say: This cup of liberty, which these, your old masters, hold to your lips, we will dash from you, and leave you to the chances of gathering the spilled and scattered contents in some vague and undefined when, where, and how. If this course, discouraging and paralyzing both white and black, has any tendency to bring Louisiana into proper, practical relations with the Union, I have so far been unable to perceive it. If, on the contrary, we recognize and sustain the new government of Louisiana, the converse of all this is made true. We encourage the hearts and nerve the arms of 12,000 to adhere to their work, and argue for it, and proselyte for it, and fight for it, and feed it, and grow it, and ripen it to a complete success. The colored man, too, in seeing all united for him, is inspired with vigilance, and energy, and daring to the same end. Grant that he desires the elective franchise, will he not attain it sooner by serving the already advanced steps toward it, than by running backward over them?

"Concede that the new government of Louisiana is only to what it should be as the egg is to the fowl, we shall sooner have the fowl by hatching the egg than by smashing it."

The President then reminds his hearers that the constitutionality of the Thirteenth Amendment, abolishing slavery, might be involved since the Constitution required its passage by three fourths of the state legislatures.

"Again, if we reject Louisiana, we also reject one vote in favor of the proposed amendment to the national constitution. To meet this proposition it has been argued that no more than three fourths of those states which have not attempted secession are necessary to validly ratify the amendment. I do not commit myself against this further than to say that such a ratification would be questionable, and sure to be persistently questioned, while a ratification by three fourths of all the states would be unquestioned and unquestionable . . ."

The President's calm reasoning and magnanimity is not altogether lost on his hearers. They applaud now and then but their hearts are not in it.

Next day the unfriendly New York *Tribune* reported that the President's speech "fell dead, wholly without effect on the audience" and that "it caused a great disappointment and left a painful impression." Other of the North's newspapers, either more charitable or more accurate, cited applause and close attention. But whatever the feeling of the listeners, there was no doubt about the reaction or the intent of a majority of Congress. Theirs was victorious Rome. To the South lay Carthage.

Not only a hostile Congress intervened between Abraham Lincoln, living and dead, and the adoption of his program for Reconstruction. Behind the hard peace advocates there stood, at the end of the fearsome blood bath, probably a majority of the people of the North. Let us look on this misted April night at a few of the many, in and out of office, whose hearts could not be moved by reason or forgiveness. Some we will meet again at closer hand and more than once. The faceless array of the others formed the chorus of tragedy: those who had suffered and those who sorrowed and those who made capital of woe.

As they had since the first year of the war, maimed, sickly men peddled to the now celebrating populace tales of horror which would multiply purposefully for many a year to come. These pitiful mendicants had a vested interest in keeping alive every fact and fable of Southern abuse of Northern soldiers, especially those who had been taken captive, for they claimed to be, and probably most of them were, survivors of the South's military prisons, Andersonville and Libby and Belle Meade and others less vengefully stamped on the mind of the North. The writers of the pamphlets and their hawkers, professional dealers in atrocity and professional survivors of the South's prison pens, had a believing readership of outraged millions. The North had not been hurt materially by the war—to the contrary, the conflict gave fantastic impetus to her industry and the general economy—but she had suffered grievously nevertheless. Three hundred and sixty thousand Yankee lads had died on the South's battlefields or of wounds or disease, a hundred thousand more than the dead of the Confederacy. Though the Union's population of 22,000,000, more than three times that of the white South, was less affected proportionately than was the conquered foe, every county and township and village in the North mourned its dead and, in the first, unforgiving flush of victory, angrily cursed a South of slavers and Rebels who, wishing to destroy the Union and perpetuate human bondage, had taken the lives of sons and husbands and brothers and fathers, had deliberately and sadistically starved their prisoners, withheld medicines and clothing from them, and subjected them to all manner of personal indignity.

These tales the people of the North believed. These tales the Northern leadership had wanted them to believe during the war. And many would continue to accept as gospel, for years afterward, even the most reckless yarn.

Some of the accounts of privation and death in Southern prisons were accurate. Most of them were not. Not a few of their vendors had never seen a Southern prison. Their authors were often ingenious inventors, none more so than a certain John W. Urban, who sold the same book under four different titles, changing only pictures and binding: *My Experiences Mid Shot and Shell, Mid Shot and Shell and in Rebel Den, In Defense of the Union or Through Shot and Shell and Prison,* and *Battlefield and Prison Pen.*

The pamphlets had considerable peacetime usefulness for pension seekers and for politicians who could so usefully equate dread Andersonville with the Democratic party.

Of course, there had been much suffering in the South's prisons. The South's ever more inadequate transportation system left her own soldiers in the field often without food; her industrial inadequacy made it impossible to clothe properly her own fighting men or her civilians. She was not inclined to treat her prisoners better than her own troops, nor were the officers in charge of the prisons selected from her military elite. Nevertheless the South had tried to supply the prisoners with rations equal to those of the prison garrisons. But the mourning North could not be expected to take such facts into consideration. The public did not know nor would it have cared that nearly as many Southerners had died in Northern prison camps as had Northern boys in the South's charnel houses. The North found it easy to believe the worst from the beginning; for a generation before the war her Abolitionist literature had presented the South as a region of monsters, indifferent to human life; and it was easy to carry over this conviction into the war years.

Too, there was an oddly humanitarian motive in the early wartime dissemination of atrocity stories. At first the federal government had refused to exchange prisoners on the theory that, since secession was unconstitutional, the Confederates were traitors and should not be dealt with under the rules of war. That meant that prisoners would not be exchanged. The Northern press, protesting this policy, soon began to relate the suffering of Northern prisoners as a means of having it changed. From the summer of 1862 the propaganda pamphlets and books swelled to an eventually torrential outpouring of more than three hundred titles, Secretary of War Edwin M. Stanton himself encouraging the poisoned stream. At his urging, the Committee on the Conduct of the War visited a hospital for returned prisoners at Annapolis and obligingly found what he had told them they would find, "the enormity of the crimes committed by the Rebels toward our prisoners," and "a deliberate system of savage and barbarous treatment." In 1864 the United States Sanitary Commission outdid the Committee on the

Conduct of the War with its *Narrative of Privations and Sufferings of U. S. Officers and Soldiers While Prisoners in the Hands of the Rebel Authorities.* The report was widely distributed and it contained every atrocity story known in the history of military propaganda. The committee left no doubt in the minds of the people of the North that the devilish Rebels stole, tortured, deliberately deprived prisoners of bedding, firewood, and food, and placed their prisoners under the command of men worse than beasts. In contrast, the *Narrative* described prison life in the North as all but luxurious.

Yet, despite the impact of prison literature upon the North, only one man lost his life after the war's end for asserted brutal behavior while in the Confederate Army, and he was undeserving of death. This lone unfortunate was Henry Wirz, a Swiss-born doctor who had lost an arm at the First Battle of Manassas and was subsequently placed in command of Andersonville Prison when it was established in 1864. Major Wirz was taken prisoner after the surrender and held in the Old Capitol Prison in Washington where he was tried by a military court on charges of excessive cruelty, of the murder of Union prisoners, and with conspiring with Jefferson Davis and Robert E. Lee to exterminate Northern prisoners. The court-martial which convicted him and sentenced him to shameful death—by hanging instead of at the hands of a firing squad—ignored all legal rules of evidence, accepted perjured testimony, and permitted the appearance of witnesses who had memorized their testimony in advance.

It is remarkable that only Wirz lost his life as a direct result of Northern conviction that the suffering of Union troops in the prisons of the South was deliberate. Long after the war the prison literature continued to keep hatred alive; and this was as useful in the political arena during Reconstruction as it was then and afterward to Union veterans who had to rely more on the nation's sympathy than upon inadequate records to insure the passage of the private pension bills that rewarded impartially the real and the pretended victims of the South's own scarcities.

The hymners of hate were motley.

Soon after the assassination of Lincoln a charlatan Washington medium named Cora Daniel, whose séances commanded the presence of many respectable believers, invoked the spirit of Theodore Parker, the Boston pulpit orator who had encouraged John Brown, to warn that President Andrew Johnson would soon arrest unfriendly Republican leaders and summon a Congress of Southerners and Copperheads—pro-Southern Northerners—while, simultaneously, Thaddeus Stevens and other good Unionists would call together a rival Congress in the West, so that another Civil War would follow.

Within a year Senator Charles Sumner of Massachusetts, the principal architect of universal Negro suffrage, would spread the story that Southerners, impersonating Yankees, were hiring Negroes on the pretext that they would make turpentine on the Gulf Coast and were instead shanghaiing them to be sold as slaves in the West Indies and South America. Throughout 1865 and 1866 *The Nation,* a widely circulated New York periodical, would run a section recording Southern crimes, particularly those committed against Negroes; so many of these stories were manufactured that the Augusta, Georgia, weekly *Constitutionalist* would sarcastically report that "a number of riots are desired in a number of prominent points in the South, such as Richmond, Mobile, Memphis, and New Orleans. If 20 or 30 Negroes, martyrs to liberty, can be killed in each of these places, so much the better for the Radical cause."

From the floor of the House of Representatives, George Washington Julian of Indiana, son of a Quaker, early an Abolitionist and advocate of Negro emancipation and enfranchisement, spoke for not a few of his fellow Radical Republicans, in 1865, when he said: "As for Jeff Davis, I would indict him, I would convict him and hang him in the name of God; as for Robert E. Lee, unmolested in Virginia, hang him too. And stop there? Not at all. I would hang liberally while I had my hand in."

Senator Wade, who later as president pro tempore of the Senate would have become President had Andrew Johnson been impeached, was even thirstier for Southern blood. "There is no doubt," he wrote privately, "that if by an insurrection they [the Negroes] could contrive to slay one-half of their oppressors, the other half would hold them in the highest respect and no doubt treat them with justice."

Even the gentle humanist, Ralph Waldo Emerson, lamented the possibility that the Southerners would not suffer enough:

" 'Tis far better that the Rebels have been pounded instead of negotiated into a peace . . . General Grant's terms certainly look a little too easy . . . I fear that the high, tragic justice which the nation with severest considerations should execute will be softened and dissipated and toasted away at dinner tables."

Unsympathetic toward the hungry South, the New York *Times* reasoned that "if we should feed them, we would make them insolent and they might think it unreasonable in us to stick bayonets in them afterwards in order to make them sincerely sorry for their rebellion."

About Robert E. Lee *The Nation* editorialized: "We protest against the notion that he is fit to be at the head of a college in a country situated as Virginia is"; and, in a more cruel allusion, wealthy, fanatical Wendell Phillips, Boston's archetype of Abolitionism, told a Cooper Union audience in New York that "if Lee is fit to be President of a college, then for Heaven's sake pardon Henry Wirz and make him professor of what the Scots call the Humanities."

Only a month after the surrender Theodore Tilton, the evangelical New

York editor of the Congregationalist journal, *The Independent,* declared to an audience at Cooper Union in New York City that Negroes were more entitled to the vote than were Irishmen and that Jeff Davis should be hanged. Boston's Elizur Wright, onetime editor of the Massachusetts *Abolitionist* and actuarial genius, commented acidly in 1865 that since it would take too long and therefore be too costly to educate the Southern whites to the point of being loyal citizens, the cheapest course would be to give the Negroes the suffrage and let them run things, for that way troops would have to be maintained for a shorter period than if an eye had to be kept indefinitely upon the white Southerners. Henry Ward Beecher, most intemperate of the old Abolitionist preachers, whose later affair with Tilton's wife in 1872 provided the nation with its juiciest postwar marital scandal, orated at Fort Sumter: "We look upon the shattered fort and yonder dilapidated city with sad eyes, grieved that men should have committed such treason and glad that God has set a mark upon treason that all ages shall dread and abhor it."

Most of such stuff was, of course, a letting off of steam or an emotional, all too human clamoring for expiation. In time, though a long time it was, the atrocity pamphlets would lose their morbid appeal; a satiated public would eventually grow weary of the demagogues' cry for blood, and the mourning fathers and mothers and wives and sweethearts and children would find that time brought an anodyne more comforting than the eye exacted for the eye.

But not now. The most potent policy-making and policy-influencing group in the North willed otherwise. It was formed of an alliance of the practical politicians and the idealistic zealots of the Republican party, the established or emerging Negro leaders, a conglomerate of economic realists who intended for the industrial North to stay on top, and a horde of graceless scavengers to whom the fallen South irresistibly beckoned. And in some among them were combined the motivations of them all.

The war did not destroy the Democratic party. Lincoln had not received a majority of the popular vote in 1860; in 1864 the Northern champions of the Democratic party were still vigorous and vocal. They had proved their loyalty. Their party appealed to the luckless Irish and Mediterranean immigrants whose slavery in New England's mills differed from the bondage of the Southern blacks principally in that they could not be sold and that they could vote—or be voted; to the discontented farmers of the Middle West whose fortunes had not greatly risen with the war; to religious minorities, mostly the Catholics; to the silent and the not so silent sympathizers with the old South; to the growing American proletariat. Now Andrew Johnson, a Democrat and a Southerner, though a loyal one, was in the White House. To the Republicans, the Democrats were very much alive and dangerous. True, the "Lincoln States" would likely rejoin the Union under Republican auspices, but how long could the white Southern Unionists be trusted? Let a majority of the white Southerners vote, let them withhold the ballot from the Negro, let the Democrats of the North unite with the unregenerate Rebels, and the Republican party which had saved the Union would be out in the cold. So reasoned Wade and Sumner and Davis, Representative Thaddeus Stevens of Pennsylvania, and the lesser party chieftains. Something had to be done. Many things.

The passions of a sorely hurt, victorious adversary, the dictates of practical politics—these the South could understand and expect. But she would not understand or accept, nor has she yet recovered psychologically from, the intent of those of her adversaries who rejoiced in the name Radicals, the only real social revolutionists ever to achieve great power in the United States.

Animated in part by an ideological hatred of the Southern aristocrats—they called them the slavocracy and blamed them alone for the war—and imbued with a notion of a racially egalitarian society, the true Radical Republicans pursued three primary and immediate goals: the elevation of the free Negro to full political equality, regardless of qualification other than manhood; punishment, both economic and political, for the leaders of the Confederacy and the foremost of their followers; and the creation out of the ashes of the old South of a shining new world, supervised by themselves, a region in which neither the Union nor the Republican party nor the Negro's place in the sun would ever be challenged.

They had a common animation, these Radicals, in their abhorrence of human bondage; but they had no common stamp. Some among them were well-born Easterners, New England intellectuals, scholars and teachers and preachers. Some were loutish countrymen, small-town lawyers, professional soldiers. In the last flaming years before the war many of them had, in the name of human freedom, condoned riot and mobbery and other violations of the public peace, challenged the rights of sovereign states, defied the nation's Constitution, tolerated and abetted insurrection and even murder, as John Brown and his raiders could have attested. In the hour of Union victory they were to be merciless and uncompromising in their demand for an immediate and punitive political equality for the black man of the South. For the black man of the North they showed considerably less concern. Among their champions in the political lists were political giants and moral pygmies. In concert with fellow Republicans of less single-minded intent they would dominate the nation's political life for a decade; but try as they would, they could not lastingly achieve their Southern program.

Other Americans in Washington and in the cities of the North—and in the South too—must have found Lincoln's conciliatory terms as repugnant as did those Republican politicians and dreamers in whose scheming they figured so greatly. These were the leaders of the freedmen, articulate, persuasive, many of them well educated, and most of them free before the war. Some were patriots and some were knaves, some selfless and many self-seeking; and, at their backs, the thousands of Negroes who crowded into Washington and elsewhere in the North in the latter years of the war, tatterdemalion refugees and black men in Union uniforms, served as an inviting reminder that in the South waited the three and a half million children of Jubilee, ready to listen to whoever else promised them the most.

Ablest of them all was Frederick A. Douglass, the brilliant Negro Abolitionist, born a slave in Maryland, who had escaped to New York in 1838 by using a free Negro friend's identification papers. Douglass was the most widely and favorably known Negro in the North, a man whom Lincoln had reputedly described as, considering his origins, the obstacles he had overcome, and the position he had attained, "one of the most meritorious men, if not the most meritorious man, in the United States." In the 1840s Douglass had written and published his eagerly read autobiography *Narrative of the Life of Frederick Douglass, an American Slave.* Beginning a new life of freedom as a laborer in New England, he had become a newspaper editor in Rochester, New York, and a dynamic anti-slavery lecturer. Implacable toward the South, he wrote of the war that it was "undertaken and brazenly carried on for the perpetual enslavement of colored men." One paragraph from his autobiography, as revised after the war, expresses the attitude so completely shared by his white Radical compatriots:

"Happily for the cause of human freedom, and for the final unity of the American nation, the South was mad, and would listen to no concessions . . . They had made up their minds that under a given contingency they would secede from the Union and thus dismember the Republic . . . They had come to hate everything which had the prefix 'free'—free soil, free States, free territories, free schools, free speech, and freedom generally, and they would have no more such prefixes. This haughty and unreasonable and unreasoning attitude of the imperious South saved the slave and saved the nation. Had the South accepted our concessions and remained in the Union, the slave power would in all probability have continued to rule; the North would have become utterly demoralized; the hands on the dial plate of American civilization would have been reversed, and the slave would have been dragging his hateful chains today wherever the American flag floats in the breeze."

So spoke Frederick Douglass, the Negro. So he felt in the hour of triumph. And when he spoke the Northern humanitarian, the Northern politician, and the three and one half million Negroes listened. And, in different temper, so did the South.

And all of the victorious coalitionists—the officeholders and the office seekers, the old Abolitionist shock troops, the more moderate Republicans, and the freedmen—had been conditioned long before the spring of 1865 by nearly a half century of unending sectional conflicts and crises, almost all of them having their roots in the institution of slavery, and by the unshakable conviction that in defending slavery and disrupting the Union the South had been as morally wrong as the North was morally right and should be made to atone. Neither before the war nor during it nor even afterward would the South comprehend the intensity of this feeling, upon which the Radical Republicans could play so successfully for ten lamentable years.

The curse of sectionalism had antedated the quarrel over slavery. Almost from the nation's birth North and South had differed in cultural attitudes, in political theory, and in economic bases. They had not disagreed initially as to the position of the Negro in the American society; no sectional division marked the Congress which in 1790 decided that only a free white person could be naturalized. Implicit here was an intent to maintain an inferior status for the Negro, and not only the slave Negro, for even the free black man was subjected to limitations of his civil rights. Nor in the beginning were the people of the Southern states unique or original in their concept of the United States as a confederation, freely entered upon and as freely to be quitted.

But the sectional lines, in respect to slavery, the nature of the Union, and the place of the Negro in the American society, soon appeared; and, ironically, an invention of inestimable value to man led directly to the fixed and opposing resolves. Eli Whitney's cotton gin and the looms of England's industrial revolution made the slave a seeming imperative for the South even as his relative uselessness to the North was recognized. And so the spokesmen for human freedom had fallen largely silent in a region whose multiplying wealth lay in cotton fields and black bodies; but the voices grew louder in the rest of the land.

The defenders of slavery were to persuade few beyond their borders. Not to the slave South but to industrial New England migrated the skilled workers of Europe, bringing with them memories of ancient serfdoms and a loathing for those who held men enslaved. Not to the region of slave competition did the landseekers migrate but to the Midwestern frontier, there to clear and till their lands and to look southward in contempt for the slavocracy; and, in time, 400,000 foreign-born would enroll in the armies of the Union. Not as a state's right but as a moral wrong did the Abolitionists interpret the system they intended to destroy, no matter the cost, and to replace with a then singular philosophy of racial equality.

The divergent cultures had hardened, and for a half century an ever more divided nation sought without success to find an accommodation. Almost every milestone was ominous, and over each hung the shadow of slavery. The Missouri Compromise . . . the Tariff of Abominations . . . the

Webster-Hayne Debate . . . the Nullification Controversy . . . the Anti-Abolitionist Laws . . . the Gag Resolution . . . the Annexation of Texas . . . the Mexican War . . . the Wilmot Proviso . . . the Compromise of 1850 . . . the Great Debate . . . the Fugitive Slave Act . . . the Kansas-Nebraska Act . . . the Dred Scott Decision . . . the Lincoln-Douglas Debate . . . the Election of Lincoln . . . the Secession of South Carolina. . . .

Always the uncompromising voices had drowned out the counseling for moderation and peace. Here is John C. Calhoun, defiantly bespeaking nullification and threatening a resort to arms. Here is Wendell Phillips, hated and hating, determined to arouse the country to forcible destruction of slavery. Here are the formidable Abolitionist senators, Wade of Ohio and Zachariah Chandler of Michigan, and Representative Thad Stevens of Pennsylvania, preaching war against all defenders of slavery. Here is William H. Seward, United States senator from New York, predicting "an irrepressible conflict with the outcome either an entire slave-holding nation or entirely a free nation." Across the years we can hear the icy denunciations of Emerson and the rhymed satires of John Greenleaf Whittier, and adamant Jefferson Davis holding immutable the institution of slavery and the right for a state to withdraw from the Union, and South Carolina's Robert Barnwell Rhett thundering for secession. And, near the end of the uneasy peace, the voice of Abraham Lincoln, certain that slavery was evil but less certain of the procedures to end it: "I have no prejudices against the Southern people . . . I surely will not blame them for not doing what I should not know how to do myself."

For nearly fifty years the drumfire voices had bespoken violence, and violence in turn encouraged the voices. Young Elijah Lovejoy, Abolitionist editor and martyr to the freedom of the press, died at the hands of a mob in Alton, Illinois. The agents of Abolitionism's underground railroads spirited escaping slaves to freedom; the slaveowners struck back; and Abolitionist mobs attacked the slaveholders who sought to regain their human property. Across Kansas raged John Brown, dedicated to murder for freedom's sake; against the rampaging Free-Soilers, armed by New England's Abolitionists with Sharp's rifles—"Beecher's Bibles" they were called—stood the Border Ruffians, and men died by the hundreds in bleeding Kansas. The sentimental story of Uncle Tom, Topsy, Little Eva, and Simon Legree, written by a clergyman's wife in the Maine town where he taught at Bowdoin College, fed impartially the hate of South for North and North for South. And in 1859 at Harper's Ferry, Virginia, John Brown, his sons, and the handful who followed them sought to arouse the slaves of Virginia to insurrection.

To the South John Brown's raid had been the final, unneeded proof of Northern madness. He had been encouraged and given aid by Massachusetts men who should have known better. The South would not soon forget the old man's raid, for its people believed almost to a man that this setting of slave at the throat of his master was planned Yankee mischief at its worst. But the Yankees who thought differently, and they were the loudest among the Yankees, made of old John Brown a saint whose soul went marching on.

So in an evil time war came. To the men of the South it was a war for Southern independence, to the men of the North a war for the nation's unity and for the black man's freedom, some of them putting the one cause ahead and some the other. Now the men of the North had won and Abraham Lincoln lay dead. Ready now for the trampling feet were the grapes of wrath. And the anguished cry of Georgia's Benjamin Hill when he learned of the murder of the President was the voice of the fallen Confederacy: "God help us if that is true. It is the worst blow that has yet been struck the South."

CHAPTER 2

"A Hell of a Git——"

A FEW *days before Lee's surrender, the story goes, a Yankee patrol flushed a barefooted Confederate straggler from a Virginia chicken house.*

"We've got you," yelled a well-fed Yankee sergeant.

The Johnny Reb, a grimy fist clenched around the neck of a tough, ancient rooster, looked upon his foeman with disdain. "Yep, you got me," he answered, "and a Hell of a git you got."

A Hell of a git——

The Yankee invaders had been thorough and often wanton in their destructiveness. Across Georgia, Mississippi, South Carolina, and Virginia, the states the worst hurt, the blackened chimneys that were called Sherman's sentinels stood guard above charred rafters where once had arisen great mansions, substantial farmhouses, trim town homes. Much of Jackson, Mississippi, Charleston, South Carolina, Mobile, Alabama, Richmond, Virginia, Savannah, Georgia, and many another smaller community had been burned. Atlanta and beautiful Columbia, the capital of South Carolina, lay in ashes. The devastation in Mississippi, spreading eastward and northward from Vicksburg, matched that of Georgia. The ante-bellum buildings of the University of Mississippi at Oxford, and part of the town itself, had been put to the torch. Wherever the Union armies had passed, the homes of many of the well-to-do and the middle classes were left almost bare of silver, paintings, books, and even clothing, anything of value or any trifle that attracted the pillager's eye. Trees, fences, and shrubbery had been felled or uprooted. Not enough ginhouses were left standing to accommodate even the small cotton crop of 1865. Men in creaking wagons drove their gaunt mules for miles to find fords across bridgeless rivers. Only one mile of railroad in three was operable.

Eliza Frances Andrews, a young Georgia woman, wrote in *The War Time Journal of a Georgia Girl* of the ruin in her state: "About three miles from Sparta we struck 'burnt country' . . . The fields were trampled down and the road was lined with carcasses of hogs, horses, and cattle that the invader had wantonly shot down . . . The stench in some places was unbearable . . . The dwellings that were standing all showed signs of pillage, and on every plantation we saw the charred remains of the ginhouse . . . total homes laid in ashes. Hayricks and fodder stacks were demolished, corn cribs were empty, and every bale of cotton burnt . . . I saw no grain of any sort except little patches they had spilled when feeding their horses, and there was not even a chicken left in the country to eat. A bag of oats might have lain anywhere along the road without danger from the beasts of the field, though I cannot say it would have been safe from the assaults of hungry men."

Young Whitelaw Reid, who would become the editor of the New York *Tribune,* the most influential of the period's newspapers, inspected the South for the *Tribune* soon after the fall of Richmond. The farmers of desolated Virginia were growing enough corn, he reported, to stave off starvation. "But in the main, between Richmond and Gordonsville, as between Fredericksburg and Richmond, abandoned fields alternated with pine forests, destroyed depots, and ruined dwellings. Imaginative writers have described the droves of wild beasts which they represent as having taken possession of these desolated regions; but the sportsman is likely to find nothing more formidable than abundant coveys of quails. . . .

"Hanover Junction presented little but standing chimneys and the debris of destroyed buildings. Along the road a pile of smoky brick and mortar seemed a regularly recognized sign of what had once been a depot, and the train was sure to stop. Not a platform or water tank had been left, and the rude contrivances hastily thrown up to get the road in running order were, in many cases, for miles and miles the only improvements visible."

The indices of the South's bankruptcy were legion. The currency and bonds of the Confederacy had absolutely no value. Congress had not granted Lincoln's request in 1864 for a constitutional amendment to provide compensation to slaveowners after emancipation; the uncompensated freeing of the Negroes had wiped out investments in human beings variously estimated at from two billion to four billion dollars. Southern insurance companies were worthless.

Louisiana had been second in the nation in per capita wealth in 1860. By 1880 she would be in thirty-seventh place. South Carolina dropped in the same twenty years from third to forty-fifth in per capita wealth; Mississippi from fifth to forty-sixth, Georgia from eighth to fortieth, Texas from ninth to thirty-sixth, Alabama from sixteenth to forty-fourth, Arkansas from nineteenth to forty-third, and Virginia from twentieth to thirty-fifth. Interest rates ranged from 18 per cent to 24 per cent throughout most of the South and rose to an incredible 35 per cent in South Carolina.

In the wake of surrender swarmed the Yankee tax collectors. Arlington, the home of Robert E. Lee, was seized for taxes. Unscrupulous agents bought distressed property themselves for resale at huge profits: a $15,000 property for $300, a $40,000 estate for $200, a complete town, Fernandina, Florida, for little more than $10,000; but confiscatory tax collection was halted in 1866, and in 1872 Congress permitted Southern owners to reclaim such properties as were still in the hands of the government.

General Sherman, as pitying in victory as he had been ruthless in war, addressed a reunion of the veterans of the March to the Sea two years after the surrender.

"Look to the South," he said, "and you who went with me through that land can best say if they too have not been fearfully punished. Mourning in every household, desolation written in broad characters across the whole face of their country, cities in ashes and fields laid waste, their commerce gone, their system of labor annihilated and destroyed. Ruin, poverty, and distress everywhere, and now pestilence adding the very cap sheaf to their stack of miseries; her proud men begging for pardon and appealing for permission to raise food for their children; her five millions of slaves free and their value lost to their former masters forever."

Nor were the North's tariff, taxation, and fiscal policies in general calculated to aid the South. The invaders had systematically destroyed the South's cotton mills, the region's only industry that threatened New England with competition, a concentration of effort which led an English observer to comment that "one can hardly harmonize the pure anti-slavery professions of the war party in the North with depredations so systematically directed against establishments employing only free labor." After the war Congress established a 40 per cent tariff on cotton mill machinery. During the war Congress had raised the tariff rates steadily with the excuse that since the North's manufacturers were being heavily taxed for war revenues they must be compensated through additional tariff protection. By the war's end the average rate on dutiable goods was 47 per cent as against 18.8 per cent in 1860.

It would be nearly a hundred years before the South, selling its cotton in an open market and buying most of its necessities in a closed one, would even partially overcome such handicaps.

The National Banking Act, passed in 1863, would do lasting damage too, through its requirement of $50,000 as the minimum capital for banks in communities of less than 6000 population and $100,000 for cities with greater population. Such capital was available in few Southern towns in 1865; even by 1893 there was only one bank for every 58,000 Southerners, although the non-Southern ratio was one bank for every 16,600 citizens. From 1865 to 1875 the South was apportioned only $9,500,000 from the more than $100,000,000 spent by the Federal government on public works. Massachusetts and New York together received $21,000,000, Mississippi and Arkansas a combined total of $185,000.

The rankest of pillagers in the postwar South were the treasury agents. During the war Congress had authorized the Treasury Department to send agents through those areas in the South which had been overrun and occupied to seize for the government "abandoned" cotton and any other "abandoned" possessions and commodities owned by disloyalists which could be sold. The agents had taken possession of some $30,000,000 worth of cotton by the war's end. The dishonesty of many of them was almost beyond belief. Of them, E. Merton Coulter wrote in *The South During Reconstruction:*

"Secretary Hugh McCulloch was forced by his conscience to remark of his brood of agents, 'I am sure I sent *some* honest agents South; but it sometimes seems very doubtful whether any of them remained honest very long.' The methods of their dishonesties were diverse. Laws and regulations allowed them from 25 per cent to 50 per cent of the proceeds of their seizures; but such profits were insufficient to satiate their cupidity. They sold either to themselves or to others through collusion, for 10¢ to 30¢ a pound, cotton worth from 60¢ to $1.20 a pound and transmitted to the government its proportion of the lower price. In Savannah alone, out of $21,000,000 worth of cotton sold, they handed over to the United States Treasury only $8,000,000. These 'rogues and fortune hunters,' who were 'privateering on land in time of peace among the vanquished,' seized all cotton in sight whether it had belonged to the Confederate government or not, but they could be bribed to desist from taking private cotton. Conversely, now and then they would deface Confederate identification markings and, through agreement with a planter on whose land it might be found, share the profits with him. Many planters honestly owned cotton bargained for by the Confederacy but not received or paid for before the Surrender; and even when cotton had been paid for, the planter repossessed it if possible, for the Confederate bonds he had received for it had now become worthless. An agent in Texas forced a woman to sell for $75 a bale her 400 bales worth $200 each, under threat that he would seize it as Confederate cotton if she did not comply. Another agent who had an interest in a steamboat refused to let a planter move his cotton unless he shipped it on the agent's craft . . . Agents who could not find cotton seized horses and mules as Confederate property, and in some parts of the South they forced planters to pay the old Confederate tax-in-kind—the 1/10th of certain farm products."

The catalogue of ruin runs almost endlessly. Not for a quarter of a century would the South's livestock equal the number of sheep and cattle and hogs that fattened in its fields and pens and meadows in 1860; not for a quarter of a century would it plant as many acres to cotton. In the war's last year and for the first few months of peace almost a million white Southerners and twice that number of Negroes lacked even the barest of necessities.

James Gill, an Arkansas slave, remembered more than sixty years later how folks got by: "Howsomever, us all lived good 'cause there was a heap of wild hogs and possums and such, and we had hid a heap of corn and us did fine. . . . Heap and heap of times the soldiers would go by us place. When the Yankees would come they would ax my mammy, 'Aunt Mary, is you seen any secesh today?' and Mammy, she'd say, 'No sir,' even if'n she had seen some of us men."

And William Colbert, a onetime Georgia slave, recalled what happened to his master: "The Yankees come in, and they pull the fruit off the trees and et it. They et the hams and corn but they never burned the houses. Seems to me like they just stay round long enough to get plenty of something to eat, cause they left in two or three days and never seed 'em since. The massa had three boys to go to war but there wasn't one to come home. All the children he had was killed. Massa, he lost all his money, and the house soon began dropping away to nothing. Us niggers one by one left the old place, and the last time I seed the home plantation I was a standing on a hill. I looked back on it for the last time through a patch of scrub pines, and it looked so lonely. There wa'n't but one person in sight, the massa. He was a-setting in a wicker chair in the yard looking out over a small field of cotton and corn. There was four crosses in the graveyard in the side lawn where he was a-setting. The fourth one was his wife. . . ."

Henry William Ravenel was a South Carolinian, as proud of his Huguenot lineage as were his fellow Carolinians of his scientific genius. A notable botanist, kindly slaveowner, and greatly successful planter, he lost in the wake of the war much of his land and all of the library that was one of the South's finest. Let these excerpts from his diary tell of the bruising of an aristocracy:

1865

May 22. We begin now to realize the ruin to property which the war has entailed upon us. All classes and conditions of men will suffer who had property, except the small farmers who owned no negroes. Confederate securities, I consider a total loss. Bank stock, confederation and private bonds, are all more or less dependent for their availability upon Confed securities, & upon the value of negro property; both of which are lost. The Rail road companies are nearly all ruined by the destruction of their roads & the heavy debt they must incur to rebuild. The only money now in possession of our people is coin in small quantities which had been hoarded through the war, & some bills of the local banks. There will be but little means of increasing this amount for some time to come, as provisions are scarce, & the cotton has been mostly burnt, captured or sold. The financial prospect is a gloomy one, & there will be much distress before our conditions can improve. My own loss (exclusive of the value of my property, & the losses from the Yankees in St. Johns, & Wheelers men up here) is as follows—$11,600 Confed. 8 per ct bonds—$6,500 Conf 8 per ct. stock—$2000 non taxable 6 per cts.—$1200 in 7.30 Treasury notes, $300 in 4 per ct scrip—$2400 in currency=$24,000 in Confed securities. I have also bonds from Charley & Peter Snowden amounting to $7770 for negroes purchased. If the negroes are emancipated I will return these bonds to them as their means of paying will be lost, & I would not wish to embarrass them with such a debt. I have 32 shares Charleston bank (par $100)—24 shares State Bank—& 90 shares Peoples bank (25)—all doubtful. $1060 in City of Charleston 6 per cts—$1050 in State of So. Ca. 6 per cts, $1500 in 6 per ct Bonds of Charleston & Savannah R.R. Co. The above with my farm (& 32 negro slaves?) is the total amount of my property. . . .

June 14. Our young men are going to work in earnest for a living. Every one sees the necessity of exertion—& as soon as business can be resumed & money begins to circulate, we hope to have more prosperous times. Parker Ravenel & Coffin have established a line of wagons, from this place to Orangeburg, from this place to Columbia, & from the latter place to Orangeburg. . . . This arrangement will go on until the Railroad is completed. The negroes are very foolishly leaving their former masters. Nearly every family in Aiken has lost some, many all their servants. The novelty of the situation tempts them to make use of it. Many who are well treated, & much better off than they can be by their own exertions, are going away. They all want to go to the cities, either Charleston or Augusta. The fields have no attractions. Mine are all still with me, that have been living here. Lander who was at Granite Ville has lost his place there & gone to look for work,—& some of the other boys are working in the neighborhood. They have all professed a desire to remain with me—There are more ˙than I need for servants or farm hands & [they] will have to provide for themselves. . . .

July 6. . . . I have taken a contract to supply 200 cords wood to the R. Road at $2.50 per cord, which I hope will bring us in a little ready money. That with my Peach & Grape crop are the only sources of income that I can see at present. . . .

October 4. . . . I am now expecting to get some kind of employment & may sell out my farm & move away. This may be the beginning of a disruption & scattering of my happy family. I have spent eleven years of my life very happily at this place—& the thought of its being brought to a close, causes sadness. . . .

October 20. . . . The great Problem now before the country is that of securing profitable Labour for the wants of agriculture. The negroes seem indisposed to work in the country, & are flocking to the towns & cities. Where they have been under contract during the past season, they have in most cases disregarded their contracts,—& have made but little provision for the coming year. The planters are without means to engage them & furnish subsistance for the year. This is the almost universal case throughout the low country. Unless some means are devised for aiding the owners of land by an advance of funds or rations, hypothecated on the coming crop,—or the lands are sold to capitalists who can furnish this advance, they must remain idle. There must also be stringent laws to control the negroes, & require them to fulfill their contracts of labour on the farms. . . .

December 3. I went over to Augusta yesterday to collect my monthly amount for wood. This woodcutting is a God-send in reality to me at this time, when I am getting nothing from any other source. I get about $40 per month clear of cost of cutting &c. Without this source of profit since the war closed, I would not have been able to provide food & clothing for my family without sacrificing some articles of silver or furniture. I took over with me an advertisement offering my farm for sale which ought to appear in the Constitutionalist tomorrow.

December 22. . . . Received a letter from Peter Gaillard to whom I had written to consult as to the practicability of getting into business in Charleston. He gives a melancholy view of the condition of affairs. A large number of men who formerly did business in the city are thrown out of employment,—every one more or less ruined in money affairs & but little business as there is but little produce to be sold. It is a struggle for life—& those who are most active & prepared by previous habits & training will secure the places—others must do what they can for a living. I have had no application yet for my farm. . . .

December 26. I replied to Mr. Walters letter yesterday, stating that I asked $15,000 for my farm—of which I would require a portion (⅓) in cash—the balance in bonds or other securities I might approve of. I have considered the propriety of selling my farm before I have a certainty of getting business—& have decided that it will be best to sell if the opportunity offers, & take the chances afterwards of finding employment.

My reasons are these—The sources from which I derived an annual income by which I supported my family are all lost—the present wood cutting business cannot last very long from scarcity of timber—my farm yields nothing except Fruit & should the seasons be unfavourable, that resource is cut off, & I will be left without any means of support. . . .

December 28. . . . I wrote today to Prof P. A. Chadbourne to offer him
my set of Mougeot & Nestlers "Stirpes Cryptogamae Vogeso—Rhenanae,"
12 vols at $100 in specie or $124 in currency—also "Grevilles Cryptogamic
Flora" at $40—also De Candoles "Prodromus" 12 vols & "Kunths Enu-
meratio Plantarum" 5 vols for $50.

1866

March 2. This day year Gen. Potters army passed through Pooshee & encamped there for the night, he making his headquarters at the house. It was
during the night of the 1st that we had the visit from the gang of black
troops, who stole my horses, & all the meats and supplies we had outside
of the house. They were at their devilish work until after 1 A.M. of the 2nd.

April 11. The negroes are busy preparing & planting their crops. My farm
was in such bad condition that I told them if they repaired the fences they
could plant whatever land they wanted. They have been for near two months
past using their spare time from woodcutting in splitting rails & making
fences. Yesterday they all came & planted my crop of potatoes (about 30
rows). I wish my land was better, so they might get a better return for their
labour. They have all behaved well, & seem to wish to get along. I believe
after a while when a more settled state of affairs exist & the demand for
labour is properly adjusted, that a good feeling generally will prevail towards the negroes. They surely have done nothing to cause any ill blood
towards them. I feel nothing but sympathy for them as a poor, homeless &
unprotected, proscribed race. That the low & ignorant classes of our white
population should feel vindictively inclined towards them, may be expected.
They will taunt & maltreat the negro, simply because he belongs to the
proscribed race, & was once a slave. Even if we felt inclined to indulge a
revengeful feeling at the loss of property in their emancipation, we should
recollect that it was through no act of theirs, that emancipation was effected.
It was simply the result of the chances of war, on which we had staked our
cause & all that we had. Let us have the magnanimity to be just, if we have
not the Christian principles of forgiveness.

June 9. We are under further obligations to the Ladies of Baltimore for
provisions received yesterday, about 1 bush flour, 2 bushels meal & ½ of
a side of bacon. These things were sent on here for distribution to certain
persons who were named & to others whom the committee might think
proper to give. I am indebted to some kind friend who presented my name
& I have received more than I had any right to expect. . . .

July 22. This morning at breakfast table the subject of early struggling in
life was discussed, & I endeavoured to impress upon my children the great
advantages of self exertion & of early habits of training in making one's
way through life. I have been thinking of it since, & record for their benefit
my thoughts on the subject. After graduating at College, where I idled the
first 18 months of my course, & made some amends in the last year, studying
pretty hard and taking one of the high appointments, I came home intending

to study medicine, & did really begin to read a work on Physiology. My father who had practised in the country & had to give it up on account of ill health dissuaded me from it, as too arduous a work for my constitution, thinking only of a hard country practice, & not estimating the advantages which I might have acquired from a knowledge of Anatomy, Physiology & Therapeutics. He offered me a plantation & negroes to begin life with. Of course the temptation to ease was strong, & I yielded. I have ever since regretted that I had not persevered in the study of medicine. It suited my previous inclination & my turn of mind. I had paid much attention to Chemistry & Natural Philosophy in College & was pleased with this glimpse I got of the world of Nature. . . .

I wish it impressed upon them that my error in the beginning was in taking to planting, a life of ease & non-exertion, instead of studying a profession by which I could have gained a livelihood through my own exertions. I would now have had that profession as a means of support. We cannot violate that primaeval law of our nature "In the sweat of thy brow shall thou eat bread" without paying the penalty in after life. . . .

July 24. Wrote to Mr. Walter in reference to the purchase of my farm by Capt Barkman. I have offered it at $10,000. . . .

November 6. I sent down today my Certificate for $1060 in City of Charleston Stock to James Wilson for sale. I hope by what I may realize from its sale to be able to commence my nursery business & make the necessary repairs on my farm. . . .

November 24. Received last night a letter from James Wilson inclosing my two certificates of Stock which he was unable to sell. . . .

1867

January 1. . . . Received last night a letter from Dr. Curtis inclosing one to him from Prof Gray, to whom he had written at my request on the subject of making collections of plants for sale. Dr. Gray writes in a very friendly manner, & although he cannot hold out expectations that the plan will pay well, offers to aid me in every way & to bring the matter to attention of botanists abroad. I think it likely I shall abandon the scheme, as one which will require too much of my time without a prospect of compensation, which I cannot now afford to devote to it. I have other employment for my time in the editing of our paper here, & in writing for Hills Magazine. . . .

1870

February 2. . . . I have put my farm in Woods' hands for sale. He does not think I can get over $8000 for it. . . .

December 20. Received last night a letter from the Librarian of University of S. C. on the subject of the purchase of my old newspapers. The Trustees had not yet held a meeting & no decision had been made. I offered the Newspapers 1865 at $200, & the old acts of Assembly &c at $25 & the old book at $25. . . .

1871

December 16. We have decided to make a change in our household arrangements. We have had Peggy cooking for us at $1.50 per week & Leah washing at $1.30 per week. We find it necessary to curtail these expenses, & tomorrow we will begin to do our own cooking in the house, & Leah, Rony & Peggy will each give us a days washing every week for house rent. I will hire Ben to do work about the house, bringing water & wood &c. . . .

December 20. . . . I wrote to Prof Gray yesterday to offer my entire Collection of Cryptogams for $1000 as follows Fungi—3000 species (& all the duplicates, enough to be used in exchange to add another 1000); Musci about 624; Hepaticae about 85; Lichens about 750; Algae about 300— total about 4760. . . .

1875

June 18. . . . This morning after breakfast I walked out to Hampton Hill to take a look at property which again was to come into my possession after 18 months' alienation. The house has been improved perhaps to the value of about $500. A stair way leading downwards & the basement rooms excavated & inclosed. The fences have been brought in so as to enclose about 35 acres around the buildings. The vegetable garden is in a neglected & ruinous condition, nothing planted there—The fruit garden grown up in weeds & grass, & needing cultivation to keep things alive—the Asparagus field mostly lost from neglect,—the outbuildings, particularly Jimmys & Stephens houses very much in delapidated [sic] & out of repair. No improvements whatever except in the house & no crop of any kind planted. . . .

1876

March 27. . . . Mary has taken Henry Smiths house, and is fitting it up for boarders. The rent is $60 the first month & $40 after. . . .

April 1. Mary made an arrangement yesterday evening with Mr. Chetfield to take two of the rooms for lodgers at $1.50 a room, & will probably take all she has furnished. A party of four ladies have taken two of the rooms, only as lodgers at $3 a day for the two rooms. . . .

April 3. Two more rooms taken by lodgers this morning—. . . .

April 10. . . . I have arranged with Henry Smith to take back the house on payment of $30. for half month. We have lost upwards of $30. by the 2 weeks operations. Enough for that speculation. . . .

April 20. Miss Blackman & Miss Beardsley came this morning to board at $15 each per week, having separate rooms. We have given up our chamber & fitted up the parlor for a bedroom. . . .

1879

December 1. . . . . Received from James Wilson yesterday a Postal card announcing the sale of my two $500. S.C.R.R. Bonds at 24½ = $245.00. This is one of the last fragments of my property from the wreck of 15 years ago—I still have one $500. bond of Sav. & Ch. R.R. which is unsalable & perhaps never will be worth any thing—& I have my Hampton Hill farm & this house & lot in Aiken. The Hampton Hill property is deteriorating yearly & I have offered it for 2 years past at $4500 but cannot get a purchaser. I find it rather hard to get on with my family of 8, with the little income I can muster. . . .

1881

April 29. . . . . Mary looks thin after her close confinement & hard work with the boarders. The last of them left on Monday. . . .

1882

March 6. . . . . I offered Hampton Hill for sale today at public auction, but could not sell. . . .

Inflation.

Phoebe Ellen Upton kept a diary too. Her Quaker father, Samuel George Upton, had been an Indiana Democrat and he had vowed that if Abe Lincoln were elected in 1860 the Uptons would leave home. And so they did. Upton sold his two Indiana weekly newspapers and locked up his law office. The family—parents, four daughters, and a son—moved to Vicksburg and endured its siege, the father serving in the commissary department, a Herculean assignment in that starving city. After Vicksburg fell, its conquerors gave Sam Upton permission to take his family up the Red River to North Louisiana on a steamboat carrying paroled troops from the Vicksburg Military Hospital to another in Shreveport. About a month before Lee's surrender, the family started out for their Vicksburg home. At first they traveled by wagons pulled by a yoke of steers and on mule back. Malaria-ridden twenty-four-year old Phoebe Ellen had a mind for costs:

Mar. 14, 1865—Paw . . . had to pay $5 per bushel for corn.

Mar. 17—Mrs. Wyatt charged us $20 (for a room) but Maw gave her 15 buttons which was $5.

Mar. 18—Paw's bill at Mr. Chatham's was $20. I sold a young lady nine sheets of note paper for $5. (At Parson Williams, only seven miles along the way, with Paw lying sick in the wagon) Here we got to sleep two in a bed, the first time since we left home, and the lady of the house has on a calico dress, very kind, hospitable people in appearance and I shall like them very if they don't charge too much.

Mar. 19—Mr. Williams charged us $25.

Mar. 20—Mrs. Webb charged us $87. Pretty high.

Mar. 21—I had my chill at night. Went to bed early. Had such good accommodations. Mr. Meredith charged us $30.

Mar. 23—A gentleman traveling from Harrisonburg could get no corn until he came into this region, two days journey from Mr. Meredith, and then could get but ten ears for $10.

Mar. 28—Mr. Daws charged Paw five dollars! for us staying all night. For five bushels of corn $25. The cheapest bill we have had yet.

April 6—These Yankee boats are chartered by two men who buy cotton at from 4 to 8¢, sell flour at $8 . . . Therefore a bale of cotton will buy a barrel of flour.

April 23—There are rumors that Richmond has fallen, and that Lee is captured, but of course it is not General Robert Lee. If it is true that Lee has surrendered, our Country is no more. We are a conquered people, subject entirely to the mercies of the U. S. Government. A system of espionage will be carried on equal to that of France. Arrests will be of every day occurence, executions for treason will not be rare. Our tax will be enormous. There will be no liberty or happiness any more in Dixie.

April 29—Eldon and Amy, [the brother and a sister] came down yesterday to get honey and meat. 10 lbs. honey $30. Meat $2.50 lb. Cheap eggs are only $5 per dozen though I got 4 doz. for $3—$12 last week . . . Lee has surrendered I am afraid . . . If all this be true, our soldiers will soon be coming home and we must soon have peace. Well, I've said no more than others, and can afford to be defeated as well, and I do not intend to trouble myself about it. I have swallowed half a glass of vinegar since my last chill, and oh! I am afraid to hope that I am to miss today's chill.

July 31—[back in Vicksburg] Paw raised $30 by dint of much trying at 33⅓% per month. Awful.

The roll call of the dead . . .

Never in modern history has a people at war suffered proportionately as high casualties as did the Confederacy. On the road from Fort Sumter to the courthouse village in Virginia 258,000 Southern fighting men had died in battle, or from wounds or disease. At least another 100,000, and probably more, had been wounded, and a fourth of these were permanently disabled. Out of the Northern prison camps, nearly as lethal as the prison pens of the South, straggled 60,000 human shells. The white population of all the seceding states had been fewer than 5,500,000 at the war's onset. At its conclusion not more than one family in a hundred had gone through the war without mourning a father, a son, a cousin, an uncle, a brother. Of the

South's white men who had been physically able to enter military service when the war began, one fourth were either dead or incapacitated. A year after the surrender, the state of Mississippi would allot a fifth of its revenues for artificial arms and legs for her veterans.

Nor was the loss in manpower to be counted alone in the number of dead, the maimed, and the disabled. By the thousands, Confederate veterans and their families migrated to the new lands of the Southwest and the Far West. By the hundreds they sought sanctuary in Brazil and in Mexico. Some of the South's principal civil officials who were liable to arrest went into hiding or fled abroad. Not a few Confederate officers sought foreign commissions.

Gallant Admiral Raphael Semmes, whose exploits as commander of the raider *Alabama* rank with those of the greatest seamen of all times, was thrown into prison for three months, despite the parole that had been granted him, on the charge, made by the Secretary of the Navy, that he had violated the rules of war in escaping from the *Alabama* after her colors had been struck in the one-sided battle with the *Kearsage* in the English Channel. Judah P. Benjamin, the Confederacy's astute, cynical Secretary of the Treasury, made his way to England, there to earn a reputation at the bar which surpassed even his prewar standing in his native Louisiana. John Cabell Breckinridge, Jefferson Davis's Secretary of War, and former United States senator whom, in December 1861, his fellows had branded a traitor, escaped to Cuba and from there to Europe, not to return until the government granted him amnesty in 1869.

And the spirit's unease.

And there was another injury which could not be assessed in vanished homes and towns destroyed, in lost wealth, or in the crosses that marked the resting places of the dead. The prideful, martial soul of the South had been dealt an appalling blow. Her people, who before the war had boasted and even believed that one Southerner could lick ten Yankees, had learned that they could themselves be licked. The extent of their dispiritedness can be gauged from careful estimates that in the last year of the war the South's armies lost three times as many men by desertion as from combat or sickness, and that by the spring of 1865 fewer than one fourth of her effectives were in the field. Mistrustful of many of their civilian leaders from Jefferson Davis on down, numbed and enervated by the material attrition of four years of a war fought on their own soil, and with the governments of the Confederate states at odds with each other, undoubtedly a majority of Southerners were ready for peace, that final spring, at almost any price. The practiced eye and analytical mind of Whitelaw Reid saw clearly in the grievous hour of defeat the chastened Southern spirit:

"The first feelings were those of baffled rage. Men who had fought four years for an idea smarted with actual anguish under the stroke which showed their utter failure. Then followed a sense of bewilderment and help-lessness . . . I speak advisedly, and after a careful review of our whole experiences through the months of May and June, in all the leading centers of the Southern influence, when I say that the National Government could at that time have prescribed no condition for the return of the Rebel States which they would not have promptly accepted. They expected nothing; were prepared for the worst; would have been thankful for anything.

"In North and South Carolina, Georgia and Florida, we found this state of feeling universally prevalent. The people wanted civil government and a settlement. They asked no terms, made no conditions. They were defeated and helpless—they submitted. Would the victors be pleased to tell them what was to be done? Point out any way for a return to the established order of things, and they would walk into it. They made no hypocritical professions of new-born unionism. They had honestly believed in the right of secession. The hatred of Yankees, which had originally aided the conspirators in starting the movement, had grown and strengthened with the war. Neither the constitutional theory nor the personal hate of their lives could be changed in a day, but both were alike impotent; and having been forced to abandon the war, they longed for the blessings which any peace on any terms might be expected to bring in its train."

Any peace on any terms. But the South hoped and even believed that the peace would be a forgiving one. Did not General Lee himself think so? Had not General Grant's magnanimity and the healing words of Lincoln been auguries of reconciliation? The Confederacy had not been a mad con-glomeration of rebels, to be treated as such, but an orderly constitutional compact among sovereign states. Its defeat and dissolution could not alter the legality of its origins. The Yankees themselves had all but set precedent for withdrawal from the Union, for, had not peace between the United States and Britain been unexpectedly achieved in 1815, New England's sea-faring traders would almost certainly have disrupted the nation because of their opposition to a conflict which was destroying their commerce. So thought the South.

But on April 14 a pistol shot echoed in Ford's Theater in Washington. And louder than gunfire resounded the words of an unforgiving, aging Pennsylvanian, whose God was the God of the Hebrew avengers:

"Grind down the traitors," thundered Representative Thaddeus Stevens. "Grind the traitors in the dust."

That summer Whitelaw Reid watched shamefacedly in his Savannah hotel while a drunken Union sergeant insisted on cutting with a pair of tailor shears the buttons from the uniform of "an elegant grey-headed Brigadier who had just come in from Johnson's army; but he bore himself modestly and very handsomely through it." That summer 85,000 Negro troops helped garrison the Southern states.

And before the year was out the South would know that the plan of Abraham Lincoln and of Andrew Johnson was not what Thad Stevens of Pennsylvania and Senator Charles Sumner of Massachusetts had in mind. Which, instead of humbling her further, would arouse the spirit that in the summer of 1865 was so nearly dead.

CHAPTER 3

Black Codes and Freedmen's Bureaus

To HIS fellow South Carolinians, Wade Hampton became in his lifetime an Arthurian legend, even though, in the raucous twilight before the war, he walked the lonely middle of the road and returned to it, in the haggard dawn of defeat, after the struggle which had cost him almost everything but his honor. Eventually the South Carolinians would listen to his moderate counsel and for a while follow him, and so win back their state; but his words were not heeded when they could have done the most good.

In the early months of peace the respected men of the middle road, who counseled compromise in the all-important issue of Negro enfranchisement when compromise was yet possible, were, in the places where they could count, only a handful. Among them were such leaders as Louisiana's Francis Tillou Nicholls and L. Q. C. Lamar of Mississippi and Alexander Stevens of Georgia. But they were not men to be listened to in the time of rebuilding, so warned the spokesmen for the South's uncompromising core, for they preached political and racial heresy.

What was this heresy?

Wade Hampton had advised the South in the summer of 1865 voluntarily to grant suffrage to all Negroes who were literate or who owned property. He was the first among the South's wartime leaders to do so. General Nicholls, who had lost an arm and a leg in the service of the Confederacy, and who would be Louisiana's first post-Reconstruction governor, argued also for the enfranchisement of the educated Negro and the disfranchisement of the illiterates of both races. Lamar, whose conciliatory spirit was rare for a Mississippian, and Alexander Stevens, who had been the Confederacy's dubious vice-president, agreed that the denial of the franchise by reason of race alone was neither possible nor desirable. Yet only the stature of the dissenters saved them from general scorn.

Above other such farsighted men Wade Hampton towered. In a state much concerned with ancestral attainments he held hereditary right to high position. His grandfather and his four uncles had served as officers in the American Revolution. The grandfather, for whom his father and he were named, won the rank of major general in the War of 1812; and so ably had the first Wade Hampton managed his South Carolina sugar and cotton plantations that he died the wealthiest planter in America. The second Wade Hampton had been one of the South's great land proprietors; and, though no office seeker himself, he was so much a kingmaker that he was known as "the great Warwick of South Carolina."

Wade Hampton III was born into a proud tradition and he added greatly to it. He was a man's man, a physical giant, a huntsman who once fought a bear with a bowie knife in the Mississippi bottoms and won. When he followed his state out of the Union, although protesting that while South Carolina's resort to secession was constitutional she lacked sufficient provocation, he was probably the richest planter in the South. In 1861 his slaves had picked five thousand bales of cotton from his Mississippi plantations alone. This cotton he offered to the Confederacy to be exchanged abroad for arms.

To war with him went Hampton's Legion, a volunteer body of infantrymen, cavalrymen, and artillerymen whom he had raised and in considerable part outfitted at his own expense. He was then only forty-three, "six feet in height, broad-shouldered, deep chested, with legs which, if he chose to close them in a grip, could make a horse groan with pain." Three times wounded —at the First Battle of Manassas, at Seven Pines, and at Gettysburg—he became, after the death of Jeb Stuart, under whom he had risen to second in command, the leader of the Confederacy's Cavalry Corps. Before the war's end he had lost a son in battle, his majestic South Carolina home had been put to the torch, and the greater part of his wealth had been forfeited. South Carolina almost chose him as governor in 1865, after a constitutional convention authorized under the Lincoln Reconstruction program which President Johnson followed while he could, despite Hampton's warning that the North would construe such an act as one of defiance.

This was the man who was the first authoritative white Southerner to speak for Negro suffrage. If a majority of the white South would not listen to Wade Hampton on such an issue, it would not listen to anyone. Nor did it. But the few who agreed with him, and the militant many who did not, were all in accord on one fundamental fact. The Negro must be adjusted to his new status, and his place in the South's political and economic life had to be determined before the region whose wealth and weaknesses alike had derived from his utilization as a slave could be rehabilitated. The urgent and unresolved question was how and under whom and in whose primary behalf all this should be accomplished.

Here, inevitably, began the new parting of the ways.

In the Lincolnian spirit and purpose President Johnson set three primary tasks for the Southern state conventions which were summoned in the summer of 1865 by the provisional governors and which, though made up of delegates elected by assertedly "loyal" citizens, were actually dominated by former Confederate leaders previously pardoned by Lincoln and himself. Slavery must formally be abolished. The ordinances of secession must be nullified in each state. Each state must repudiate the Confederate war debts. Once these requirements were met the erring sisters could be joined again to the Union.

Except for Texas, which took no action at all until April of 1866, and South Carolina, which refused only to repudiate its war debt, the constitutional conventions in the Southern states fulfilled Johnson's three requirements. But these conventions and the legislatures which they created ran afoul of the Radicals, already denouncing Johnson's Reconstruction policies, for four principal and other lesser reasons, as being too soft.

The white Southerners selected in general their wartime leaders to guide them toward political rehabilitation. Not a single Southern state gave the vote to the former slaves, although Andrew Johnson had recommended—without insisting upon it—that educated and property-holding Negroes be enfranchised. Legislative representation was apportioned on the basis of white population alone. And in all but two states, Arkansas and Tennessee, where Negroes were the fewest in the South in proportion to population, statutes of varying severity, relative to the conduct and the rights of free Negroes, were enacted. These were to be known collectively as the Black Codes.

This was enough and more than enough for the Radical Republicans. The South had learned nothing from defeat. Her refusal to enfranchise the Negro, her citizens' loyalty to the Confederacy's civil and military leaders, the adoption of the Black Codes presented the Radicals with precisely the weapons they needed to negate the Lincoln-Johnson policy of conciliation and thus transform Reconstruction into a travesty of the course that Abraham Lincoln had charted.

Ironically enough, the Northern states were singularly dilatory in granting suffrage to their own Negro citizens, even though these were but small minorities and included a far higher admixture of technically skilled, literate, and long-time free men than did the South's Negro population. But their numbers in the North were politically negligible. Also, the North had won.

Perhaps, as W. E. B. Du Bois, the Negro historian, asserts in *Black Reconstruction,* the Radical leadership would have modified its early and even its later Reconstruction attitudes had even one Southern state offered the ballot to literate or property-owning Negroes and to those who had served in the Union Army. It is at least likely that, had the South given the franchise to qualified former slaves and freedmen, the Democratic party in the South and in the nation would have shared in the practical rewards of their enfranchisement; the Radicals would not have had as ready-made a chamber of Southern horrors and shortcomings; and Reconstruction politics would not have been so sadly characterized by racial cleavages.

The water was soon over the dam. When the Thirty-ninth Congress refused to approve Johnson's program, the stage was set for Radical Reconstruction.

What actuated the Southern resistance to Negro suffrage and the South's insistence upon rigid supervision of the freedmen?

The one arose in part from a valid belief that the Negro masses were unready for self-government, the other almost wholly from the conviction that the uprooted slave posed a serious threat to law and order and to the South's agricultural economy. And, no matter how literate the free Negroes might have been, the white Southern majority was emotionally unready to incorporate in the restoration of normal political life a race it considered in multitude to be not only unready for suffrage, which it was, but innately inferior. Moreover, the fear of bloodshed and economic disaster should the Negroes not be brought under control in the summer of 1865 was very real.

The Negroes in the South would have been superhuman indeed if most of them had not become intoxicated by the ferment of their wondrous new condition. Yet, in the main, the ignorant freedmen were, before mass enfranchisement, more an exasperating nuisance than a Jacobean menace. Perhaps because they had been conditioned by 250 years of enforced docility, perhaps because of the knowledge of sure, if extralegal, white retaliation, perhaps because of the presence of regulatory Union troops in the South, the freed Negroes committed comparatively few major crimes in the first year of peace, and certainly not as many as did Southern white bushwhackers and deserters and other brigands in the last year of the war.

Every Southern state had its true tales of horror: tales of white men murdered, white women raped, and white homes burned or pillaged; but there were no mass assaults upon the white people and no wholesale challenge to established law. What the Negroes did by the tens of thousands —while other thousands of older, more stable and religious-minded Negroes stayed put—was to go on a prolonged emotional binge. They abandoned the plantations and farms where they had been slaves; their favorite pastime, besides carousing, seems to have been the holding of camp meetings which were considerably more pagan than Christian.

Eda Harper, a former Mississippi slave, never forgot:

"When the war ended, a white man come to the fields and tell my mother-in-law she free as he is. She drops her hoe and danced up to the turnroad and danced right up into old master's parlor. She went so fast a bird could of sot on her dress tail. That was in June. That night she sent and got all the neighbors, and they danced all night long."

Patsy Moore, also a Mississippi slave, remembered too:

"When freedom come, folks left home, out in the streets, crying, praying, singing, shouting, yelling and knocking down everything. Some shot off big guns. Then come the calm. It was sad then. So many folks done dead, things tore up, and nowheres to go and nothing to eat, nothing to do. It got squally. Folks got sick, so hungry. Some folks starved nearly to death. Times got hard. We went to the washtub—onliest way we could all live. Maw was a crippled woman. Paw couldn't find work for so long when he mustered out."

And Felix Hayward, raised a slave in Texas:

". . . we knowed freedom was on us, but we didn't know what was to come with it. We thought we was going to get rich like the white folks. We thought we was going to be richer than the white folks, 'cause we were stronger and knowed how to work and the whites didn't; and they didn't have us to work for them any more. But it didn't turn out that way. We soon found out that freedom could make folks proud but it didn't make 'em rich."

The more fearful white Southerners had nightmarish premonitions that the bloodletting of a Haiti or a Santo Domingo might be re-enacted in an Alabama, a Georgia, a South Carolina.

Here appears a contradiction in Southern folklore which is more apparent than real. On the one hand, the happy slave bows and scrapes, contented, loyal, and grateful, to his kindly master. On the other lurks a savage and persistent threat to the safety of the white man—and the white woman—in the South. The answer to the seeming contradiction, of course, is that the stereotype of devotion does not exclude the fearsome other. Nor was either necessarily related to the kindness or to the cruelty of the individual master, for the docile and the recalcitrant slave, the house servant and the field hand alike must have been stirred by the thought of forbidden freedom.

Time and again, and long before the Abolitionists encouraged revolt, the slave had risen in the South. More than 250 organized though rarely widespread risings brought panic, murder, rapine, and merciless retaliation in a like number of years between slavery's inception and the War Between the States; and this despite the multiple safeguards of armed overseers and masters, roving patrols, and the concentrations of militia companies and volunteer home guards.

As early as 1526 a hundred slaves in what would become South Carolina rose against their Spanish masters, in the first slave revolt in North America, and fled, after bloody fighting, to the Indians. Not until 1663 did the English colonies witness insurrection—of Negro slaves and white indentured servants—but as the number of slaves increased during the eighteenth century, so did the number of risings . . . in New York City in 1712, "the conspirators tying themselves to secrecy by sucking ye blood of each others hands." . . . in Charleston in 1720, in Virginia and Louisiana and again in Charleston in 1730 . . . thrice again in South Carolina in 1775. . . .

In the early nineteenth century the revolts mounted in number and, if possible, in the indiscriminate brutality with which they were entered upon and put down. The gigantic slave Gabriel massed a thousand fellow slaves on the outskirts of Richmond in 1800; but he and his fellow conspirators had already been betrayed on the very day they planned to strike. Other insurrections during the half century also involved ominously large numbers . . . under the freed mulatto Charles Deslondes in Louisiana in 1811 . . . under Denmark Vesey in South Carolina in 1821 . . . under Nat Turner in Virginia in 1831. No slave state was immune to the contagion.

And in 1856, in the wake of Abolitionism's persistent urging to insurrection, almost the entire South was alerted to the likelihood of regionwide uprisings. The slave unrest in that year was extraordinarily strong. Conspiracies were discovered from North Carolina to Texas; in some instances the Negroes were aided and encouraged, whether through discontent, criminality, or sympathy, by white men. Plots were exposed in Louisiana, Kentucky, Tennessee, and Missouri, in Georgia, Maryland, Alabama, the Carolinas, and Florida. Hundreds of slaves were executed.

In the North the extremists welcomed the crisis. Frederick Douglass wrote: "Resolved, that while we deeply oppose the necessity of shedding human blood . . . we should rejoice in a successful slave insurrection which would teach the slaveholders the wrong and danger involved in the act of slave-holding." The Abolitionist, A. J. Grover of Illinois, proposed that William Lloyd Garrison's group aid every effort at insurrection because "Revolution is the only hope of the slave; consequently the quicker it comes the better."

Small wonder then that the South, reacting like hornets to the flaming torch, was ready to fight when it learned that behind John Brown was Massachusetts money. This was the ultimate in evil, the arousing of the Negro against the white South by the white men of the North.

Nor were Southern fears altogether allayed during the war itself, even though the Negro seldom took advantage of the unprotected rural home, in fact often serving as protector himself. Into the armies of the Union went two hundred thousand former slaves, many to be employed some day as occupation troops. Uncounted thousands of others served in nonmilitary working crews, adding their brawn to the already one-sided strength of the North, and still other thousands fled the plantations, thereby striking another and as effective a blow.

The South found little consolation in the relatively small incidence of wartime Negro violence. It was enough that the capability was there, enough that at the Negro's side and behind him, sometimes urging him on, stood the invaders, in and out of uniform.

Many Southerners, unafraid of massacre, believed that the behavior of the freedmen bore witness to the folk belief that the Negro was per se a shiftless, childlike sub-human. And almost all of the whites, the fearful and the contemptuous and the vengeful, agreed also that unless the roaming Negroes were taken off the highways, run out of the towns and cities, and sent back to the fields to make a crop, the apocalyptical horsemen would stalk the land.

The Black Codes were born in 1865 and 1866 of such conviction. In the aggregate they represented a backward-looking effort to deal with a desperate new problem. Yet the Codes were neither original nor unique. Their conglomerate inspiration derived from a past in which the slave Negro had neither political nor civil rights. They were a hodgepodge pieced together from Northern and Southern prewar vagrancy statutes; from British laws applicable to the West Indies; from national statutes relative to the free Negro; from the Union Army's makeshift regulations for the former slaves in the occupied South; and from the initial rules of the Freedmen's Bureau, the Congress-created agency for the care of the freed Negroes, which came into being a month before the war's conclusion and which did not become a regulatory and political force itself until after the Radical and general Northern reaction against the Codes.

The liberating Union forces had themselves been both humanitarian and stringent in governing the Negro in the occupied areas of the South before the end of the war. On the humanitarian side the Army ordered compensation of from $3 to $10 a month as well as rations, clothing, living quarters, and medical attention for the free laborer, and prescribed that the sick and unfit must be cared for on the plantations where they had worked. School for Negro children had to be maintained at the planters' expense. Corporal punishment was forbidden and the working day limited to a maximum of ten hours. The free laborer was to be given a small plot for cultivating his garden. Overseers who abused Negroes could be punished by military authority, and the provost marshal had the power to settle disputes between employers and workers.

But the employee was required to fulfill his labor contract, usually of a year's duration, and he could be punished by the military for disobedience or insolence. A freedman needed a pass to go from one plantation to another, and military inspectors were empowered to search Negro cabins in a generally vain effort to reduce wholesale thievery. Moreover, the Army enforced strict vagrancy laws in several states, even to the point that a Negro could not travel on the highways without his employer's permission. In some Southern cities the Army also made Negroes who refused other employment work on the streets without pay.

The Black Codes were so short lived that they served only to threaten rather than to punish. The Army and the Freedmen's Bureau soon superseded state authority in handling most of the eventualities with which the Codes sought to deal. But they lasted long enough to give proof to the Northern voting majorities that the South was impenitent.

Mississippi's legislature enacted the first, the most severe and the most pugnaciously phrased of the Black Codes. That state's body of laws relating to the freedmen was approved after a campaign in which the question of admitting Negroes as witnesses in court was the principal issue and in which a majority of lawmakers opposed to the acceptance of Negro testimony were elected. Mississippi had also irritated the Radicals and others by electing as its first postwar governor a still unpardoned Confederate brigadier general, Benjamin G. Humphreys, who had said, however, that he was desirous of renewing his allegiance to the United States and who had been an anti-secessionist Whig until Mississippi took its first walk. Johnson's presidential pardon had arrived just in time for his inauguration on October 16, 1865.

On that day Humphreys addressed the Mississippi legislature. What he said was not likely or intended to win friends and influence people up North:

"Under the pressure of federal bayonets," Humphreys declared, "urged on by the misdirected sympathies of the world in behalf of the enslaved African, the people of Mississippi have abolished the institution of slavery, and have solemnly declared in their state constitution that 'the legislature should provide by law for the protection and security of person and property of the freedmen of the state, and guard them and the state against any evils that may arise from sudden emancipation . . .' We must now meet the question as it is and not as we would like to have it. The rule must be justice. The Negro is free, whether we like it or not; we must realize that fact, now and forever. To be free, however, does not make a citizen or entitle him to social or political equality with the white man. But the constitution and justice do entitle him to protection and security in his person and property."

The governor fired a parting salvo at the Yankees for "four years of cruel war conducted on principles of vandalism disgraceful to the civilization of the age," which were "scarcely more blighting and destructive on the homes of the white man, and impoverishing, degrading to the Negro than has resulted in the last six or eight months from the administration of this black incubus."

The legislature then went about setting things straight. In so doing it went out of its way further to antagonize the North.

Here, at random, are some of the provisions of Mississippi's Black Code.

Negroes could not testify in court. They could own property only within towns and cities. Negro orphans under eighteen, and children of parents who would not or could not support them, could be bound out by probate courts as apprentices, with their former owners having first choice, the owners to support such children and to see that they were taught to read and write.

The apprenticeship law was not unlike those in the North and applied to both races; but only the freedmen and prewar free Negroes and mulattoes were singled out in the vagrancy law. Miscegenation was forbidden, and any white person who assembled with freedmen, free Negroes, or mulattoes on terms of equality or who lived in adultery with a Negro woman could be punished with a $200 fine and six months' imprisonment. The offending Negro could receive a maximum fine of $50 or ten days' imprisonment. A Negro was defined as a person having at least one eighth Negro blood.

The Mississippi Black Code forbade the giving or lending of weapons, ammunition, or liquor to freedmen and included the first Southern statute which made segregated public conveyances obligatory. Mississippi's freedmen, free Negroes, and mulattoes were required to have a lawful home or employment after the second Monday of January 1866 and to be able to give proof of residence and job pay that day and annually thereafter. If a laborer quit work without sufficient cause before his contract of employment ran out, his wages were forfeit up to the time of quitting; he could be arrested and brought back, and the arresting officer could be paid a reward by the employer. The reward would be deducted from the Negro's wages. Employers who enticed Negroes, or who knowingly hired a freedman who had left a job, or who even sold him food or supplies, were guilty of misdemeanor and could be sued for damages. Negroes could suffer special penalties for maltreating animals, making dangerous speeches, preaching without a license, selling liquor, trespassing, or rioting. White citizens who sold liquor or firearms to Negroes could be fined and placed in prison.

Mississippi's Black Code was the first and, from the Northern viewpoint, the worst. But Alabama prohibited Negroes from engaging in any trade or business, save farming, without a license; Florida authorized whippings as punishment for misbehaving freedmen, and South Carolina, whose Black Code was almost as onerous as Mississippi's, ordained that "no person of color shall migrate into and reside in the state unless within twenty days after his arrival within the same he shall enter into a bond with two freeholders as surety . . . for his good behavior and for his support." A freedman in South Carolina had to pay anywhere from $10 to $100 for a license to engage in any labor except that of farmer or servant, and such licenses could be withdrawn upon complaint.

Louisiana demanded that all farm laborers enter into labor contracts for the ensuing year within the first ten days of the new year, such contracts to be in writing and to be binding not only on the heads of families but on all minors. The worker "shall obey all proper orders of the employer or his agent, take proper care of his work mules, horses, oxen, stock; also, of all agricultural implements; an employer shall have the right to make a reasonable deduction from the laborer's wages for injuries done to animals, and for agricultural implements committed to his care." One-dollar fines were prescribed for failure to obey reasonable orders, for neglect of duty, and for leaving home without permission. Except in case of proved sickness, lost time meant a fine of twenty-five cents an hour and absences from the home place without leave a fine of two dollars a day. The dishonest laborer had to pay his employer twice the value of any hogs, sheep, poultry, or any other property of the employer stolen by him, and also for willful destruction or injury to property, one half of the double amount to be kept by the employer and the other half to be paid into a general fund which would be divided at the end of the year among other workers.

Undeniably the Codes reflected in part a reckless defiance of the victorious government. But it is probable that in 1865 the Southern lawmakers did not realize how fixed was the Radicals' determination that the Negro should have full civil rights. These unyielding Southerners saw themselves in a life-and-death struggle with political and economic realities created by the fact of emancipation. Not their conquerors but they themselves had everything to lose if the Negro would not return to work. They alone would be the white victims of racial disorder. Being human and resentful and afraid, they did weigh their Codes in favor of the white employer.

The North forgot or was unaware of such attitudes as that of the state of Illinois, for instance, which only in February 1865 repealed a twenty-year-old statute authorizing a $50 fine for free Negroes who entered the state and stipulating also that, if the Negro failed to pay, his services could be sold to the man who would pay the fine in exchange for the shortest period of labor, with one half of the sum going to the informer.

And, while Mississippi's Black Code required that Negro apprentices must be taught to read and write, Illinois made no such stipulation. Moreover, the vagrancy laws of Maine, Connecticut, Rhode Island, and New York were as severe as or more severe than were any adopted in the South. But the South's legislation was directed almost exclusively against a people whose enslavement had been in part responsible for the catastrophic war that had been waged. In 1865 that made an important difference.

And so it was that, in behalf of the Black Codes, Mississippi's special commission to recommend laws to govern the free men would suggest sarcastically that those who found them unbearable "might flee and take sweet refuge in the more inviting bosom of the state or community who may cherish a more lively and congenial fellow feeling . . . for that class. . . ."

And so it was that a bombastic Northern newspaper, the Chicago *Tribune,* would warn that "We tell the white men in Mississippi that the men of the North will convert the state of Mississippi into a frog pond before they will allow such laws to disgrace one foot of soil in which the bones of our soldiers sleep and over which the flag of freedom waves."

And so it was that the admonition of Wade Hampton of South Carolina, trying his greathearted best to bring together two harried peoples, would not be heard:

"As a slave he was faithful to us; as a free man let us treat him as a friend. Deal with him frankly, justly, kindly, and my word for it, he will reciprocate your kindness, cling to his own home, his own country and his former master."

Paternalistic, yes; unrealistic, maybe. But neither more paternalistic nor unrealistic than the workings out of the Freedmen's Bureau which in a limited sense preceded and then encompassingly superseded the Black Codes.

I went down to Augusta to the Freedmen's Bureau to see if 'twas true we was free. I reckon there was over a hundred people there. The man got up and stated to the people: "You all is just as free as I am. You ain't got no mistress and no master. Work when you want."

—Willis Benfield, slave in Georgia.

At another time and under different circumstances the most fervid Southerners could have liked the kindly, one-armed man from Maine, General Oliver Otis Howard. But it was his lot that his name would become synonymous with the Bureau of Freedmen, Refugees and Abandoned Lands, popularly—and unpopularly—known as the Freedmen's Bureau, the nation's first Federal welfare agency, an organization conceived in humane concern, nurtured on ineptitude and political manipulation, and destined to die of material and spiritual corruption; and so he became anathema to the South. For if the Black Codes were repugnant to the North, the expanded Freedmen's Bureau and the so-called Loyal Leagues, which the Bureau's agents encouraged, were to the white South the very creations of Beelzebub.

The placing of men in positions of extravagant political authority has, inevitably, the chanciness of a poker deal. Had General Sherman, in wartime the South's scourge and during Reconstruction its understanding friend, stood in the place of Oliver Howard—or for that matter, and not inconceivably, in the place of President Ulysses S. Grant—the history of the American nation could have been mightily altered. The deal didn't go that way.

Howard was a deeply religious, humanitarian, and well-intentioned man, but he was the wrong man for the difficult and important job to which two presidents assigned him.

His record before and during the war had been generally good. The son of a Maine farmer, he had put himself through Bowdoin College by teaching during vacations. He had entered West Point in 1850 and in 1854 had been graduated fourth in his class. Two months after Fort Sumter was fired upon he had resigned as instructor in mathematics at the Academy to become colonel of the Third Maine Regiment, and before the year was out he had risen to brigadier general of Volunteers with the brevet rank of major general in the regular Army. He had fought well at Bull Run and on the Peninsula. At Fair Oaks he had lost his right arm; but he was back in the field in a matter of weeks, to take active part, as commander of the rear guard, at the Second Battle of Manassas. He saw action at South Mountain, at Antietam, at Fredericksburg where he led a division, at Chancellorsville where he bore the onus for the initial Union reverses, and at Gettysburg where, although his personal courage was marked, his indecisiveness as a commander contributed to the Union defeat in the first day's battle. After participating in the fighting around Chattanooga he was made a corps commander, then commander of the Army and Department of the Tennessee and of the right wing of Sherman's Army on the march from Atlanta to the sea. Shocked by the outrages then committed by Union troops, he had summarily punished looters and criminal marauders.

Unfortunately for the South and the nation, General Howard's military and personal virtues were overshadowed by his weaknesses as commissioner of the Freedmen's Bureau, a post to which Lincoln had appointed him upon its creation in March 1865 and to which Andrew Johnson had reappointed him in May. The pious man whom the Union had admired as "The Christian Soldier" was a poor executive, a naïve, too-trusting administrator in an agency which would become uncommonly tainted by fraud, inefficiency, and gross political misconduct.

For these and other less valid reasons Oliver Howard was not to be altogether admiringly remembered even in the North as the first peacetime guardian of the free Negroes' rights and minister to their material needs. In its original enterprises the Freedmen's Bureau was to be a monument to his good will; in much of its later aspects, a memorial to his own frailties—dishonesty was not among them—and to the misdirection and abuse of an essentially noble purpose.

Congress passed the first Freedmen's Bureau bill, establishing the agency as an adjunct of the War Department, on March 3, 1865. At the time of its creation Senator Lyman Trumbull of Illinois, the scholarly moderate whose determination to protect the freedmen would lead him later to transform the Bureau into a partisan weapon, saw the Bureau as "only designed to aid these helpless, ignorant, unprotected people . . . until they can provide for and take care of themselves." The Army's own prior efforts to care for and keep under some sort of control the multitude of Negroes whom war and their own first purposeless intoxication with freedom had made destitute had been uneven and without central direction. The need to supplant or correlate the relief work of the Freedmen's Aid Society and the American Missionary Association and other church and philanthropic organizations was acute.

General Howard divided the South into ten Bureau districts, each with an assistant commissioner at its head. These assistants were military men who already had experience in caring for the freedmen within the Union lines. Some of them were as prejudiced against the former masters as they were devoted to improving the lot of the former slaves. Under these administrators, local agents in every Southern county tried to untangle the war-knotted threads of everyday living, provide food and clothing for the needy, and direct the work of Negro rehabilitation. The original agents were usually commanders of small military garrisons and were, in general, abler men than the political appointees—"men who are too lazy to work and just a little too honest to steal"—who would follow them after the Bureau's powers were explosively expanded.

Had the Bureau continued to function within its initially prescribed limits, the good it undeniably accomplished in its first purposeful guise could have been lasting. As Dr. W. E. B. Du Bois summarizes its Herculean assignment, the Bureau was authorized "to make as rapidly as possible a general survey of conditions and needs in every state and locality; to relieve immediate hunger and distress; to appoint state commissioners and upwards of 900 Bureau officials; to put the laborers to work at regular wages; to transport laborers, teachers and officials; to furnish land for the peasants; to open schools; to pay bounties to black soldiers and their families; to establish hospitals and guard health; to administer justice between man and former master; to answer continuous and persistent criticism, North and South, black and white; to find funds to pay for all this."

The early efforts to accomplish these tasks were both imposing and heartening. The local Bureaus acted variously as employment agencies and relief centers for distributing food and medicine to the needy, as supervisors of labor contracts between former masters and former slaves, and as disciplinarians of Negroes unwilling to work. They opened and operated schools for the Negroes and provided them with hospital care. The national Bureau's zeal for education, coupled with the educational programs of other Northern welfare groups, had the effect, naturally resented by white Southerners, of giving Negro children and their parents and even their grandparents better opportunities for education than were afforded the poorer white children of the South. The local agencies kept close watch on agricultural labor contracts—land rental for cash by the most fortunate Negroes, land rental by payment of fixed shares of the crop, and sharecropping. They fixed money wages for farm laborers whose employers could and would pay in cash and they saw that the employer provided a basic food allowance of salt pork, meal, and molasses.

The Bureau's relief work, both during its period as an emergency unit and later, was, for the times, stupendous. More than 21,000,000 rations were issued, mostly between 1865 and 1867; 15,500,000 of them to Negroes and the rest to destitute whites. Of the issuance of Bureau rations in Atlanta, a Southern reporter wrote: "I cannot help but remark that it must be a matter of gratitude as well as surprise for our people to see a government, which was lately fighting us with fire and sword and shell, now generously feeding our poor and distressed. . . . There is much in this that takes away the bitter sting and sorrow of the past. . . . Even crippled Confederate soldiers have their sacks filled and are fed."

In the six years beginning with June 1, 1865, $5,262,511.26 of Bureau funds went into Negro public schools. By 1870 the Bureau could count 3300 teachers and 149,581 pupils in day and night classrooms. It founded or gave substantial sums to the first Negro colleges and universities. This educational activity was its finest and most lasting contribution to the dream that Reconstruction could be real reconstruction.

When it was necessary the early assistant commissioners and their local agents could be stern in handling the malcontented or trifling Negroes. Thousands of such vagrants were put to forced labor on public works. In Georgia, General Davis Tillson, the assistant commissioner, withheld government rations from able-bodied Negroes who refused to work.

But not even the most disciplinary commissioner or agent could still the heady rumor that before Christmas of the first year of independence every freedman would receive forty acres and a mule. General Rufus Saxton reported from South Carolina, late in 1865, that the impression was universal among the freedmen that they would receive their forty acres in January and that his agents, despite every effort, had not been able to "disabuse so deep seated a conviction." The rumor had spread from the pledge made by Thaddeus Stevens in 1865 that the land of all Confederates owning more than 200 acres would be confiscated and the 300,000,000 acres involved divided among the freedmen in forty-acre plots. Wishful or mischievous local agents and clerks, Radical troublemakers, and political self-seekers and some teachers spread the fantastic promise. And the free Bureau rations were no inconsiderable factor in helping to aggravate the labor chaos which the Bureau sought to end.

On February 6, 1866, Congress approved a bill of which Senator Trumbull was the author, broadening and extending the functions of the Bureau and giving it extraordinary judicial powers in white-Negro relations and disputes. It was, in effect, a warning to the South that its Black Codes were not to govern the Negroes' conduct.

Senator Trumbull's bill was proposed as a guarantee to the Negro of his rights as a free citizen; but in its plan for such a guarantee it clearly violated the civil rights of the white Southerners. If a Negro believed that civil equality was not accorded him or that he was not being justly treated, he could complain to the agent of the Freedmen's Bureau in his county. The agent, serving as a court, could determine without a jury whether the accused was guilty and impose upon him a fine or prison sentence. Behind the Bureau agents stood the Army.

President Johnson vetoed the bill on February 19, 1866. The act, his veto message said, contained unconstitutional provisions, notably one authorizing trials by military court-martial from which no appeal could be made even to the United States Supreme Court. The penal provisions were harsh. The civil courts were bypassed. The bill itself gave to a President too much patronage. There was no necessity for unlimited Federal assistance to the Negroes. The Negroes themselves would be unduly encouraged to idleness. The eleven states most affected by the bill were not represented in the Congress which enacted the measure. The old law itself had more than a year yet to run. So Johnson argued.

The veto message was conciliatory, reasoned, notable for its adherence to constitutional principles. But the Radicals were in no mood for reason, compromise, or constitutionality. On July 16, 1866, Congress, after an earlier failure, passed the Freedmen's Bureau expansion bill over the presidential veto.

With the establishment of the Freedmen's Bureau as a political force and the prior or concurrent return to civil life of many of the Army officers who had directed the local agencies, it became a happy hunting ground for political timeservers and highhanded or corrupt agents whose behavior destroyed in short order whatever Southern respect had been won by the genuine reformers, the teachers, and the decent administrators; for, though many of these good folk remained, or came later, their work was overshadowed by men whose unforgivable sins, from the Southern viewpoint, were their open and unscrupulous political activity and their pro-Negro bias in court.

The Freedmen's Bureau itself was not directly responsible for what was to the whites the most detested and alarming aspect of the freedmen's entry into the South's political life. But Bureau agents and lesser employees were the principal organizers of the Southern chapters of the Union League of America, whose clubs in the South were known as the Loyal Leagues.

The parent Union League of America had been founded in the North in 1864 in a dispiriting time of Southern military success. The membership had then been made up only of loyal white citizens, most of them strenuously anti-Southern, determined to punish the secessionists after the war and to keep the Republican party in power forever. Until after the showdown between the Radicals and Johnson the Southern branches that were established after the war were made up principally of white Northern and Southern Unionists. But politically astute Republicans recognized that if the Negro could be shaken out of his political apathy and be voted as a bloc, the party to which he could ascribe his freedom could hold power in perpetuity.

The character of the established Leagues changed. Their memberships and that of the new clubs which spread throughout the lower South became overwhelmingly Negro. Their leaders were either Negroes or Northern whites. Their stated objectives were: "To preserve liberty and the Union . . . to protect, strengthen and defend all loyal men, without regard to sect, condition or race; to elect honest and reliable Union men to all offices of profit or trust in national, state and local governments; to secure equal civil and political rights to all men."

The Leagues were skillfully designed to remind the Negroes of their new importance and their obligations to the Republican party as the author of their freedom. They were organized in secret, mumbo-jumbo ritualistic lodges. The password was the four L's—*Lincoln, Liberty, Loyal, League.* Elaborate prayers and incantations enlivened the meetings. The flag, the Bible, and copies of the Declaration of Independence and the Constitution were prominently displayed. The dues were usually ten cents a month, with the initiation fee running as high as five dollars.

The Loyal Leagues fanned the fires of racial discord. Their assemblies were characterized by denunciations of the Southern whites. Negroes who through loyalty to their former masters were reluctant to turn against them or become Republicans were threatened with death; many were badly beaten and some were murdered. The Loyal Leagues in places organized military units and drilled along the highways; inevitably clashes between the armed Negroes and armed whites were frequent.

White and Negro organizers promised that the land of the white Confederates would be confiscated and divided among the Negroes; no less important personages than Thad Stevens and Ben Butler, the organizers said, were advocating such redistribution, which was true enough.

It was not long before hosts of the South's adult Negroes, entranced by the colorful rituals and the dazzling vision of forty acres and a mule and with their gratitude to the Republican party as continuously encouraged as was their resentment against the white Southern Democrats, belonged to the Loyal Leagues. Negro women members of the League vowed that they would not consort with or marry men who would not join.

The white organizers went to unusual lengths to enlist League members. They drank and mingled with the recruits at dances, picnics, and joint political and League gatherings. Incendiary organizers and white League officials, often employees of the Freedmen's Bureau, encouraged Negro members to turn upon the Southern whites, so that the Loyal Leagues contributed more than any other Negro activity to the spread of the Ku Klux

Klan. One of the worst of the organizers was a self-styled colonel, James Stewart Sinclair, who also called himself "The Fighting Parson." Ostentatiously mingling with League members, he urged the Negroes to hate and insult their former masters and told them that within ten years the only Southern problem would be the Negro's decision as to what he would do with the whites.

Not all such troublemakers were from the North, or were Bureau workers. Few were more rabid than James W. Hunnicutt, a South Carolinian who migrated to Virginia. Hunnicutt was a preacher, a former editor of a religious newspaper and a onetime slaveowner who had supported secession. He had later deserted from the Confederate Army and had become a Radical Republican editor in Richmond. Hunnicutt's venom was deadly, his invitation to lawlessness brazen: "There is corn and beef and flour and bacon and turkeys and chicken and wood and coal in the state," he wrote in one editorial, "and the colored people will have them before they will starve." And again: "If the next Congress does not give us universal suffrage, we'll roll up our sleeves, pitch in and have the damndest revolution the world ever saw."

Some Northern observers gave warning, among them Harriet Beecher Stowe, who wrote from her postwar home on the St. Johns River in Florida that "corrupt politicians are already beginning to speculate on the Negroes as possible capital for their schemes and to fill their poor hands with all sorts of vagaries. . . ." Mrs. Stowe had endorsed Johnson's Reconstruction program and agreed with her brother Henry who "takes the ground that it is unwise and impolitic to endeavor to force vigorous suffrage on the South at the point of a bayonet."

Oliver Howard stubbornly refused to believe that any of his Bureau officials were guilty of the fraud, inefficiency, and graft with which it was honeycombed or that, by 1868, its usefulness had been all but completely impaired by his agents' political activity and their pitting of Southern Negro against Southern white. He ascribed to race prejudice and politics all criticism of the Bureau's personnel and policies. He had only good words for Radical Reconstruction, even for the South Carolina legislature of 1868, possibly the most venal aggregation of men ever brought together anywhere at any time in a democratic setting.

"These men were in earnest," he wrote of that body. "They were educating themselves to legislation by legislating. Every pulse of the heart of the majority beats for the flag, for the Union. And who would substitute for such a legislature even extraordinary ability and learning, coupled with disloyal sentiments and intense conviction of the righteousness of state supremacy?"

Howard's rejection of criticism of the Bureau's political role, his sentimentality, and his indifference to proper business methods contributed greatly to the disesteem in which the Bureau was held by a considerable body of Northerners as well as nearly universally in the White South before it closed up shop. The Trumbull bill had provided in 1866 that the Bureau should disband after two years. Its life was subsequently extended to 1872, but, except in Negro education, its usefulness had ended before then.

Howard himself became the object of serious charges in Congress in 1870 and again in 1874—this time by William W. Belknap, Grant's own later discredited and dishonest Secretary of War, an odd person, indeed, to accuse anyone of misfeasance or malfeasance in office. The charges against Howard included misapplication of public funds, sanction of incomplete and incorrect records, responsibility for some minor defalcations by Bureau officers, and failure to put into effect a suitable system of payments to Negro veterans. A congressional committee absolved him in 1870; later a special court of inquiry, appointed by Grant, exonerated him of the offenses of which Belknap had accused him.

The Bureau itself was posthumously tainted by the failure of the Freedmen's Savings and Trust Company because of its unofficial but close ties with the ill-fated bank. The Freedmen's Savings and Trust Company had operated, under a charter granted by Congress, as a private organization; but its president for most of its life had been John W. Alvord, general superintendent of education in the Freedmen's Bureau, and Howard himself had been an influential director.

The bank was organized as an idealistically conceived means to teach the freedmen to save and was popularly identified with the Bureau, both during the years of its success and at the time of its failure. Before it closed its doors the bank had thirty-two branches in the South. Between 1865, when it was organized, and 1874, when it failed, free Negroes deposited in it nearly $20,000,000. It fell victim to bad bookkeeping, ill-advised loans, and corruption; and although the federal government should have accepted a moral obligation to do so, it did not compensate the depositors. They were eventually paid only sixty-two cents on the dollar.

By then the Freedmen's Bureau had wound up most of its affairs. From 1868 to 1872 it engaged only in the operation of schools and collecting pensions and bounties for Negro veterans. The Bureau had failed in what should have been its primary objective, that of bringing together the white man and the Negro in the South. It had, instead, the opposite effect. And the Loyal Leagues, which its agents had organized and encouraged, died because their organizers and leaders, who had counseled racial hatred and violence, were engulfed and destroyed by the vastly better organized and more determined counter-violence of the white Southerner.

But the Bureau cannot be dismissed as a bureaucratic miscarriage. In the famine-ridden postwar years of 1865, 1866, and 1867 it fed the hungry and clothed the naked and succored the sick, "a great and indispensible work of mercy and relief, at a time when no other organization or body was in a position to do that work." Throughout its checkered existence it was the principal medium through which the free Negro could be educated.

Two assignments in Oliver Howard's later military career reflected an ironic contradiction which was more than simply a personal one. The "Christian soldier" who had ministered to one dark-skinned people after the liberation he had helped to win for them would not draw his sword again except to crush another. Placed in command of the Department of the Columbia in 1874, he led in 1877 an expedition against the Nez Percé Indians and another, in 1878, against the Bannocks and the Piutes. If the contradiction disturbed him or many of the Abolitionist and Radical survivors in the Congress which by then they no longer ruled, they largely managed to keep their misgivings to themselves.

It is kindlier then, to a kindly man, to remember Oliver Howard, who was a teacher before he was a soldier, not for his military record, his partisanship, or his lackluster administration of an unprecedented venture in government, but because of his zeal in educating the Negro, and not only in secondary schools. Not that the white South, as will be noted, loved him any the better for that.

CHAPTER 4

Pardons for What?

JUST as the enactment of the Black Codes infuriated the North and created a quick suspicion that the South intended to continue slavery in very thin disguise, so did the Northern assumption that, in seceding, the South had been collectively and individually guilty of the crime of treason embitter the losers. Especially angered were the more than 150,000 Southerners who were excluded from the original amnesties granted first by Lincoln and then by Johnson, and who were forced to the humiliating alternatives of submitting to political and even economic discrimination or of seeking a pardon for having done what they had believed to be their constitutional right to do. They had been loyal to their respective states. They had served and defended the confederation of these states. The issue had been decided not by law but by arms.

Their outrage was matched, at the least, by the conviction of the Radicals that amnesty and individual pardons gave the military and civilian leaders of the Confederacy, and its slaveholding aristocracy, a too easily secured absolution for the high crime of treason.

Caught in the middle between the unforgiving Radicals and the unrepentant Secessionists stood President Andrew Johnson, the suspect Democrat in the White House.

Lincoln's successor issued his own first General Amnesty Proclamation —but not the first since the beginning of hostilities—on May 29, 1865. It differed in two significant respects from Lincoln's General Amnesty Proclamation of December 1863. Lincoln's offer was made to a people at war, primarily to weaken their will to fight, and it excepted only six classes of persons: ". . . all who are or shall have been civil or diplomatic officers or agents of the so-called Confederate government; all who have left judicial stations under the United States to aid the rebellion; all who are or shall have been military or naval officers of said so-called Confederate government above the rank of colonel in the army or lieutenant in the navy; all who left seats in the United States Congress to aid the rebellion; all who resigned commissions in the (United States) army or navy . . . and afterwards aided the rebellion; and all who have engaged in any way in treating colored persons, or white persons in charge of such, otherwise than lawfully as prisoners of war . . ."

Andrew Johnson was offering amnesty, upon their taking the required oath of allegiance, to a defeated people who could no longer wage a war; but his anger and grief at the murder of Lincoln, his strong dislike for the propertied, slaveholding Southerners, and the mood of Congress and the people influenced him to add to Lincoln's original six exceptions eight others, including one which Lincoln had also tacked on later, namely Confederates under restraint of federal authorities. Johnson's other exceptions were "all persons who have been or are absentees from the United States for the purpose of aiding the rebellion; all Confederate military and naval officers who were educated at West Point or Annapolis; all persons who held pretended offices of governors of states in insurrection against the United States; all persons who left their homes within the jurisdiction of the United States to aid the Confederacy; all persons who have been engaged in the destruction of the commerce of the United States; all voluntary participants in the rebellion and the estimated value of whose taxable property is over $20,000; and all who have taken and later violated Lincoln's amnesty oath or the oath of allegiance to the United States."

Some fifty occupations were represented in the excepted classes: planters and businessmen, postmasters and mail contractors, cotton agents, state and Confederate judges, district attorneys, state printers and customs officers, governors and congressmen, tax assessors, members of the secession conventions—in sum total, the majority of the surviving upper-class Secessionists of the South.

Without a pardon none among the proscribed group could take part in the political rebuilding of the South. Unpardoned, none could buy or sell property, obtain copyrights or patents, or recover his lands and possessions if they had been seized as abandoned or enemy property. Under a strict—and never-invoked interpretation of the proscriptions—none of the proscribed could be certain even that he was legally married.

But to those excluded from amnesty Lincoln and Johnson alike gave both the hope and, in generous measure, the reality of pardons. Had they not, a considerable majority of the South's most responsible, best-educated and relatively well-to-do citizens would have found themselves, from 1865 to 1867, beyond the pale of the region's political and, to a degree, its economic life.

Consider then, as a small but meaningful footnote to the story of amnesty and pardon during Reconstruction the unusual but not unique case of Anna Maria Hennen Jennings—Mrs. Needler R. Jennings—of New Orleans, whose presidential pardon for being the widow of her late husband now adorns the hallway of a great-grandson's home.

Save in one respect, this handsomely printed, two-page document is similar to some 13,500 others which Andrew Johnson signed in 1865 and 1866. On Mrs. Jennings's pardon almost everywhere that the printed pronouns *he, him,* or *his* appear, they are scratched out and the substitutes *she, her,* or *hers* are scrawled in ink above them. The omissions of changes in gender here and there can be ascribed to a clerk's carelessness or haste.

The pardon reads as modified:

ANDREW JOHNSON,

PRESIDENT OF THE UNITED STATES OF AMERICA,

TO ALL TO WHOM THESE PRESENTS

SHALL COME, GREETING:

WHEREAS, Mrs. A. M. Jennings of New Orleans Louisiana, by taking part in the late rebellion against the Government of the United States, has made himself liable to heavy pains and penalties;

AND WHEREAS, the circumstances of ~~his~~ *her* case render ~~him~~ *her* a proper object of Executive clemency;

NOW, THEREFORE, BE IT KNOWN, that I, Andrew Johnson, President of the United States of America, in consideration of the premises, divers other good and sufficient reasons me thereunto moving, do hereby grant to the said *Mrs A. Mc Jennings* a full pardon and amnesty for all offences by ~~him~~ *her* committed, arising from participation, direct or implied, in the said rebellion, conditioned as follows:

1st.   This pardon to be of no effect until the said *Mrs A. Mc Jennings* shall take the oath prescribed in the Proclamation of the President, dated May 29th, 1865.

2d.   To be void and of no effect if the said *Mrs A Mc Jennings* shall hereafter, at any time, acquire any property whatever in slaves, or make use of slave labor.

3d.   That the said *Mrs A. Mc Jennings* first pay all costs which may have accrued in any proceedings instituted or pending against his person or property, before the date of the acceptance of this warrant.

4th.   That the said *Mrs A. Mc Jennings* shall not, by virtue of this warrant, claim any property or the proceeds of any property that has been sold by the order, judgment, or decree of a court under the confiscation laws of the United States.

5th.   That the said *Mrs A. Mc Jennings* shall notify the Secretary of State, in writing, that she has received and accepted the foregoing pardon.

IN TESTIMONY WHEREOF, I have hereunto signed my name and caused the Seal of the United States to be affixed.

Done at the City of Washington, this _Tenth_ day of _November_

A. D. 1865, and of the Independence of the

United States the _Ninetieth_

(SEAL)

By the President: _Andrew Johnson_

William H. Seward Secretary of State

Mrs. Jennings must have been a much-relieved woman that November when Andrew Johnson granted executive forgiveness for being widow and heir of a Louisianian who had been worth $20,000 or more. But neither she nor the five young daughters whom the Battle of Shiloh had orphaned nearly four years earlier would soon forgive in turn the government which required her to implore such an instrument. Resolute, proud Anna Maria Jennings had not wanted to seek a pardon, but she had to recover her property if only because there were the children to feed and clothe and educate.

She knew that her middle-aged, patrician husband had not thought himself a traitor when he entered the Confederate service as a lieutenant colonel. He had been a cultured citizen of his adopted city, New Orleans, to which he had come from Virginia as a young man, a leading spirit in the Lyceum, a volunteer in the Mexican War, and a moderate Whig and disbeliever in secession. Like many another Southern man, he had reluctantly gone with his state and the Confederacy to his death. And she knew that no traitor either, though also excluded from amnesty, was her aged father, Justice Alfred Hennen, a revered pioneer among the Americans in New Orleans. A Kentuckian, he had settled there in 1807, soon after finishing the study of law at Yale University, and had entered upon the practice of his profession. He had prospered at the bar and later had become a member of the State Supreme Court.

In 1815, when Andrew Jackson's nondescript army fended off and destroyed the British at the Battle of New Orleans, young Alfred Hennen had been one of the general's picked American bodyguard. His two sons had served their country in the Mexican War, and one of them, a lawyer too, had unsuccessfully defended William Mumford, the high-spirited gambler who was hanged, on order of General Butler, for tearing down the flag of the United States after the capitulation of New Orleans in 1862. The Hennens and the Jenningses and their kin and their kind had been, according to their lights, as upright and patriotic as they had been prosperous and prideful folk in the prewar South, and they were not in the habit of asking pardon from man or government.

Yet more than 16,000 Southerners among those excluded from Andrew Johnson's first amnesty sought pardons as soon as they were offered. With a generosity in singular contrast to his attitude before he became President, Johnson granted pardons to some 13,500 of these applicants. His magnanimity won him no friends among the infuriated Radicals, who accused him of being too soft, pro-Southern, even corrupt in his pardon policy.

Long before the surrender Lincoln had pardoned hundreds of affected Southerners in Arkansas, Tennessee, Louisiana, and elsewhere in the border states and in the occupied South. With the setting in 1865 of the Southern state conventions required for putting into motion the machinery of reunion under the Lincoln-Johnson plan, thousands of Southern men—and a few women—descended upon Washington in person or by proxy, bearing letters and often supporting petitions explaining just how and why and to what extent they had been loyal to the Confederacy and why they thought they should be forgiven. Among them were many former Confederate generals and holders of high civilian office in the Confederacy. But never Jefferson Davis, President of the Confederate States of America.

Not all of their applications would reflect the dignity with which Robert E. Lee made his own unsuccessful request:

Richmond, Virginia, June 13, 1865.
His Excellency Andrew Johnson,
President of the United States.

Sir: Being excluded from the provisions of the amnesty and pardon contained in the proclamation of the 29th ult., I hereby apply for the benefits and full restoration of all rights and privileges extended to those included in its terms. I graduated at the Military Academy at West Point in June, 1829; resigned from the United States Army, April, 1861; was a general in the Confederate Army, and included in the surrender of the Army of Northern Virginia, April 9, 1865. I have the honor to be very respectfully,

Your obedient servant,

R. E. LEE

Though his concern for the disposition of Arlington, his wife's family estate where they had lived in luxury before the war, offered a family motivation, Lee's primary reason for urging Southerners "to take the oath of allegiance and accept in good faith the amnesty offered," and recommending that the members of the excepted classes apply for pardons, was patriotic. "I believe it to be the duty of every man to unite in the restoration of the country and the re-establishment of peace and harmony," he explained. "Those considerations governed me in the counsels I gave others, and induced me on the 13th of June to make application to be included in the terms of the Amnesty Proclamation. . . ."

Few other applicants stated their cases so briefly. Many offered excuses that must have been proffered with tongue in cheek. A North Carolinian recounted how he had consented "reluctantly and with bleeding heart" to vote with other delegates for the ordinance of secession in his state. The engineer of the Confederate raider *Alabama,* begging "clemency and pardon for the wrong he had committed," pled that he had been the "misguided dupe and tool of others." An Alabama petitioner, declaring that he had been forced to do military service as a member of the fire department in a provost guard, hardly knew how else he had participated in the late rebellion "unless the passing of Confederate currency may be considered as participating therein."

The oath required of all was as brief as was Lee's application. "I, ———, do solemnly swear (or affirm) in the presence of Almighty God, that I will henceforth faithfully support, protect and defend the constitution of the United States and the Union of the states thereunder, and that I will in like manner abide by and faithfully support all laws and proclamations which have been made during the existing rebellion with reference to the emancipation of slaves. So help me God."

But there were outnumbering thousands of others who would not seek pardons at all. They would remain pariahs, at least theoretically, until Johnson's final, universal amnesty of Christmas Day, 1868. It was for them and himself that Innes Randolph, an aristocratic Virginia lawyer and journalist, wrote *The Good Old Rebel,* which was circulated anonymously. Its first verse read:

> *Oh, I'm a good old rebel,*
> *Now that's just what I am;*
> *For the 'fair land of freedom,'*
> *I do not give a damn;*
> *I'm glad I fit against it,*
> *I only wish we'd won,*
> *And I don't want no pardon*
> *For anything I done.*

Inevitably scandals would smirch the pardoning process.

Whether they wanted to regain property, to occupy public office, or to participate in political rehabilitation, quick action was imperative for most of the applicants for pardon. And how better to get such action than by going to persons with influence—to the right general or congressman, to a military governor, or, better still, to a pipeline to the White House itself?

One lamentable result was that, despite the press of other business more vital to the nation, much of the time of the President, the Department of Justice, and the Department of State was almost completely taken up, throughout the summer of 1865 and well into the fall, with the consideration and granting of pardons; so much so that the President's health was for a time seriously impaired by the strain. The New York *Herald* noted caustically on July 31, 1865: "The scene at the President's reception today was most remarkable. The anteroom was crowded with senators and representatives of the late Rebel Congress, seeking interviews with the President and beseeching that their pardons might be hurried up."

From nine to three daily the President's door was open to Southerners seeking pardons and to job-hunting Northerners and Southerners. Nevertheless, relatively few pardons had been granted by the middle of August, for Johnson had planned to study personally each petition. And the applications could not be really carefully studied even after the appointment of a pardon clerk in the Attorney General's office to examine petitions and arrange them for higher consideration.

Obviously a pardon board should have been set up. Even more practical was a suggestion by the New York *Tribune,* soon echoed by the *Herald,* for the issuance of "a simple proclamation setting forth that certain Rebels for the good of the country are expatriated, and all the rest admitted to the rights of citizens." But Johnson did not set up a pardon board and he was not to issue another amnesty proclamation for two years, by which time only a relatively few among those in the excepted classes who had sought pardons had not received them.

Instead, as the appeals piled up, there came into being a new and generally unsavory profiteer, the pardon broker or attorney; and in short order gossip and even formal accusations brought the White House itself into the clouded picture. The pardon brokers, whose usual fee was $150, busied themselves in the Southern state capitals as well as in Washington. The provisional governors appointed by Johnson were also besieged by applications for pardons, by pleas for support of such applications, and by supplications for political jobs from Southerners made abject by their ambition or their poverty.

The son of the nation's twelfth·president was to look back with contempt upon the Washington in which the pardon brokers flourished in 1865. Understandably, General Richard Taylor, who on May 4 had surrendered the last Confederate army east of the Mississippi, and who was the son of the late President Zachary Taylor, was prejudiced. Though he worked ceaselessly to aid his compatriots who sought pardons, never would he apply for a pardon himself. When his father was President, General Taylor had known many Whigs who were now influential Republicans, and perhaps because he thought some of them might be helpful, he went to Washington in the summer of 1865 to try vainly to obtain the release of Jefferson Davis and of several Confederate governors, all held in military prisons. In Washington he called upon President Johnson and found him "a saturnine man, who made no return to my bow," but who "had now somewhat abated his wolfish desire for vengeance." Taylor did obtain permission from Johnson to visit Davis at Fortress Monroe, but days were required to accomplish even this, days during which time he was sickened by what he saw about him. Of the period he wrote later in his *Destruction and Reconstruction:*

> Meantime, an opportunity to look upon the amazing spectacle presented by the dwellers at the capital was afforded. The things seen by Pilgrim in a dream were at this Vanity Fair visible in the flesh: "all such merchandise sold as houses, lands, trades, places, honors, preferments, states, lusts, pleasures; and delights of all sorts, as bawds, wives, husbands, children, masters, servants, lives, bloods, bodies, souls, greenbacks, pearls, precious stones, and what not." The eye of the inspired tinker had pierced the darkness of two hundred years, and seen what was to come. The martial tread of hundreds of volunteer generals, just disbanded, resounded in the streets. Gorged with loot, they spent it as lavishly as Morgan's buccaneers after the sack of Panama. Their women sat at meat or walked the highways, resplendent in jewels, spoil of Southern matrons. The camp-followers of the army were here in high carnival, and in character and numbers rivaled the attendants of Xerxes. Courtesans swarmed everywhere, about the inns, around the Capitol, in the antechambers of the "White House," and were brokers for the transaction of all business. Of a tolerant disposition and with a wide experience of earthly wickedness, I did not feel called upon to cry aloud against these enormities, remembering the fate of Faithful; but I had some doubts concerning divine justice; for why were the "cities of the Plain" overthrown and this place suffered to exist?

The pardon brokers in this Vanity Fair and elsewhere in the nation were blatant influence peddlers. They advertised their talents in newspapers throughout the South, much as did two Georgia attorneys named Briscoe and Graffenreid who proclaimed in Milledgeville's *Southern Recorder* that they could "give special attention to the preparation of applications for pardons" and that they could also "make arrangements with professional parties at Washington City to attend to all such cases." This pair's fees ranged from an average of $150 to $500 in very special cases.

No evidence exists that Johnson and the cabinet members involved in the granting of pardons ever directly encouraged the pardon brokers, although the New York *Herald* probably overstated the case when it wrote of the Attorney General in September 1865 that "any intimation that money can assist a petition is a gross insult to his whole office from himself to his humblest messenger." There were enough minor officeholders in the Department of State and the Department of Justice and even in the White House who, recognizing an easy dollar when they saw one, could be persuaded to bring a client's petition before the pardon clerk, the Attorney General, or the Cabinet secretaries themselves, and through one such highly placed official or another to the attention of the President himself.

One notorious case, involving a woman pardon agent, had Washington gossiping for months about sexual immorality within the White House. The factional versions of the case of Mrs. L. L. Cobb, an attractive woman with the habit of talking too much about her easy access to the White House in search of pardons, leave few facts undisputed. The principal unchallenged fact is that the man who sought to trip her up, and to discourage the operations of certain other women brokers whose characters he questioned, was an unpleasant, partisan, but exceptionally able detective. He was General LaFayette C. Baker, a highhanded forty-year-old adventurer and chief of the National Protective Police, the organization which would become the United States Secret Service; and he was likely less motivated by moral scruples than by his antagonism toward the President, his close connections with some of the congressional plotters against Johnson, and his opposition to the general pardoning of Southerners.

Baker had been a vigilante in San Francisco before the war. He had been captured and held as a spy when on a secret mission for the Union to Richmond, the capital of the Confederacy, but he escaped and returned to Washington. There his Richmond adventure won him employment as a detective. Later he was commissioned a colonel and was appointed in 1862 as special provost marshal of the War Department; by 1865 he held the rank of brigadier general. Indifferent to such constitutional guarantees as due process and warrants for arrest and search, he had been indefatigable in running down pro-Southern Washingtonians, bounty jumpers, war speculators, and real or alleged plotters against the government. He had ably planned and directed the expedition that captured the dying John Wilkes Booth and his accomplice, D. C. Herold, after Lincoln's assassination.

Whatever his motivations, the capital's super-sleuth determined to prove that Mrs. Cobb was, to say the least, guilty of irregularities in securing pardons. Washington was then gossiping that President Johnson's son Robert, who had a reputation as a woman chaser, was the manipulator of Mrs. Cobb's easy access to the President. Whether Baker simply intended to persuade Johnson, through his evidence, to bar the White House to Mrs. Cobb or whether he sought also to embarrass the President remains a matter of debate.

One of Baker's operatives, posing as a former Confederate in immediate need of a pardon, secured from Mrs. Cobb a promise in writing that she would deliver the needful document to him the very next day, together with a receipt for two $50 bills which he paid as a retainer's fee. The bills were marked. The pardon was not delivered on schedule, Mrs. Cobb blaming her failure on the President's illness and Secretary Seward's absence. On the second day she handed to Baker's man a pardon signed by the President, together with a receipt for four more marked $50 bills for a total fee of $300. Baker then appeared dramatically and demanded of Mrs. Cobb the four marked bills. White-faced with anger, she surrendered them, meanwhile upbraiding the general and vowing that he would be discharged and indicted for false arrest, or so runs Baker's version in his autobiographical *History of the United States Secret Service.*

In his story Baker also relates that he then warned the President three times that Mrs. Cobb, among others, was obtaining pardons irregularly, but that the President replied after the third conference that he himself could not possibly know "the character of the females visiting his house" and asked for a report on which an order to exclude questionable persons from the White House could be based. Mrs. Cobb then told the President her version of her experience with Baker, alleging persecution. Johnson gave Baker a tongue-lashing for interfering with matters which, said the President roundly, did not lie within the province of the National Protective Police.

In a letter to the New York *Times* in April 1866 Mrs. Cobb's loyal husband defended her reputation, setting forth in part: "This famed pardon brokeress, a Yankee girl, gave much of her best strength as a nurse . . . in the Union hospitals, and also sacrificed . . . an only brother, who fell as color bearer . . . at Gettysburg." And Colonel A. K. Long, Johnson's private secretary, later testified under oath before the House Judiciary Committee during the impeachment proceedings against the President that Mrs. Cobb had obtained only three pardons and that the President did not even know her, the pardons having been obtained through third parties.

Baker's departure from public life was inglorious. He resigned and Mrs. Cobb brought suit against him. A jury convicted him of false imprisonment in a trial in which the President apparently showed unusual interest. Baker paid a fine and costs of $36. He died in mid-July 1868, less than a year after giving highly questionable testimony against the President during the impeachment proceedings.

The pardon brokers, male and female, went merrily on until Johnson's second amnesty proclamation, on September 7, 1867, left only some 300 persons unpardoned. This amnesty excluded only (1) the Confederacy's president, vice-president, heads of departments, foreign agents, those above the army rank of brigadier general and the naval rank of captain and the governors of the Confederate states; (2) all persons who in any way treated otherwise than as prisoners of war persons who in any capacity were employed in the military or naval service of the United States; and (3) all who were "actually in civil, military or naval confinement or legally held to bail either before or after conviction. . . ." Since the summer of 1865, 13,500 pardons had been granted. Still unpardoned until the second amnesty were as many as 130,000 Southerners who could be legally included in the previously excepted classes, but who hadn't asked for clemency.

On Christmas Day, 1868, Johnson proclaimed universal amnesty for all former Confederates. In so doing he solved a long-irritating problem.

In the years between, one man became in his time of adversity a symbol to his fellow Southerners of the South's martyrdom and courage. Jefferson Davis, the imprisoned president of the Confederacy, had not endeared himself to many among the ranking civilian and military leaders of the South while he held office; he was given to small bickerings, associates had complained; his dislikes were unwavering; to the Confederacy's harm he fancied himself a military genius; he was a moody, sensitive, and aloof man. But Jefferson Davis, a maltreated prisoner for two years at Fortress Monroe, had become a folk hero in whom the South could imagine she saw her collective self.

On May 2, 1865, upon evidence flagrantly false, President Johnson had charged Davis with conspiring in the assassination of Lincoln and put a $100,000 reward upon his head. Three weeks later the president of the destroyed Confederacy was arrested while in flight and lodged in Fortress Monroe, Virginia. There he remained until May 13, 1867, when he was admitted to bail. For the first five days of his captivity Davis's hands were manacled, his feet fettered. He was forced to keep a light burning in his cell so that his guards could watch him night and day; every fifteen minutes the officer of the guard inspected him. Not until October 1865 was he given comfortable quarters, and in those quarters he would remain long after every other Southern leader had been released.

Iron-willed Jeff Davis never asked for mercy or pardon; nor did he ever forgive Johnson for wrongfully charging him with plotting Lincoln's murder. About him had raged a battle of petitions, especially in the early months of his imprisonment, those from the North almost universally demanding severe punishment, even the death penalty, those from the South asking for mercy for the fallen leader and denying passionately that Davis or any other Confederate was a traitor.

The South's resentment of the North's interpretation of the act of secession was deep and lasting. The seceders had believed secession to be a constitutional right of the states. So also Thomas Jefferson had believed and Madison and many another among the founding fathers. As a congressman, Abraham Lincoln himself, in defending in 1848 the revolution of the Texans against Mexico, had said:

"Any people anywhere, so inclined and having the power, have the right to rise up and shake off the existing government and form a new one that suits them better. This is a most valuable and sacred right—a right which, we hope and believe, is to liberate the world. Nor is this right confined to cases in which the people of an existing government may choose to exercise it. Any portion of such people that can may revolutionize and make their own of so much of the territory as they inhabit. . . ."

Never in his life would the man so ill-used in Fortress Monroe waver in his belief in the right of a state to secede. The war had proven to him only that the North was militarily stronger than the South. And Andrew Johnson would always believe in turn that Jefferson Davis should have been tried for treason. Publicly he stated that he would never pardon Jefferson Davis until the Confederate chieftain himself asked for clemency. And, privately, in August 1868, he had written Benjamin C. Truman, his wartime aide in Tennessee and his confidential agent in the South after the war, only four months before the universal amnesty: "I shall go to my grave with the firm belief that Davis, Cobb, Toombs and a few others of the arch-conspirators and traitors should have been tried, convicted and hanged for treason. . . ."

Fifteen years later, on March 10, 1884, Jefferson Davis was to have the last word. Addressing the cheering, weeping members of the Mississippi legislature, the old Confederate leader gave defiant voice to what must have been in the hearts of a majority of the sixteen thousand who had long before sought forgiveness and in the hearts of the unreconstructed hundred thousand and more who had refused to come to Andrew Johnson as suppliants:

"It has been said that I should have applied to the United States for a pardon, but repentance must precede the right of pardon and I have not repented. Remembering as I must all which has been lost, disappointed hopes and crushed aspirations, yet I deliberately say, if it were to do all over again I would again do just as I did in 1861."

It is easier now than it was then to assess the North's moral and political perplexities which led to the ready pardons and, at the end, to universal amnesty; and it is chilling to speculate upon what might have happened had the North, in time of war and in time of peace after victory, determined to guide itself by the Constitution's own definition of treason and to mete out the punishment prescribed for such treason. Under the Constitution treason against the United States can be committed only by "levying war against them or in adhering to their enemies, giving them aid and comfort," and is punishable by death. Yet, although the government of the United States officially regarded the war as an insurrection, it could not make up its mind as to what kind of war this really was—a rebellion, a civil war, or, as the dilemma worked itself out in practice, a war between belligerent nations, each of which would be treated on the field of battle as a lawful enemy.

The gap between the constitutional definition of treason and the North's practical compromise was later succinctly described by Judge John C. Underwood of the Federal Circuit Court for the District of Virginia, when he was considering the case of Jefferson Davis in May 1867: "It is a little remarkable that in the midst of a gigantic civil war, the Congress of the United States changed the punishment of an offense from death to fine and imprisonment; but under the circumstances it was very honorable for the government of the United States to exhibit clemency and moderation."

The first modification of the North's concept of the conflict came on July 31, 1861, in an Act of Congress which set forth that anyone found guilty of conspiring to overthrow the United States government or to have interfered with the carrying out of its laws "shall be guilty of a high crime, and upon conviction thereof . . . shall be punished by a fine not less than $500 and not more than $5000 or by imprisonment (for no more than six years) or by both such fine and imprisonment." Soon thereafter supplementary laws made liable to confiscation any property used for "insurrectionary purposes," provided fines and imprisonment for anyone recruiting soldiers and sailors to serve against the United States, and set forth that users of slave labor "shall forfeit the claim to such labor."

As the war proceeded Congress provided as punishment for treason "that every person who shall hereafter commit the crime of treason against the United States, and shall be adjudged guilty thereof, shall suffer death . . . or, at the discretion of the court, he shall be imprisoned for not less than five years and fined not less than $10,000." Here was a practical as well as merciful alternative.

The President was also authorized to seize the property of the rebels and to use the proceeds to support the Army and Navy. Lincoln, disturbed over even this much severity, persuaded Congress to resolve that "no proceedings under said act shall be construed as to work a forfeiture of the real estate of the offender beyond his natural life." The confiscation act was even further softened. Its thirteenth section provided that "the President is hereby authorized at any time hereafter by proclamation to extend to any persons who have participated in the existing rebellion in any state or part thereof, pardon and amnesty with such exceptions and at such time and on such conditions as he may deem expedient for the public welfare."

Under that authority Lincoln and Johnson acted generously and wisely. But the South could not bring itself to believe that its leaders had, in the words of Jeff Davis, anything to repent. Nor could the Radicals, on the other hand, see any virtue in continuing after the war the "clemency and moderation" which marked the wartime government's interpretation of the nature of the conflict itself.

And so on fertile ground fell new seeds of discord.

CHAPTER 5

All in the Name of God

As the hickory withes sliced bloody crisscrosses upon his back, perhaps the conviction that he was on God's side sustained Henry Neal. Perhaps, also, the east Tennesseans who had waylaid Preacher Neal as he rode horseback to Axley Chapel near Morgantown were sure that they were God's chosen instruments for vengeance. After all, good Union men had warned this Southern Methodist blasphemer not to preach at Axley Chapel or anywhere else in hill country; he had a whipping coming to him.

Henry Neal's offense in 1869 was that he was a preacher of the Methodist Episcopal Church, South, in this unforgetting and now ascendant stronghold of Unionism. And, although the whipping that spring morning left him scarred for a lifetime, he was luckier than had been some other preachers on both sides of Methodism's splintery fence during the thirty years of church division that had its origins in the issue of slavery and the right of the states to secede.

The east Tennesseans who bushwhacked the Reverend Mr. Neal were thoroughgoing. One dedicated, cursing churchman jammed a revolver against his chest and told him that if he opened his mouth his brains would splatter the road. Preacher Neal dismounted. As he did, several other men sprang from the bordering woods. After they had blindfolded him one of the band struck him with a pistol on the back of the head, laying open the scalp for two inches. Thickskulled Henry Neal came to in a few seconds; whereupon his captors began pushing him through the woods, and whenever he fell, as he did two or three times, they jerked him to his feet and kicked him.

After the forest hid them from the road they roped him to a tree and, one man to a side, began beating him with heavy switches, several gripped together in the hands of each man. The beating continued until the withes were frayed to uselessness. Having thus made clear the lesson that it was unhealthy for a Southern Methodist preacher to be caught spreading the gospel or anything else in east Tennessee, Henry Neal's abductors forced him to lie face downward and left him bleeding in the woods.

Preacher Neal was not the only secessionist man of God who was punished after the war in east Tennessee. There was Jacob Brillhart, an aged venerable divine, who was seized at Cedar Springs and ridden on a rail, and Jacob Smith, so severely beaten over the head with pistols and clubs at Logan's Chapel that he was forever afterward a cripple. For good measure the injured man was beaten again the next month when he persisted in holding services. Other preachers, more fortunate than these, were let off with warnings or coats of tar and feathers or the burning of their churches.

The Methodist war in the name of a sectional God had not started in Tennessee; and it had long antedated the Reconstruction days of reckoning among the people of a state which had divided over secession with the western and middle Tennessee secessionist majority arrayed against the mostly Unionist, non-slaveholding small farmers and mountainfolk of east Tennessee. The beginnings of the national church's divisive disputation lay so far back in the history of the slave controversy itself that only the older clergymen of Reconstruction could remember the earliest wrathful schisms in the flaming time when the Abolitionist circuit riders first preached freedom in maddened Kansas and Missouri and the rest of the disputed West.

But there was one fact upon which both sides could agree, the one in accusation and the other with pride. The Methodists of the North and the border states had formed the spearhead of Abolitionism's all-out assault upon the institution of slavery. Close behind them came the fewer Congregationalists, rooted in New England and not significantly divided over slavery. The other principal evangelical churches, notably the Baptist and the Presbyterian, had also split over the issue, leaving only the Protestant Episcopalians and the Roman Catholics, small in number and better disciplined, still united at the war's beginning.

The North's Methodists also had their catalogue of martyrs. In it the name of the Reverend Anthony Bewley might well have led all the rest.

Almost alone, Mr. Bewley had sided with the national church when the members of the Missouri Conference, meeting in 1845 at Columbia, followed their bishop out of the church and into the dissident Methodist Episcopal Church, South. What happened to him afterward tells in microcosm the story of a half century of excesses which characterized American Protestantism's cleavage over slavery and secession. In that division no other political or religious group equaled the ardor with which the Northern Methodist circuit riders, bishops and laymen assailed slavery, so much so that Yankee Methodism became synonymous in the South with Abolitionism and Radicalism and the advocacy of miscegenation, before, during, and after the war. The Methodists of the North, stimulated by their single-minded clerical missioners, were the shock troops of the anti-slavery army, the most uncompromising and the most effective of those militant churchmen, North and South, who proclaimed their alliances with God in the conflict they so effectively helped to bring about.

The remembrance of Mr. Bewley's martyrdom must have quickened many a Northern Methodist preacher as, his church triumphant, he preached brotherly affection and aid for the former slaves and condign punishment for the masters and for the preachers to whom the masters had listened.

Mr. Bewley remained in the '50s, as a loyal minister, in the Southwestern Conference, serving variously in Arkansas and Missouri. The feeling against him and the few other Conference preachers who represented the Northern church was intense. His children were not allowed to attend school. He and his fellows were accused of being slave enticers and fomenters of rebellion, rapscallions who used their clerical garb as a cloak for their misdeeds. Some pro-slavery counties forbade the anti-slavery, Union Methodist preachers to preach and provided extralegal penalties of tarring and feathering for the first offense and hanging for the second. A minor martyr of the Northern persuasion was the Reverend J. E. Gardner, who, two months after Fort Sumter was fired upon, was hoisted upon a "Lincoln rail," derided as a "nigger thief" while tar and feathers were prepared, the mob meanwhile shouting for a rope, and then tarred and ridden on the rail. As he clung painfully to his perch he alternately "preached Christ to them" and, oblivious, perhaps, to his own painful journey, sang animatedly:

> *"Children of the heavenly king,*
> *As we journey let us sing . . ."*

Bewley escaped physical punishment for a while; but in the spring of 1860, when he was busily preaching in Texas, the story spread that he and a companion had been engaged in burning homes of Texas pro-slavers and even entire towns and that they were plotting slave insurrections. Bewley had then been in Texas for about two years and had accepted reappointment to his district despite the evident danger. But in the wake of these accusations he decided to leave the state and go to Cassville, Missouri, where he would be among friends. His departure was discovered almost immediately; his flight was well publicized, and he was trailed through Texas and western Arkansas. When he reached Barry County, near Cassville, eight Texans caught up with him and told him that Texas had offered a thousand-dollar reward for his return. His captors, soon joined by other pursuers, took him in September to Fayetteville, Arkansas, with the announced intention of returning him to Texas. There a cursing mob tried to lynch him. One report has it that he was rescued by the sheriff. He was kept chained to one of his guards the next night. On September 5, 1860, he wrote his wife from Fayetteville that a group of vigilantes would set out with him for Texas that night.

A week later a mob seized him at Fort Worth and hanged him. Another Northern Methodist preacher, then living in Texas, described his murder in understandably biased words: "Shortly after dinner they marched him off to Fort Worth. At the regular hour for supper he went to the tavern and ate his last meal with a set of bloodthirsty assassins of the South. He was then taken a short distance from town by a party of those demons, and there, with a rope entwined around his neck, he was suspended between heaven and earth like a dog, to die by the hands of his fellow men. After letting him remain all night in this position, a hole was dug by two Negro men. The dead victim was then taken down by these two Africans and thrown in without coffin or box, the dirt being thrown upon him scarcely covering his body . . . During a period of four years . . . I have accompanied this good man from one appointment to another but never did I hear him hint anything that would prejudice the Negro against his master, nor did I ever hear him preach an Abolition discourse. But the whole matter was he was a member of the old Church . . . There is not now in Texas a member of the old Methodist Episcopal Church that dare own his membership."

Some three weeks later Mr. Bewley's remains were dug up, according to contemporary church reports, stripped of their flesh, and laid out upon the roof of the storehouse of a Captain Eph Daggett.

The South did not mourn Mr. Bewley's passing. Upon receiving news of his death the pro-slavery *Christian Advocate,* a Texas journal of the Southern Methodists, commented:

"We published in our news column a paragraph of four lines stating that a Reverend Mr. Bewley of the Northern Church had been hung at Veal's Station after having been condemned by a jury of three hundred men. . . . There are cases in which lynch law is expedient, necessary, and just. We are not now prepared to declare that Mr. Bewley's was one of these cases nor that it was not. He fell a victim to his lawlessness which he and others of his kind have for some time been laboring to inaugurate and promote in Texas. He was . . . formally warned by a large committee of Southern men that anti-slavery missionary operations among us would certainly result in bloodshed and that if he persisted he would be regarded as an aggressor and treated accordingly. . . ."

A month before Bewley's murder the New Orleans *Christian Advocate,* another organ of the Southern dissenters, had commented, with equally rapturous dislike, on the behavior of their Northern brethren:

"Abolition doctrine has been the direct cause of both the John Brown and the Texas conspiracies, together with all similar disturbances . . . [in Texas] the men, the old women, and the children were all to be killed, and the young women to be devoted to a far more horrible fate. And this is the fruit of Abolitionism—of anti-slaveryism—of the teaching of the anti-slavery press, in pulpit and rostrum. . . . These conspirators are the advance guard of the Black Republican party to which Doctor Abel Stevens professes to belong, and which the majority of Northern Methodists, it is said, will support in the ensuing presidential election. . . . The blood of the revolution of Santo Domingo, of Kansas, of Harper's Ferry, and of this Texas infamy rests on the head of these modern Tories and incendiaries. . . . How can a man teach Abolition doctrines, or support the Black Republican party and not be a villain . . ."

For years before Anthony Bewley's martyrdom and the manhandling of Mr. Gardner, the Northern Methodists' espousal of freedom for the Negro and the South's reaction to it had agitated the nation's political cauldron. Despite earlier admonitions of their bishops, the New England Methodists had become identified with the Abolitionist movement almost from its inception. The freedom of the Negroes soon became the Northern churches' paramount earthly concern. As a foreseeable result, the Methodist Church had divided in 1844 and 1845 into Northern and Southern branches, and each branch immediately set out to capture the border states and territories. Their behavior soon became unruly, especially in Kentucky, western Virginia, and Missouri, where mobs of one branch often raided and broke up the church services, manhandling ministers and worshipers alike.

The ante-bellum division between the Northern and Southern churchmen was complete and unyielding; and so enduring would it be that nearly a century would pass before a reunion could be effected. By the beginning of hostilities the members of the Northern Methodist Church were all but unanimous in their opposition to slavery, the only exceptions being found among a few slaveholders in the border states, most of whom nevertheless maintained their memberships in the Northern branch. Almost to a man they were staunch Unionists.

Northern Methodism's nigh-fanatical espousal of the Abolitionist movement before the war, its making of loyalty to the Union a test of Christian intent, and its later identification with Radical Reconstruction in the South had great import for the South and for the nation. The Methodists were a uniquely powerful sect. The Episcopalians and the Presbyterians in the South and the Congregationalists in New England could count among their members a majority of the upper-class industrial, agricultural, and professional groups. The yet chaotic Baptist expansion, until recently concentrated in the frontier, was most effective still among the least secure and less well-educated citizenry. The ably led Methodist Episcopal Church was the most dynamic, the fastest growing, and, excepting the minuscule Quakers and the sectionally limited Unitarians and Congregationalists, the most dedicated to social reform of the nation's organized churches. Methodism's greatest initial appeal had been to the solid middle classes of America's towns and cities and to her yeomen farmers, but throughout the first half of the nineteenth century the church had been winning converts among all social groups. When the Methodist bishops and preachers spoke, politicians listened no less attentively than did their congregation. The church's army of circuit riders was so inured to hardship as to be all but unstoppable.

But when the Methodist Church's missionary vigor became diverted and divided over slavery, Northern and Southern communicants parted company. Southern Methodist mass meetings declared the Yankee church to be "a nuisance, a stench in the nostrils of our people." Southern Conference resolutions found that "a secret viper works in our midst, known as the Northern Methodist Church. . . ." John C. Calhoun said of the breaking of the cords that bound the Union: "The first of these cords which snapped [under the stress of the slavery question] was that of the powerful Methodist Episcopal Church. . . . They are now arrayed into two hostile bodies, engaged in litigation about what was formerly their common property."

Neither side had a monopoly on rash statements or outrageous behavior. Yet except in eastern Tennessee, where the loyalist Methodists of the highlands had been hounded by the temporarily ascendant Confederacy, the South was not the aggressor in the religious disunion that was engendered by slavery, nurtured on war, and prolonged by Reconstruction. Armored in the belief that the true church was loosing against the forces of Southern darkness the Lord's own fateful lightning, Northern Methodism was the foremost trampler of the vintage where the grapes of wrath are stored, not only during the war but afterward. The early postwar historians of Northern Methodism may have been too exuberant in the claims they made for the church's part in the winning of the war. But it is certain that the militancy of Methodist preachers and the patriotism of Methodist laymen in the doubtful states of Missouri, Kentucky, and Maryland were greatly responsible for the failure of those states to secede when, from a military standpoint, they still could; and the respective Southern and Union strength in West Virginia in 1861 could have been measured and located by determining the respective memberships and locations of the various churches of the Methodist Episcopal Church, South, and the Methodist Episcopal Church.

The ministerial fervor sometimes found oddly unchristian expression, as in the sermon of a Reverend Mr. Black, whose church was situated in Newport, Kentucky, across the river from Cincinnati. One Sabbath day, early in the war, Mr. Black decorated his church with the United States flag and figures of eagles, chose as the day's hymns "The Star-Spangled Banner," "The Red, White, and Blue," and "Hail Columbia," and, in the course of his sermon, delivered himself of these sentiments:

"I trust our troops will rally and wipe the disgrace of Manassas, though it costs the life of every Rebel under arms. Let Davis and Beauregard be captured, to meet the fate of Haman. Hang them up on Mason's and Dixon's line, that traitors of both sections may be warned. Let them hang until vultures shall eat the rotten flesh from their bones; let them hang until the crows shall build their filthy nests in their skeletons; let them hang until the rope rots, and let their dismembered bones fall so deep into the earth that God Almighty can't find them in the day of Resurrection."

Nor even elsewhere than in Tennessee were the Northern Methodists inclined to relent after victory. A resolution passed by the Boston Methodist Preachers Meeting in 1865 declared that "never will the nation feel its sense of honor and justice vindicated until the leaders of this unprovoked and wicked rebellion shall have surrendered and suffered condign punishment, the penalty of death." The meeting also resolved:

"That no terms should be made with traitors, no compromise with Rebels; that the surrender of Rebels should be held to the strict justice their crimes have merited;

"That we hold the national authority bound by the most solemn obligation to God and man to bring all the civil and military leaders of the rebellion to trial by due course of law, and when they are clearly convicted, to execute them;

"That in the Reconstruction of Southern states no man should hold office who held a commission in the Rebel army or in the Confederate government, nor shall he be allowed to vote. . . ."

Perhaps the South's churchmen would have been less resentful had the Northern evangelists restricted themselves, in war and in peace, to similar hell-fire sermons and resolutions. But as early as October 1862 the Methodist Ministers Association of Boston decided to send missionaries to selected Southern communities which had fallen to the federal armies, there to take over churches vacated by Southern Methodist ministers. Other Northern Methodist conferences followed suit. So did the Northern Presbyterians and the United Brethren. The implacable Methodist bishop, Edward R. Ames of Boston, persuaded Secretary of War Stanton to go much further. At Bishop Ames's behest Stanton ordered the Union generals in command of the several occupied areas of the South to place at Ames's disposal all houses of worship belonging to the Methodist Episcopal Church, South, "in which a loyal minister, who has been appointed by a loyal bishop," was not officiating. The generals were also directed to provide Bishop Ames and his clerk with transportation and subsistence wherever possible.

Neither the bishop nor Secretary Stanton seems to have been troubled by this unusual relationship between church and state. Uniformly the generals obeyed Secretary Stanton's order. Southern Methodist ministers and laymen bravely but bootlessly denounced the seizures. In 1864 a convention of Southern Methodist ministers, meeting in Louisville, Kentucky, behind the federal lines, protested Stanton's order as "unjust, unnecessary and subversive alike of good order and the rights of a numerous body of Christians. . . ." They saw in the appropriation of church property and the replacement of Southern ministers with loyal Northern Methodists a scheme of the Northern church to absorb Methodism's secessionist branch. A few more conservative Northern Methodist clergy were themselves disturbed and lent their influence, late in the war, to an unpopular and unsuccessful effort to reunite the divided branches, not in a spirit of victory but of forgiveness. In a pastoral letter distributed throughout the South at the close of the war the bishops of the Southern Methodist Church themselves shut the door to reunion by denouncing the Northern Methodist bishops and preachers who had usurped their churches and refused to surrender them.

Abraham Lincoln had no sympathy for these annexations of church property. In January 1863 he protested to the commanding general of the department of Missouri, where a Southern minister had been banished from his pulpit. ". . . I believe he does sympathize with the Rebels; but the question remains whether such a man of unquestioned good character . . . can with safety to this government be exiled upon suspicion of his secret sympathies . . . The United States government must not, as by this order, undertake to run the churches. When an individual, in a church or out of it, becomes dangerous to the public, he must be checked; but let the churches, as such, take care of themselves. It will not do for the United States to appoint trustees, supervisors, or other agents for the churches."

Later the President wrote to friends of the deposed minister who had appealed to him: "I have never interfered nor thought of interfering as to who shall or who shall not speak in any church, nor have I knowingly or believingly tolerated anyone else to so interfere by my authority."

Not until after he had dispatched these letters did Lincoln learn of Stanton's order in behalf of Bishop Ames. He protested in exasperation to Stanton, telling him of his embarrassment at so belatedly learning of the War Department's order and asking his devious secretary for an explanation. Stanton then somewhat modified his order by making it apply only to the "rebellious states." Lincoln wrote a pacifying letter to the Missouri minister who had first written him about the ouster, quoting Stanton as saying that the order was never intended as anything but a means of rallying Methodists in favor of the Union in areas where the rebellion had scattered them.

Lincoln was a much angrier man in March 1864 when he wrote to the Union commander in Memphis regarding a similar controversy: "If the military has need of the church building, let them keep it, otherwise let them get out of it, and leave it and its owners alone, except for causes that justify the request of any one." Soon thereafter he addressed the same general: "I am now told that the military were not in possession of the building. This, if true, is most extraordinary. I say again, if there be no military need of the building, leave it alone, neither putting anyone in or out of it, except on finding someone preaching or practising treason, in which case lay hands on him, just as if he were doing the same thing in any other building, or in the streets or highways."

The President's order, if such it was, remained more honored in the breach than in the observance. Northern churchmen defended the occupation of Southern churches and the appointment of Army chaplains, as in

New Orleans, to fill Episcopalian pulpits. The Northern Presbyterians argued that many Southern pulpits were vacant because their former occupants had either abandoned them or had been driven from them and that, since the government would not allow any but loyal men to take their place, the Northern clergymen were only obtaining permits from the government "to go into all the South and preach the gospel to every people." The analogy was not likely to please Southerners.

Neither could Southern churchmen be moved to Christian fellowship by the preachments of the Reverend John T. Newman, General Grant's personal pastor and friend, and later a bishop of the Northern Methodist Church. Soon after Mr. Newman took charge of the church in New Orleans he told his congregation of Unionists: "We are denounced as church robbers, or charged with having robbed the people of the South of their church properties. My answer is: the right of church property has never been disturbed as far as we are concerned. The general government has seen fit to seize these churches but it has not conveyed their title to us . . . We do not own an inch . . . If there has been any robbing, the accusation lies against the general government. But the government has committed no robbery. They were aware that these churches were occupied, so far as they were occupied at all, by congregations united by disloyal sympathies and by teachers disposed to implement treason."

But though the Northern ministers did possess the churches, their white Southern congregations were small except in the random pockets where Union sentiment had existed and persisted. East Tennessee could count the most of these.

The Methodist churchgoers of the Tennessee mountains had been fortunate before the war, as far as intra-denominational strife was concerned, in that while two out of three of its citizens opposed secession, they were not animated by a moral compulsion to erase slavery from the land. The mountain people had impartially disliked Negroes and the highfalutin' men who owned them. Andrew Johnson and William G. Brownlow, the principal Unionist leaders whom east Tennessee produced, came to their anti-slavery views late in their lives. When the Southern Methodists seceded from the general conference in 1844—after Bishop James Andrews of Georgia had been dismissed by vote of the Northern-dominated majority because he had not freed the slaves of the widow whom he had married—east Tennessee Methodism's Holston Conference had gone along all but unanimously with the seceders. From 1844 to 1860 the east Tennessee Methodists, whether pro-Union or secessionist, pro-slavery or anti-slavery or indifferent, got along together tolerably well. But on the eve of war the Conference had expelled several ministers without trial, in the absence of the ministers themselves and contrary to church law, because they were Union men. That action hopelessly and belligerently separated the east Tennessee Methodists from the Southern Methodists and assured the flogging, nine years later, of the unfortunate Henry Neal.

One of the angriest and assuredly the most active of the Unionist clergymen of Tennessee was William G. Brownlow—"Parson" Brownlow—leader of the state's loyalists, who had long since subordinated his ministerial duties to a stormy career as a pro-Union pamphleteer and newspaper publisher. Brownlow was the man who, after federal troops overran east Tennessee, had called for the organization of the loyal Methodists into a new Holston Conference. The formal summons for the convention first appeared in May 1864 in Brownlow's *Whig*. No brotherly love for the secessionist Methodists could have animated by then the organizers of the new, loyal conference. East Tennessee was a ravaged land, wasted by guerilla warfare and Confederate incursion, and preyed upon by indiscriminate bushwhackers less interested in a man's loyalties than in his purse. Now, in 1864, Yankee soldiers protected the loyal men. The pro-Unionists, in and out of the churches, were in the saddle, and the leader of loyal Methodism was Parson Brownlow, provisional governor of the occupied state.

The east Tennesseans were behind him. Even when Tennessee, reversing itself after Lincoln had called for troops, had voted by a majority of 57,671 to secede, east Tennessee had remained one-sidedly loyal, thanks greatly to the leadership of Andrew Johnson and the pen of Parson Brownlow. Now, with the Union in the saddle, it was the turn of the Brownlow men to set the Lord's house in order.

Provisional Governor Brownlow journeyed North early in 1864 to discuss with Methodist bishops at Philadelphia, Cincinnati, and elsewhere the reorganization of the church in east Tennessee. He reported that a canvass of the region had disclosed that sixteen ordained traveling and local ministers were ready to join the Northern ranks as were sixty-five others not ordained. These and the loyal laity hastened to even scores with the Southern Methodists. In one of the earliest acts of the revived Holston Conference under Brownlow the General Committee denounced Southern Methodism which "at an early period in this wicked rebellion . . . took her stand upon the treasonable and therefore false foundation of secession; her pulpits bellowed with more terrific thunder on the side of disunion than those of almost any other church, hurling fiery invective at the Union and the North—carrying the most of her leading and influential ministers and members into the unhallowed embrace of treason . . . It therefore remains to us and the loyal thousands of our brethren similarly situated to do one of three things—either to remain in the wilderness, not of Judea, but of Dixie; or, next, to form ourselves into a separate and independent organization; or, last of all, to seek a reunion with the Methodist Episcopal Church of the United States, whose usages, doctrine, and faith are in accord with ours and in the enjoyment and practice of which we desire to live and die."

Within a year the reorganization of the Holston Conference had been completed. Only twenty-nine ministers of the Southern church went along with the reunion. From then on the unforgiving posture of the Loyalists throughout the period of Brownlow-dominated Reconstruction in Tennessee was all that he could have desired.

Meanwhile and afterward the Southern Methodist Conference gave voice to its impotent wrath at the seizure and retention of the Southern church's property, especially in Tennessee. In May 1868 it even presented a memorial to the general conference of the Northern Methodists in Chicago: ". . . to set forth . . . the wrongs which we are suffering at the hands of agents of the M E Church . . . and also to devise some means by which an end may be made to these outrages . . . Our churches seized by the ministers and members of the M E Church are still held by them and used as houses of worship. To give the semblance of legality to these acts . . . trustees have been appointed . . . and these churches are annually reported by your ministers in their conferences statistics . . . Our ministers are either excluded and driven out or allowed only joint occupancy with your ministers . . . [some] are driven by mobs and threatened with death should they attempt to return . . . A presiding elder and the preacher in charge of the circuit . . . were arrested and marched fifteen miles amidst indignities and insults; at another an aged Godly minister was ridden upon a rail . . .

"Our parsonages have also been seized . . . $3600, appropriated upon our application by the United States Government for damage to our church in Knoxville . . . was by some sleight of hand movement passed into the hands of the minister of the M E Church . . . Surely if the United States Government does not confiscate the property of those who are called Rebels, the M E Church in her highest legislative assembly will hardly set a precedent by claiming this property of her Southern brethren."

It must not be supposed that the postwar church quarrels were limited to Tennessee or to Methodists or to the single issue of expropriation of church property. Southerners of all denominations resented Northern assumption of moral superiority, but the Northern Methodist ministers did bear the brunt of Southern wrath. They were, to an angry Georgian who spoke for many another, ". . . preachers blating hypocrisy with their lips, with the venom of the devil in their hearts, missionaries of wrath, stirring up strife, kindling hate, and sowing the seeds of damnation in the soil of hate, come amongst us in clerical robes, spotted with sin and dripping with crime, their Bible a league with hell, their text the enmity of man, and the gospel of lust as their creed, only that Radical orthodoxy may be accepted and acknowledged by the South."

And though few responsible Northern churchmen or laymen echoed him, most white Southerners believed that the Reverend Gilbert Haven, Massachusetts Abolitionist and scholar of the classics, who would later become a bishop, spoke for all Northern Methodists when he joyfully predicted that "the hour is not far off when the white-hued husband shall boast of the dusky beauty of his wife, and the Caucasian wife shall admire the sun-kissed countenance of her husband as deeply and as unconscious of the present ruling abhorrence as is his admiration for her lighter tint."

No wonder that the Northern Methodist proselyters gained during Reconstruction almost no Southern white members except in the mountain strongholds where few Negroes lived. Three fourths of the estimated 200,000 postwar converts to Northern Methodism were Negroes. The failure of the Northern Methodists to win Southern followers must have been disappointing, for their bishops and missionaries had labored under the belief that the Southern white masses were resentful of the leaders who had plunged them into disastrous war and that they were ready to flock to the Northern church.

The reaction of the white Southern churchmen was summed up at the Southern Conference of Methodist Bishops meeting in 1866, even before Radical Reconstruction was really under way. The Southern bishops noted that "a large proportion if not a majority of Northern Methodists have become incurably radical. They teach for doctrine the commandments of men. They have incorporated social dogmas and political beliefs into their church creed." Some Southern churchmen would be saying much the same things and for much the same reasons more than eighty years later. And the Northern church, in the plaintive words of the New York *Christian Advocate* in 1865, just couldn't understand why "there is no moral sense of its great crime apparent in the South. It returns acknowledging only its failure, not its sin."

The disillusioned Northern Methodist missionaries soon turned almost wholly to the Negroes. Their labors in this unworked vineyard, both in the secular and religious education of the Negro, were generally laudable. A congressional report on the Freedmen's Bureau in 1872 pointed out that many of the Bureau's employees "had been selected as being the most devout, zealous, and loyal of that religious sect known as the Northern Methodist Church"; and a Southern clergyman observed that "the colored Methodists in the South who have had the advantage . . . of your [Northern Methodist] training are far in advance of any colored people in that section."

The Northern church soon all but abandoned its secondary schools and turned to supporting Negro seminaries, normal schools, and colleges, with the intention of training Negro teachers to instruct the young. It was a realistic policy which would greatly benefit the Negro for generations to follow.

In American Christianity's prolonged civil war the Negro stood aside. Even had the Northern churches pressed strenuously for integrated worship, it is unlikely that the mass of Negroes would have gone along during Reconstruction. To the contrary, they had had enough of the white man's churches as slaves listening to the white man's preachers in the reserved balconies or in the slave quarters. As Molly Finlay, an Arkansas slave, remembered such preaching, "He just say 'serve your masters; don't steal your master's turkey; don't steal your master's chicken; don't steal your master's hog; don't steal your master's meat; do whatsomever your master tell you to do.' "

Except for the African Methodist Episcopal Church, whose ministers were the best educated among the Negro clergy and who maintained fairly close ties with the Northern church, the free Negro Protestants went their own way, not ungratefully, but certain that only through separateness could they find religious freedom. And while some of their preachers during Reconstruction were educated or deeply spiritual self-taught men who had answered an inner call, many of them were so self-seeking, so lacking in education, religious training, or spiritual grace that in the folklore of both races in the South they came to be represented far more often as men of cunning than as men of God. In many, if not in most, of the separate Negro churches, and notoriously in the rural churches, the established forms and dogmas of Protestant worship degenerated into primitive, near-orgiastic rites, day-and-night-long travesties of the backwoods revivals of the early nineteenth century, sometimes even into a partial reversion to voodooism.

Yet the free Negro worshipers did identify their life stories with the sufferings of Jesus Christ. The spirituals they sang were the folk songs of slavery and of persecution. *Tell old Pharaoh let my people go . . .* The Beatitudes had personal meaning. *Blessed are the poor . . .* The humble origins of Jesus were familiar. *For there was no room in the inn . . .* Not many of the white folks could understand, only a few, such as Anthony Bewley, who had died for their sakes, and Henry Neal, whose abductors had struck in the name of the avenging Jehovah and not the forgiving Christ. These two would have understood the singing in the backwood shanties that passed for churches:

> *Po' little Jesus,*
> *Yes, Yes,*
> *They boun' him wid a halter,*
> *Yes, Yes,*
> *An' whipped him up de mountain,*
> *Yes, Yes,*
> *Wasn't that a pity and a shame?*
> *Lawd, Lawd,*
> *Wasn't that a pity and a shame?*

BOOK **II**

THE RADICALS
TAKE OVER

Men in Collision

R<small>ETURN</small> now to the summer of 1865 and an all but one-sided renewal of a debate as old as the Republic itself; to the joining of a new issue, already ordained in blood, and to the raising of a dark ghost which has not yet been laid. For a time postpone judgment on the protagonists. Among them, on all sides—for there were more than two sides or three— moved honest men and rogues and in-betweens, dreamers and schemers, altruists and narrowly political partisans. Most of them showed a toughness of spirit, a resoluteness which, if it could have been expressed in concord for the national good, might have brought about the still unachieved miracle of intersectional amity.

The resumed debate, which the war had not ended but only interrupted, had to do with the constitutional rights and relationships of the separate states within the union. The new issue—one to be argued among the victors, with the vanquished having no voice—concerned the treatment of the de- feated secessionist states, especially with respect to the terms upon which they would be permitted to rejoin the national body politic. The specter, political too, and menacing to most Southern whites, whether Democrats or old-line Whigs, and to the Northern Democrats, was a potential black phalanx of a half million mostly illiterate Negro voters, their political awareness limited only to a folk awareness that they owed their freedom to Mr. Abe Lincoln, the Republican party, and the military might of the Union.

The specter and soon the sporadic fact of a mass Negro electorate were to determine the white South's reaction to Reconstruction. The rest the South could have and would have peacefully if resentfully accepted: a strong cen- tral government as against the diffusion and separation of powers; a purga- torial interlude between the day of defeat and the day of forgiveness; military occupation, political proscription, punishment of its principal mili- tary and civil leaders; a long term of political servitude to the conqueror. Universal franchise for the freedman was the revolutionary cornerstone of Radical Reconstruction and the lasting incentive for Southern resistance to the Radical program.

Abraham Lincoln was not yet in his grave when the architects of political revolution began drawing their blueprints for the new order; indeed, they had begun even before he became President. The voices of Abolitionism's social and political revolutionaries in mid-nineteenth-century America had not been as clamorous, as threatening, or as aggrieved as those of Europe's rebels against autocracy, but they had been as insistent and as uncompromising. The war had not quieted the apostles of a raceless Utopia; and allied with them now were more practical and powerful and successful planners who were thinking considerably less of man's brotherhood than of the perpetuation, world without end, of Republican domination of the nation and of the opportunities for personal power, economic manipulation, and regional exploitation which that domination would assure. Between them and the promised land would stand only Andrew Johnson—and he not at first—a minority in and out of Congress, almost all of them Democrats, politicians too, and the five and a half million whipped Southerners who, so thought the men of the North, would have precious little to say or do about it all.

The job that summer seemed almost ridiculously easy. Lincoln and his "soft-headed" plan for a moderate Reconstruction were both dead. The very night after the President's death Senator Sumner had conferred with Andrew Johnson in behalf of universal Negro suffrage and emerged confident that, Southerner and Democrat though he was, Lincoln's successor would go along. Johnson, Sumner knew, was a good Union man who only a year before, during the presidential campaign, had been violent in his denunciations of the Rebel South and in his demands for confiscation of Rebel property and punishment of the Confederacy's leaders. The Tennessean had been highly critical, too, of Grant's generous terms at Appomattox.

"Treason is a crime," he had said, "and must be punished as a crime; it must not be excused as an unsuccessful rebellion. . . ."

When the Radical leaders conferred with Johnson the Sunday after the assassination Ben Wade said enthusiastically: "Johnson, we have faith in you! By the gods, there will be no trouble running the government." There was no doubting which way the Radicals meant for the government to be run. General Butler, scheming for appointment as Secretary of State, spoke for most of them in those first confident days when, with specific reference to Virginia but with obvious inclusion of every Southern state, he said, "The time has not come for holding any relations with her but that of the conqueror to the conquered."

Vengeance, the anticipation of spoils, perpetuation of Republican political supremacy, a determination to reshape the South—whatever the motive or combination of motives which animated these men—the vote of the Southern Negro would do the trick. It was as simple as that. The Abolitionist Wendell Phillips minced no words in making the case for the Negro voter.

"The Negro must be given the franchise because we have no other timber to build the [Southern] states with," he said at the annual meeting of· the Massachusetts Anti-Slavery Society in 1865, "and unless we build with him, we must postpone Reconstruction for so many years that the very patronage of territorial government would swamp Republican institutions. . . ."

There were strong, unexpected voices in the North, warning against indiscriminate and immediate enfranchisement. General William T. Sherman said that the Negro must first be trained in citizenship. Louis Agassiz, perhaps the nation's most noted scientist, echoed Sherman's proposal. Henry Ward Beecher, the militant Yankee preacher, warned that civilization for the Negroes could not be "bought nor bequeathed nor gained by sleight of hand. It will come with sobriety, virtue, industry, and frugality." And even the arch-Abolitionist of them all, William Lloyd Garrison, had not demanded enfranchisement as the immediate reward of freedom. Writing in his *Liberator* before the war had ended, he said of universal suffrage for the Negro: "According to the laws of development and progress, it is not practical. To denounce or complain of President Lincoln for not disregarding public sentiment, and not flying in the face of these laws, is hardly just. Besides, I doubt whether he has the constitutional right to decide this matter. Ever since this government was organized, the right of suffrage has been determined by each state in the Union for itself, so that there is no uniformity in regard to it. In some free states, colored citizens are allowed to vote; in others they are not. It is always a state, never a national matter." And Garrison predicted that if the Negro were enfranchised through the use of military force the ballot would only temporarily be his.

Some among the opponents of presidential Reconstruction honestly resented what they believed to be executive encroachment on the powers of Congress. Some were moved by personal animosity toward the President and by their resentment at the ease with which former Confederates would be able to return to power in the South. Some were animated by belief in the principle of universal manhood suffrage regardless of color or capability. But the overriding consideration was the perpetuation of Republican rule through the Negro vote in the South.

That summer Andrew Johnson, the commoner who hated the slave-owning aristocrats and had stood by the Union, took a second look; and Andrew Johnson, the Southerner, Democrat and believer in states' rights within the framework of the Union, set himself courageously, stubbornly, hopelessly against the Radicals.

By mid-May Johnson had made up his mind which way he would go. He knew for a certainty what he was in for. Nonetheless, beginning on May 29, he issued a series of proclamations, in the manner of Lincoln, setting up additional provisional governments, first in North Carolina and subsequently in Mississippi, Georgia, Texas, Alabama, South Carolina, and Florida. By July 13 all of the "Johnson governments" in the Southern states had been authorized.

None of the proclamations required that the Negro participate in the Reconstruction process; instead, only loyal white citizens were authorized to draft and ratify the new constitutions and elect the state legislatures whose principal initial duties would have to be the repeal of the ordinances of secession, the repudiation of the Confederate debt, and the ratification of the Thirteenth Amendment. As has already been noted, Johnson also granted amnesty to all former Rebels—except for the fourteen excepted classes—on condition that they take the oath of allegiance.

The conventions themselves were to determine the qualifications of future officeholders and voters, the states' rights Tennessean proclaimed, since this determination was "a power which the people of the states have rightfully exercised from their origin of government to the present time."

By December 1865 every former Confederate state except Texas had complied with the Lincoln-Johnson formula for return to the Union; Texas would comply the following April. And so, when the Radical-dominated Thirty-ninth Congress convened on December 4, 1865, began the first of Reconstruction's three political phases, the showdown in Washington between President and Congress. Almost from its beginnings the Radicals would have their way. Though neither subdued nor destroyed, Andrew Johnson would be rendered politically impotent and with him the white South under military government. The second phase, the years of the locust, would encompass Grant's first term, during which Radical Republican administrations would govern almost every Southern state and leave behind them the most hateful memories in all our history. In the third phase, from 1872 to 1876, would come the progressively successful Southern counterattacks; in these waning years of Radical Reconstruction the white South would nullify the Negro vote through intimidation, terrorism, and overt persuasion and so end Republican rule.

Andrew Johnson was lifelong a defiant spirit. Successfully he defied origins as humble as were Andrew Jackson's and Abraham Lincoln's, the adolescent stigma of a bound apprentice and runaway orphan, and a lack of education which left him in his early manhood no more than an illiterate tailor. He defied politically the slave-owning secessionist Democrats and the Republican mountain men of Tennessee, and the threat of violent reprisal against himself, the Union Democrat who accepted from Lincoln the wartime post of provisional governor of his occupied state. He defied the ill will of Northern masses who cried out for punishment of the fallen enemy, and the purposeful congressional majority which would become more intent upon chastising the President than the South from which he came. He

defied the most forbidding weapon in democracy's legal arsenal, impeachment itself, which he alone among all American presidents would have to
stand up to, a final, triumphant defiance which was crowned seven years
later by his return to Washington as a United States senator from Tennessee when almost all of the raging partisans who had sought to destroy him
as President were either discredited or dead. A tough, stubborn man, rasp-
tongued and short of temper, this tailor from Tennessee, and a President
deserving far more recognition in his own time and in the annals of the
nation than has been accorded him.

Andrew Johnson was only three when his father, variously a bank porter,
a sexton, a city constable—an honest man of scant ability—died while saving
two persons from drowning. He was still a child when he was apprenticed to
a tailor. Soon, because he had broken a window and feared punishment, he
ran away from the job which was to pay him only in food and clothing until
he reached his majority, and was advertised as a runaway.

In 1826 Andrew Johnson and his mother and stepfather forsook North
Carolina for Tennessee; and there, after a period of fitful wandering, young
Andrew settled in Greeneville, where he opened a small tailor shop. Before
he was nineteen he married plain Eliza McCardle, a shoemaker's daughter,
and it was she who set him on the road to success. Eliza Johnson taught her
unlettered husband to read and write and bore him three sons and two
daughters. Avid for learning, the tailor paid men six cents a day to read to
him as he stitched, and at night Eliza took up where the readers had left off,
while her husband continued at his work.

The tailoring shop throve, and by the time Johnson reached his thirties
he had achieved modest financial success. The black-haired, grim-faced bull-
dog of a man had also developed a liking and a talent for politics. The tailor
shop became a political forum where the community's Jacksonian Democrats began to gather to talk politics. It wasn't long before Andrew Johnson,
a crudely powerful debater, became the champion of the little men, the
mechanics and small farmers and minor tradesmen who stood up to the
Tennessee aristocrats, and whose class prejudices he appealed to and shared.
He was an alderman at twenty-seven, victor over a blue-blooded Whig, and
then mayor of Greeneville. In 1835 he went to the legislature, and in 1840
he was a Democratic candidate for elector-at-large, convassing for Martin
Van Buren and building up a tremendous following among the mountaineers
and workingmen of east Tennessee. In 1843 he was elected to the Twenty-
eighth Congress as a representative of Tennessee's First District; and he
served continuously in the House of Representatives for ten years until a
Whig legislature gerrymandered him out of his district.

As he grew politically so waxed his hatred for the slave-owning aristocracy; as his principal political rival in Tennessee, Isham G. Harris, put it:
"If Johnson was a snake, he would lie in the grass to bite the heel of the rich

man's children." But he was no defender of Abolitionism. As a congressman he once said prophetically that if the Abolitionists were to free the slaves and turn them loose on the South, "the non-slave holder would join with the slave owner and extirpate them," and that "if one should be more ready to join than another, it would be myself."

Tricked out of his congressional seat, he ran for the governorship of Tennessee in 1853 and won. He was re-elected in 1855, and two years later the Tennessee legislature sent him to the United States Senate. As governor his popularity was not sectional but general. He secured Tennessee's first tax levy for public education and was responsible for the establishment of a state library and a state board of agriculture. When he ran for his second term, against an anti-Catholic, Know-Nothing candidate, he showed the courage which would have to be summoned again and again; at a political gathering at which he had been warned not to speak on pain of death, he taunted from the stump: "Show me a Know-Nothing and I will show you a loathsome reptile on whose neck every honest man should set his heels."

On the eve of war Andrew Johnson went to the United States Senate, a Democrat but a Union man who would risk his life in the nation's behalf, a stern critic of centralized federal power and of monopoly and the privilege of wealth, a proponent of popular election of United States senators, and sponsor of a homestead law which would provide 160 acres to every head of the family who would settle in the public domain. His advocacy of that law further earned him the dislike of the Southern slaveholders who wanted no small non-slave-owning settlers in the territories of the West. On December 18, 1860, when the secession convention of South Carolina was being held in Charleston, Johnson completely alienated the Southern firebrands when, in a portentous address to the Senate, he declared his allegiance to the Union. Andrew Johnson remained in the Senate when all the other Southern senators withdrew; and when he compounded his defiance with a savage excoriation of his Southern colleagues, and especially Jefferson Davis, whom he hated as the personification of the slavocracy, and insisted that the Union must be preserved, he became simultaneously hero to the North and traitor in the South.

As for slavery: "My position is that Congress has no power to interfere with slavery," he had told the Senate, "[and] that it is an institution local in its character and peculiar to the states where it exists, and no other power has the right to control it." He believed with Lincoln that there should be no emancipation unless freed Negroes were subsequently transported to Africa or elsewhere. But slavery was repugnant to him, and he spoke as a Southern poor white when he said of the Emancipation Proclamation that it would break down "an odious and dangerous aristocracy and free more whites than blacks in Tennessee." Of John Brown he had said: "John Brown stands before the country as a murderer. The time has arrived when these things ought to be stopped; when encroachments on the institutions of the South ought to cease; when the sovereign states and their institutions should be let alone; when you must either preserve the Constitution or you must destroy the Union. Those may make him a God who will, and worship him who can—he is not my God and I shall not worship at his shrine." To the North's own extremists he had cried: "We do not intend that you shall drive us out of this house that was reared by the hands of our fathers."

And, pleading to the South to remain in the Union after Lincoln's election: "I voted against him, I spoke against him, I sent my money to defeat him; but still I love my country; I love the Constitution; I intend to insist upon its guarantees; there and there alone I intend to plant myself, with the confident hope and belief that if the Union remains together, in less than four years the now triumphant party will be overthrown."

When war came he did his best to make it as merciful a conflict as possible; in the Senate he introduced resolutions setting forth that the struggle should not be carried on in a spirit of oppression of the South "nor for any purpose of conquest or subjugation, nor purpose of overthrowing or interfering with the rights or established institutions of those states, but to defend and maintain a supremacy of the Constitution and all laws made in pursuance thereof."

In March 1862, when Johnson was serving in the Senate, Lincoln asked him to accept appointment as military governor of Tennessee.

Had all of Tennessee been held by Union forces, the assignment might not have been as perilous. West and middle Tennessee, predominantly secessionist in sympathy, had been occupied after the capture of Fort Henry and Fort Donelson, the routing of the Confederate armies in western Tennessee, and the occupation of Nashville. East Tennessee, Johnson's own region where Union sentiment was strong, lay under Confederate martial law. Johnson took up his duties in antagonistic Nashville. There he behaved admirably; and, after all of Tennessee came under federal control, he secured the restoration of civil government under loyal men in spite of the opposition of Union military commanders.

Neither Andy Johnson's courage nor the political advantages which this loyal Southern Democrat offered to the Republican administration were lost on Lincoln and his fellow political strategists. When Lincoln was grudgingly renominated at the so-called National Union Convention in 1864, the Republicans dropped the party name and nominated Johnson as the President's running mate, not only in recognition of his heroic service but as a means of silencing Northern Democratic criticism that the party in power was only a sectional hodgepodge. Thus did the Jacksonian Democrat from Tennessee become vice-president and, three months later, by the dreadful mischance of assassination, President of the United States.

Andrew Johnson did not stand altogether alone. At his side was ranged the Democratic minority in Senate and House. He wielded the considerable patronage power of the executive branch. Intermittently he could count on Republican conservatives in Congress. Even so, he was a near-solitary and suspect figure. Not so the men who went at him tooth and nail. In every sense they represented the majority. They were the spokesmen and the manipulators of the party in power and of the people who stood behind that party, and among them were some who would have been conspicuous in any American political gathering at any time in our history. Few can receive more than passing recognition here, but three among these antagonists of Andrew Johnson must be singled out: Thaddeus Stevens, the Radical whom the South hated the most, then and for generations to follow; Ben Butler, the Radical man most despised in the South; and Charles Sumner, the only man among them all who would eventually earn the South's grudging respect.

In August 1868 a wasted, implacable, and disappointed old man lay dying in Washington. Beside Thaddeus Stevens's deathbed waited a mulatto woman, old too, but not as old as he. Her name was Lydia Smith. For many years, both before and after the death of her husband, a Negro barber, she had been the housekeeper of the bachelor congressman from Pennsylvania, and, so said his enemies and some among his political associates, much more to him than that; a handsome, light-skinned woman who lived in Thad Stevens's two-and-a-half-story brick house in Lancaster and accompanied him to Washington when Congress was in session. It was Lydia Smith who opened the door to old Thad's gambling friends in Washington and prepared the food for their all-night sessions of faro. Newspapers, North and South, had printed stories accusing the pair of adultery and miscegenation. Not once had Thad Stevens brought suit for libel against his accusers, not even when the Lancaster *Intelligencer,* his home-town Democratic newspaper, published one of the most insulting comments on a man's personal life ever to appear in an American newspaper.

The *Intelligencer* was outraged because Thad Stevens, having purchased a cemetery lot, had returned the deed upon discovering that Negroes were forbidden to be buried in the cemetery:

> Nobody doubts that Thaddeus Stevens has always been in favor of Negro equality, and here where his domestic arrangements are so well known, his practical recognition of his pet theory is perfectly well understood. . . . There are few men who have given to the world such open and notorious evidence of their belief in Negro equality as Thaddeus Stevens. A personage not of his own race, a female of dusky hue, daily walks the streets of Lancaster when Mr. Stevens is at home. She has presided over his house for years. Even by his own party friends, she is constantly spoken of

as Mrs. Stevens, though we fancy that no rite of Mother Church ever gave her a right to it. It is natural for men to desire to sleep their last with those they love in life. If Thaddeus Stevens insists on being buried side by side with the woman he is supposed to have taken to his bosom, it is entirely a matter of taste. But why did he not purchase a lot in an African burying ground at once? There no white man's bones would have jostled his own and she who has so long been his most intimate associate might have been gathered to his side without exciting public scandal.

Few besides Lydia Smith were with Thad Stevens in his final hours, and only she and his nephew at the moment of death. Two Negro Sisters of Charity in a Providence hospital he had helped found and two Negro ministers came to pray with him. The night that he died a company of Negro Zouaves stood guard beside his bier, and many more Negroes than whites accompanied his body to the rotunda of the capitol where it lay in state.

The tombstone in the small graveyard in Lancaster where agnostic Thaddeus Stevens was buried bears the epitaph he wrote for himself: *I repose in this quiet and secluded spot, not from any natural preference for solitude, but finding other cemeteries limited by charter rules as to race, I have chosen this, that I might illustrate in my death the principles which I advocated through a long life—Equality of Man before his Creator.*

Thus in life and in death did the leonine boss of the Radical Republicans make full and unashamed acknowledgment of the trait which was the most inexplicable and hateful to the white South he so rabidly hated in turn—a genuine and fanatic belief in the equality of the races. Andrew Johnson did not share that belief, nor did Lincoln; and this divergence alone made it inevitable that the Tennessee Democrat and the Pennsylvania Republican, commoners who in other times and with other issues at stake might have been allies, should engage in no-quarter political combat.

Few American politicians of less than presidential rank have so tempted biographers; fewer have been as contradictorily presented. The who and the what of Thad Stevens's life are clear enough; the whys have been obscured by partisanship and the personal convictions of the biographers. Born in Danville, Vermont, in 1792, he hardly remembered his father, a ne'er-do-well shoemaker who ran away from his wife and four sons, the youngest of whom, Thaddeus, was sickly and blighted with a deformed foot which made him the butt of his playmates. Sally Morrill Stevens was a redoubtable, persevering woman who, because she wanted her children to have a better chance for education, moved from Danville to Peacham, where an academy had been established a few years earlier. Completing the academy's courses, Stevens then attended Dartmouth, sandwiching in a term at the University of Vermont. Before graduating from Dartmouth he read law, and after winning his degree, continued to do so while teaching at an academy in York, Pennsylvania.

To short-cut the time requirement for admittance to the Pennsylvania bar he took his law examinations in Maryland, and having passed easily, he settled down to the practice of law in Gettysburg. He was then an aristocratic-looking young fellow, though already a hater of aristocrats, friendly-eyed, with an aquiline nose and a wide, thin mouth, stylishly dressed, and despite his crippled foot, an avid huntsman and rider to the hounds and a powerful swimmer. Young Thad Stevens was not immediately successful, but after he won freedom for a man charged with murder, with the then unusual plea of insanity, he made a reputation as a defense lawyer.

It was in Gettysburg, so close to the slave state of Maryland, that Thaddeus Stevens made the cause of the Negro slave his own, defending many fugitive slaves without fee and even spending $300, with which he had hoped to add to his law library, to purchase the freedom of a Negro hotel servant who was to be sold away from his family. He soon became known for his ferocious hatred of slavery and of slavers and as a caustic critic of Andrew Jackson and "Jacksonian Democracy," and as a successful businessman as well as lawyer—he entered the iron business in 1826—and a political hopeful who was described in 1830 as "a firm and undeviating Federalist." In these years he developed a dislike for the Masonic order which was almost as intense as his detestation of slavery. At the Anti-Masonic party convention in Baltimore in 1831 he became overnight a nationally prominent if not universally admired political figure because of an invective-larded denunciation of secret organizations. Two years later he was elected to the Pennsylvania House of Representatives on the Anti-Masonic ticket, and there he served until 1841, with two years time out between 1835 and 1837.

As a legislator Thad Stevens introduced all manner of anti-Masonry legislation, described the order as a "secret, oath-bound, murderous institution" which endangered the continuance of the government. Stevens wanted to exclude Masons from juries and disqualify Masonic judges in cases where Masons were on trial. He won a legislative inquiry into "the evils of Masonry," an unavailing effort because the empowering resolution did not provide for contempt proceedings against untalkative witnesses. He was almost as zealous in his espousal of free education, a principal advocate of an act in 1834 extending the free school system of Philadelphia throughout Pennsylvania, and foremost among the defenders of free education when Pennsylvanians, angered by the additional taxes required for a free system, sought the repeal of the law. In the House he denounced class hostility as being responsible for the opposition to public schools, characterized the repeal act as "an act for branding and marking the poor," and succeeded in winning over the House and bringing about a reversal in the Senate. He also sought larger appropriations for state colleges, espoused the right of petition and a constitutional limit on the state debt. In 1836–37 he introduced a resolution for the abolishment of slavery and the slave trade in the

District of Columbia, as a Pennsylvania legislator, and in the State Constitutional Convention of 1837 he refused to sign the constitution as finally
adopted because it denied suffrage to Negroes. Eventually the Whigs and
the Anti-Mason party united to elect an Anti-Mason governor, to whom
Stevens became the principal adviser. His subsequent persecution of Masonry revealed the psychopathic anger which he was able to summon against
the institutions and the people whom he abhorred. By 1840 he was one of
the most powerful men in Pennsylvania. Moving to Lancaster in 1842, he
purchased a two-story brick house in an unfashionable part of town. Lydia
Smith occupied a cottage in the back yard; some time after Smith died she
took up residence in Thad Stevens's house.

Stevens spent the next several years recouping his fortune, for his iron
works had not yet prospered and he was some $200,000 in debt. Through
his extraordinarily successful law practice he paid off all but $30,000 of his
obligations in six years; and this $30,000 he still owed when, finding the
call of politics and the fight over slavery irresistible, he sought and won
election to Congress in 1848 as a Whig. A fiery Free-Soiler, Stevens taunted
Southerners in the grossest terms; Virginia's slaveowners devoted their lives,
he said, "to selecting and grooming the most lusty sires and the most fruitful
wenches to supply the slave barracoons."

In 1853, disgusted with Whig middle-of-the-roaders, he quit Congress
but not politics. Foremost in Pennsylvania in the organization of the Republican party, he led the twenty men who formed the party locally in
Lancaster in 1855 and was a delegate to the national convention in 1856.
In 1858, at the age of 68, he was re-elected to Congress as a Republican,
and for the ten years until his death he would be the harshest and the most
uncompromising of the Radical Republicans. After Lincoln's nomination
his was the strongest congressional voice in opposition to any concessions
to the South, opposing pacific proposals as "the coward breath of servility
and meanness," and warning the South to secede at its own peril. He predicted that if the slave states sought to destroy the Union "our next United
States will contain no foot of ground on which a slave can tread, no breath
of air which a slave can breathe." So intemperate were his tirades that
friends more than once had to shield him from bodily harm.

The vengeful old man was one of two House members who voted in
1861 against the resolution declaring that the war was not to be prosecuted
for conquest or subjugation. From the beginning of the conflict he advocated
confiscation of all property that could be used to aid the Southern insurrection and the arming of the Southern slaves and ridiculed Lincoln's plan for
compensated emancipation as "diluted milk and water gruel." As the war
progressed the South's destruction became his single goal. In 1864 he even
described as a necessity the extermination of the Rebels, the desolation of

the South, the erasure of its state lines, and its colonization by Yankee pioneers.

He may have been in part moved to such imprecations by the destruction of his Caledonia ironworks, near Chambersburg, when Lee invaded Pennsylvania in 1863. Assuredly, the Confederates took special pleasure in laying waste Thaddeus Stevens's property. The invaders would have been something less than human had they not. The Southern troops took all stores and supplies from the works and then burned most of the settlement itself; as Stevens indignantly reported, "They took all my horses, mules, and harness, even the crippled horses." Two tons of Stevens's bacon and barrels of molasses helped feed the Confederates, and the Rebel cavalry horses enjoyed $2000 worth of his grain. The sawmill, forges, bellows houses, rolling mill, and furnace were put to the torch, and the plant's bar iron was hauled off to be converted into horseshoes, together with about $4000 worth of wagons. So thorough a job did the Southerners do that Stevens had to provide personally for the families who had been dependent upon the works and who became almost the only Northerners to know firsthand, as the Southerners by tens of thousands knew, the destructiveness of war.

Not that the baleful Pennsylvanian needed such a goad. Lincoln's "Ten Per Cent" plan for Reconstruction was intolerable to him. In an acrid speech objecting to the seating of the congressmen from Louisiana, elected before the war's end under the President's Reconstruction formula, he declared the South lay outside of the Constitution and that only the law of nations should limit the North in deciding upon the conditions of its restoration to the Union. The Southern states were nothing but "damned Rebel provinces" to be carved up, said the raging old boss of the House, and the estates of leading Rebels should be divided into forty-acre plots and sold to former slaves at $10 an acre.

"I have never desired bloody punishment to any great extent," he cried, in probably the most revealing summation of his attitude and intentions toward the South. "But there are punishments quite as appalling and longer remembered than that. They are more advisable, because they would reach greater numbers. Strip proud nobility of their bloated estates; reduce them to a level with plain republicans; send them forth to labor and teach their children to enter the workshops or handle a plow, and you will thus humble the proud traitors."

He denounced as "sickly humanity" a proposal that the United States lend $50,000,000 to the South after the war on the grounds that both sections had been responsible for slavery. The South's principal military and political figures he would have hanged; he was determined to crush any man who pursued a gentler course.

Thad Stevens hated as has no other man in our public life, and no other man in public life has been as hated in turn. He was a lonely, cynical misanthrope, gifted with a mordant wit; a brilliant, earnest orator whose denunciatory tongue knew no limits. To a visitor who called as he lay dying and who remarked that his appearance was poor, he answered, "It's not my appearance but my disappearance that troubles me." Of a fellow representative, pacing up and down the House aisles as he spoke, "Do you expect to get mileage for that speech?" Even of Daniel Webster he once said, "I could cut his damned heart out." But for the psychopathic quality of his hatred for the South of slavery and secession he could have been remembered for his political genius and his championship of the freedman. Instead, he is notable in our history as the engineer of the program of punitive Reconstruction and as a congressional dictator who would destroy even a president if he stood in his way.

Close at the side of malevolent Thad Stevens stood General Benjamin Franklin Butler, representative from Massachusetts, "grotesquely ugly, grotesquely complex and controversial," an opportunistic sail trimmer, yet a remarkably resourceful lawyer, a shrewd investor, and, for whatever reasons, an early champion for improvement of the miserable lot of the New England millworkers. The unscrupulous politician was also a reformer who even went so incredibly far as to advocate, as a thirty-five-year-old Massachusetts legislator, reduction of the work day to ten hours, a revolutionary proposal indeed in a day when the white industrial slaves of Yankee millowners—men, women, and children—worked under conditions which, save for the fact that they were not legally enslaved, were as intolerable as the lot of the worst off of the South's Negro slaves.

Ben Butler had entered politics as a Democrat. In 1853, when he was thirty-five, he was elected to the Massachusetts House of Representatives and then the Senate, principally through the support of the laborers and the immigrant Roman Catholic voters of his textile mill constituency. He was suspect by his own party's leaders; in the Democratic National Convention of 1860 he supported Jefferson Davis for president and then bolted to the Kentuckian, Breckenridge, who was like himself a Jacksonian Unionist. Interested in military affairs—as a youth he had sought but failed to receive a West Point appointment and thereafter hated the regular Army—he somehow wrangled election shortly before the war as a brigadier general of Massachusetts militia.

When Sumter was fired upon, Butler's militiamen and money were ready. As a military figure, he was throughout the war the center of unending controversy. He offended the regular army commanders with sometimes brilliant and imaginative proposals—among them balloon observation—which were matched by a disastrous ineptness in the field. As with Andrew Johnson, his position as a Democrat active in the Union's behalf kept him in the public eye; he liked it that way because his own crossed eyes were on a presidential nomination.

Ben Butler's military career began auspiciously enough. His 8th Massachusetts relieved blockaded Washington; then with only nine hundred troops Butler peacefully occupied Baltimore a month after the opening of hostilities and was rewarded with promotion to major general of volunteers. As next in command at Fortress Monroe, Virginia, he proved himself a capable administrator, and he dealt with the problem of slaves fleeing to the Union lines simply by describing them as contraband. He was badly outgeneraled and defeated in the Battle of Big Bethel; after minor successes as commander of joint military and naval forces in an attack on the forts at Hatteras Inlet, and a political squabble over authority to enlist troops in Massachusetts, he was put in command of the land forces in the expedition against New Orleans.

There, under the guns of the federal fleet, he landed on May 1, 1862, and there he earned the lasting contempt of the South and the opprobrium of much of the rest of the world. He hanged the young gambler, William Mumford, for hauling down the United States flag on the day of occupation. Highhandedly ignoring the federal government, he assumed full control of tax collections and expenditures and, more than incidentally, gave New Orleans the most thorough physical house-cleaning and sanitation program that the indifferent Creole city had ever known. Almost every European government protested strongly when he seized from the French Consulate $800,000 in bullion which belonged to Southerners who had put their money in the hands of the French Consul. Some of the gold was not turned over to the United States itself until the nation had been aroused over its whereabouts.

If Butler took advantage of his position as military ruler of New Orleans to enrich himself, he managed to cover his tracks; but his brother, Andrew Jackson Butler, was one of the profiteers from such corrupt practices as dealing with the enemy, and this with Butler's covert support. Even his most partisan biographer, James Parton, writing in 1864, admitted that "The general's brother was one of the lucky men who chanced to be in business in New Orleans at the critical moment . . . Later in the year, came the confiscation of Rebel property, with frequent sales at auction of valuable commodities. Of this business, too, he had an ample share—just the share his means and talents entitled him to." Among Brother Butler's assets were all the private capital which Ben could raise for him to speculate in cattle and other provisions and confiscated steamboats; and Ben gave him military protection on his upriver trading trips through enemy lines, one or two companies of infantry to a steamboat, to sell salt and medicine to the enemy in exchange for cotton and sugar which were then sold for four or five times as much as the value of the goods he traded.

The general's own men hated him because of the brutality of his discipline. So readily did he execute deserters that Lincoln himself once ordered him to suspend sentences of death until further notice. In his presence the braver bluecoats would call from the ranks, "Who stole the silver spoons?" in reference to the popular tale that he stole the silverware from the New Orleans home he commandeered. And when he visited the Yankee prison camp at Point Lookout the Confederate prisoners shouted at him: "You damn lobster-eyed son-of-a-bitch," and, "Pay me the money you stole in New Orleans," and, "Why don't you fight men and not women?"

The jibe about warring on women was related to the most notorious of Butler's acts as military commander of New Orleans and one which would bring him lasting odium. It was the "Woman Order," General Order Number 28 of May 15, 1862. Many women of New Orleans had behaved insultingly toward the conquerors from the first days of the occupation. In retaliation, General Order 28 was issued: "As the officers and soldiers of the United States have been subjected to repeated insults from the women (calling themselves ladies) of New Orleans, in return for the most scrupulous non-interference and courtesy on our part, it is ordered, that hereafter, when any female shall, by word, gesture, or movement, insult or show contempt for any officer or soldier of the United States, she shall be regarded and held liable to be treated as a woman of the town plying her avocation."

When the mayor of New Orleans objected he was removed from office and committed, together with some of his aides, to prison. In England public opinion shifted after the order to the Southerners. On the floors of the House of Commons and the House of Lords, members of Parliament demanded that the British government protest. Jefferson Davis, in an extraordinary proclamation which cited Mumford's execution, the imprisonment of New Orleans citizens and paroled soldiers, the arousing of slaves, the plundering of New Orleans, and, above all, the Woman Order, pronounced "said Benjamin F. Butler to be a felon, deserving of capital punishment. I do order that he shall [be considered] . . . but as an outlaw and common enemy of mankind, and that, in the event of his capture, the officer in charge of the capturing force will cause him to be immediately executed by hanging." Another Davis proclamation included as "robbers and criminals, deserving death" all commissioned officers in Butler's command.

That summer Butler wrote his wife that "I am changing my opinions. There is nothing of the [Southern] people worth saving. I am inclined to give it all up to the blacks. There is such lying, meanness, wrong, and wickedness, that I am inclined to think that the story of Sodom and Gomorrah a myth, else why not rain fire and brimstone upon this city? I am afraid the Lord will do so in the shape of the Negroes."

Lincoln removed him from his command in December 1862 and in 1863 put him in charge of the occupied Districts of Eastern Virginia and North

Carolina with command of the Army of the James. There Butler showed marked interest in the welfare of Negroes. He took a census of the Negroes in his districts, provided shelter and medical care, made farm lands available to some of them, and set up a rudimentary educational system. As for Virginians in general, he said, "I never saw a loyal Virginian who was worth a curse whose skin was lighter than the ace of spades." As Commissioner for the Exchange of Prisoners Butler managed to effect some exchanges and to force the Confederate government to admit that the United States' Negro troops had military status. Up to his old tricks, he encouraged trading with individual Southerners. He botched one independent military venture which led to the bottling up of his army at Bermuda Hundred by a numerically inferior Confederate force.

All the while Butler's mind had been more on the presidency than on the prosecution of the war itself, and, but for his own decision, he might have been Lincoln's Vice-President. The President had determined that his running mate in 1864 should be a Democrat, and politics, if not personal liking, made Butler a likely prospect. To the embattled North he was a champion of the Negro, a humbler of the South, a soldier whose record was, as far as the public was concerned, a good one. The Radicals saw in his behavior in New Orleans an offset to Lincoln's moderation. As a Democrat he could be counted upon to make inroads among the Northern Democrats, just as Andrew Johnson was to do. And it is quite probable that Lincoln and his political strategists figured that it was better to have Butler with the President than as an active candidate against him. He could be a very real menace; Lincoln's secretary, John Hay, described him as "the smartest damn rascal that ever lived." But Butler declared that there was nothing in the vice-presidency, and so the nomination went to Andrew Johnson, who would become the South's friend, instead of to the Massachusetts politician-soldier who, to the white South, was Caliban.

Late in the war, for reasons that were never explained, Grant relieved Butler of his command in January 1865 and ordered him to return to Massachusetts. Butler, by now a Radical Republican in all but name, made the first of his many party switches. To a New York audience he said of Lincoln's assassination with hypocritical piety on the very day that the President died: "Perhaps I may say reverently that this dispensation of God's good providence is sent to teach us that the spirit of the Rebellion has not been broken by the surrender of its armies." Immediately thereafter he joined the Radical Republicans whose leaders in caucus promised to endorse him as Secretary of State. At this gathering Butler said emphatically that Johnson "must not administer the estate of Lincoln," though toward Johnson himself, perhaps in the hope that he could be persuaded to a harsh peace, he was outwardly friendly; and even when Johnson lay ill in the summer of 1865, Butler, according to Gideon Welles, Lincoln's Secretary of the Navy, "pushed his way to the very door of the sick room to insist on the execution of Davis and Lee and to urge severity."

Ben Butler was elected to Congress in 1866 as a Republican, and as a Republican he served until 1875. As Thaddeus Stevens declined in health Butler increasingly became the House's leading spokesman for punitive reconstruction. In his autobiography he would later succinctly set down his program: "With the Radical Republicans of my party I held the proposition . . . that the Rebel states should be held as territories under military government until all possibility of a race war or race dissensions between white and black should be obliterated, and that then these Territories might be admitted into the Union as states when the Negro had learned how to be a citizen, and the white man had learned how to be a loyal one. . . . I would have confiscated the real estate of all those who had voluntarily taken an active part in the rebellion. I would have permitted all to run away who desired to and expatriate themselves as they had tried to do by bloody war—and some of them by so going away justified the propriety of my suggestion. Their lands so forfeited I would have divided among the private soldiers of the army to be theirs at the end of five years of occupation."

The *Independent* of March 14, 1867, contained a memorable description of the Representative Butler of this time: "Make the best of it you can, it is a terrible face, this of Butler's; it looks like a pirate's—the strong, unscrupulous, cruel face, the low wide head, the crossed eyes, the hatchety Roman nose, the thin lips, make a combination powerful and pitiless. Yet we know this man has room in him for large magnanimities, for gentle charities, for good will and tenderness. Only this is not the nature he faces the world with. He meets that with the brain of a master, with the will of a tyrant, and the ambition of a spirit which can brook no superior. . . . As a politician Ben Butler is overreaching, self seeking, and will be content with no less than the highest prize in the political game."

Butler never won that highest prize but, because of Stevens's feebleness, he became the dominant figure in the management of Johnson's impeachment by the House of Representatives; and, in one memorable demonstration, he created by his performance on the floor a phrase which echoes angrily even today. After an Ohio Carpetbagger was flogged in Mississippi, his bloodstained shirt was included in an exhibit assembled in Washington in proof of Southern atrocities. Butler, in a warning on the floor of the House that the South would be punished for its misdeeds, waved the garment over his head. From then on "waving the bloody shirt" was to be part and parcel of the American political lexicon.

Butler's political role after the failure of the impeachment proceedings was all but anti-climactic, although he remained foremost among the advocates of stern measures in the South until the Democratic tidal wave of 1875 swept him out of office. He was elected to Congress again in 1878 as a Greenbacker, and while in Congress he ran three times for governor of Massachusetts, twice as a Republican, in 1871 and in 1872, and as a Greenbacker in 1878, with some Democratic support. Finally in 1882, with the full support of the Massachusetts Democratic party, and profiting by the national reaction against the Republicans, he was elected governor by a small majority of 14,000, the only victor on the Democratic ticket. Defeated for re-election in 1883, he sought the presidency in 1884 and was nominated by a new splinter party, the Anti-Monopoly party, and by the Greenbackers; and he sought that same spring the Democratic nomination as well. In the election he received only 175,000 votes, nearly one fourth of them in Michigan.

Never again did Ben Butler seek political office. He died in Washington in 1893, leaving behind him a fortune of some $7,000,000 and a record for audacious political conduct never surpassed in American politics.

Andrew Johnson and Thad Stevens were commoners. Ben Butler was of the New England middle class. Charles Sumner was a Massachusetts blue blood whose tongue was scarcely less venomous than was Butler's and whose concern for the welfare of the Negro as ragingly idealistic as was Stevens's. It was Sumner who denounced the Louisiana state government, organized under the Lincoln Plan in 1864, and which did not grant universal suffrage to the Negro, as "a mere seven months' abortion, begotten by the bayonet, in criminal conjunction with a spirit of caste, and born before its time, rickety, unformed, unfinished, whose continued existence will be a burden, a reproach and a wrong."

The ascetic, scholarly Bostonian's talent for personal invective had almost cost him his life six years before the war. During the passionate, hate-ridden debate over the Kansas-Nebraska Act he indulged in galling assaults upon the Democrats, the South, and slavery. Two days after his speech, while he sat at his desk, he looked up to see standing over him a young stranger, Representative Preston Brooks of South Carolina, who, after saying, "I have read your speech twice over carefully; it is a libel on South Carolina and Mr. Butler [Senator Andrew Pickens Butler of South Carolina] who is a relative of mine," beat him mercilessly with a heavy cane until he fell to the floor unconscious and covered with blood. Never did he fully recover from his injuries. For three and one half years he was absent from the Senate, seeking in Europe and at home relief from the continuous pains which had reduced him to near-invalidism.

Meanwhile he was re-elected by the almost unanimous vote of the Massachusetts legislature. When he returned to the Senate he determined upon "an assault on American slavery all along the lines" in the face of Southern aggressiveness which had secured the passage of Senator Jefferson Davis's resolutions affirming the sanctity of slave property in the territories.

From the outset of the war Sumner sought the emancipation of the Negroes on moral grounds, and absolute civil equality; and no man had done more to win presidential and public approval of these goals. His antagonism toward the South and his insistence that Congress should initiate and control Reconstruction led him to the proposition that the seceded states had abdicated all rights under the Constitution; had, as he phrased it, committed suicide, and should come under the jurisdiction of Congress, to be treated as "conquered provinces and its proud nobility . . . subjected to retaliation which would be longer remembered than death." On the last day of his life Abraham Lincoln told his Cabinet that Sumner, more than any other man, had prevented the recognition of Louisiana under his plan; and his outpourings against Johnson, before, during, and after the impeachment proceedings, in which he went so far as to name the President the century's "enormous criminal," were without congressional parallel.

Yet he was no single-minded fanatic. Perhaps the most widely traveled member of Congress, and almost certainly having the widest knowlege of international affairs of any American of his time, he succeeded as wartime chairman of the Senate Committee on Foreign Affairs to kill off resolutions, following United States seizure from a British ship of the Confederate emissaries, Mason and Slidell, and afterward, which almost surely would have embroiled the United States in war with Great Britain and with France.

Understandably he would get along no better with Johnson's successor, Ulysses S. Grant, for, though they were of the same party, they were almost completely antipathetic. In time he would denounce the Union's war hero as furiously as he had inveighed against his Democratic predecessor; he and Grant were at opposite poles in training, in education, in temperament, and in governmental experience. They became extreme personal antagonists, engaging in a running fight which ended with the most senseless of all congressional humiliations of the period, Sumner's demotion as chairman of the Foreign Relations Committee.

Quixotically, the man whose goal of "absolute human equality, secured, assured and invulnerable," had led him to utter the wildest political extravagances in and out of Congress displayed in his later years a magnanimity toward the South and an honest man's contempt for the plunderers of the Grant administrations. In December 1872 Sumner introduced a bill providing that inasmuch as "national unity and good will among fellow citizens can be assured only through oblivion of past differences, and it is contrary to the usage of civilized nations to perpetuate the memory of civil war," the names of battles waged against fellow Americans should not be continued in the Army Register or inscribed on the regimental colors of the United States. This and other gestures of kindness and sympathy for the South won him, before his death, the respect and even the admiration of much of the onetime Confederacy; and after he succumbed from a heart attack in March 1874, at the age of sixty-three, Senator L. Q. C. Lamar, the Democratic Senator of Mississippi, delivered on the senate floor the most moving of any senatorial tribute to the man who, as W. A. Dunning observed in *Reconstruction, Political and Economic,* "would shed tears at the bare thought of refusing to freedmen rights of which they had no comprehension, but would filibuster to the end of the session to prevent the restoration to the Southern whites of rights which were essential to their whole concept of life."

Thad Stevens, the South's most hated foeman, Charles Sumner, in time its most respected, and Ben Butler, the most despised, dominated the politicians whose common goal was the continued possession of the South by the Republican party. But men far less zealous or maligned or basely motivated than they could have found reason for partisan alarm as the summer of 1865 gave way to autumn.

CHAPTER 2

Showdown in Washington

A REPUBLICAN President and a Republican Congress had governed and guided the Union through its most perilous years; through a war which, while slavery was the great moral and emotional issue, was made inevitable by conflicting political theories of the indissolubility of the Union and the constitutional right of a sovereign state to leave that Union. Now, in the first summer of peace, a Southerner and a Democrat was President.

In the Southern night Yankee boys had chanted around their campfires the most haunting and meaningful of American battle songs, and they had died by the tens and the hundreds of thousands with the song's burden in their hearts:

> *In the beauty of the lilies Christ was born across the sea*
> *With a glory in his bosom that transfigures you and me;*
> *As he died to make men holy let us die to make men free . . .*

Now in the summer and fall of 1865 unrepentant Rebels were fashioning the Black Codes.

True enough, the "loyal conventions" in the South were uniformly amenable to the ratification of the Thirteenth Amendment which gave constitutional authority to the established fact of Negro freedom; but conventions and citizenry were showing a striking preference for leaders who had worn the gray and a reluctance toward Negro suffrage so marked that, despite the pleadings of white Southern moderates, not a single state granted suffrage even to the small minority of Negroes who might be considered qualified by education, by prewar free status, by property ownership, or by military service.

Now the ascendant industrialists of the North, whose mills and foundries and factories had meant the difference between triumph and stalemate or defeat, and who dreamed of a vaster economic empire, might again be plagued by the ridiculous Democratic idea of tariffs for revenue only, nonsense which could become reality if to the Northern Democrats' ranks could be added Democratic majorities in the Southern states. Few of these men of substance thought much of the schemes of Stevens's band of genuine Radicals to confiscate the lands of other men of property for division among Negroes; such a procedure would endanger the institutions in which they believed the most. But if old Thad and Ben Butler and their cohorts could keep the Southern Democrats under their heels, more power to them.

And for the politicians and those rare creatures, the political theorists, there remained the question, underscored by Lincoln's vast wartime extension of executive actions, of where the powers of the President ended and the powers of Congress began. In its practical application the answer would determine the techniques of Reconstruction. Would they be formulated by the Democratic President who held out the olive branch to the South or by the Congress, a majority of which intended to punish the Rebels and perpetuate the victorious party's glorious hour?

In the inevitable and unequal contest Andrew Johnson would suffer every political humiliation save the ultimate indignity of expulsion from office by a hostile Congress. He was not without allies, personal and political, or lacking in considerable popular support. Andrew Johnson's supporters were a heterogeneous lot, held together by party ties and sectional sympathies and, on the part of the working-class Democrats of the urban North, so many of them newcomers from Europe, by a sense of kinship for Johnson the commoner, a dislike for the potential or actual Negro competitor, and an antipathy for Republican industrial leadership that had its origins in class struggle and, especially in New England, in religious ill will. Among them were the Democrats of the border states which had not seceded, less loyal now as the Radical scheme began to unfold itself than they were in war; the Copperheads of the middle and western states, whose Southern heritage or sympathies had brought them during the war to the brink of treason; political mercenaries, held together by the not inconsiderable patronage of the executive branch; a few men of the caliber of statesmen, Democratic by conviction before and during the war; and all of them together a suspect minority in the victorious Union.

When President Johnson proclaimed amnesty for all former Confederates save for the excepted groups at the end of May 1865, and followed this up with successive proclamations setting up provisional governments in North Carolina, Mississippi, Georgia, Texas, Alabama, South Carolina, and Florida, his actions made inevitable all that would come later.

By December 1865 every former Confederate state except Texas had complied with the provisions for readmission: the drafting and ratification of new constitutions by loyal white citizens in convention assembled and their election of state legislatures, which, as required, repealed the ordinances of secession, repudiated the Confederate debts, and ratified the Thirteenth Amendment. When, in that same December, the Thirty-ninth Congress convened, the Radicals were ready for Andrew Johnson, the constitutionalist who believed each state had the right to set its own qualifications for suffrage, and whose program made no mention of immediate and full acceptance of the Negro in the nation's political affairs.

Throughout the fall the Radicals had been busy undermining Johnson by seeking to destroy his reputation. They had been as busily engaged in proving that the South was unrepentant and unable or unwilling to prevent violence against the freedmen. To the old canards—that the President was secretly a Roman Catholic or, contradictorily, an atheist—they added some new ones. High among these was the accusation that Andy Johnson was a chronic drunkard. An unfortunate incident made the story stick throughout his term as President and for a long time afterward.

Ill in Nashville before his inauguration as vice-president, he had wanted to take the oath there, but Lincoln knew it would be good politics to have his Southern running mate sworn in at the capitol. Johnson arrived in Washington a day or so before the inaugural and very probably drank too much at a party the night before the ceremonies. The next day, just before the inaugural, he asked Vice-president Hannibal Hamlin for a drink, saying that he felt faint, a euphemism for a hang-over. In a very little while he drank three glasses of brandy; and when he entered the Senate chamber to be sworn in, the heat of the chamber, the three quick drinks, and the excesses of the night before combined to so befuddle him that he did make a sorry public spectacle of himself. But he was not a drunkard in a day of hard drinkers, though he did like a few drams of Tennessee whisky on occasion. Even his uncompromising Tennessee political opponent, Parson Brownlow, defended him against the charges of alcoholism. "Nobody in Tennessee ever regarded him as addicted to the excessive use of liquors," Brownlow testified; and Lincoln said, soon after the inaugural: "I have known Andy Johnson for many years. He made a bad slip the other day but you need not be scared. Andy ain't a drunkard."

Within his own official family a spying double-crosser did his best that summer and afterward to destroy the President. He was Lincoln's Secretary of War, Edwin M. Stanton, whom Johnson had unwisely retained. Stanton kept the Radicals informed of what was going on in the executive branch, even fabricating a tale that Johnson intended to reorganize Congress and turn over control to Southern and Northern Democrats. In mass meetings and in their own private caucuses the leaders of the Radical majority decided well in advance of the gathering of the Thirty-ninth Congress that the Johnson program must be nullified and the Southern states readmitted to the Union only on the Radical terms.

When Congress convened in December the Radicals authorized the appointment of one of the strangest committees ever created in Washington. Known as the Joint Committee on Reconstruction, it was composed of six senators and nine representatives, all Republicans, with Stevens as chairman. The committee collected testimony from 144 witnesses as to the continued rebellious spirit of the South and the unwisdom of permitting the presently elected state governments, under Southern white control, to continue to function. In his message to Congress on December 6, 1865, Johnson announced that the Union had been restored under the Lincoln-Johnson plan. In Washington delegates from the former Confederate states awaited admission to Congress. To the surprise of no one the all-Republican Joint Committee found that the South had no legal state governments, since, by "committing suicide," the seceding states had, upon defeat, put themselves under the control of Congress and that Congress alone could restore them and determine the conditions for their readmission. In that same month, in brazen contradiction, the Thirteenth Amendment was formally proclaimed to be in effect, having been ratified by the requisite number of states—but eleven of the ratifying states were the same Southern states which the Joint Committee and the Republican majority behind it had declared to lack properly constituted governments.

Now began a series of presidential vetoes of congressional Reconstruction acts and of congressional repassage of most of the measures over the vetoes, a frustrating contest between the executive and the legislative branches which presaged from the beginning political degradation and economic blight for the white South, and which would almost bring about the impeachment of Andrew Johnson on grounds which no student of American government justifies today.

Though it was unfolded piecemeal, the Radicals' over-all program for Reconstruction was definite and encompassing. We have witnessed earlier some of the impact of that program upon the whites and the Negroes of the South where the debates and the legalisms and the political maneuverings in Washington, culminating in the sordid drama of impeachment, were translated into abominable reality for the one and, for the other, into a chimerical hour of triumph. Through a procession of constitutional amendments, military intervention and congressional legislation, the Radicals were to embody emancipation into the Constitution and transform the modestly conceived Freedmen's Bureau into a judicial branch of the Army empowered to supervise Negro schools and health agencies and to maintain special courts for the protection of Negroes. They would abolish the South's postwar codes for the supervision and discipline of the former slaves, enfranchise the untutored Negro mass only two years away from slavery while disfranchising some 150,000 former Confederates, and bar any states from interfering with the Negro's right to vote through a constitutional amendment that imposed Negro suffrage upon such loyal Union strongholds as Ohio, Michigan, and Kansas, which after the war had rejected proposals for Negro suffrage.

At every turn Andrew Johnson battled the Radicals, stubbornly, unavailingly, tooth and nail. In April 1866 Congress passed the epochal first Federal Civil Rights Act, a measure its leadership considered to be needful because the Dred Scott decision had held, in effect, that the Negro had only subhuman rights. It extended citizenship to all persons born in the United States without regard to color—unless they were Indians, the only non-whites in the United States who on their own had fought their exploiters until their near-extermination—and granted to such citizens the rights to make contracts, to hold property, to enjoy equal protection under the law, and to be subject to like punishment. A provocative harbinger of the future, the act gave federal courts jurisdiction in suits arising from its violation, and the President was authorized to use the armed forces to enforce it. Johnson vetoed the measure as an unwarranted intrusion upon states' rights; inherent in the veto message was his philosophy that the freed slaves did not yet merit full equality.

Early in June 1866 the Joint Committee offered the Fourteenth Amendment, citing the general doubt as to the constitutionality of the Civil Rights Act itself; and Congress almost immediately authorized the submission of the amendment to the states. This, the most controversial and far-reaching of the several amendments to the Constitution, conferred citizenship on every person born or naturalized in the United States, thus including Negroes among the citizenry for the first time; it authorized the reduction of representation in Congress for states which deprived the Negro of the ballot; it debarred from national and state office former Confederates if they had held similar governmental posts before the war; it repudiated the Confederate debt and affirmed the validity of the United States debt. One section abrogated the "three-fifths clause," whereby a Negro was counted as only three-fifths of a person in determining a state's population, a decision which increased the South's representation in the House by about a dozen seats. Another provided a proportionate reduction in representation—never actually enforced—when a state denied the vote "except for participation in rebellion or other crime."

Of the former states of the Confederacy only Tennessee, firmly in Radical hands, ratified the Fourteenth Amendment and accordingly was restored to the Union in July 1866. The other ten states overwhelmingly rejected the amendment. So did Kentucky, Ohio, Delaware, and Maryland and New Jersey. Not until July 28, 1868, would sufficient approval be mustered in the Southern and border states for ratification; and in the objecting Southern states the conditions under which ratification was secured were such as to make the legality of the amendment debatable.

That legality is a moot question now. Yet its employment in the Supreme Court's ruling in 1954 on school segregation brought the argument to the fore again among those who protested the mid-twentieth-century interpretation of the Fourteenth Amendment. And whatever the usefulness of the debate, the argument as to the dubiousness of the amendment's origin is an intriguing one. Article Five of the Constitution, so the challenge runs, establishes the procedures for the submission and ratification of constitutional amendments. The end decision rests with the states; in the final version of Article Five the authors of the Constitution inserted a provision forbidding the deprivation to any state of equal suffrage in the Senate without that state's consent. But through the Committee of Fifteen the Radicals excluded from the Senate the senators elected from ten Southern states, thus making it possible to obtain in the "rump senate" the two-thirds majority vote needed for submitting the proposal for the Fourteenth Amendment to the states. The excluded states had complied with a presidential Reconstruction program, were being governed by elected legislators, and had participated in the ratification of the Thirteenth Amendment. If their senators had been seated, submission of the Fourteenth Amendment would not have been authorized when it was, or for years later—which is exactly what Thad Stevens knew. When ten of the eleven former Confederate states rejected the Fourteenth Amendment the Radical answer was not long in coming.

Meanwhile, in June, the Committee of Fifteen had reported, as expected, that the Confederate states were not entitled to representation and set forth the proposition that Congress and not the President was empowered to draw up the terms of Reconstruction.

From the opening of the Thirty-ninth Congress to the end of his term Andrew Johnson, as truculent and as intemperate in his denunciations as were any of his foes, would lead a minority in the most uncompromising and bare-knuckled, and longest lasting of any contest between President and Congress in our history.

On Washington's Birthday, 1866, following a mass meeting of his supporters in a Washington theater and a serenade and processional march, Andy Johnson tossed down the gauge which the Radicals were quick to pick up. The Committee of Fifteen, he roared, had consumed every power of Congress. "I am opposed to the Davises, the Toombs, the Slidells," he said in a reminder that he, too, though a Southerner, had supported the

Union. "But when I see on the other hand men still opposed to the Union, I am still for the preservation of these [the Southern] states. I look upon as being opposed to the fundamental principles of this government and as now living to destroy them, Thaddeus Stevens, Charles Sumner and Wendell Phillips." Later he would say of the Civil Rights Bill that the safeguards it proposed for "the security of the colored race" were "another step toward or rather a stride to centralization and the concentration of all legislative power in the national government." This was his answer to Stevens, who had raged in the debate over the Civil Rights Bill that if his amendment for the disfranchisement until July 4, 1870, of all persons who had supported the Confederacy were not adopted, "that side of the house will be filled with yelling secessionists and hissing Copperheads. . . . I do not hesitate to say at once that the section [of the amendment he proposed] is there to save or destroy the Republican party." In the ensuing debate Stevens added that if the Southerners "undertake to come here, we will shoot them down." The Senate considerably softened Stevens's amendment.

After Johnson's reckless speech of February 22 no hope for compromise remained. In reality there never had been any real hope. Each side now set about to prove or disprove that the South seethed in turmoil and that no Negro's life was safe. Radical investigators reported atrocity upon atrocity, the torture of young Negro girls, the discovery of bodies of scores of Negroes in lonely bayous and rivers, the mistreatment of Union men, and the existence of plots to renew the war.

Johnson's own investigators of Southern conditions, notably Benjamin Truman, the gifted journalist who was his personal aide, and such objective reporters as Whitelaw Reid, found no mass disorder. The Radicals found plenty. The antagonists alike looked to the congressional elections to be held in the fall of 1866 for vindication and they took their causes to the people.

Throughout the summer and fall of 1866 the South had been contributing, however inadvertently, to its own doom by rejecting the Fourteenth Amendment, by establishing the Black Codes, and by setting itself against the military commissions of the Freedmen's Bureau. That summer a series of race riots, the worst of them in Memphis and in New Orleans, gave the Radicals all that they needed to back up their contention that the South was unsubdued and determined by whatever means to keep the Negro down. Which, of course, was true enough.

The first riot occurred on April 16, 1866, when a parade of Norfolk freedmen, celebrating the passage of the Civil Rights Bill, tangled with irate whites, and two men on each side were killed. Far worse was the insensate three-day conflict in Memphis, which began on April 30 with a brawl between Irish policemen and Negro soldiers and developed into widespread race rioting in which more than forty Negroes were killed. That same spring a Negro garrison in Brenham, Texas, burned down the town after a fight between drunken Negro troops and white residents; in Victoria, Texas, Negro soldiers terrorized the town; the Negro garrison at Fort Macon, in Beaufort, North Carolina, rescued Negro soldiers charged by civilian authorities with raping and attempting to rape white women.

But the most savage, one-sided, and consequential rioting of the year, with probably the greatest toll in dead and wounded of any Reconstruction affray, was that which flared in New Orleans in July.

Louisiana had re-entered the union in 1864 under Lincoln's "Ten Per Cent" plan and with a constitution written and approved by white loyalists in convention; but after the war's end former Confederates and other secessionist Southerners assumed control of the state government and of the city of New Orleans. The white Radical leaders decided in 1866 that they had better call a new convention, disregarding what they themselves had already done, draw up a government for the "territory of Louisiana," and then ask Congress for readmission as a new state. After Congress rejected Louisiana's elected representatives, the state's Radicals were supported in their plot by Governor J. Madison Wells who had been the nominee in 1864 of the Radicals and Conservatives alike. The Louisiana Radicals were aware that Johnson would veto any congressional act which would readmit Louisiana under such a scheme and that the act probably could not be repassed over his veto. Accordingly they took advantage of a very small loophole, provided by the state convention of 1864, as a way to write a new constitution which would place political power again in their hands.

The convention of 1864 had adopted a vague, last-minute resolution authorizing its president to "reconvoke the Convention for any causes, or in case the constitution should not be ratified, for the purpose of taking such measures as may be necessary for the formation of a civil government in the state of Louisiana." This resolution had no validity in 1866. The constitution had been in effect for two years, and, under its provisions, civil government had been set up. Nor was the resolution ever a part of the constitution, for it had not been ratified by popular vote; and whatever its asserted authority, it provided that only the president of the convention of 1864 could reconvene that body. Judge Edward H. Durell, the former president, did not himself act under the resolution to reconvene the convention. Instead the secretary, in behalf of "several members of the convention," as well as the governor, called upon the delegates to meet on June 26 without semblance of legality.

On that day some thirty to forty members—considerably fewer than the required quorum of seventy-six—met in New Orleans without Judge Durell in attendance. R. K. Howell, a Radical who had resigned as a member of the earlier convention, was elected president in Durell's stead; and, without constitutional authority, Howell summoned the convention to meet again on July 30 to "revise and amend the constitution and to consider the adoption of the 14th Amendment." Forthwith he hurried to Washington to enlist congressional and military support for the coup. By now it was generally known in Louisiana that the plotters intended to so amend the constitution as to enfranchise the Negroes and disfranchise the former Confederates, to void the elections held under the constitution of 1864 and order new ones, and to elect a Radical government which would then be approved by the congressional majority.

Even the anti-Southern General Philip Sheridan, in command of federal troops in Louisiana, reported to General Grant that, prior to the convention, "political agitators and revolutionary men" made inflammatory addresses at Negro mass meetings. The worst of such demagogues was Dr. A. P. Dostie, a Northern dentist who had hung out a shingle in New Orleans. This is what Dr. Dostie said, in part, to one such mass meeting, three nights before the convention was to gather:

> "I want the Negroes to have the right of suffrage and we will give them this right to vote. There will be another meeting here tomorrow night, and on Monday I want you to come in your power. I want no cowards to come. I want only brave men to come, who will stand by us and we will stand by them. Come, then, in your power to that meeting. . . . We have 300,000 black men with white hearts. Also 100,000 good and true Union white men, who will fight for and beside the black race against the hell-bound Rebels, for now there are but two parties here. There are no Copperheads now. Colonel Field, now making a speech inside, is heart and soul with us. He and others who would not a year ago speak to me, now take me by the hand. We have 400,000 to 300,000 and can not only whip but exterminate the other party. Judge Abell with his grand jury may indict us. Harry Hayes, with his posse comitatus, may be expected there, and the police, with more than 1,000 men sworn in, may interfere with the convention; therefore, let all brave men and not cowards come here on Monday. There will be no such puerile affair as at Memphis, but if we are interfered with, the streets of New Orleans will run with blood. . . ."

Meanwhile Mayor John T. Monroe of New Orleans had notified General Absalom Baird, temporarily in command of the military district in Sheridan's absence, that the convention delegates would be jailed "unless the convention was sanctioned by the military." In turn, General Baird warned the mayor that the convention was not to be interfered with, although he had no instructions to that effect, his argument being that if the body were legally constituted it had a right to meet, and if it were not, the United States Courts would declare its acts to be null and void. But the Louisiana Conservatives knew that the Radical Congress would not be deterred by any court action from accepting what would be the inevitable results of the convention. Louisiana's civil government would be turned over to the Radical Republicans.

Two days before the convention was to meet, Governor Wells was conveniently absent from the temporary state capitol in New Orleans. In his stead the lieutenant governor and Mayor Monroe told General Baird that if the convention delegates persisted in meeting their indictments would be sought, and, if they were indicted, the sheriff of Orleans Parish would be ordered to arrest them. The general replied that his troops would release the delegates if they were arrested and telegraphed the War Department for further instructions. His telegram was not answered. Secretary of War Stanton showed the telegram neither to President Johnson nor to the rest of his Cabinet.

Early in the morning of July 30 Mayor Monroe issued a proclamation entreating that peace and order be maintained. In midmorning the lieutenant governor asked General Baird to furnish troops to preserve order. The general was willing enough to comply, but somehow he held the mistaken belief that the convention would open at six o'clock in the evening instead of at noon. The troops who could have averted the imminent tragedy remained at Jackson Barracks.

Thus was set the stage for what the Radicals called the "St. Bartholomew's Day of New Orleans."

The delegates convened at the Mechanic's Institute at noon. Discovering that little more than one third of a quorum was in attendance, they adjourned until one o'clock. During the recess a parade of Negro supporters of the convention formed near by and, under the national flag and to the martial beat of drums, began marching across Canal Street, the city's principal business thoroughfare, toward the Institute. Few of the paraders were armed, but more than a few had been drinking. Most of the mob of whites who blocked their way were armed and many of them were also drunk. A few whites and Negroes scuffled. Someone fired a shot. But the procession went on its way, and after regular and auxiliary police arrived it appeared for a few minutes that nothing untoward would happen. Then a policeman arrested a newsboy who had been making trouble; he was fired upon, whether by a white man or a Negro never being determined. The mob went for the Negroes with guns, clubs, and knives, driving them into the hall of the Institute, which they then surrounded and stormed. Probably most of the police joined forces with the attackers; some policemen butchered Negro prisoners who surrendered to them; others tried to do their duty.

Dr. A. Hartsuff of the United States Army reported that thirty-four Negroes and "one disloyal white" were killed, as were Dr. Dostie and the white minister who had opened the convention with a prayer. Eight convention delegates were wounded, according to this report, as were nine loyal whites, ten policemen, and 119 Negroes. Almost certainly the Negro casualties were considerably greater. The mayor and the lieutenant governor listed forty-two policemen killed and wounded.

The bloody affair was short-lived. When General Baird's troops arrived at 2:40 P.M. most of the rioting was over and the police were maintaining a semblance of order. General Sheridan reported to Washington that what had occurred that terrible day was no riot but "an absolute massacre." A congressional committee of investigation divided in partisan fashion. Its majority, echoing General Sheridan's comment, found in "St. Bartholomew's Day" proof positive that loyal men were not safe in Louisiana. The Democratic minority reported that the Radicals had planned to provoke the riot, expecting its suppression by the federal troops before any white Radical leaders could be molested, but not before the trouble would provide reason for congressional interference in Louisiana's affairs.

Whoever was to blame, the rioting in New Orleans foreshadowed the shape of things to come.

Thad Stevens's announced alternative to the adoption of the Fourteenth Amendment was military occupation until the South gave in. Doggedly the President determined to go to the people who, he believed, would throw out the Radical Republican majority and in so doing give their approval to Lincoln's and his program. Accordingly he recommended a National Union Convention which would join the nation's moderates, North and South, in a new party. Despite the sure reprisals which had been threatened at a Republican caucus in July when Stevens offered a resolution demanding that any Republicans who supported Johnson's convention be read out of the party, the National Union Convention, summoned by Johnson, did meet in Philadelphia on August 14.

For the first time since Fort Sumter, former Confederates and Unionists joined in a political meeting, Democrats and Republicans sharing the leadership. A Confederate and a Union officer marched arm in arm down the meeting-hall aisle. The delegates were reminded of the equal right of states to representation, of the right of states to formulate voting qualifications, and of the constitutionally prescribed requirement that amendments to the Constitution could be made only through a favorable vote of two-thirds of the states. Resolutions declared slavery to be dead and that the Negroes should have "equal protection and every right to personal property." Johnson's leadership was praised.

Armed with their resolutions, a committee of the delegates went to Washington to proffer their support to the President. In a brief, bristling speech at the White House accepting the resolutions, Johnson further antagonized the Radicals, if that were possible, by again severely upbraiding the congressional majority in phrases so extreme that the Radicals skillfully and falsely interpreted his words as meaning that the President intended to force Southern representation upon Congress by military force.

The Radical answer was a Loyal Union Convention in Philadelphia at which they emotionally equated the Republican party and the Union cause. To Philadelphia from the South flocked white and Negro Radical spokesmen. Never would the bloody shirt be waved more successfully than in the ensuing congressional campaign. The Radicals implicated Johnson in the New Orleans "Negro massacre." Indiana's Oliver P. Morton, a powerful politician who only a short time before had opposed mass enfranchisement of the Negro and had challenged other Radical objectives, shouted this wicked description of the Democratic party:

"Every unregenerate Rebel calls himself a Democrat. Every bounty jumper, every deserter, every sneak who ran away from the draft calls himself a Democrat. Every man who murdered Union prisoners, who invented dangerous compounds to burn steamboats and Northern cities, who contrived hellish schemes to introduce into Northern cities yellow fever, calls himself a Democrat. Every dishonest contractor, every dishonest paymaster, every officer in the Army who was dismissed for cowardice calls himself a Democrat. In short the Democratic party may be described as a common sewer and loathsome receptacle."

Wealthy Senator Zachariah Chandler of Michigan, potent Republican boss, added, "Every man who murdered and stole and poisoned was a Democrat"; and Senator Roscoe Conklin of New York thundered that in the South women and children were being shot down for decorating the graves of Union soldiers and that "the rich traitor is courted and caressed and the poor Unionist butchered with the connivance of Andrew Johnson."

Ben Butler had his own prescription. If the President were to call on the Regular Army for support, the Union veterans of the war would turn against that army and "sweep it away like cobwebs before the sun." Even Lincoln's sensible first-term vice-president, Hannibal Hamlin of Maine, by now collector of customs in Boston, declared from the stump that Johnson had been responsible for the New Orleans rioting.

The President countered with a speaking tour, the first in the now usual tradition, with the Chicago tomb of Stephen A. Douglas as his ultimate destination. With him in the "Swing Around the Circle"—under some compulsion—went General Grant, Admiral David Farragut, and several cabinet members. In Maryland and Delaware Johnson was enthusiastically received. In Philadelphia he was heckled and all but mobbed. In Camden, Trenton, New Brunswick, and Newark, New Jersey, he won some applause when he pleaded for the restoration of peace and friendship between North and South. In his most memorable and successful address, at a banquet at Delmonico's in New York—the highlight of what was more often than not an unsuccessful, angry, and maladroit succession of appeals to the public—he said movingly:

"Let me ask you, are we prepared to renew the scene through which we have passed? Are we again prepared to see these bare fields drenched in our brothers' blood? Are we not rather prepared to bring from Gilead the balm . . . ? They are our brethren, part of ourselves. They have lived with us and been part of us from the establishment of the government to the commencement of the rebellion. They are identified with our history, with all our prosperity."

Throughout New York State he ranged, speaking for peace and preservation of the Constitution. But though he was often well received, the organized heckling of the Radicals grew worse. In Cleveland, the home of Ben Wade, he lost his temper.

"Let the Negroes vote in Ohio before you talk about Negroes voting in Louisiana," he shouted. "Take the beam out of your own eye before you see the moat that is in your neighbors'. You are very much disturbed about New Orleans, but you won't let a Negro go to the ballot box to vote in Ohio." All true, of course, but unpalatable.

In Indianapolis, Radical mobs shouted him down, and a man was killed in the general street fighting which followed. The Republican governors of Indiana, Illinois, Michigan, Ohio, Missouri, and Pennsylvania refused to listen to the President of the United States. The city officials of Baltimore, Philadelphia, Pittsburgh, and Indianapolis declined to tender him an official welcome. The vital Midwest, though its economic interests were closer to those of the South than to the industrial East, was, as any casual observer could have reported, safely in Republican hands. Johnson had been unable to capitalize on the discontent of the western farmer and the Republicans had succeeded in identifying the President with near-treason and with the worst sentiments of the unregenerate South. In the November elections the Republicans returned a better than two-thirds majority in Senate and House. Thad Stevens, Charles Sumner, Ben Butler, Ben Wade, and their allies would now run the country.

They wasted no time in showing their hand.

When the second session of the Thirty-ninth Congress convened in December, the emboldened Radicals supported Senator Sumner's bill granting unrestricted Negro suffrage in the District of Columbia, although the Negro could vote in only six Northern states. The President vetoed the bill. In an election that same month the District itself rejected the proposition 7,337 to 36. But Congress passed the Sumner bill over the President's veto.

If the Radicals had thought to overawe Andy Johnson by the ferocity of their assault, their disregard for precedent and the intensity of their purpose, they could not have been more wrong. In as one-sided a battle royal as was ever staged the Tennessee tailor stood toe-to-toe with his adversaries, slugged it out, and by a political miracle was still on his feet when the completion of his term signalized the end of his personal fight though not a resolution of the issues over which he had battled the Republican majority.

An uninformed visitor might have wondered at the start of the epic session whether the primary intent of Congress was to obliterate the presidency, as represented by Andrew Johnson, or to remodel the South. As fast as Senate and House, prodded by Sumner and Stevens, could act, they ramrodded a group of bills designed to force the South into approving the Fourteenth Amendment and to reduce the President to political impotence.

On February 13, 1867, Stevens guided the First Reconstruction Act through the House by a vote of 109 to 55. It divided the Southern states into five military districts—Virginia, the First, North and South Carolina, the Second, Georgia, Alabama, and Florida, the Third, Mississippi and Arkansas, the Fourth, and Louisiana and Texas, the Fifth. In the Stevens bill the military governors of these districts were to be selected by General Grant, the first General of the Army since George Washington, and by now the Radicals' man. These governors were to have near-despotic power in their districts. The bill described the civil governments of the Southern states as "pretended." To be restored to the Union the occupied states were required to call new constitutional conventions, the delegates to be elected by universal manhood suffrage, which were to frame constitutions that allowed Negro suffrage. These constitutions had to be acceptable to Congress. Qualified voters, Negroes and "loyal" whites, were to elect state legislators pledged to ratify the Fourteenth Amendment. Former Confederates who were disqualified under the proposed amendment would be excluded from voting. Each Southern state, after complying with these provisions, could apply to Congress for representation. Congress reserved to itself the right to review each case, to determine whether continued military rule was necessary, and to seat or refuse to seat the new representatives.

The bill was somewhat moderated in the Senate, thanks to a tiny coalition of four Democrats and two conservative Republicans. Their modifications, minor as they were, infuriated Stevens. The Senate's version, which finally became law, included the general provisions, but more mildly described the governments of the Southern states as "not legal" rather than "pretended," permitted the President to name the military commanders, and prepared the way for the states to get out from military rule. The Stevens version had not suggested any way for return to statehood.

Thad Stevens furiously accepted most of the modifications, but he stiffened the Senate's conditions under which the states would be admitted. On Washington's Birthday the House's final version was accepted by the Senate. Its title was "An Act to Provide for the More Efficient Government of the Rebel States." Among its unexpected supporters was Reverdy Johnson of

Maryland, who, after speaking against the bill in the Senate, voted for it, explaining that there would be a worse bill if this one was not accepted.

Andrew Johnson, denouncing the measure as "a bill of attainder against nine million people," vetoed it. On March 2 the act was passed over his veto.

Also in March, Congress proceeded to reverse a constitutional practice of eighty years by passing, again over a presidential veto, a Tenure of Office Act, providing that any officer whose appointment required Senate confirmation, including Cabinet officers, could be removed only by the Senate's concurring approval.

The Secretaries of War, Navy, and State were holdovers from the Lincoln administration; and, under the terms of the bill as passed, the President obviously had the right to remove them since they had not been confirmed by the Senate during his administration. This important distinction was brought out during debate on the bill but, at the time, was allowed to stand unchallenged. It was to be a vital issue during the impeachment. Secretary of War Stanton, the schemer whose removal set off the long-plotted impeachment proceedings, was not, in reality, protected by the bill.

On March 2 the President sent his veto of the Reconstruction and the Tenure of Office Acts to Congress. Both were immediately repassed, as was also the Command of the Army Act, which required the President to issue all military orders through the General of the Army.

The "Sinful Ten" Southern states refused to call new conventions under the terms imposed by the Committee of Fifteen. Congress, in the next few months, passed supplementary Reconstruction statutes. The first of these set up the machinery by which the military commanders would inaugurate new voter registrations. These voters, made up only of those who had signed a long and complicated oath, would alone be eligible to vote in an election for a constitutional convention. At least half the eligible voters in each state would have to approve the constitution the convention would draw up.

In vetoing this act, which made explicit the procedures required under military Reconstruction, the President wrote: "When I contemplate the millions of our fellow citizens of the South, with no alternative left but to impose upon themselves this fearful and untried experiment of complete negro enfranchisement—and white disfranchisement, it may be, almost as complete—or submit indefinitely to the rigor of martial law, without a single attribute of freemen, deprived of all the sacred guarantees of our Federal Constitution, and threatened with even worse things, if any worse are possible, it seems to me that their condition is the most deplorable to which any people can be reduced."

Congress repassed the bill on March 23, 1867.

In the second supplementary act Congress gave the military commanders the right to go behind the oath and bar from registration anyone they chose to believe was not swearing honestly as to his loyalty. The registrars thus completely controlled the registration lists.

Finally, when the Southern whites hit upon the device of registering in large numbers and then not voting, thereby preventing the constitutions from being accepted by vote of half the registered voters—as stipulated— Congress added the clincher: each constitution would be considered affirmed if only half of those who voted endorsed it.

Despite his antagonism toward these measures and his doubts as to their constitutionality, Johnson was conscientious in his execution of the will of Congress. Forthwith he appointed the military commanders. They occupied the South with 20,000 regular troops and additional Negro militia, a revealingly small number for a region whose congressional critics had described as still being in a state of insurrection.

The Johnson governments were replaced by the military. In the ten states 703,000 Negroes and 627,000 whites were registered as voters. In five states, Alabama, Florida, Louisiana, Mississippi, and South Carolina, Negro voters constituted a majority; in the six other former Confederate states, including Tennessee, Negro-white coalitions were necessary to keep the Republicans in office.

For the sake of chronological clarity it is needful here to continue to outline this phase of Reconstruction, at least in its legislative and judicial aspects, beyond what was its most dramatic episode, the impeachment of Andrew Johnson. Considerably before impeachment, and even before the first of the Reconstruction Acts, the South had defied the Radical program; long after the impeachment had failed that defiance continued.

Under the prodding of the military governors and with the objecting white Democrats temporarily helpless against the native white and Negro coalitions and the congressional provision that only a majority of the votes cast sufficed to put a state constitution in effect, the Southern states had, by late 1867, voted to call the requisite conventions. These met in 1868 and, under Radical domination and with Negroes taking a principal part in every convention, drew up the necessary constitutions. In themselves most of these constitutions—except for their guarantees of civil rights for Negroes, universal manhood suffrage, and the disqualification of former Confederates— were not objectionable to the white South; they were similar to the more advanced instruments already long in force in the North. Most of them would survive, with few changes, after Reconstruction's end.

In June 1868 Congress admitted seven states—Arkansas, Alabama, Florida, Georgia, Louisiana, North Carolina, and South Carolina—each having satisfied the requirements of the Reconstruction Acts to the Union. Georgia was returned to military rule when, after the federal troops were withdrawn, the white Democrats, with the aid of some white Carpetbaggers and Scalawags, expelled every Negro from the state legislature. Mississippi,

Texas, and Virginia remained under military rule; a majority of the voters of Mississippi and Texas had failed in their respective elections in 1868 to approve the clauses disfranchising certain classes of Confederates. Virginia's military governor had refused to submit her new constitution to the people on the grounds that it was too harsh.

Not until March 1870, having ratified the Fifteenth Amendment, forbidding the denial of the vote by any state to any citizen because of race, color, or previous condition of servitude, were these three holdouts readmitted; and on July 15, 1870, Georgia, having been compelled by an act of Congress to ratify the Fifteenth Amendment for readmission, became the last of the Southern states to be returned permanently to the Union. It is of passing note that the Fifteenth Amendment was rejected by New Jersey, Delaware, Maryland, and Kentucky, which had also turned down the Fourteenth Amendment, and by California, and that Oregon and Tennessee did not act upon it.

Meanwhile the Radicals, succeeding in all else, had set about to accomplish the final degradation of Andrew Johnson.

CHAPTER 3

How to Mob a President

EDWIN McMASTERS STANTON, a gifted and energetic lawyer, occupies a unique and unenviable place among Americans of note. He served one President in the time of the nation's direst peril and played that President's successor false in the nation's most difficult period of readjustment; and he considered himself superior both to Abraham Lincoln and Andrew Johnson. He was an efficient and undoubtedly a patriotic man; but he had no patience for anyone who stood in his way, not even presidents.

Lincoln chose him as the successor to rich, ruthless Simon Cameron, the shady boss of Pennsylvania's Republicans and his Secretary of War, and in that wartime post Stanton conducted himself tirelessly and despotically. But this restless Ohioan, whose ambition first led him to Washington as a practitioner before the Supreme Court, cannot justly be remembered best for his very real services to the nation, among them his success in 1858, as special counsel for the United States Government, in resisting fraudulent claims to lands worth $150,000,000, which spurious plaintiffs declared had been deeded to them by the Mexican Government before the Mexican War. His name is not inscribed on the pages of our history because of his undeniable ability, but for the unforgivable weakness of a man who was willing to be informer and conspirator against Andrew Johnson, the second of the Presidents who had entrusted him with the then most vital cabinet post. As Secretary of War he would become the immediate provoker of the most reprehensible assault upon the rights and powers of the executive branch of our government upon which any Congress has ever engaged.

The tragedy of bewhiskered, big-nosed Edwin Stanton, an unusually able and versatile wartime administrator, was that his undeniable talents became subordinated to his taste for duplicity.

Andrew Johnson had turned frequently for advice to Stanton, against his own better judgment. He had entrusted to him the naming of the generals to head the five military districts. That those generals would be in full sympathy with the Radicals' plans rather than with the President's policies should have been foreseeable. Almost from the beginning Johnson knew that he had blundered greatly in retaining Stanton. But the President, procrastinator that he was, continued to put off the day of decision so long urged on him by his confidants. It was not until early August 1867 that he took the step which formed the basis for the impeachment charges against him.

Throughout 1867 an unsuccessful impeachment plot had been in the making. During debate on the President's veto of the District Suffrage Bill, Representative James M. Ashley, of Ohio, whose detestation of slavery and of Johnson's middle course led him to fanatic excesses, offered, and Congress passed, a resolution that the Judiciary Committee investigate the President's acts to ascertain if there were grounds on which he could be impeached. Though not a committee member, Ashley became its goad, creating and following up rumors which he urged the committee to investigate. Within the committee the industrious politician, George S. Boutwell, of Massachusetts, who saw in impeachment "not necessarily a trial for crime but a political remedy for political differences," kept the investigation alive.

The most evil of the inspired rumors against Johnson had it that he had torn out certain pages missing from John Wilkes Booth's diary to hide incriminating evidence that he had conspired in the assassination of Lincoln so as to become President. Another was that John Surratt, son of the wrongfully executed Mrs. Mary Surratt, could implicate the President in the conspiracy. Ashley believed he had lined up one Sanford Conover, a perjurer then in jail for trying to implicate Jefferson Davis in the assassination of Lincoln, to testify that Johnson had been a conspirator. Incredible people presented incredible testimony.

Early in June the committee voted against a recommendation of impeachment. Boutwell asked for more time to dig up evidence. The hearings continued.

Finally, in November, the committee reversed itself, and recommended impeachment by a 5–4 vote. Joined to the two Democrats who voted against the recommendation were two Radicals, James F. Wilson, of Iowa, the committee chairman, and Frederick E. Woodbridge, of Vermont. After two days of debate the House disapproved the report by a vote of 108 to 57. Congress was not yet ready to impeach unless it were "for some offense known to the law, and not created by the fancy of the members of the House."

But prior to the voting down of this resolution of impeachment the President had provided his enemies with ammunition for new and more effective charges. For two years Johnson had known of Stanton's disloyalty to him. At the end of July 1867 he learned that Stanton had drafted the Supplementary Reconstruction Act which Congress had just enacted. He had already discovered that Stanton's wishes, not the President's, were being carried out by the military commanders. On August 1 he asked Stanton in writing for his resignation but delayed sending the note to him.

Then on August 5 the President made the appalling discovery that a recommendation for mercy for Mrs. Surratt, with which the Military Commission had concluded its report of the trial of Lincoln's assassins two years before, had never been shown to him. The President could conclude only that the commission's recommendation had been withheld from him by Stanton through his immediate subordinate, Judge Advocate General Holt.

On receiving the President's note, Stanton replied in writing that he refused to resign "before the next meeting of Congress."

The President "suspended" Stanton on August 12. Next he persuaded General of the Army Grant to accept an ad interim appointment as Secretary of War, a maneuver which, under the controversial Tenure of Office Act, was legal as long as Congress was not in session.

The removal of Stanton meant, for the moment, an improvement of conditions in Louisiana and Texas. The President removed General Sheridan from the command of the Fifth District where Sheridan highhandedly had removed almost every civil officer in the two states. Johnson also transferred General Daniel E. Sickles from command of the Second District, embracing North and South Carolina, when the general continued to place his own authority above that of a United States Circuit Court.

In further expression of executive prerogative and in defiance of the Radicals, Johnson issued in the autumn his second amnesty proclamation. Radical rage mounted when Pennsylvania, California, New Jersey, and New York elected Democratic governors and Negro suffrage was rejected by Minnesota, New Jersey, Ohio, and Kansas. Thad Stevens's home town went Democratic. Congress was still in the hands of the Radicals, but the election reflected popular approval of the President. As one newspaper put it, "Impeachment died at the polls."

Early in January 1868 the President sent a message to the Senate explaining his suspension of Stanton as required by the Tenure of Office Act. The message made a good impression on the nation. Especially telling was

Johnson's revelation that Stanton had contributed to the New Orleans riot of 1866 by failing to reply to the request for instructions made by General Absalom Baird, in command in Louisiana during General Sheridan's absence.

Senator Howard of Michigan drafted the Senate's reply to the President's message. The Radical senators would not accept Johnson's right to remove Stanton. Despite the extended discussion led by the Democratic senators, it was obvious that the Radical position would prevail.

The vote was set for Monday, January 13.

From the President's point of view, it was of utmost importance that, if the Senate decided that he did not have the right to suspend Stanton, the acting Secretary of War should be a man who would refuse to acknowledge the Senate's authority over removal of Cabinet officers. Such a man would continue to act as Secretary ad interim until the constitutionality of the Tenure of Office Act could be tested in court. Johnson apparently believed that General Grant understood what was expected of him: that he should either hold the secretaryship under those terms or resign immediately so that the President could replace him with someone who would agree to participate in a court test.

On Monday the Senate ordered Stanton's reinstatement by a vote of 36 to 6, with 13 not voting.

When Grant learned of the Senate's action he locked up the Secretary of War's offices, handed the key to an adjutant general, and returned to his offices in the Army Headquarters Building. Stanton, already waiting at the War Department, re-entered the Secretary's offices. The immediate opportunity for testing the constitutionality of the Tenure of Office Act had ended.

Johnson realized that Stanton would not issue his orders, but he entertained hope that, as Commander in Chief of the Armed Services, he could issue them through General of the Army Grant. At first Grant seemed willing to comply. But his Radical associates, now seeing him as their probable candidate for the presidency, warned him of the political consequences of thus supporting the President.

Soon Grant was writing Johnson in such terms as to disassociate himself from the President's effort to rid himself of Stanton. He declared that he had accepted the ad interim appointment only to make sure no one was appointed "who would, by opposition to the laws relating to the restoration of the Southern States . . . embarrass the Army in the performance of duties specially imposed upon it by these laws."

Johnson, who had instructed Grant verbally to ignore orders from the War Department unless "such order is known by the General commanding the Armies of the United States to have been authorized by the Executive," put his instructions in writing on January 29. Grant coldly replied that since Stanton had received no mandate from the President "limiting or impairing his authority to issue orders" he would continue to accept the Secretary of War's directions.

"When my honor as a soldier and integrity as a man have been so violently assailed," he wrote, "pardon me for saying that I can but regard this whole matter . . . as an attempt to involve me in the resistance to law."

If the President were resisting the law he was certainly open to impeachment. The House passed a resolution requiring the Secretary of War to produce the Grant-Johnson correspondence. This Stanton did. The Radicals rejoiced in what appeared to be Grant's recognition of the President's culpability. The President was able to counter by producing statements from all his Cabinet members that at a Cabinet meeting after Grant had turned over the keys to Stanton, Grant had admitted that he had promised the President not to do so and had, therefore, shown he believed it proper to follow the Executive's orders. The Radicals were frustrated again.

To Johnson it was obvious that he had to test in the courts the constitutionality of the Tenure of Office Act. For a month he tried to find someone willing to accept the ad interim appointment. He had previously recalled to the post of Adjutant General, General Lorenzo Thomas, whom Stanton had assigned to inconsequential duties outside Washington. In February General Thomas accepted the ad interim appointment as Secretary of War.

Now the tempo of the conflict of authority quickened.

General Thomas himself bore to Stanton the President's second letter of removal. Stanton replied verbally that he needed time to think things over and immediately prepared to retain physical possession of the War Department Building. He formally notified Congress of Johnson's order and directed Grant to place guards around the building. There he remained, night and day, behind barricades during the tense weeks that followed his challenge of the President.

The Senate hurried into executive session. It emerged with a resolution declaring that "under the Constitution and the laws" the President had no right to remove the Secretary; the resolution was tantamount to an article of impeachment though emanating, incorrectly, from the Senate instead of the House.

In the House reviling Radical leaders saw a special symbolism in the fact that the next day was Washington's Birthday. Thad Stevens summoned his Reconstruction committee to meet that day, and the House voted that it, too, would not take a holiday.

Rumors and counter-rumors spread through the city. Vain old General Thomas bragged that night, while dressing for a masked ball, on his way to the ball, and at it, that he would use force to evict Stanton if force were required. Orderlies appeared at social gatherings to announce that all officers of the Fifth Cavalry and officers under command of General Emory, the Washington post commandant, must report at once for duty.

Stanton, on hearing of General Thomas's posturings, prepared an affidavit which related that Thomas was planning to remove him from office by force, that such a threat violated the Tenure of Office Act, and that Thomas was therefore guilty of a high misdemeanor. A Stanton emissary hurried through the night to the Radical Chief Justice of the Supreme Court of the District of Columbia, David K. Carrter, who issued a warrant for General Thomas's arrest. Early the next morning Thomas was arrested. The general made $50,000 bail and called on his old friend Stanton to plead with him to turn over his office. Thomas made no mention of force, and they parted cordially after Stanton gave the general a drink upon his complaint that he had not yet breakfasted.

Now it appeared that the President had his case, ready made by the Secretary. But Judge Carrter, seeing the implications of the affair, dismissed the Thomas case a few days later without trial.

If there had been talk of force, it was not the President's talk.

But on whose authority had General Emory ordered his officers to their posts? Summoned to the White House, the general said that the General of the Army had issued the command and that he had obeyed, in compliance with a rider to the previous spring's Army Appropriation Bill which provided that all orders for military operations must go through the General of the Army whether issued by the President or the Secretary of War. The President asked Emory if this meant that the President of the United States could give an order only through the General of the Army.

When Emory reported the conversation to his Radical friends he made it appear that the President had directed him to disobey the orders of his superior. Secretary Stanton's version, which he gave to newspapermen, was that the President had commanded Emory to send soldiers to eject Stanton, that Emory had refused, and that Johnson had then asked Navy Secretary Gideon Welles to send a company of Marines to do the job.

Washington's Birthday, Friday, February 22, 1868. . . .

More reports, more rumors. Rumors that troops were about to eject Stanton, that troops were ordered out to protect him, that Confederate veterans were advancing on Washington from Maryland. Newspapermen, politicians, bankers, citizens of every sort and description crowded into the Capitol, or jammed the hallway before the House Reconstruction Committee room where the committee was formulating the resolution of impeachment, or squeezed into the galleries, waiting. . . .

At high noon two flags were run up above the halls of Congress. The senators flocked to the House to witness the opening of the impeachment proceedings. Ben Wade, president pro tem of the Senate, was invited to sit on the dais by the side of Speaker Colfax. In the quiet that momentarily followed the chaplain's prayer a Democrat got the floor and moved facetiously that Washington's Farewell Address be read and that the House adjourn in honor of the day. His jest was not appreciated.

With the dying Thad Stevens limping feebly at its head, the Committee on Reconstruction entered the House. Speaker Colfax ordered silence. Haggard and trembling, Stevens read the Committee's resolution "that Andrew Johnson, President of the United States, be impeached of high crimes and misdemeanors in office." The old man then said he was ready for the vote but claimed the right of rebuttal "if the other side must speak."

Most assuredly the Democrats did wish to speak.

They prolonged the hopeless debate so long that the House had to adjourn until Monday without voting on the resolution. But the Radicals, anxious to achieve the drama of impeaching a President on the first President's birthday, set the House clock back so that the journal's entries on February 24 would still read as of February 22.

Even larger crowds than on Saturday milled for blocks outside the Capitol when debate was resumed on Monday. Every Capitol policeman, every member of the city police force was on duty to maintain order. In the House Congressman Ashley renewed the Radical accusations, followed by Boutwell. Judge Woodward of Pennsylvania spoke for the Democrats. At 4:30 Stevens mounted to the speaker's platform to read his own diatribe. His body, tense with hate and wracked with illness, was not strong enough to carry him through the impassioned oration. A clerk finished for him.

And then the vote.

Outside the noise of the crowd sounded like a raging storm, as the members of the House of Representatives recorded predictably their party affiliations. But there was little excitement when the results were announced: 126 for impeachment, 47 against.

At 1:10 the next afternoon Thad Stevens, leaning on the arm of John A. Bingham, his face a death mask, solemnly informed the Senate that "the people of the United States" had impeached Andrew Johnson.

Beyond Washington, even some among the followers of the Radicals were becoming disturbed by the extreme attitudes their leaders in Congress were taking. From all over the country telegrams of confidence were dispatched to the outwardly unperturbed President. Mass meetings of his supporters were held in various cities. Within Washington the frenzy of politicians and people approached mass hysteria. Symptomatic was the reaction to a letter to Speaker Colfax from the New York City Chief of Police. A large amount of nitroglycerin had disappeared from New York. Perhaps, the chief suggested, it has been spirited away for use in Washington. The House immediately adjourned so that a search of the building could be made.

Only the White House, the center of the vortex, remained calm. The President felt he had done his best to defend the powers of the executive branch of the government as the founding fathers had outlined them in the Constitution. If the legislative branch were permitted to override the Constitutional division of duties the American system would collapse. Yet, as long as the legal forms of impeachment were maintained, the Congress was acting within its rights to vote impeachment. If Congress should vote to suspend or arrest him before the trial had been completed, as some of his confidants feared, the President was resolved to resist. In the meantime he caused consternation by appearing as a matter of course at Chief Justice Chase's Wednesday Evening, a social event to which the Radical leaders were accustomed to repair.

The grounds for impeachment, the "particular articles" which would be argued before the Senate, remained to be stated. This assignment was entrusted to the seven managers of impeachment: John A. Bingham, George S. Boutwell, Benjamin F. Butler, John A. Logan, Thaddeus Stevens, Thomas Williams, and James F. Wilson, of Iowa, Radicals all.

The managers drummed up eleven Articles of Impeachment. The first nine were reported out by the House committee. Of these, eight accused Johnson of having removed Stanton from office in violation of the Tenure of Office Act and of the Constitution, and that he had conspired with General Thomas to break other laws. A ninth charged that the President had given General Emory illegal instructions preliminary to seizing control of the government through a coup.

At the last moment, in fact after the House had already notified the Senate that it was ready with the Articles of Impeachment, the tenth and eleventh articles were added.

The tenth was the creation of Ben Butler, which he had unsuccessfully attempted to get the committee and the House to accept. This article objected to three presidential speeches. In the first Johnson had called Congress "a body hanging on the verge of government" and a Congress "of only a part of the States." In the second he had accused Congress of trying to break up the government. In the third he had mockingly compared Thad Stevens to Christ. The Butler article charged that in these speeches the President had attempted to bring Congress into "disgrace, ridicule, hatred, contempt and reproach," and had degraded the presidency "to the great scandal of all good citizens."

The eleventh article, the so-called "Omnibus Bill," was ascribed to Stevens. Almost every charge made in the other ten bills was repeated here. It was intended to be so full and so long that in its vagueness each senator would be able to find some aspect which would extenuate his voting impeachment.

The Senate received the Articles of Impeachment on March 4. The organization of the Senate as a court was undertaken the next day.

In the Senate chamber were placed seven large leather chairs to be occupied by the seven managers of impeachment. To the Senate dais was invited Speaker of the House Colfax, to sit side by side with Ben Wade, who would be President of the United States if the Senate found the President guilty of any of the charges.

What was planned was nothing more than a political lynching. But the Chief Justice of the United States, Salmon Chase, who would preside during the hearing, soon tried to make it clear that the Senate could not treat lightly the judicial process.

The Chief Justice was an unusual and an enigmatic man. Raised a devout Episcopalian in Ohio, and of New England birth, he had been a school-teacher and, before and after his admission to the Ohio bar, a literary dilettante. So whole-souledly had he defended escaping slaves before the war that he was ridiculed as the "Attorney General for runaway Negroes." Early a Whig, he espoused in the '40s the splinter Liberty Party and later the Free-Soilers; and a coalition of Ohio Free-Soilers and anti-slavery Democrats sent him to the United States Senate in 1849. His anti-slavery, pro-Union convictions drew him into the new Republican party, and as a Republican he served for two terms as governor before being elected to the Senate in 1860. In 1861 he resigned to become Lincoln's Secretary of the Treasury, but he did not get on well with the President, considering him to be lacking in force, and became a leading anti-Lincoln manipulator and an avid if unannounced candidate for the Republican presidential nomination in 1864. That summer Lincoln accepted his resignation; but when Chief Justice Taney died in October, Lincoln appointed Chase in his place. As Chief Justice after the war, he advocated manhood suffrage for Negroes but was adamantly opposed to military usurpation of civil government and favored dismissing the indictment of Jefferson Davis for treason. And in the impeachment proceedings he was obviously determined that he would be no figurehead accomplice to a partisan travesty.

Each senator in his turn was required to take the selfsame oath. There was no hitch to the process until Senator Thomas A. Hendricks of Indiana, a fighting Democrat who would be Samuel Tilden's running mate in 1876, raised the question whether Senator Wade could possibly "do impartial justice" because of his extraordinary stake in the outcome. Joining Senator Hendricks in his protest were Senator Reverdy Johnson of Maryland, a Democrat, and Senator Dixon of Massachusetts, a conservative Republican. The Senate, however, voted that the senator from Ohio had the right to serve as a member of the Court of Impeachment.

Justice Chase, essaying to demonstrate the difference between a court and the Senate's political functions, urged that procedural rules for the court adopted while the Senate was acting as the Senate be readopted by the members acting as a court. Over some objection this was done. The House managers were then notified that the Senate was ready to hear their articles.

The President was summoned to appear when the court reconvened on March 13.

Meanwhile Congress approved on March 11 the final revision of the Reconstruction Acts which made it possible for a simple majority of those voting on a state constitution to confirm the constitution, rather than a majority of all those registered.

President Johnson had picked his counsel with the help of Cabinet members and personal advisers. They decided first that Attorney General Stanbery, a member of his official family, should head the defense. To answer criticism that the President was using public funds in his own interest, Stanbery resigned as Attorney General the day before the Senate reconvened as a court.

It was also agreed that the other defense lawyers should come from different political groups. Benjamin Robbins Curtis of Boston, a former justice of the United States Supreme Court who had been a dissenter in the Dred Scott case, was next selected. The President asked for the inclusion of Jeremiah Sullivan Black, a Democrat; to balance him, William M. Evarts, a near-Radical Republican, was chosen. The President personally selected Judge T. A. R. Nelson of his home town, Greeneville. Because of the public issues involved all counsel served without pay.

During the course of the trial illness forced Stanbery to give up the direction of the defense. Evarts then became chief counsel and, in the eyes of contemporary and later lawyers, the hero of the proceedings. To the case he brought a thorough knowledge of the Constitution, acquired in the prewar years when he was counsel in several cases of interest to fellow Abolitionists. In 1867 he had been one of the lawyers employed by the government in the trial of Jefferson Davis for treason. His friendship with Republican leaders proved an asset. He had long been party to their thinking, and he realized that for some of them a stumbling block to a vote for acquittal might be the fear that Johnson, if acquitted, would flagrantly flaunt the powers of Congress. To allay this fear, he suggested that the President offer the post of Secretary of War to the greatly respected General John M. Schofield. He then persuaded the general to agree that his name could be sent to the Senate for confirmation at any time during the hearing. When this was done, late during the trial, it had the effect Evarts had anticipated.

Evarts's wit was proverbial and often demonstrated. A guest for Sunday dinner in Senator Sumner's home during the trial, he complained that he was having to work even on the Sabbath in the President's behalf. Chided by his host for disregarding the commandment against working on Sunday, he replied: "Is it not written that if thine ass falleth into a pit, it is lawful to pull him out on the Sabbath day?"

On March 14, the day after the Senate reconvened as a court, Jeremiah Black resigned as a counsel for the President. Although his departure created a sensation and one adverse to the President, his resignation had nothing to do with the merits of the impeachment. Instead it reveals the cynical opportunism of some of the President's loudest adversaries.

Black represented clients who wanted the United States to enforce its claim to a guano-rich island, also claimed by Santo Domingo, by dispatching a warship to seize it. Black had arranged for Senator Ben Butler to receive compensation from his clients if he would write a letter to the President, with the concurrence of three others of the seven managers of impeachment, setting forth Butler's conviction that the government should seize the island. The implication was clear that if the President played ball with the managers they would play ball with him. When the President refused to order out the warship Black resigned as a defense lawyer, sending the President a note saying that "unless you can do something for your friends, it is useless for me longer to apply my personal and professional powers when defeat stares us in the face."

William S. Groesbeck of Ohio replaced Black as counsel.

The court convened on March 13, with Chief Justice Chase presiding. Loudly, then, the Senate's Sergeant at Arms called out: "Andrew Johnson, President of the United States; Andrew Johnson, President of the United States, appear and answer the Articles of Impeachment exhibited against you by the House of Representatives of the United States."

To this call there was no answer. In the impressive silence that followed Stanbery, Curtis, and Nelson filed in, and Stanbery read the President's authority for his counsel to enter his appearance and also his request for forty days in which to prepare his answer to the Articles of Impeachment. At no time during the trial did the President appear in court in person.

Ben Butler argued strongly against so long a delay.

"It took the Almighty only forty days to destroy the world by flood," he said. "Who could say what Johnson might not do with his executive power during a similar period?"

Answering him and the other managers, Stanbery marveled that a case of such magnitude should be treated "as if it were a case before the police court." By a majority of one, an immediate trial was averted and the President was given ten days in which to prepare his defense. The trial would be held after the House had prepared its replication to Johnson's answer. Fundamentally, in this first and only impeachment trial of a President, the question was whether the men who made up the Senate would agree with Sumner that the Senate was only "a political body—and with a political object" or, with Chief Justice Chase, that it was in fact a court.

The actual trial began March 30 with the opening argument read by Ben Butler who, because of Stevens's illness, became in fact though not in name the director of the managers. Attired, though in the afternoon, in an impressive evening suit in recognition of the importance of the occasion, Butler gave a monotonous reading of the speech which had taken him three days to write.

Impeachment, he droned, was a political, not a legal, proceeding; senators were bound by their constituents, not by their consciences, and the President had to carry out laws enacted by Congress until those laws were declared unconstitutional. Butler defined an impeachable crime as "one in its nature or consequences subversive of some fundamental or essential principles of government, or highly prejudicial to the public interest; and this may consist of a violation of the Constitution, of law, of an official oath, or of duty, by an act committed or omitted, or, without violating a positive law, by the abuse of discretionary powers from improper motives, or for any improper purpose." That covered just about everything but an unshielded cough.

Wilson then presented all the documentary evidence on which the managers would build their case—including the President's message to the Senate revealing why he had suspended Stanton and the Senate's own journal recording that it did not concur in the suspension; Johnson's message to the Senate on February 21 relating that he had removed Stanton; and the Senate's resolution that the President had no right to remove him. Later the managers cynically referred to the Senate's resolution as a proof of Johnson's guilt.

For twenty-three days the managers presented their evidence. Questions of admissibility were raised and answered. At one point Chief Justice Chase voted on a question of admissibility to break a tie. Sumner and other Radicals furiously questioned the presiding jurist's right to vote, and Sumner moved that the Chief Justice could not vote. His motion was voted down. That evidence of respect for the judicial process bothered the Radical leaders.

The managers' witnesses were principally clerks, summoned only to attest the genuineness of the documents presented. One of the few witnesses testifying directly regarding a charge was General Emory. His testimony concerning his talk with the President was remote from the distortion which had produced the rumor that the President was preparing to seize the government by military force. One Article of Impeachment collapsed with his testimony.

General Thomas was not called to testify, though several who said they had heard him the night of February 21 did appear. Under cross-examination their testimony revealed nothing but the general's garrulity.

At last the President's counsels had their day. Curtis opened the case for Andrew Johnson on April 9, giving emphasis to the serious nature of a senatorial court of impeachment. He narrowed the eleven charges down to two: the President's removal of Stanton, and the omnibus conglomerate of other crimes. Stanton, he argued, was not covered by the Tenure of Office Act. During the House and Senate debates members of the Radical group in both houses had expressly stated, while the bill was being argued, that Stanton, as a holdover from Lincoln's Cabinet, was not covered. But if the law did apply to Stanton, Johnson had only attempted to remove Stanton and had failed; and even if the President had in fact succeeded in ejecting the Secretary, he was within his rights, for the Tenure of Office Act was certainly unconstitutional—which a Supreme Court would decide many years later. Finally, if the Tenure of Office Act was constitutional, the House still must prove that the President willfully intended to misconstrue and violate the act. If the President did not refuse to carry out an act he considered unconstitutional, Curtis asked, how else would its constitutionality ever reach the court?

Secretary of the Navy Welles was prepared to testify that the President's consultants had voted 29 to 20 that they believed his removal order against Stanton was constitutional. The managers of impeachment hastened to block the presentation of his evidence. Some senators, normally Radicals, declared that the evidence should be heard, but the managers' opinion prevailed. This arbitrary suppression of testimony was remembered when the critical votes on impeachment were cast.

Manager Boutwell recommended that Johnson's punishment should be that he should be "projected into the vast hole in the skies near the Southern Cross where no powerful telescope has ever found nebulae, asteroid, comet, planet, star or sun." In this unfinished chaos he should "forever . . . exist in a solitary as eternal as life. . . ." Groesbeck, speaking in behalf of the President, reminded the court that the Senate could have terminated the President's ad interim appointment of General Thomas simply by considering the name of the man he had sent to the Senate for confirmation. Stevens's argument, presented by Ben Butler, was that the House's vote of condemnation had already committed the Senate. Stanbery, weak from illness, but believing that his feeble effort might be as important as the shepherd's pebble, took the floor to emphasize that the President, confirmed in his position, would not abuse his powers. Both Bingham and Evarts talked for three days.

Evarts's plea unanswerably brought out the legal points involved. The oath of the President of the United States, he said, was a vow to defend the Constitution, not to execute the laws of Congress. The people of the United States, learning that the President had been impeached, might reasonably conclude that he had been punished for bribery or for surrendering military or state secrets to a foreign power. Certainly they would not agree that a President's removal of a member of his Cabinet was reason for impeachment. Nor had the President used force to try to remove the Secretary. Instead he had relied upon approved civil procedures.

In reference to Boutwell's proposed celestial punishment for the President, Evarts's wit reduced friend and enemy to helpless laughter. Since

Boutwell alone knew where this spot was to which the President should be consigned, Evarts said, it should be Boutwell's job to take him there. "With the President made fast to his broad and strong shoulders, and having essayed the flight by imagination, better prepared than anybody else to execute it in form, taking advantage of ladders as far as ladders will go to the top of this Capitol, and spurning then with his foot the crest of Liberty, let him set out upon his flight, while the two Houses of Congress and all the people of the United States shall shout *'sic itur ad astra!'"* The problem for Boutwell, Evarts added, then would be how he would get himself back. Perhaps for the rest of time the impeacher and the President, beyond the power of Congress, would continue their contest.

As the day for the vote approached the managers of impeachment anxiously went over the list of fifty-four senators. Two thirds of them would have to support at least one of the House's accusations to throw Andrew Johnson out of the White House.

The nine Senate Democrats would vote against impeachment, as would three already committed conservative Republicans, James Dixon of Connecticut, James Rood Doolittle of Wisconsin, and Daniel S. Norton of Minnesota, each of whom had stood steadfastly by the President. So important was every vote that in the last few days the legislature of Maryland, which had for months been represented by only one senator because the Senate would not seat her junior Democratic senator, Philip F. Thomas, on grounds that he had been disloyal, now withdrew his name and elected George Vickers, and then dispatched an icebreaker up the frozen Chester River to return Vickers to a special train which rushed him from Baltimore to Washington.

Sure to lose twelve votes, the managers could afford to concede only six more. Every man who called himself a Radical had to vote with his party or commit political suicide. And yet, as the day of decision approached, some remained who either said definitely that they would vote their consciences or hesitantly admitted that they had not yet made up their minds.

The undecided few would have to be brought into line by whatever means were required. From their states were summoned Radical politicians to drive home to them the certainty that their political futures were at stake. Constituents deluged them with letters. The Radicals, caucusing twice daily in the ornate home of Kansas Senator Samuel C. Pomeroy, who had bribed his way into office in 1867, searched carefully for weaknesses in each doubtful senator's character which could be played upon to gain an affirmative vote.

There were twelve in all upon whom the Senate lynchers could not yet count: William Pitt Fessenden and Lot Myrick Morrill of Maine, Lyman Trumbull of Illinois, James W. Grimes of Iowa, William Sprague and Henry Bowen Anthony of Rhode Island, Joseph O. Fowler of Tennessee, Peter G.

Van Winkle and Waitman T. Willey of West Virginia, George Franklin Edmunds of Vermont, Edmund G. Ross of Kansas, and John B. Henderson of Missouri, Radicals all.

Fessenden had written a friend: "Whatever I may think and feel as a politician, I cannot and will not violate my oath. I would rather be confined to planting cabbages for the remainder of my days." And Grimes was saying that he could not believe that the President had committed those "overt, flagrant and corrupt acts that constitute high crimes and misdemeanors." In the Senate's executive session on May 11, when each senator, as in a jury room, had the opportunity to express an opinion, the Radicals discovered the need for even greater pressures.

In Chicago the Methodist General Conference, then in session, prayed that every senator—meaning especially Methodist Senator Willey—might be saved from error. Carpetbagger Governor Holden of North Carolina asked by telegram: "In the name of humanity, liberty and justice, can it be possible that Andrew Johnson will be acquitted?" A majority of Missouri's eight Republican House members called on Senator Henderson to demand that he vote for impeachment. The Radical-dominated Tennessee legislature passed a resolution demanding that Joe Fowler vote for impeachment. Rhode Island's Sprague was emphatically told that his re-election to the Senate depended on his voting with the Radicals. Anthony, close friend of Chief Justice Chase, became fearful that a vote against impeachment might weaken his friend's chances for the Republican nomination for President.

The most unexpected holdout was Ross of Kansas. Ross, an old-time Abolitionist who had voted consistently with the Radicals, was a poor man and an ambitious one. His political advancement depended upon his vote. Yet he had indicated that he might vote against impeachment.

From Kansas arrived a telegram: "Kansas has heard the evidence and demands the conviction of the President," signed, "D. R. Anthony and 1,000 Others." To this ultimatum Ross replied: "I do not recognize your right to demand that I vote either for or against conviction. I have taken an oath to do impartial justice according to the Constitution and laws, and trust that I shall have the courage to vote according to the dictates of my judgment and for the highest good of the country."

The Radical leadership achieved a four-day postponement, using the sudden illness of Michigan's extremist Radical Senator Jacob M. Howard as an excuse for time in which to put more pressure. The delay worried the President's friends.

Senator Ross recalled that on May 16, the day of decision, "The galleries were packed. Tickets of admission were at an enormous premium. The House had adjourned and all of its members were in the Senate chamber. Every chair on the Senate floor was filled with a Senator, a Cabinet Officer, a member of the President's counsel or a member of the House." The members of the House of Representatives entered behind the managers of impeachment. Thad Stevens was carried into the chamber in a chair. Senator Howard, draped in a shawl, was brought up the stairs on a stretcher. James Grimes of Iowa, stricken with paralysis three days earlier, was helped to his seat just before the vote was taken.

Ben Wade was so sure of the outcome that he had already formed his Cabinet. The Radical caucus was equally confident. Certainly one of the only remaining doubtful seven senators would give way.

In the omnibus indictment rested the Radicals' best chance for conviction. Though it was eleventh in order, they maneuvered to have it considered first.

The roll call began. . . .

With the tally eleven for conviction and six for acquittal, tall William Pitt Fessenden of Maine, first of the doubtful Republicans to be polled, states his conviction: "Not guilty." Joe Fowler of Tennessee in his turn almost inaudibly breathes his answer. Was it "Guilty" or "Not guilty"? He repeats his decision, firmly and loudly, "Not guilty." The paralyzed Grimes is the third of the question marks. He struggles to his feet. "Not guilty." John Henderson of Missouri follows, "Not guilty."

Now it is the turn of Edmund Ross of Kansas, the senator whom popular opinion had selected as the man most likely to bow to Radical pressure. Conscious that "friends, position, fortune, everything that makes life desirable to an ambitious man, were about to be swept away by the breath of my mouth, perhaps forever," he casts his die:

"Not guilty."

The Radicals' best hope has failed them. Lyman Trumbull of Illinois votes "Not guilty," as expected. So does Peter Van Winkle of West Virginia.

Seven Radical Republicans have proved themselves more true to country than to their party.

There remained a chance of conviction on one of the other articles. The Radicals obtained a ten-day recess in which to harangue, to distort, to raise doubts, to win over at least one of the recalcitrant senators. The House voted the managers the power to investigate "improper or corrupt means used to influence the determination of the Senate," the purpose of the delay being to find evidence that some of the senators had been bribed. The managers intercepted telegrams, culled through wastepaper baskets, examined bank records. Their efforts yielded no provable charges, but the deviationists were effectively tainted.

Not one of the "Sinful Seven"—the Southern states which had rejected the Fourteenth Amendment had been as unimaginatively labeled the "Sinful Ten"—ever again held elective office.

On May 26 the Senate voted on the second article. Again the unfortunate Ross was considered to be the holdout most likely to give way. But he voted "Not guilty" on the second article and again on the third.

Rather than undergo the humiliation of having each of the remaining articles voted down, the Radicals hastily called for adjournment of the Senate court. They had failed to lynch judicially a president.

To assure that the record would incorporate what had actually transpired, Chief Justice Chase ordered the Senate clerk to make the entry that the impeachment effort had not succeeded. Secretary Stanton quitted the War Department. General John M. Schofield, the President's nominee, was confirmed. William Evarts became Attorney General.

What came after was anti-climactic.

The Republicans, in convention assembled in Chicago on May 20 and 21, nominated General Grant on the first ballot, even though Ben Butler was very much available, as the party's choice for the presidency, with the Indiana Radical, Schuyler Colfax, Speaker of the House during the impeachment proceedings, as his running mate. The Republican platform endorsed the Radical Reconstruction program, equivocated on the unpopular question of Negro suffrage and the tariff, advocated payment of the national debt in gold, and unmeasuredly denounced the Democratic party and especially Andrew Johnson.

The Democrats, meeting in New York on July 4 through July 9, nominated Horatio Seymour, a former governor of New York and a hard-money man, as their presidential candidate and Francis T. Blair of Missouri for vice-president. The Democratic platform attacked the Radical Reconstruction program and endorsed the so-called "Ohio Idea" for the payment of the national debt in greenbacks. The Southern Democrats had a high time. North Carolina's Zebulon Vance delighted the crowds in Union Square with his repetition, time and again, of a jibing verse:

> To every Southern ribber
> Shall Negro suffrage come;
> But not to fair New England,
> For that's too close to hum.

The Republicans waved the bloody shirt, accusing the Democrats of wholesale slaughter of Negroes and white Unionists in the South. The Democrats countered with denunciation of the Republicans for espousing social equality of the races. Blair, the Democratic vice-presidential nominee, made a serious blunder in writing public letters declaring that he would not accept Reconstruction.

Behind Grant were lined up almost solidly his "Boys in Blue" and the registered Negro voters in the South. Even so the election returns were surprising. Grant won the electoral votes of twenty-six of the thirty-four states, but his popular majority was only 306,000. Probably a majority of the white voters of the nation had supported the Democrats.

In the middle of the campaign Thad Stevens died. For the South that was something of a consolation prize.

CHAPTER 4

The Years of the Locust

THE Yankees, *the boy's grandmother told him time and time again, believing every burning word of it, came back again with their bayonets, the war being over and us with most of our men dead and so many of the living sick and crippled. They came down because old Thad Stevens wanted to put the colored people on top. It seemed like they stayed forever, and they stole us blind, the Carpetbaggers and the uppity blacks and some of our own folks too, the filthy Scalawags. They ran things to suit themselves, and General Grant—he was President by then—backed them up; and he and those fine Republican friends of his helped themselves all over the country to everything that wasn't nailed down. But it was worst of all down here and it still would be if our Southern men hadn't got together in the Ku Klux Klan to run them out. Your grandfather, God bless his memory, was one of them. And we hadn't been married more than a year when I sewed his robe together for him and out he would ride, night after night, night after night. Terrible times they were, but we won out in the end.*

The old lady died, believing. The grandson who is past fifty, and who can be multiplied by the tens of thousands, still believes the stories his grandmother told him; that is, when he thinks about them, and he does more often now than he did, say, twenty years ago or even five years ago.

What is germane is not the proportion of fact to fancy in the memories of a soft-voiced, shrunken old lady who carried her indignation with her to the grave, but that the white people of the South did remember Reconstruction as a nightmare is remembered, even as the Negroes of the South all but forgot Reconstruction as an unbelievable dream is forgotten; what is germane is that the tales told by the old people, who were once young and hot-eyed and furious, to their children and their grandchildren were spun from the substance of truth.

It is useful for those who are not the inheritors of bitter fact and legend to know something of the tenure and the employment of the Yankee bayonet in the South of Reconstruction; something of the nature and durations of the civil governments which ruled the Southern states in Reconstruction; something of the response of many men, white and black, Yankee and former Rebel, Republican and Democrat, to the vast, national opportunity for public plunder; and something of a political president who had been an unpolitical general, and of the men who surrounded him, and of the odorous times in which they lived and governed and stole or permitted stealing.

The Yankee bayonets . . .

Most of the Southern states did not remain long under military rule. Five years after the war every former state of the Confederacy had been re-admitted to the Union, though under terms which, save in divided Tennessee, were universally repugnant to most of their white citizens.

As military occupations go, the administrations of even the worst of the military governors were more highhanded and pettily autocratic than brutal. The behavior of almost all of the white regulars, officers and men alike, was so acceptable that Northern Carpetbaggers complained of the fraternization between the Southerners and their conquerors, of Yanks and unreconstructed Rebs drinking together, of Southern families inviting and Yankee officers and soldiers accepting invitations to social events and to homes. In the infrequent clashes between Southern whites and Negro troops the Northern white officers and men were likely either to look the other way or to side with the whites; and even the misbehavior of the Negroes themselves, during the brief period they were used as occupying troops under the Reconstruction Act, was more spontaneous and individual than concerted. Grant recalled the Negro soldiers soon after he became President.

The troops who occupied the South from March 1867 to June 1868 were concentrated in the principal communities, so that for most Southerners their presence was sensed rather than seen. And many a white Southerner, writhing later under the Radical Republican civil governments, which the Reconstruction Acts and the symbolic bayonets had brought into being, would remember with an odd sort of yearning the days of the bluecoats.

The President's initial commanders of the five military districts, as selected by Secretary Stanton, were General John M. Schofield, the First; General Daniel E. Sickles, the Second; General George H. Thomas, the Third; General Edward O. C. Ord, the Fourth, and General Philip H. Sheridan, the Fifth. Among these commanders and their successors the worst were the violently irascible Sickles and the hot-tempered, South-hating Sheridan, General John Pope, a Kentuckian and West Pointer who had been a poor field soldier during the war and who replaced General Thomas in the Third, and General E. R. S. Canby, a trouble-shooting regular from Kentucky, who was dispatched to whatever place in the South other administrators were in difficulty. Johnson soon replaced Sheridan and Sickles. The principal offense of the generals was their often wanton usurpation of civil administrations. The governors of Virginia, Mississippi, Georgia, Louisiana, and Texas were removed arbitrarily by the commanders; countless lesser officials were similarly expelled from their posts and replaced by military officers; time after time the generals unnecessarily substituted military commissions for existing civil courts.

Except that the President of the United States had to approve any death sentence, the power of the commanders was absolute. They could and did remove civil officials, replacing them with military personnel or with Loyalists. They regulated labor and laid down rules for the preservation of the health and the prevention of epidemics, principally by halting the congregation of freedmen in the towns. They forbade the carrying of concealed weapons. In most of the districts they stayed, because of widespread impoverishment, all proceedings for the sale of land, crops, stock, implements, and the like where the debt was contracted prior to January 1, 1866. They could and often did deal sternly with the freedmen, insisting that they live up to fair labor contracts and support themselves and their families and avoid political activity until they were registered as voters. On the other hand, whipping as punishment for a freedman's crime or misdemeanor was prohibited; civil officers were forbidden to collect taxes on freedmen that were not imposed upon all persons; the Freedmen's Bureau was required to investigate all charges against landholders of driving freedmen off their lands, and the removal of crops was forbidden until the laborers' share could be ascertained and assigned.

Actually, despite the Radicals' prior contention that no loyal citizen's life was safe in the South, the generals had little violence to contend with save in Texas and western Arkansas where the turmoil was inherent in the frontier, with little relationship to race or politics. Save for the riots in New Orleans and in Memphis, there had been no major interracial collisions before the military occupation and there were none of consequence between white and Negro citizens during it. The Ku Klux Klan had been organized only three months when the troops arrived and was still simply a frolicsome society. Even at the zenith of their successful employment as instruments of reprisal, terrorism, and demoralization of Radical politicians, the Klansmen and their counterparts never pitted themselves against the white regulars. Except in the Southwest, the Army's judicial and supervisory chores were for the most part prosaic; and the frequency of military trials for theft of horses, mules, and other agricultural equipment and supplies indicated desperate need rather than unruliness.

Most of the offenses tried by the military commissions in the South were for such thefts, and at least as many offenders were Negro as white. The larceny of a horse or mule could result in sentences of from six months to five years. In the Second District a white man was sentenced to three months in the Dry Tortugas, a military prison in the Gulf of Mexico, sixty-five miles west of Key West, for "disloyal utterances and deterring Negroes from registering." In the same district one unfortunate miscreant was sentenced to five years at hard labor in the Dry Tortugas for stealing five mules and three others were given the same term for the larceny, respectively, of one horse, three horses, and twelve horses. A white man was sentenced to two years for "insulting the flag" and another to ninety days at hard labor in the Dry Tortugas for saying that, if he could, he would blow the government to atoms, that the Negro registration was a "humbug," and that no honorable Southern man could or would take the oath of allegiance. The murder of a Negro by a white man was punished by a sentence of ten years; a Freedman's Bureau agent who illegally collected fines and obtained money under false pretenses won the strange verdict of "Guilty, but acquitted." Another agent found guilty of bribery and illegal charges for services was imprisoned for ten months and fined $50. Acquittals for theft, larceny, and even murder were apparently as frequent as were convictions; but some soldiers who committed robbery and assault with intent to kill were sentenced to ten years and given dishonorable discharges.

Prosaic the trials were for the most part, but not always. Mississippi, whose editors seemed to have a special penchant for running afoul of the military, provided two notable and highly controversial cases. One involved Colonel W. H. McCardle, the editor of the Vicksburg *Times*, who made no bones about his detestation of General Ord, the military commander of the Fourth District, and of the Republicans in Congress. In November 1867 a lieutenant led a squad of soldiers into the *Times* office, arrested the editor, and lodged him in a military prison in Jackson. Soon thereafter Colonel McCardle was tried before a military commission on charges of denouncing General Ord as a usurper and a despot, with defaming the character of an agent of the Freedmen's Bureau, and with advising voters to remain away from the polls at the time of the election at which it was to be ascertained whether a majority of Mississippians desired a convention to gain readmission as a state, all contributing to a general charge of impeding the execution of the Reconstruction laws.

Colonel McCardle applied to the United States Circuit Court for a writ of habeas corpus. At the hearing Judge Robert A. Hill held that the question involved the constitutionality of the Reconstruction Acts, decided that those acts were constitutional, that the powers vested in the commanding general had not been transcended by him, and that Colonel McCardle was subject to arrest and trial before a military commission without being indicted. Accordingly the editor was returned to the custody of the military authorities. He then appealed to the Supreme Court of the United States under a congressional act which authorized appeals in such cases; but before the Supreme Court could reach a decision Congress passed another act depriving the court of jurisdiction.

The second case arose from a senselessly aggravated episode. Colonel Joseph G. Crane, the military mayor of Jackson, ordered the sale of a piano in the home of E. M. Yerger, editor of the Jackson *News,* to satisfy a tax assessment against Yerger's residential property. The family proved to the military marshal who served the writ of attachment that the piano had belonged to Mrs. Yerger before her marriage. Nevertheless, Colonel Crane ordered the execution of the service and the sale. Yerger, who was out of the state, was apprised of Colonel Crane's action by telegram. He requested Crane by return telegram to suspend proceedings until his return. Crane paid no attention. Shortly after he came back to Jackson, Yerger, a man whose temper when aroused was all but maniacal, accosted Colonel Crane on a Jackson street and stabbed him to death.

The slaying of Colonel Crane was the principal, individual *cause célèbre* of the period of military occupation. Here, stormed the North, was murderous proof of Southern intractability. Here, answered the South, was the inevitable result of military bullying. Yerger was brought to trial before a military court. His chief counsel and kinsman, Judge William Yerger, rushed to Washington and presented his application for a writ of habeas corpus to Chief Justice Salmon Chase, in a historic test of the jurisdiction of the court-martial in time of peace and of the constitutionality of the Reconstruction Acts. An Associated Press dispatch of July 13, 1869, is revelatory as to what the Mississippi historian, Colonel J. S. McNeily, described as "another pollution of the stream of law, as in the McCardle case":

> Arguments in the Yerger case for procuring its removal from the military commission, and bringing it before the Supreme Court, were concluded yesterday. Attorney-General Hoar strenuously combatted the jurisdiction of the court. Important questions in the petition for a writ of habeas corpus have induced the Attorney-General to enter into written stipulations with petitioner's counsel to put the question in such form as may be considered and determined before the Supreme Court next October. The present application to the Chief Justice to remove was suspended. The President authorized the Attorney General to say that no sentence of a military court will be executed until the final determination of the [Supreme] court. This meets the approval of Chief Justice Chase.

Obviously the Supreme Court believed it had jurisdiction; but if it rendered a decision the whole Reconstruction program would have been endangered and possibly annulled as being unconstitutional. Instead the military trial was summarily brought to an end. No sentence was pronounced, although it was generally known that the court-martial had agreed on the death penalty. Yerger was held in prison until civil government replaced the military regime and finally was turned loose without a trial on the grounds that his life could not twice be placed in jeopardy for the same offense.

No other judicial episode of military Reconstruction approached these two in constitutional importance or matched them in dramatic quality. The bored majors and captains and lieutenants and the occasional colonels and generals dealt mostly with the humdrum of everyday human conflict. The South's everlastingly remembered insult was not the replacement with military appointees of justices of the peace, circuit clerks and probate judges, constables, circuit judges, sheriffs and aldermen, mayors and magistrates and county treasurers, recorders and assessors by military appointees. The unforgivable reality was not that military rule was unbearably strict or unreasonably long but that it had been imposed at all; what counted was that the bayonets glittered among a people who had complied, whatever their reluctance or misgivings, with the Lincoln program for Reconstruction, only to find that the rules changed as the political balance shifted. What mattered was not so much the trials before military tribunals, but that the men in blue uniforms spelled out an intolerable choice between military occupation or a return to the Union on terms to which the whites were almost totally opposed.

Even had every trial of a white Southerner ended with a verdict of not guilty; even had the generals appointed their former foemen to every major and minor office, and applauded every critical editorial in a Southern newspaper; even had every officer been the soul of courtesy and sympathy—yet, since the ultimate responsibility of the district commanders was to register the new electorate, seeing to it that the freedmen voted and that great numbers of the white Southerners did not—the memory of the bayonets would not die. The bayonet became and the bayonet remains a durable and unendurable symbol in a 150-year-old debate as to the rights of the several states and the overriding rights of the American citizen.

As Benjamin H. Hill of Georgia, an early advocate of as phlegmatic acceptance as possible of the results of defeat, now despairingly protested: "Every proposition in these military bills has been originated since the war; not one of them was demanded during the war or was made a condition of the surrender."

Old Thad Stevens wanted the colored people on top. . . .

The generals were especially zealous in the registration of the new electorate. The second of the military Reconstruction Acts required the commanders to compile before September 1, 1867, lists of qualified voters whose ballots would determine whether the Southern states would comply with the requirements for re-entering the Union. Each commander divided his territory into registration districts, appointing three-man registration boards, all of whose members had to take an ironclad oath that they had always been loyal. Some of the commanders specified that one registrar in each registration district must be a Negro. Few white Southerners could swear honestly that they had never voluntarily borne arms against the United States or had never given aid or encouragement to persons so engaged; that they had never sought or accepted any office in the Confederate government or in the Confederate states or had never voluntarily supported such authority. Thus most of the registrars were federal soldiers, Negroes, and Freedmen's Bureau agents, many of whom were paid specified sums, ranging from fifteen to forty cents, for every name they secured.

No persons were permitted to register who had been "disfranchised for participation in any rebellion or civil war against the United States," who had taken part in the war after having held a civil office in the United States, or who refused to take the oath of allegiance or whose oath was disbelieved by a registrar. Registrations were begun in June, and when they were completed about 150,000 leading white Southerners could not vote and 703,000 Negroes had been registered as against 627,000 whites; and in five states—South Carolina, Florida, Mississippi, Alabama, and Louisiana—the registered Negro voters outnumbered the whites. Significantly the whites temporarily abandoned the designation of Democrat; for before the war it had been a divisive characterization, and the prewar Whigs and Democrats could not afford to be divided now. They united as Conservatives, sometimes as Conservative Democrats.

In the elections on the question of holding constitutional conventions and for the selection of delegates to such conventions, tens of thousands of white persons refused to vote—only a tenth of the registered whites in Florida and South Carolina, a third in Alabama, and nowhere more than one half—thus making the outcome in each state a foregone conclusion. Conventions were authorized in every state except Texas, where an election was not held until 1868. A majority of the delegates in every state was Radical. Every state delegation included Negroes, their number ranging from nine in Texas to seventy-six in South Carolina, where, as in Louisiana, they constituted a majority. Not all of the minority of whites who voted for the conventions were Radicals; for while most of the Conservative leaders advocated white nonparticipation in the elections in the vain hope that Congress itself might recoil from the resultant elevation of the ignorant, the venal, and the incompetent, other Southerners, equally sincere and concerned, urged that the whites who were permitted to register should vote for delegates and then vote against the conventions. Still others, a practical-minded minority, believed that the whites should vote for the best qualified among the candidates and for the conventions. These dissenters from the white majority were variously animated. Some were convinced that the South's only hope lay in admitting to itself and to the nation that it was at the mercy of the conqueror and to seek the best terms the Radicals would allow; some thought that by taking part in the machinery of Reconstruction, as candidates or as open supporters of candidates, they could sway enough Negro voters to win for the white Conservatives some semblance of participation in Reconstruction; some were still convinced Unionists; and still others were driven by desire for personal advancement. Most of the whites who did vote supported the conventions.

The conventions themselves produced constitutional documents more acceptable than the most sanguine white Conservatives had expected. As was to be expected, the delegates were grossly extravagant with the taxpayers' money, and many of them deliberately stole from the public treasury through spurious travel and other expense claims and the extension of salaries. Interminable bickering among the Carpetbag-Negro-Scalawag majorities caused costly delays. A historian of Reconstruction in Texas estimated the state treasury paid out more than $200,000 for a five months' session during which only one month was spent in actual consideration of the constitution. In most states a majority of the Conservative white delegates, outnumbered, impotent, and outraged, withdrew from the sessions before they ended. White Southerners crowded the galleries, taking mordant, belligerent delight in the burlesques of parliamentary procedure, in the pompous, bombastic orations of the more foolish Negro delegates—probably most of them could not read—and in the entire travesty of democratic self-rule which was being imposed upon the South and for which the South would have to pay. Before the several convention sessions were ended some Negro members were expelled for their behavior, some were discovered to be fugitives from justice, and others were jailed for extracurricular theft.

Some of the zanier constitution makers tried to abolish by law the use of such words as "Yankee" and "nigger." More dangerous were efforts in four states to force integrated school systems upon the white citizens, ventures foredoomed by massive white resistance in which some Carpetbaggers themselves joined. There was no general effort to give constitutional approval to mixed marriages or to challenge white ascendancy in the purely social or economic realms. The really revolutionary aspects of the Radical constitutions were the establishment of universal manhood suffrage regardless of race or color and of universal free public school education.

The adopted constitutions, greatly patterned after those of the Northern states, were more truly democratic than those under which the South had lived before the war; and, save for their unacceptable inclusion of the Negro in the electorate with no other qualification than manhood, they were sufficiently approved to be retained, with little change, for years after Redemption. Their innovations—innovations as far as the South was concerned—would not seem revolutionary today: free education for all, nonimprisonment for debt, universal manhood suffrage, homestead exemptions, use of the total population as the basis for representation, shorter terms of public office. All of them gave the governors greater power than they had enjoyed in the South or elsewhere; most of the constitutions enabled the governors to appoint many local officials. Five states—North Carolina, South Carolina, Georgia, Florida, and Texas—did not deny any white men either the vote or the right to hold office, whatever their roles in the Confederacy.

The constitutions of Virginia and Mississippi excluded most Confederate sympathizers from holding office, but no binding restrictions were placed upon their votes. Arkansas and Alabama forbade the vote or the holding of office to all men who had opposed military Reconstruction or had aided the Confederacy after holding civil office in the Union; Louisiana denied the vote and the holding of office to almost everyone who had aided the Confederacy; and these latter three states actually disfranchised and disqualified as officeholders many white and Negro Democrats whether or not they had aided the Confederacy. When the electorates of Mississippi and Virginia voted on their constitutions, the sections on disabilities and disqualifications were voted upon separately and defeated. The end result was that among the ten states to come under the Reconstruction Acts only in Arkansas, Alabama, and Louisiana were restrictions on white suffrage and office-holding actually prescribed in the constitutions as adopted.

Early in 1868, with ten Southern states still under military government, but with civil rule near, the constitutions of eight of these states were submitted to the voters for ratification. Texas had not yet drawn up a constitution. Virginia's military governor deemed her constitution's restrictions too harsh; it was not submitted, and she remained under military rule.

For the white South the ratification of these new state constitutions meant government by the vote of the Negro, allied with what were mostly poor whites, and dominated by Northern Carpetbagger and home-grown Scalawag leaders. For the Republicans their adoption meant a Republican South and all but assured a Republican president in 1868.

Only two of the eight states whose dubiously qualified electors voted upon the constitutions and for candidates for office failed to approve the constitutions or to put Radical slates in office. One was Mississippi which, by hook or crook, although the Negro voters outnumbered the whites three to two, rejected the new constitution itself; the other was Alabama in which less than one half of all registered voters participated as required in the Second Military Reconstruction Act—a congressional provision animated less by political morality than by concern whether the Supreme Court might otherwise hold the adopted constitutions invalid. The Radical congressional majority could not drag Mississippi into the Union since a majority of votes was cast against the constitutions; but by passing the Fourth Military Reconstruction Act, which repealed the second act's provision that at least one half of the registered voters must vote, Congress again broke faith with the white South and Alabama was rejoined, willy-nilly, to the Union. Only Virginia, Mississippi, and Texas remained outside the fold ,and under military rule.

Thus ended, for most of the South, the military phase of Reconstruction.

It seemed like forever, and they stole us blind, the Carpetbaggers and the Negroes and some of our own folks too, the filthy Scalawags, and those uppity colored people running things to suit themselves. . . .

A phlegmatic Southerner might have consoled himself during the early days of Reconstruction with the reminder that military rule had been historically the lot of the defeated until the conqueror willed otherwise, and that the South had been more fortunate than most occupied nations or rebellious areas. Other Southerners, aware that their region had loitered well behind the rest of the nation before the war in economic and democratic aspirations and attainments, might have welcomed, save for the mass-enfranchisement provisions, the progressive provisions of the new constitutions. But no white man of education or of property, or with a sense of history, however genuine his democratic faith, could have applauded the legislative, judicial, and executive aberrations that came in their immediate wake.

It is easier to separate the facts of Reconstruction's corruption from fiction when the plundered dollar has not been filched from the evaluator's own pocket and when he has not himself undergone the experience of having those pockets rifled while a policeman looked on. It is easier to muse upon the good that accompanied the evil and of the old wrongs that led to the new ones when the muser does not stand by, all but helplessly, while the planners of Utopia, alien of skin and region and politics, sets about to remake his cherished, ruined world. And it is far easier to philosophize about the swift passage of even the most unendurable hours and days and years, and about the inescapable penalties of people whom the fortunes of war have cast as the losers, when a century has intervened.

Yet it is the detached philosophers and evaluators and musers—and among them is every serious contemporary American historian—who have brought the Reconstruction picture into focus; and whether their re-estimations will end all the tales that the grandparents told, which is doubtful, they have scaled down the computations of Radical thievery to something like life-size and have enabled us to perceive more clearly the economic and political rigors of Reconstruction. It is important to know that the dollar cost of Reconstruction to the white South came more from the extravagance and wastefulness of the Radical legislatures in spending the tax dollar for good ends than from the purse lining of dishonest officeholders and railroad speculators, legion though they were; to ascertain that greater by far than the combined cost of Radical wastefulness, extravagance, and personal dishonesty was the basic cost of these newfangled ideas which the Carpetbaggers brought with them and wrote into the state constitutions or made into state laws: free public school systems for all children of all races; a tremendous extension of public improvements, and a dramatic revision of the agricultural South's rudimentary concepts of governmental benefits and social responsibilities.

The usurpers built poorhouses and insane asylums and hospitals and roads and bridges, some as replacements in the wake of war but most of them new creations, and almost the entire tax burden was carried by the white landowners. They also improved and extended the judicial systems, and that cost more money too; for the courts were open now to the Negro, as plaintiff or defendant, and a lot more money was needed for Ol' Cuffey to come before judge and jury than to be let off, as he was before the war, with twenty good licks by the master or overseer who was both judge and jury and who charged the taxpayer no money for his services.

The taxes did soar, but they were high principally in contrast to what the planter-dominated legislatures spent meagerly before the war *pro bono publico* and what the economy-minded Bourbons would permit to be spent after the Redemption—which was how the white Conservatives proudly described their eventual victory. And even relative taxation figures can be misleading; for instance, Mississippians paid, under the Republicans in 1875, 9½ mills in state taxes and 10¾ mills in county taxes. Two years later, under the Redemptionists, the state taxes had been reduced to 5 mills, but county taxes had been raised to 16 mills, so that the Democrats actually increased the combined state and county taxes from 20¼ to 21 mills. Moreover, in that state, as James W. Garner, its most qualified historian of Reconstruction, took pains more than a half century ago to admit, "there were no great embezzlements or other cases of misappropriation during . . . Republican rule."

Garner could find in the whole Reconstruction period in Mississippi only three cases of embezzlement: that of a white Republican treasurer of a hospital in Natchez who took $7251, a colored librarian who stole books, and a native white treasurer who embezzled $61,962. It can be argued, moreover, that the ignorance of many whites as well as of the mass of Negro voters, the inexperience of Radical administrators, and the low level of officeholders in town and county governments, where decent Republican leadership was hard come by, contributed perhaps as much to the cost of Radical government as did the legislative programs themselves or the dishonesty of officeholders in a position to capitalize upon their powers. And though the Negro politician is credited with much of the thievery, in actuality his Carpetbagger and Radical political mentors got the loaf and he the crumbs. If any Negro Radical retired wealthy during or after Reconstruction, he covered his tracks well.

The Southern white was affronted by more than simply the waste and corruption that accompanied Reconstruction; and the Southern inheritance of indignation has been kept alive not so much because of moral principle, though that had been contributory, as through more personal and emotional reasons that can be summed up in the story of the politician's Everyman, Bill Brown, who was seeking to persuade a more naïve fellow citizen to vote again for old Tom Jones.

Old Tom's right to continue in office had been challenged by the upstart Harry Smith. Time and again old Tom's champion brought up the political immorality of the challenger. Finally the undecided citizen was moved to comment. "I don't see why you keep bringing that up," he protested. "Everybody knows that old Tom is nothing but a crooked son-of-a-bitch himself."

"I know," old Tom's supporter answered, "but he is our son-of-a-bitch."

Whatever the cost of Reconstruction, the Conservative whites paid most of the bill and they didn't share in the graft; that is, if the pervasive corruption of the railroad speculators, dollar-blind to race, party, or region, is considered apart. Increases in public expenses during Reconstruction stood at 200 per cent in Alabama and Florida, 500 per cent in Louisiana, and 1500 per cent in Arkansas. The ad valorem tax rate rose 400 per cent in Alabama, 1600 per cent in Louisiana, and 1400 per cent in Mississippi, while property values declined as much as 75 per cent and hundreds of thousands of acres were sold for taxes. The estimated public debts of the Southern states grew greatly: South Carolina's from $7,000,000 to $29,-000,000, Alabama's from $7,000,000 to an estimated $32,000,000, Louisiana's from $14,000,000 to $48,000,000, all figures which have been challenged by modern contemporary historians. Radical treasurers either kept records so poorly, or so effectively destroyed them before the white Conservatives were restored to power, that even the approximate amounts of the state debts are impossible to determine. No one can really decide what state debts were secured by railroad or other property and which represented outright waste. Bond issues in the millions were eventually sold at fractions of their face values. It is as impossible to assess the total debts of the cities and counties. In 1870 real property in the eleven former Confederate states was valued at less than half of its assessment in 1860, while taxes amounted to four times the levies of 1860. Yet even at their worst the tax rates in the Reconstruction South were little higher than were prescribed in most Northern states. The Illinois rate in 1870 was 45 mills, for example, while the Southern average was only 15 mills.

The South was hard put to pay off. Large landowners, unable to meet their taxes, had to surrender part, or infrequently all, of their acreage to the state and thus make it eligible for the promised if usually unfulfilled distribution in small lots to the Negroes and poor whites who made up the Radical rank and file.

Worst ridden of the eleven states were South Carolina, Louisiana, and Arkansas. The cost of a Louisiana legislative session before the war had been about $100,000; under the Radicals it rose to almost a million dollars, of which half went for salaries and mileage expense for members and clerks. Louisiana spent $1,500,000 for public printing under the Warmoth regime. For a capitol building the Louisiana Radicals bought for $250,000 a hotel which had recently been sold for $84,000; and Louisiana's chief justice was a party to the sale of a state-owned railroad for $50,000 after more than $2,000,000 had been spent developing it, the jurist joining in refusing to ·sell at a fairer price to unfriendly bidders. The Florida legislature sold 1,100,000 acres of public land held in trust by the state, at five cents an acre, to the right people. An Arkansas Negro political leader was paid $9000 for repair of a bridge which had originally cost the state $500. The South Carolina legislature paid $700,000 for land worth only $100,000, for resale to Negro farmers. After the Radical speaker of the South Carolina House had lost $1000 on a horse race, the House voted him a $1000 bonus for his efficient services as presiding officer. Legislators charged such items as women's garments, whiskies, wines, and dinners and coffins to legislative expense. The same legislators issued $1,590,000 in state bonds to redeem $500,000 worth of bank notes. These are only random items.

Political preferment became the exclusive property of the Radicals. From the very beginning the majority party's delegates to the constitutional conventions managed to place themselves in the most lucrative of the thousands of public offices vacated under the Reconstruction Acts, though a few Conservatives managed, in some states, to secure some minor political positions. The governors filled most local offices by appointments. The Radical legislatures could declare offices vacant and fill them as they wished. After General Grant became President, the Radicals' state bosses were able to add to the elective offices which they could control through legislatures or by state appointment such plums as federal judgeships and collectorships of internal revenue and customs and postmasterships and the like. An unsavory procession of crudely partisan, even crooked federal judges appeared on the Southern horizon. Governors, through their almost unlimited powers of appointment, created Radical political machines which must have seemed invincible.

Nor were some Southern Democrats immune from temptation. The Democratic administration of Governor Robert Lindsay of Alabama, from 1870 to 1872—in between two Radical regimes—was little if any less dishonest than the Radical regime which preceded and followed it. In Georgia the editor of the Augusta *Weekly Chronicle and Sentinel* wrote of his state in disillusion: "It is a mortifying fact that the extravagance of Bullock's administration—we say nothing as to the corruption—benefited about as many Democrats as Republicans."

And in that most refined and profitable branch of public plundering, the multifold railroad development schemes, dependent upon state aid, Southern Democrats, impeccable in their social and political antecedents and in their loyalty to the Confederacy, were only too frequently willing to join forces with the political enemy for their common personal gain. Some railroaders were honest. But most of them, the Northern and Southern speculators alike, exploited, corrupted, and robbed outright the Southern states in the near-sacred cause of railroad development.

The pilfering of the worst of the run-of-the-mill Radical politicians was dwarfed by the profits from the assortment of railroad promotion schemes, some outrightly fraudulent, some legally concocted to benefit primarily the promoters, whose harmony in the interest of quick profits was not disturbed by either sectional animosity or political differences. State aid for the building of railroads, so greatly needed in the South before the war and more desperately afterward, was a practice neither new nor in itself wrong. The state either loaned its credit or directly participated in the building of railroad facilities. Before the coming of the railroads the states had aided in developing inland waterway and turnpike systems, and where the theory of state participation had been honestly and sensibly applied to railroad building its benefits were evident. Under the usual procedures the state either endorsed the bonds of the railroad, present or projected, retaining a lien on the property for the state's protection, bought the issues outright, or loaned the builders an agreed-upon sum for each mile constructed, generally from $10,000 to $15,000 on a mile.

In conspiratorial hands the bond issues were something else again. Railroad promoters and speculators bribed state legislatures, notably in Georgia, South Carolina, and Florida, to sell railroad holdings for next to nothing. An Alabama editor charged that "inside the state capitol and outside of it, bribes were offered and accepted at noonday and without hesitation or shame," the effect being "to drive capital from the state, paralyze industry, demoralize labor, and force our best citizens to flee Alabama as a pestilence, seeking relief and repose in the wilds of the distant west."

Some legislatures loaned more to the promoters per mile than the finished railroads were worth; and when they were surrendered to the state, which was often, the state generally suffered heavy losses. Some state officials even delivered state bonds before the railroads were built, for sale by the promoters for whatever they would bring; most such roads were not completed and in instances were not even begun. Records were poorly kept. Alabama has never discovered the amount of her railroad issues, the estimates ranging from $17,000,000 to $30,000,000. Twenty men in Arkansas controlled the charters of eighty-six railroads, securing state loans of $5,350,000 for their construction or extension and another $3,000,000 in levee bonds given to the railroads upon their claim that the built-up roadbeds could also serve as levees. Only Mississippi, whose constitution forbade state aid, was not greatly victimized; but even there the legislature circumvented the constitution by voting gifts of land and money to selected companies.

Some of the manipulations were fantastic. In North Carolina the legislature had authorized by 1869 a total of $27,850,000 in bonds supposedly for the aid of railroads, of which $17,640,000 had been issued and sold for whatever the market would bring. In later investigations twenty-two legislators were listed as having received more than $200,000 in bribes during the big year. But no deal approached that made in Florida by General Milton S. Littlefield, a former Union officer, who led the North Carolina speculators, and who betook himself and his talents to Florida after the debacle of North Carolina's bonds. In alliance with another promoter, George W. Swepson, General Littlefield began his Florida operation by taking advantage of the financial woes of the Pensacola and Georgia Railroad and the Tallahassee Railroad. Before the war these lines had received aid from counties which they served, the counties accepting their bonds as security. Because of wartime destruction and the early chaos of peace, the two railroads could not meet their obligations; and in February 1869 they were advertised for sale at auction for the benefit of the bondholders. When the auction opened Swepson was there with a million dollars of the line's first-mortgage bonds which he had bought from the counties at from thirty to thirty-five cents on the dollar and which he put up at face value for two thirds of his winning bid. For the nearly half-a-million-dollar balance he gave what turned out to be a worthless check. Even the money with which the bonds had been acquired from the counties had been embezzled from North Carolina.

The swindlers consolidated their two railroads, in June 1869, into the Jacksonville, Pensacola, and Mobile Railroad, for which they solicited and were awarded state aid to the tune of $4,000,000 worth of 8 per cent state bonds. The railroad put up its bonds, in like amount, as security to the state. The proceeds of the sale of the state bonds were to be spent to complete, equip, and maintain the road. Bonds in hand, General Littlefield took an extensive trip. In New York, London, and Amsterdam he peddled the state bonds at approximately seventy cents on the dollar, most of the buyers being Dutch.

Of the nearly $2,800,000 thus raised, the railroads of Florida received altogether only $309,000, the balance being expended in commissions and expenses. Governor Harrison Reed of Florida, whom rival Radicals tried four times to impeach, was accused of having been paid $223,750 by the swindlers. He finally reported to the legislature: "It appears that the bonds of the company were entrusted to one of the firms of swindlers who abound in New York, who by fraud and villainy have diverted the proceeds from the work for which issued."

And that is probably as good a way as any to end this account of Reconstruction thievery.

But even had not one Radical administration been tainted with an iota of rascality, and even had not these regimes been preceded and punctuated later by military occupation, the Reconstruction decade would have been abhorred by most white Southerners and as abhorrently remembered by their sons; for what galled the spirit even more than federal bayonet and the light-fingered adventurers was the composition of the governing coalition.

Those moderate Southern white leaders who in 1865 had asked the pre-Reconstruction constitution makers to enfranchise such Negroes as were qualified through literacy or property ownership had won few white supporters. Now the ignorant mass of Negroes had the vote; and that was and would remain intolerable for generations in a region which steadfastly refused to recognize even the educated Negro as a political man. Unacceptable also to the white Conservatives were the fellow whites whom they looked upon as renegades to race, to region, and to party: the native Southerners, not all of them riffraff, who joined forces with the South's Negroes for personal profit, or in revulsion against the slave-owning upper- and middle-class Southerners with whose slaves they had competed and who had led them into the war; or, as with so many of the upland folk of the Carolinas and Virginia, Tennessee and Arkansas and elsewhere, because they had been good Union men before and during the war and now saw both political and personal opportunity in an otherwise unnatural alliance.

Since only in five Southern states were Negro voters in the majority, Radical control in the other six depended upon the combined votes of Southern Negroes and whites, new Yankee settlers, and the few thousand Northern political adventurers who guided them; and this willingness of fellow whites to make common political cause with former slaves and the Yankee was almost as execrable to the Conservatives as was universal Negro suffrage.

Politically repugnant too, although less emotionally so, were the Carpetbaggers, the political adventurers from the North and the Midwest. The South could accept and even welcome the nonpolitical Yankee settler after the war; but save in relatively few instances she did not and would never hold out her hand to these Republican politicians who, save in Tennessee, dominated the Southern Republican organizations. It was not so much what they did but what they were that counted against the Negro-Scalawag-Carpetbagger alliance whose destruction was the be all and end all of Conservative political thinking, political planning, and political and extralegal action until the last of the Republican rings had been broken up.

For some the end was not long in coming.

Only Virginia, among the eleven Confederate states, never experienced Radical Republican rule. She remained under military Reconstruction until her compliance in 1870 with the congressional formula. Fortunately Virginia's Republicans then split into irreconcilable factions, putting up rival gubernatorial candidates in the first election after her readmission; and the Conservatives, rallying behind the more tolerable candidate, Gilbert C. Walker, were instrumental in electing him.

In that same year of 1870, in Tennessee, North Carolina, and Georgia, the Conservatives either regained control or made a beginning that would have the same result. In Tennessee, Parson Brownlow, believing the state to be as firmly in his grip as it was when he became its wartime provisional governor, had determined in 1869 to relinquish the governorship and move on up to the United States Senate. The governor's office had to be filled by a special election. As they had done in Virginia and would do elsewhere, the Republicans split, each faction nominating two candidates; the Democrats supported the more acceptable candidate, DeWitt C. Senter, who was elected. A new constitutional convention the next year granted universal suffrage, thus returning the vote to thousands of disfranchised Democrats, and Radical Republicanism was dead in Tennessee.

In each of these first three states to overturn Radical administrations the Ku Klux Klan made a fearfully potent contribution, both prior to and during the fateful election year. The Republican Congress, aroused by the threat that the Klan and kindred organizations posed Republican domination of the South and incensed by its murderously effective resort to lawlessness, passed in May 1870, and subsequently in April 1871, the Ku Klux Klan Acts, in order to put teeth into the enforcement of the Fourteenth and Fifteenth amendments and to empower the use of troops against secret organizations. But among the states which rose up against Radical Republicanism, only in North Carolina did the state administration employ military force to try to break up the Klan.

Governor William W. Holden, the North Carolina native political changeling whom we will meet again, bent upon routing the hooded horsemen, placed a thousand North Carolinian militiamen—one regiment of white mountaineer loyalists and another of Negroes—under the command of Colonel George W. Kirk, who had led a regiment of North Carolina Union troops during the war. "Kirk's Lambs," as the militiamen were mockingly dubbed, roamed the countryside, pillaging, arresting and torturing to gain confessions; so irresponsible were they that they almost collided with regular United States troops. But despite—or perhaps because of—Kirk's brutality and the exodus from North Carolina of hundreds of white citizens to escape prosecution as Klansmen, the Democrats elected in August 1870 five of seven congressmen to be chosen for full terms and one of two for unexpired terms and won more than a two-thirds majority in both houses of the legislature. Judge George W. Brooks of the United States District Court, deciding that he had jurisdiction, issued writs of habeas corpus for the prisoners arrested by Kirk's ruffians. President Grant refused Holden's telegraphed plea for aid. Judge Brooks discharged all of Kirk's prisoners; in September a continuing legal battle ended with the disbandment of Kirk's mountaineers and Negroes. Kirk and his second in command surrendered to the United States Circuit Court to avoid suits brought against them in state court. Obligingly a circuit court judge discharged the cases against them; and, evading state officers, they made their way to Washington where they received minor federal jobs as their rewards.

The Democratic legislature impeached Holden and removed him from office. Lieutenant Governor Todd R. Caldwell replaced him and was returned in 1872; but though the worst of Radical Reconstruction was over in North Carolina, political power was still closely divided and the Democrats did not gain complete political mastery until 1876, when they placed wartime Governor Zebulon Vance in the governor's chair.

In 1870 Georgia became the fourth state to break the back of Radicalism and the first to establish complete and lasting Democratic control. After Radicals and Conservatives in the Georgia legislature had joined in 1869 to expel its Negro members, Rufus B. Bullock, the Carpetbag governor, had persuaded Congress to return the state to military government. When that purgatory ended the Radicals divided, as in Virginia and Tennessee. A Democratic legislature was elected in 1870, and when it met in 1871 Bullock fled to escape almost certain impeachment. James M. Smith, a Democrat, replaced him after a special election which was held before the year was out.

President Grant's enforcement acts—notably the act of February 1871, putting congressional elections under the control of federal authorities, and the Ku Klux Act of 1870 and 1871, giving the President military power to send federal troops to suppress violence in the Southern states—failed to halt the South's rebellion against Radicalism. In 1873 the old story of Radical inability to maintain a united front led to the election of Richard Coke, a Democrat, as governor of Texas. Alabama, which in 1870 had elected a Democratic governor only to have the Radicals regain control in 1872 through the combined contributions of the Ku Klux Act, federal troops and marshals, and a poor Democratic record, found two more years of Radical misrule more than enough; a majority of Alabamians, many Negroes among them, voted Democratic in 1874.

In Arkansas a Radical division, which eventually and inevitably pitted opposing Republican factions against each other in guerilla warfare and small pitched battles in which more than two hundred men were killed, led to Democratic victory in 1874. In 1872 the Arkansas Democrats, uncertain as to what course to follow, had not contested as a party and had split their support between the two Radical factions. The two Republicans, Joseph Brooks and Elisha Baxter, contested the governor's office by force of arms for two years, in what became known as the Brooks-Baxter War; and in 1874 the Democrats nominated their own candidate, Augustus H. Garland, and won.

Only four states now remained under Radical control, Mississippi, South Carolina, Florida, and Louisiana. Ever since her belated readmission into the Union in 1870, Mississippi's Democrats had sought unsuccessfully to become a balance of power between the two Radical factions which sought ascendancy. In the state's first gubernatorial election under the Reconstruction Acts the Democrats supported President Grant's own brother-in-law, Lewis Dent, a Johnny-come-lately Conservative Republican, against their own fellow citizen, General James L. Alcorn, prewar Whig and wartime general of Mississippi troops whose reasons for embracing Radicalism we shall survey later. Alcorn won; but when the Democrats supported him for re-election over General Adelbert Ames, who had been the third of her military governors, Ames won. In 1874, with intimidation as their principal weapon, the Democrats took over the legislature; and when impeachment proceedings were initiated against Ames, he promised to resign if they were dropped. They were, and he did.

South Carolina and Louisiana suffered most at the hands of the Radicals; and they, together with Florida, would not throw off the Republican yoke until after the presidential election of 1876. Not once during South Carolina's ten-year ordeal were the Democrats able to break the Republican hold, despite the Radical record. The two-term Carpetbagger governor, Robert K. Scott, had to resort to bribery to avoid impeachment even by a Radical legislature; her home-grown Scalawag Franklin J. Moses, Jr., was even worse; only his successor and the last of the Republicans, Daniel H. Chamberlain, an honest New Englander, gave South Carolina a decent administration so far as he was able. By 1876 the white South Carolinians were prepared as a last resort to engage in open civil war.

Florida's situation differed in that her Democrats were unable to capitalize successfully upon a continuing division in the state Republican party, even though the total white population, Democrat and Scalawag, exceeded the Negro population. For ten years Republican governors, Republican legislative majorities, and Republican senators and congressmen had their almost undisputed way. In 1875 a Democrat did go to the United States Senate after his own ballot in the legislature broke a tie vote for the office.

Not even South Carolina endured such corruption as did Louisiana, where federal troops were used to protect the Radicals in their debauchery, by direction of President Grant who, in the words, amply backed by the evidence, of the Southern historian, E. Merton Coulter, "maintained for the next four years [1872–76] a reign of irresponsible lawlessness unequaled in the history of civilized peoples."

In 1868 Henry Clay Warmoth, a resourceful, ambitious young Illinois Carpetbagger with a good war record, was elected governor with the backing of the more uncompromising and self-seeking white and Negro Radicals. But, as everywhere else in the South, the Radicals soon divided into warring groups. President Grant supported the worser faction, which was known as the Customs House Ring, against Warmoth's group; and Warmoth, refusing to make peace with probably the most odious political machine ever to function in the South, supported the Democratic candidate in the 1872 election, John McEnery, for whom the State Returning Board found a 10,000 majority. Backed by the most powerful figure in the state, Stephen B. Packard, the Customs House gang's federal marshal, and by the dishonest federal district judge, Edward H. Durell, who had been president of the Loyalist convention of 1874, the Radical Carpetbagger candidate, William Pitt Kellogg, succeeded in overriding the Returning Board's verdict and secured the governorship. Kellogg, like Warmoth a former Union officer, then manipulated a questionable impeachment of Warmoth and, as now-undisputed boss of the state, put Warmoth's mulatto lieutenant governor, P. B. S. Pinchback, in for the remainder of Warmoth's term.

After two years of political turmoil, with the native whites resorting to last-ditch violence, the Democrats and the Radicals each claimed a majority in the 1874 legislature; and when the whites banded together in the White Leagues, loosely-knit organizations of military character, President Grant returned to Louisiana General Philip Sheridan, the most ruthless of the former military district commanders. He promptly asked Grant's permission to declare the rebellious Louisianians to be banditti and to treat them as such. A congressional committee of investigation worked out a compromise under which Kellogg's regime was guaranteed until the end of his term in 1877; and so matters stood when the nation's electoral votes were counted in the election of 1876.

Thus, in brief, passed the years of Reconstruction in the South. We shall later more closely inspect some of the more meaningful figures and events and issues of these years. Here we have been concerned principally with the duration and the ending of Reconstruction in the several Southern states. No other ten years in our history have left such a mark; they were, to the Southern Negroes in the days before disillusion and defeat, the years of Jubilee; to the Carpetbagger and the Scalawag adventurer they were the years of good pickings; and, to the honest visionaries among them, they were the years of needful reform. To the white South they were and remained the unforgettable years of the locust.

CHAPTER 5

The General Is Challenged

It could not be expected that the angry men of the South would have been acutely aware of or, being aware, would have been solaced by the shameful and significant fact that Reconstruction thievery was but one expression of the materialism, the boom psychology, and the indifference in high places and low to dishonesty in public and in private life that characterized the national spirit. The air that the young American giant breathed as he flexed his war-hardened industrial muscles and dreamed of dazzling wealth to come was tainted by more than the outpourings from factory smokestack and steel furnace and the locomotives that charged the buffalo.

The robber barons whom Stewart Holbrook so joyously impaled in *The Age of the Moguls* had not waited until now to appear. They had been there all along, and in a variety of guises: in the money markets of the East, among the town builders of the prairies, among the Jacksonian land grabbers and New England's textile giants. But the robber baron came of age in the twenty years after the Civil War, and the first ten of those years coincided with Radical Reconstruction. The arrogant despoilers who through those years dominated the national scene, the Republican party, and American industrial expansion made pygmies of their envious fellow rascals in the South in all save common amorality.

Perhaps no man in public life in the heyday of the robber barons could have prodded or shocked or shamed or angered the people of the United States into successful rebellion against their overlordship. The man who was President of the United States for eight of those first ten years did not even try.

In a way that few would perceive until much later the South of Reconstruction could have felt curiously grateful to President Ulysses S. Grant, the general who had destroyed on the field of battle her aspirations for nationhood, the conqueror whose magnanimity in the hour of victory had lifted her spirit with a short-lived presentment of further generosity; for, as President of the United States, Grant's indifference to public plundering, his choice of intimates and governmental aides, and his endorsement of the Radical state governments of the South and of military force as a means of

perpetuating them actually hastened rather than postponed the South's redemption. The beginning of the end of the South's humiliation originated
not so much in a sectional as in a national revulsion against what came to be
called Grantism, whether it was manifested in the whisky ring or in the military posturings of Sheridan in Louisiana.

By 1872 the handwriting was already blazoned on the wall. Foremost
among those in whose composite hand the indictment of Grantism was written was Horace Greeley, the eccentric, quixotic, honest, and ambitious editor
of the New York *Tribune,* the nation's most powerful newspaper. Greeley
had been a sulphurous champion of emancipation and of universal suffrage,
a belligerent reformer whose name had been anathema in the South in the
decade before the war, during the war years themselves, and well into
Grant's first administration. To complete the tale of the corruption and the
disintegration of Radical Republicanism let us meet now the foremost
needler of the nation's conscience and the President whom conscienceless
men betrayed.

The tragedy of Horace Greeley's life was a late compound of crushing
political defeat, the loss of the editorship of the newspaper he had made
great, and the death of his wife, all coming only weeks apart and leaving
him so broken in mind and body that he died insane on November 29,
1872, in the very month of his supreme challenge, as presidential nominee
of a liberal Republican and Democratic coalition, to Grantism. The President's own personal tragedy was more prolonged and complex; he died
lingeringly of cancer, and through most of the nine years between his leaving
office and his death he would be plagued by lack of means, business failures,
and calumny from which even members of his own party would not spare
him. These two men, the Union's greatest editor and the Union's greatest
soldier, stood high above their respective journalistic and military contemporaries of the North. Yet each of them, as their lives neared their end, may
well have wished that they had never escaped their humble origins.

Grant, the general who pounded the Confederacy to pieces, does not
come within the province of this story; nor does the earlier Grant, the hard-
drinking regular, veteran of the Mexican War, who resigned his commission
in 1854 after a warning from his commanding officer about his habits and
thereafter, until his appointment as brigadier general of Illinois Volunteers,
was by turn a ne'er-do-well farmer, a real estate agent, a minor political
candidate, customhouse clerk, and an employee in his brother's Galena
leather store. Neither are we concerned with the Grant of his three pre-
presidential years as the Union's hero and General of the Army, considerately
supervising the military enforcement of the Reconstruction Acts and then
breaking with Johnson and permanently aligning himself with the Radicals.

Even in treating of Grant the President we cannot do so in the entirety, for
no more than passing acknowledgment can be made of those solid though

few constructive achievements of his two administrations which are remembered today as being tainted with unrelieved fraud, ineptitude, and calculated connivance in the humiliation, plundering, and political enslavement of the South. Instead, we must be limited to the Grant of Grantism, the unsure, blundering soldier-in-politics. Against him the honest liberals within the Republican party turned, sick at heart, before his first term was out, and not as unavailingly as Horace Greeley must have believed in the hour of his political and personal crucifixion.

The near-incredible irony is that Grant himself was as honest personally as was his predecessor and foe, Andrew Johnson, as honest as the crusading editor who would turn against him. He moved as an honorable soldier moves, but, behind and beside him, for four years of war and for three years of peace, in his world, prowled small men and big men alert to the main chance: the colonels who accepted fat railroad bribes for moving their men by roundabout routes; the speculators in secondhand Army carbines, billed as new, which had an unfortunate tendency to blow up when shot; the canners of meat which usually did not kill but only made a man unfit for active duty for days and even weeks; the manufacturers of bluecoats from material so shoddy that it would disintegrate in the southern rain.

Small men and big men: Jay Cooke, brilliant financier of the war to the Union's great advantage and to his own greater one, planning his empire-to-be and mercifully unaware of the empire's aftermath; Simon Cameron, whom Lincoln permitted to resign as Secretary of War, boss of Pennsylvania, fashioner of state governments for a chosen few. And the most magnificent of all ravishers of the public domain, Collis P. Huntington and Mark Hopkins, Leland Stanford and Charles Crocker, none of them too old but all of them too smart to fight for a nation which offered such opportunity to speculators in railroad ventures; four men who pyramided $200,000 in bribes to congressmen into a gross of $79,000,000 in railroad stocks, government bonds, and cash from localities hungry for a railroad terminal and a profit of $36,000,000 in money, mines, forests, townsites, farm acres, leaving the federal government with a $24,000,000 bag, investors with beautifully printed bonds, and uncounted congressmen with hungry memories of their bribe dollars.

But because of, more than in spite of, incalculable corruption, industrial America came of age and the American expansion was assured.

Against the American background three years after the war's end moved a stocky, stoop-shouldered hero who disliked politics and war as well and, having no fixed affiliation, permitted himself in the spring of 1868 to become the Republican nominee for President—"Let us have peace," he said in his brief note of acceptance—and so became President of the United States, winning the electoral votes of all but eight states but with a popular majority made possible only by the Negro voting masses of the South.

From the beginning Grant was victim of his own faulty judgment and political ignorance, of the times, and of men smarter than he. Almost everything seemed to go wrong. The over-all caliber of the President's cabinet was the worst in history; he chose them to suit himself, with no regard for fitness, or worse, from an orthodox politician's viewpoint, without primary reference to party loyalty. He ran or tried to run the White House as an Army headquarters in wartime, with delegation of too much authority to military aides. Naïve in politics—he had voted only once for a President and that time for Buchanan—he came soon under the influence of Ben Butler and others of the less scrupulous of the Republican Radical leaders. The most notable exception in his Cabinet was Hamilton Fish, Secretary of State for almost the whole of Grant's term of office, whose diplomatic skill established Anglo-American relations, at dangerously low ebb during the war and afterward, on the most harmonious plane.

Throughout both terms Grant stood by friends and political associates unworthy of his loyalty, notably his private secretary, Orville E. Babcock, and his Secretary of War, William Belknap, who was proved to have accepted bribe money from a western post trader and whom Grant, by permitting him to resign, protected from the consequences of impeachment. Unwarily he welcomed as friends the notorious speculator, Jubilee Jim Fisk, the Pennsylvania Camerons, and the ubiquitous Roscoe J. Conkling, to whom he even offered the post of Chief Justice of the Supreme Court. The President had a peculiar knack for dismissing the best of his advisers, and when Charles Sumner scrupulously denounced the Grant-endorsed attempt to annex the Dominican Republic in 1869, Grant forced him to relinquish the chairmanship of the Senate Committee on Foreign Relations. Members of his official and even his personal family would be involved throughout both terms in nauseous scandal and fraud.

The magnanimous commander who had won the gratitude of Robert E. Lee and the South at Appomattox would come full circle, not simply to an accommodation with the Radicals in their Reconstruction policy, but to near-unqualified endorsement, even to the employment of federal troops to keep alive the most venal of the Southern administrations. Wise and moderate and honest men within the Republican party shook their heads at the decisions, or the lack of them, which permitted or encouraged the debauchery of a Louisiana and a South Carolina, and of the nation itself. Some among them were more disturbed with the Southern policy than with the scandals which were to become worse in the second administration. To others the scandals themselves provided the primary issue of Grantism—bribery by the railroad kings, the peccadilloes of Jay Gould and Jim Fisk, the whisky ring, Crédit Mobilier, the gold-corner deal involving the President's own brother-in-law, which boomeranged when the President refused to agree to prevent the government from selling gold to break the corner; one after another after another. . . .

Among these shocked stalwarts of the crusading wing of the Republican party none was more profoundly disillusioned than was Horace Greeley, none was in such a commanding position to make his grievances known, and none set about doing something with a stronger will.

No other American editor, before or after Horace Greeley, played so uncommon a scold to the American conscience; none ever appeared less suited to that rule than the absent-minded, shambling man, his mild baby pink face half circled by throat whiskers, his white overcoat and socks invariably awry, his twisted cravat and shapeless unpressed trousers and wide-brimmed hat making of him a caricaturist's delight. No other American editor traveled a harder road to journalistic heights than did the New Hampshire-born son of an itinerant farmer and day laborer. His formal schooling was irregular and short-lived, ending at fourteen when he was apprenticed to the *Northern Spectator* of Poultney, Vermont. He was only nineteen, and journeyman printer and already an omniverous reader, when the *Spectator* gave up the ghost. He walked most of the way to Erie County, Pennsylvania, where his impecunious parents had finally settled down; and after a year of working as a printer in Pennsylvania and upstate New York, with no foreseeable chance for advancement, he set out for New York City, with his personal possessions tied in a handkerchief and some twenty-five dollars in his pocket, a twenty-year-old country boy, "tall, slender, pale and plain," as he described himself later, and of "unmistakably rustic manner and address." He knew "only so much of the art of printing as the boy will usually learn in the office of a country newspaper"; of the art of newspaper writing he knew almost nothing.

For several weeks young Greeley vainly sought work as a printer, his capital disappearing at the rate of $2.50 a week for room and board. Then came the first of a succession of jobs, the eye-straining task of setting up a New Testament in small agate type. Subsequently the *Evening Post* hired and then discharged him because only "decent looking men in the office" were wanted. One minor printing job followed another until 1833 when he entered upon a printing partnership, putting up as capital the few dollars he had saved. His first partner drowned in July of that year. His successor, Jonas Winchester, and Greeley printed two lottery organs; and Greeley, determined to become a journalist, began contributing to these two publications and to the city's newspapers. Soon Greeley began to make a reputation for himself as a writer, and in 1834 he and the redoubtable James Gordon Bennett founded the *New Yorker,* a literary weekly and news journal. The *New Yorker,* ably edited and well printed, trebled its list of subscribers in three years; but the partners were never able to get it out of debt, and though Greeley's editorship greatly enhanced his professional reputation, the magazine failed.

Greeley next became editor of a Whig campaign weekly, *The Jeffersonian,* which he edited for one year at a salary of $1000. *The Jeffersonian,* whose circulation was 15,000, had considerable influence, and Greeley established some long-lasting political friendships. Even more successful under his editorship was the *Log Cabin,* a Whig newspaper, with a first issue of 48,000 and circulation mounting quickly to 90,000.

In April 1841, with an invested capital of some $2000—one half of it borrowed and the other half represented by printing materials—Horace Greeley founded the New York *Tribune,* "a journal removed alike from servile partisanship on the one hand, and from gagged, mincing neutrality on the other." The acquisition in July of a partner, Thomas McElrath, gave the *Tribune* the business management it needed and Greeley enough time and the financial independence to make the *Tribune* live up to its stated purpose. In the fall the *New Yorker* and *Log Cabin* were merged with the *Tribune;* by 1846 the *Tribune* was the best newspaper in New York City and in the nation. Its powerful editorials and intellectual appeal were unique for its day, and Horace Greeley's then-revolutionary viewpoints on many public matters made the *Tribune* a champion of idealistic causes and experiments in democracy.

Greeley endorsed the agrarian goal of free distribution of government lands to small settlers. He attacked railroad land grants as monopolistic, denounced the soullessness of the corporations and the cannibalistic business competition of his time. The wage slavery of the Northern mills he opposed as strongly as he did the bondage of Negroes; no Abolitionist, he argued in their behalf for freedom of speech and of the mails early in the history of those controversial zealots. He was an advocate of labor unions and co-operative shops, the first president of the New York Printers' Union, an opponent of capital punishment, and a foe of landlordism, the dominance of class, and monopoly. As the 1850s neared their stormy end the *Tribune* was the country's greatest paper, covering the nation—save for the South, where it was an abomination—with a daily, weekly, and semiweekly circulation of 287,750, a political Bible for most of its subscribers, who were convinced of Greeley's moral earnestness and held by the clarity of his editorials and his brilliant interpretation of the North's convictions.

The South had another opinion of the Horace Greeley who had opposed the Mexican War and endorsed the Wilmot Proviso and who, in 1850, had told the South that he would prefer that "the Union be a thousand times shivered rather than that we should aid you to plant slavery on free soil." Determinedly opposed to the carrying out of the Kansas-Nebraska Act, he assisted in the arming of the Free-Soilers and approved of forcible resistance to the Fugitive Slave Act as the best means of securing its repeal. Among the first of the North's editors to join the Republican Party, he attended the national organization meeting in Pittsburgh on Washington's Birthday, 1856. A year later Southern tempers rose when they read his editorial belief that the Dred Scott decision "is entitled to just so much moral weight as would be the judgment of a majority of those congregated in any Washington barroom."

Indefatigably Greeley lectured, traveled, wrote books as well as editorials and, time after time, sought political office, a field in which he would always be notably unsuccessful. His pungent phrases—"Go West, young man" was and remained the best known—were on the tongues of thousands of his fellow citizens.

When the war came Greeley gave to the Radical anti-slavery group in the Union the backing of the *Tribune* and his own personal support. Extinction of slavery he regarded as the irrevocable purpose. He was impatient with Lincoln's moderation toward the South, and though he was later to hail the Emancipation Proclamation as re-creating a nation, his delay in supporting Lincoln, and his advocacy in 1863 and again in 1864 of peace through mediation, did not add to his reputation in the North and lessened his influence in the government. Greeley himself was away on a western tour when the *Tribune* reported with intemperate zeal the impeachment of Johnson, but he got the discredit for the managing editor's course of action. Yet he did favor general amnesty. He called for an end of sectional antagonism in a speech at Richmond in May 1867, a day after he had signed the bond for Jefferson Davis's release from Fortress Monroe, a generous gesture which cost the weekly *Tribune* more than half of its circulation and brought upon Greeley the strident wrath of thousands of Northerners who wanted Jeff Davis's head.

When Grant was elected President the *Tribune* rejoiced. For two years the newspaper supported Grant, but during that time Greeley's own estimate of Grant and his policies began to change. For one matter, though a lesser one, the editor believed that one term was enough for a President, and by 1870 it was certain that Grant and his regulars planned a second term; for another, Greeley's wing of the New York State Republican party had been challenged and in 1871 was defeated with Grant's aid by the Conkling-Cornell machine. But far more important than these considerations was Greeley's conviction that Grant was not only incapable of providing good government but was indifferent to the corruption about him and to needed government reforms, in error or worse in his Santo Domingan venture, and dead set against any liberalization of the Southern policy.

Greeley was not the first of the genuine Republican liberals to be disillusioned. The reaction had first spread through Missouri where Carl Schurz broke from the regular Republican party in 1869 and set up a liberal coalition which elected him to the United States Senate. The list of party rebels included such old-time Republican idealists as Gideon Welles, Charles Francis Adams, Lyman Trumbull, George W. Julian, and many another, united as Liberal Republians. The *Tribune's* first publicly expressed opposition came in May of 1871 in an editorial questioning the wisdom of a second term. In December the *Tribune* came out unequivocally against the President's renomination. Moreover, Greeley abetted the Liberal Republicans during the congressional session of 1871–72 in their groping toward a new party. On March 13, 1872, he wrote a friend that he was determined to fight Grant to a finish though "I know how many friends I shall alienate by it and how it will injure the *Tribune*, of which so little is my own property that I hate to wreck it."

The opposition of the *Tribune* and the thunderings of its editor did not now have their prewar cataclysmic effect, nor were Greeley and the newspaper of which he was still editor so indivisible in the public mind. The fire was still there, but Greeley was not writing nearly as much. By 1871 his control was only partial; the stock was held by twenty owners, and there were other good newspapers now, though none with so great a name. It was too late for Greeley and the *Tribune* to make a President of himself. In the formative days of the Liberal Republican party Greeley had asked that his name not be mentioned as a possible presidential candidate in 1872; but, as the movement spread, his unhappy penchant for seeking political office induced him to contest for leadership in a cause which was showing great promise of success. Feelers regarding a coalition with the Democrats had met friendly responses from important segments of that party, including those Southern Democratic leaders whose collective point of view was known as the New Departure. They were practical-minded men who thought it fruitless to continue to fight against facts of political life that were now rooted in the Constitution. Georgia's Senator Benjamin H. Hill spoke for them when he said he did not believe that Southerners in general wished "to see society thrown into a state of fomentation by trying to reconstruct Reconstruction."

Not all of the members of the new Liberal Republican party were as liberal as they were political. Most of the true Liberals wanted as their candidate either the distinguished diplomat and son of a president, Charles Francis Adams, or Lyman Trumbull, who time and again had demonstrated his political independence. The more political-minded leaned to Greeley; and when the Liberal Republicans met in Cincinnati the delegates stampeded to Greeley. For Vice-President they chose Benjamin Gratz Brown, Radical Republican leader in Missouri during the war, who as a United States senator had turned from the party's excesses and as a Liberal Republican had won the governorship of Missouri in 1870.

In July the delegates to the Democratic National Convention, meeting in Philadelphia, unenthusiastically endorsed Greeley. So did the Liberal Colored Republicans in Louisiana in September. Many Democrats bolted because of his earlier hostility to the party and to the South and formed a fourth party of straight Democrats with Charles O'Conor of New York and John Quincy Adams II of Massachusetts as their candidates. Greeley eloquently accepted the nomination, declaring that the old adversaries were "eager to clasp hands across the bloody chasm." He relinquished the editorship of the *Tribune,* though he intended the retirement to be only temporary, and set out on a speaking campaign that concentrated upon Pennsylvania, Indiana, and Ohio. Especially did he plead for reconciliation of North and South through the removal of political disabilities and joint achievement of national and regional reforms. The inarticulate Grant, aware that he could not answer from the platform the vigorous and brilliant attacks of his critic, remained inactive. "I am no speaker and don't want to be beaten," he wrote. Horace Greeley's reasoned addresses drew great crowds, but the audiences were no augury. He was doomed from the start by the solidarity of the Southern Negro vote, the allegiance of the treasury-raiding Union veterans, Grant's "Boys in Blue," to the Grand Old Party, the apathy of so many unforgiving Democrats, and the widespread conviction that, whatever his honesty and brilliance and courage, he was weak in his judgment of men and erratic in his espousal of policies. If Grant did not speak others spoke for him. The personal abuse of Greeley set an all-time low in American politics. Thomas Nast mercilessly cartooned him; the regular Republican orators so vituperatively and continuously denounced him as an ignoramus, a crank, a fool, and a traitor that Greeley remarked that he sometimes wondered whether he was running for the presidency or for the penitentiary.

Only the one-sidedness of Grant's victory was surprising. Greeley won only six border and Southern states and he received 2,834,125 of the popular vote to Grant's 3,597,132. Exhausted by his speaking campaign, unnerved by the personal vilification he had suffered, he had cut short his campaign tour to watch at the bedside of his wife until she died on October 30. And when, as "the worst beaten man who ever ran for high office," he returned to the *Tribune* in the month of defeat, he learned that the brilliant and energetic Whitelaw Reid was in control and had no thought of surrendering the editorial reins. On November 29 Horace Greeley died, a madman. A nation shocked that so much had been said so harshly paid him in death a tribute never accorded another American newspaperman as such. The President, the Vice-President, Cabinet members, and governors and other thousands of his fellow citizens whom his quill pen had long aroused attended his funeral.

Horace Greeley died, too, without knowing that even in defeat he and the Liberal Republicans had accomplished much toward the reconciliation of North and South and the breaking of the Republican strangle hold, and toward making unpopular, to the point of inevitable destruction, the Radical Reconstruction policies in the South. He had helped to bring the Northern and Southern hands together across the bloody chasm. He had exposed the rotten core of Grantism. However reluctant, the coalition of Northern Republicans and Southern Democrats under the banner of Liberal Republicanism had proved that there were at least as many issues which could bring Northerners and Southerners together again as there were to divide them. Two years later the Democrats won control of Congress, and by the end of that year of 1874 only four Southern states remained captive to Radical Republicanism. And in 1876 Samuel J. Tilden of New York would actually win the presidency only to see the nation's highest office forfeited to the Republicans so that the Conservatives could regain political control in the last three of the Southern states which had endured Radical rule and Grantism.

CHAPTER 6

Experiment in Education

SOON *after the war William Lloyd Garrison asked himself a question and answered it to his own satisfaction.*

This was his question: "How can these masses of human beings, black and white—for there is virtually no difference in moral conditions at present —be raised to a fit position in the Republic?" And his answer: "A government should teach the South line upon line, precept upon precept, by military garrisons, by Bureau courts, by Congregational churches, by Northern settlers, by constitutional amendments, by Christian missionaries, by free schools, lectures, newspapers and reading rooms, what be the first principles of social order, political eminence, moral worth and industrious success."

Others in the North put the case for mass education in the South more diplomatically. In a free country, they said, the ballot should be available to every citizen, a schoolroom open to every child.

But no matter how gently the Yankee determination expressed itself, the plain fact of the matter was that the white South thought it knew better. Put a schoolbook in the Negro's hand? Ridiculous, put a hoe handle in it. That's what he needs. Education, the Southern doggerel went, is the ruination of the nigger generation.

The arguments of the adversaries in a discussion which long antedated the war were alike logical enough. In denying education to the slaves the South was, according to its lights, practical and sensibly self-protective. Even a docile slave could hardly remain satisfied once literacy had opened by the minutest crack the door to Jefferson's illimitable freedom of the human mind. And if education were to buttress and encourage his discontent, a spirited slave could become a serious threat to white security.

In keeping with such logic the South prohibited the slave by law from learning anything except the skills of the craftsman, the artisan, and the mechanic. But a considerable number of slaves, whose masters were more indulgent or humane or animated by blood ties, were passably well educated, and a continuing few were extraordinarily learned. These fortunate ones were illegally instructed by their masters or mistresses, by the tutors who were employed to teach the masters' children, by the children themselves, by white pastors, sometimes by fellow slaves. And though there are no records in proof or disproof, it is probable that a majority of the 250,000 free Negroes, most of whom lived in the South, were functionally literate.

But the temptations of the printed word were generally removed from the Negro slave. In addition to such practical considerations as the maintenance of tranquillity, God himself had ordained in Holy Writ that the sons of Ham must be the hewers of wood and the drawers of water, so why confuse them in their ordained task by teaching them to read and write?

Beneath its cloak of vituperation Garrison's case for mass education was reasonable. Lumped together, the free, illiterate Negro and the illiterate Southern poor white represented an agglomerate of ignorance which did constitute a hazard to democratic government. Up to the racial cutoff point, thoughtful Southerners would agree before and after the war with the premise that democracy could not succeed without a literate citizenry. But the white Southerner of Reconstruction was not generally ready to include the Negro, educated or not, as a participant in the functioning of a democratic government. So why educate him? And Garrison and some of his fellow advocates of mass education in the South made the mistake of recommending Negro education as punishment for white wrongdoing. The designation of military garrisons and Freedmen's Bureau courts and Northern clergymen as aids to the education of the South gave ammunition enough and to spare to the white South, to the upper-class minority which was opposed to public education on principle because of the taxation and philosophy involved, and to the majority which believed that the Negro did not need and should not have book learning.

The vehemence of Northern criticism and the South's own postwar reluctance and financial inability to embark upon so revolutionary an undertaking as mass education of the Negro combined to create during the Reconstruction period and afterward an assumption of Southern indifference to education in general which was to persist far beyond the period itself.

Undeniably the white South had been cool to the idea of mass education at public expense, even for white children, before the war. In this attitude the region did not stand alone. Great Britain herself would not approve universal public education until 1871. The reasons were varied. Wealthy Southerners were disinclined to pay taxes to educate the children of the poor. Among the lower-income Southerners there persisted the frontiersman's scorn for formal education; moreover, the difficulty of bringing together in schools the children of a scattered rural population was great and discouraging. The result was a far higher rate of white illiteracy in the South than in the North, as is strikingly indicated in the census of 1850, which showed an illiteracy rate of more than 20 per cent among the Southern whites over twenty years of age against only 3 per cent for the middle states and less than one half of 1 per cent for New England.

The South's achievement in higher education was something else and reflects its prewar caste system. In 1860 the Southern states spent twice as much on higher education as did the New England states. At that time some 25,000 students were enrolled in the South's 260 public and private colleges, half of the students and half of the colleges in the nation. Virginia, in 1857, had one college student for every 666 white citizens and Massachusetts one for every 944.

The South's tradition of higher education went back far. Virginia's William and Mary was the second college in the country; Georgia had issued in 1775 the first state university charter; the University of North Carolina was the first state university actually to open its doors; and the University of Georgia, South Carolina College, and the Universities of Alabama, Tennessee, Mississippi, and Louisiana had been founded well before the war. Two out of three Americans admitted in the prewar period to the Inns of Court in London were Southerners. Denominational colleges abounded. The United States had not yet won its freedom when the Presbyterians of the South founded Hampden-Sydney College in Virginia in 1775 and Washington College—which would become Washington and Lee University—in 1749. The education-minded Presbyterians had also established North Carolina's Davidson College, Erskine in South Carolina, Centre College in Kentucky, and Oglethorpe in Georgia. The Methodists were close behind with Randolph-Macon in Virginia and Emory in Georgia, Trinity in North Carolina, and Wofford in South Carolina. The Baptists, though less well-to-do, were responsible for Wake Forest in North Carolina, Mercer in Georgia, Richmond College in Virginia, and Furman in South Carolina.

Tradition to the contrary, higher education for women was not overlooked. Mississippi's Methodists chartered the Elizabeth Female Academy in 1819. The Georgia Female College, established by that state's Methodists, offered degrees to young ladies in 1836. There were others, among them Mary Baldwin and Hollins in Virginia, La Grange Female College in Georgia, Science Hill in Kentucky, and Warrenton Female College in North Carolina.

In yet another educational field the ante-bellum South was also active. Wealthy citizens frequently endowed private secondary schools, generally known as academies, which operated under state charters. Although sometimes partly supported by state and church, they were principally maintained by student fees and contributions from their sponsors. Below the college and the academy levels were the elementary "old field schools," also privately supported, and the tutorial systems under which the sons and daughters of well-to-do planters were taught, generally by young New Englanders, at home.

It is, of course, fallacious to emphasize quantity and duration and overlook the qualitative factors, as W. J. Cash makes crystal clear in *The Mind of the South,* that most penetrating of all analyses of the Southern character. Here is his disturbing evaluation of the historic lack, less apparent in the ante-bellum years than later:

> I know the proofs commonly advanced by apologists—that at the outbreak of the war the section had more colleges and students in those colleges, in proportion to population, than the North; that many planters were ready and eager to quote you Cicero or Sallust; that Charleston had a public library before Boston, and its famous St. Cecilia Society from the earliest days; that these Charlestonians, and with them the older and wealthier residents of Richmond and Norfolk and New Orleans, regularly imported the latest books from London, and brought back from the grand tour the paintings and even the statuary of this or that fashionable artist of Europe; that, in the latest days, the richest among the new planters of the deep South began to imitate these practices; that in communities like those of the Scotch Highlanders in the Cape Fear country there were Shakespeare libraries and clubs; that Langdon Cheves of South Carolina is reported by Joseph Le Conte to have discussed the idea of evolution in private conversation long before *The Origin of Species;* and so on *ad infinitum.*
>
> But such proofs come to little. Often, as they are stated, they are calculated to give a false picture of the facts. Thus, the majority of the colleges were no more than academies. And of the whole number of them perhaps the University of Virginia alone was worthy to be named in the same breath with half a dozen Yankee universities and colleges, and as time went on, even it tended to sink into a hotbed of obscurantism and a sort of fashionable club, propagating dueling, drinking, and gambling.
>
> Thus again, the general quoting of Latin, the flourish of "Shakespeare says," so far from indicating that there was some profound and esoteric sympathy with the humanities in the South, a deliberate preference for the Great Tradition coming down from the ancients, a wide and deep acquaintance with and understanding of the authors quoted, really means only this,

it seems to me: that the great body of men in the land remained continuously under the influence of the simple man's almost superstitious awe for the classics, as representing an arcanum beyond the reach of the ordinary.

And over and behind these considerations lies the fact that the South far overran the American average for [white] illiteracy—that not only the great part of the masses but a considerable number of planters never learned to read and write, and that a very great segment of the latter class kept no book in their houses save only the Bible.

So much for that cultural hot potato. What about public secondary school education in the old South?

Even though some progress was made prior to the war in the establishment of public school systems, the education of the children of the ordinary Southern whites was badly neglected. Thomas Jefferson had fathered in Virginia a "bill for the more general diffusion of knowledge," and his proposal for education at the common expense "without regard to wealth, birth or other accidental condition or circumstance" became law in 1796; but his dream faded because local officials thought such a program too expensive and too dangerous. Other Southern states had given some recognition to the need for public education. North Carolina was the second and Georgia the third Southern state to provide for public school education in their constitutions, with Tennessee following in 1835 and Virginia in 1851. Save for Louisiana, the new states of the Southwest declared for public education in their own constitutions upon being admitted to the Union. Louisiana made similar provisions in 1841.

But in practice general public education had made little headway in the South before the war. The moneyed groups were not eager to see the costly innovation; and the popular concept of public schools as essentially charitable or pauper undertakings made many parents refuse to enroll their children in them. Yet some principal communities of the South had created public school systems which rivaled those of the North. By 1860 the South was spending about two and one half million dollars to educate 425,600 white children, or one in every seven, as compared with one child educated at public expense out of five beyond the South's borders. But for the war the rise of men of middle-class origins to political prominence during the decade which preceded it might have brought the South's public school system to something approaching equality with the rest of the nation.

The war did more than simply halt the slow development of public education. Almost all of the colleges and universities of which the South had been so proud were, in one way or another, victims of the conflict. Some institutions, among them the University of Alabama and the University of Mississippi, were burned. Others, lacking funds and student bodies, closed their doors either temporarily or for all time. During Reconstruction the University of North Carolina shut down for five years because white students would not study under the politically appointed faculty. At the University of South Carolina the enrollment of Negro students and the presence of a part-Negro faculty caused the withdrawal of white faculty members and students. The Universities of Georgia and Louisiana were not so badly impaired; but in general the private and church colleges, relatively immune from Carpetbagger-Negro control, came through war and Reconstruction in much better shape than did the state-supported universities. By 1884 there were sixty-seven colleges for men, mostly church supported—far too many for their pitiful endowments—in six Southern states; in the New England states there were only twenty-seven men's colleges, most of them nondenominational, but with a total endowment far greater than that of all the Southern private and church-supported institutions together.

In the few months after the war, before the decision was taken away from them, the Southern states made no move to educate the Negro children. They were hard enough put to try to restore the meager white educational systems to what they had been. But even had the South been inclined and financially able to educate adequately the freedmen or even their children— and it was not—neither the Radical political leadership nor the evangelical churches of the North would have entrusted such a task to the Negroes' former masters.

These partisan and diverse sponsors of Negro education, animated by a curious blending of Abolitionist equalitarianism and vengefulness, a sense of divine mission, a considerable degree of political realism, and no little sentimentality, launched an invasion such as the world has never seen. Its purpose was the conquest of the citadel of Negro illiteracy and of white prejudice against Negro education. Its generals were a hodgepodge of inexperienced idealists, professional, mostly young educators, Christian zealots, and political ragamuffins. Its rank and file, made up of young and not so young middlewestern and New England schoolmarms, usually unmarried, and some Northern free Negro teachers, had in common the courage to serve in a hostile land and a dedicated impulse to lift the lowly. The schoolbook armies would win the first battles; but because of Southern hostility, the incompetent and unfixed purposes of their generals, and the disinclination or the inability of teacher and student to settle down for a long campaign against mass illiteracy, they lost, at least in their own time, the war itself.

Of the hundreds of Yankee schoolteachers who, in a spirit of adventure or in answer to the call of conscience, went South to teach the Negro, only a few left even fragmentary records of what they did or thought or saw. Laura M. Towne, an Abolitionist suffragette spinster of Philadelphia, was one of these. Mary Ames, a young Springfield, Massachusetts, Unitarian, was another.

The hardy stuff of which these teachers were made comes through clearly in the letters and diary of Miss Towne—one hesitates even now to call her Laura—who early in the war volunteered to teach in the Sea Islands of South Carolina.

When Union troops captured Port Royal on November 7, 1861, Beaufort and the Sea Islands became Union territory. The Carolina planters fled, and the federal government found it had on its hands several thousand helpless, ignorant field Negroes. Edward L. Pierce of Massachusetts, dispatched to the area by the Secretary of the Treasury to see that there would be a cotton crop the following year, wrote back for teachers and clothing. Miss Towne and a friend, Ellen Murray, were among those who responded.

On April 17, 1862, shortly after her arrival at Beaufort, Miss Towne had some acidly forthright comments to make:

"I think a rather too cautious spirit prevails—anti-slavery is to be kept in the background for fear of exciting the army, and we are only here by military suffrance. But we have the odium of out-and-out abolitionists, why not take the credit? Why not be so confident and freely daring as to secure respect! It will never be done by an apologetic, insinuating way of going to work."

She recorded also her pained astonishment at the conditions under which the Negroes lived, in cabins built of rough boards, ventilated by small glassless windows and with floors of sand and lime. The older people, she reported, slept in bunks, the children on the floor. All cooking was done in a single pot with long oyster shells for spoons; and "when the family has finished scraping the pot, the dogs lick it clean for the next meal." That first year the teachers did more than teach. An epidemic of smallpox broke out; the Yankee teachers went nursing from cabin to cabin.

At first Miss Towne acted as housekeeper for Pierce at The Oaks plantation, the government headquarters. Then, after teaching a few children on the plantation, she and Miss Murray opened a school in September 1862 in a brick church. They had eighty dark-skinned scholars.

"They had no idea of sitting still, of giving attention, of ceasing to talk aloud," the diary tells. "They lay down and went to sleep, they scuffled and struck each other. They got up by the dozen, made their curtsies, and walked off into the neighboring field for blackberries, coming back to their seats with a curtsy when they were ready. They evidently did not understand me, and I could not understand them, and after two hours and a half of effort I was thoroughly exhausted."

Soon the Pennsylvania Freedmen's Aid Association sent down a schoolhouse in sections. This was set up opposite the brick church and was called "The Penn School."

Miss Towne was disgusted with her friends and relatives in the North who let smaller things distract them from the worth-while tasks they could be doing. In a letter home to her sister she wrote:

"I am sorry too that you are sewing. I wouldn't touch a needle. You will find the world wags on if you don't—if not so well, yet, after a while you don't see the difference. I think fancy work and all that an invention of the Devil to distract artists and others from their true work."

On April 14, 1865, in Charleston, she wrote in her diary:

"I have seen the same old flag raised on Sumter by General [Robert] Anderson himself, Garrison, George Thompson, Tilton, Beecher, and a host of abolitionists being present. It was a most beautiful and glorious sight."

When word came of the assassination of Lincoln she and Miss Murray tore up a black bonnet and gave a piece of crape to the children to wear in school.

As teachers, the Misses Towne and Murray received soldiers' rather than officers' rations. She comments that people wouldn't starve on the government rations, but "sometimes they arrive so late that people do starve between arrivals."

With the end of the war Miss Towne, being of independent means, bought the old mansion and estate of Frogmore on the eastern shore of St. Helena. Here she and Miss Murray made their permanent home, and here she set up a school which for a while received Freedmen's Aid Association assistance.

In 1867 she protested the founding of a church for white people only.

"I think this whole church plan a snobbish affair, and that there will probably be more rigid exclusion of blacks from all equality and civility than in the most snobbish of Northern or Southern churches, for there is no hater of the negro like these speculating [Northern] planters, but I am going to attend for a while and watch matters."

By then Miss Towne was supervisor of teachers on the island for the Freedmen's Bureau. At church service she noticed two Southern white teachers. "They were tawdrily dressed—one of them in a pink silk—and were in the war undoubted rebels. Indeed, we hear that they whip the children in their school and make them call them 'massa' and 'missus' as in the old time. But they are 'nigger teachers,' so I did my duty by them as agreeably as I could. They send their reports regularly and so do their duty by me."

There was no question in her mind that free public schools were imperative. On March 3, 1867, she wrote in her diary:

"The long lost Moses, who walked all the way from Wilmington, N.C., to this village to find his mother, is our little waiter . . . Moses intended to remain in Wilmington and 'take his schooling' for a year, but the school was made a pay school, and he had no money so he came here. So it will be if ever that false plan is pursued—the best and the brightest will be cut off, many of them, from school privileges."

That same year she was irritated by what the politicians were doing to reduce the status of the Negro women while elevating the men.

"In slavery the woman was far more important, and was in every way held higher than the man. It was the woman's house, the children were entirely hers. . . . Several speakers have been here who have advised the people to get their women into their proper place—never to tell them anything of their concerns, etc., etc.; and the notion of being bigger than the women generally is just now inflating the conceit of the males to an amazing degree."

By now interest in educating the Negroes began to wane in the North, so in April 1868 Miss Towne wrote a friend:

"Tell me something about the prospects of the Penn. Branch supporting the school another year. Doesn't it look dark? Is interest dying out? I do want some clothing for my 'mudderless' if any is going, but I won't beg it if I never get it."

Aid from the North failed fast in the months that followed. But Miss Towne continued her school until her death in 1901, and it has survived as a community center.

Not all of the teachers came with such stern resolution or adamant convictions. Mary Ames and her friend, Emily Bliss, started out blithely to the same Sea Islands of South Carolina just at the war's end. Mary—it is easy to so address her—likewise recorded their experiences in her diary and reminiscenses.

"Our families ridiculed our going and tried to stop us, prophesying our return in less than a month," Mary wrote gleefully. "We made our preparations which were not elaborate—a chair, a plate, knife, fork and spoon; cup and saucer, blanket, sheets and pillow cases, and sacking for a bed of hay or straw to be found wherever we should be situated, and we added some crackers, tea, and a teapot."

Sailing from New York on the steamer *Fulton* on May 1, 1865, the young Yankee girls arrived at Hilton Head on the morning of the fourth day and went immediately "to the place where we took the oath of allegiance to the United States." But as there were already five or six teachers in Hilton Head, they were sent on to Charleston on a small steamer loaded with soldiers.

"There was no place for us. We had to sit the long night through, on a bench with no back, surrounded by soldiers smoking, playing cards, and telling stories—the longest night I ever knew."

At Charleston, "discouraged, weary, and homesick," Emily threw herself into the arms of a kindly man from Massachusetts to whom they reported, and at once "he took in the situation, called an ambulance, and put us in charge of a sergeant with a note to his wife." The wife made them comfortable in "one of the most elegant mansions in Charleston; the furniture, pictures, and ornaments were all as their owner had left them. The garden was a delight. I never saw finer roses."

Revived, and realizing after a survey they were too inexperienced to teach in Charleston, they accepted a position on one of the islands to which several thousand Negroes had been sent after Sherman's march.

"That suited us and we were ordered to leave in two days," Mary wrote.

May 10, 1865
At one o'clock we left Charleston on the propeller *Hudson,* for Edisto Island. Sailing along the shore and up Edisto River, we reached the landing place just at sunset. . . .

We brought on the boat a hundred and fifty negroes, who, as soon as they landed, built fires to cook their supper—the live oaks in the background, with their hanging moss, had a very picturesque effect.

We spent the night on the boat, the captain giving us his stateroom. We had a visit from a Mrs. Webb and one of the officers of the 32d Regulars, colored infantry, two companies of which are stationed here to protect the island from guerillas. We were asked to breakfast at headquarters, about half a mile from the landing.

May 11
At seven we started for camp, which was on the plantation formerly owned by William Seabrook. They gave us a good breakfast; then the Colonel placed at our disposal a large army wagon, drawn by four horses, to take us with our trunks and boxes to find a place to live. The drive was delightful, the road shaded and cool, winding under immense live-oak trees covered with moss; the wild grape was in bloom, and the air filled with its perfume. We passed several houses crowded with negroes, and could not make up our minds to stop at any. We drove on some three or four miles further and, as it began to be very warm and uncomfortable, we decided to stop at the very next house, negroes or no negroes. Soon we reached what must have once been a pretty avenue, now rather forlorn. Driving in, we found negro cabins on either side, and a large house at the end.

The inhabitants of the cabins came flocking out to welcome us with howdys, and offers of service to the missis. The former owner of the plantation was Dr. Whaley, the possessor of a hundred slaves, many of whom were now returned and living in the cabins. He deserted the place four years before, and the house had a desolate appearance—the windows gone, and shutters hanging by one hinge. Our trunks, box, and chairs were placed on the piazza and the army wagon was driven away. We looked at each other; our hearts were full, and if we could have seen any honorable way to escape and go home we certainly should have gone.

With the help of a Negro, his wife, and his six children who were living in the big house they cleaned up two rooms for their own use. There were no brooms or mops, so they used moss and water to clean the floors. Not realizing that their bed ticking could be filled with moss and not finding any straw or hay, the girls lay down for the night on their bed sacks on the hard floor. As there were no locks on the doors, Mary "got out the hammer we had brought in our box and kept it in my hand all night, ready to beat out the brains of any one attacking us."

After the terrors of the night the first thing the girls did in the morning was to hang out the American flag in front of their door.

Four miles away was the commissary. Two miles closer were two other teachers. They and a few officers were the only white people on the island; the rest of its inhabitants were some ten thousand Negroes.

The girls chose a nearby abandoned church as their schoolhouse and started school on Monday, May 15.

"We opened school at nine o'clock, with fifteen scholars, nine boys, and six girls. Some were decently clad, others filthy and nearly naked. One or two knew their letters. None could read. We dismissed early, as the children seemed tired and we were decidedly weary."

Soon they were holding night school for adults two evenings a week on the piazza of the house.

Mary Ames recorded that "Every noon I take home with me a troop of children, to whom I give thread, needles, and pieces of cloth, that they may have their garments patched at home. We are trying to teach cleanliness as well as reading and spelling, but it is a tough job, for the poor creatures have lived so long in a filthy condition that they don't know what it is to be clean."

Barrels of clothes arrived from the North and the young teachers distributed them: Zouave suits, coats, trousers, pantalettes, a blue Garibaldi.

The girls found life hard. They papered their bedroom with newspaper to seal holes a rattlesnake had been using. They were glad that the family of Negroes lived in a part of their house, for their nearness gave them a feeling of protection. The near neighbors "stretch out at night on the floor in front of the fire and have no bedding of any kind. They have a bowl, one plate, one spoon, and take turns using them." The annoyances and plagues included wood ticks, mosquitoes, fleas, chicken snakes, grass snakes, rattlesnakes. Many of the children had smallpox.

For three weeks the girls had only tea for breakfast and supper. When their rations arrived from Army headquarters they opened the large soapbox and found "beans at the bottom, covered by a piece of dirty paper, then a layer of brown sugar, and on top of all a bar of soap and six candles. Some ground coffee in a paper, a smaller bag with fat bacon and salt pork, and a half barrel of flour.

"Emily came down and viewed the lot, burst into tears and wished that the grave we had seen hoed out at the church was to lay her in."

Then, rallying, the girls exchanged some of the rations at the sutler's store for condensed milk, butter, corn meal, and other more welcome edibles.

The days became intolerably hot. On order of their Freedmen's Bureau supervisor they closed school for the summer on June 30 and betook themselves to a South Carolina beach for the vacation months. In October they returned to the Seabrook place and there conducted school in a building once used for billiards. Of the hundred children in their class only three knew their ages. "One large boy told me he was 'three months olds!' "

In the spring many of the Negroes who had been removed to the island after Sherman's conquest abruptly fled when they were told they would have to work for the original landowners. These planters, returning to the island to make their arrangements, "were entertained at our table, but when they were in possession and were joined by their families, it was different. The women ignored us."

> The white people of Edisto have indeed suffered, but now their homes are to be given back to them. The island negroes and those brought here by our bewildered, blundering Government have had, and will have, harder days than their masters. Among those that we have known, however painful their experience, and whether accustomed formerly to easy routine as house-servants or to rougher field service, not one among them would choose ease with servitude rather than suffering with freedom.
>
> In May we moved to the bay with our school benches and books, and had a large school there, but a month later the Freedmen's Bureau was dissolved and we were notified that our services were no longer needed.

The girls kept the school a few months longer as Mary's twenty-dollar-a-month salary was paid direct by Charles Hubbard of Boston, "whose pleasure it was to be responsible for one teacher." Then they "sent to Governor Aiken his furniture which we had bought from the negroes; one piece was the armchair given him by his mother when he was elected governor of South Carolina." Shortly thereafter they returned to Springfield.

So ended the adventures of two among the hundreds of Yankee heroines of Reconstruction, some of them granitelike in their purpose and inflexibility, others—young, adventurous, friendly—wanting mostly to help. Whatever their motives or behavior or belief, few were welcomed by their kind when they came, for they were revolutionaries in a revolutionized land.

These teachers, sent in as close behind the Army as safety would permit, were at first subject to the direction of the military commandant in the area. But, with the creation of the Freedmen's Bureau, they looked to the Bureau instead of to the military for transportation and for the very buildings in which they taught. Their salaries continued to be paid by the benevolent societies which sponsored them.

After its activities and powers were extended in the summer of 1866 the

Bureau was authorized to lease or construct school buildings for the Negroes and to staff them. As one means of raising funds, it was also empowered to sell or lease such former Confederate government property as foundries, hospital buildings, warehouses, blockade runners, and cotton gins. From such sources and from rentals of "abandoned" property the Bureau realized about $5,000,000; these sales were not calculated to win any white Southerners to the cause of Negro education. The Freedmen's Bureau spent altogether $16,000,000 on Negro schools.

The schools, under the over-all supervision of the Bureau's national Superintendent of Education, whose headquarters were in Washington, were a heterogeneous lot. Within a year after the war 366 assorted societies and auxiliaries for Negro education were active; each of them would send from one to ten teachers to the South. Principal among these societies was the nonsectarian American Missionary Association; almost as active was the Freedmen's Aid Society of the Methodist Episcopal Church, formed in Cincinnati in 1866.

In its first two years the Freedmen's Aid Society sent out 126 teachers and spent more than $67,000. On a smaller scale the Quakers, the United Presbyterians, the Old-School Presbyterians, the United Brethren, and the Protestant Episcopal Church raised money among their church members for Negro education. The American Missionary Association contributed 353 teachers and $377,027.78 in cash and supplies in 1866. In 1868 it sent out 532 teachers. Though the society was nonsectarian, most of its leadership came from members of the Congregational Church, which, as a national body, had been the first to authorize the society to be its agent among the freedmen; but the society also represented, among others, the Wesleyan Methodists, the Reformed Dutch churches, and the Free Will Baptists.

The Freedmen's Bureau worked closely with these philanthropic and religious groups. General Howard would proudly report that "from the first I have devoted more attention to this than to any other branch of my work." The exact number of teachers supported by the religious societies and the Bureau is unknown. An estimated 1300 teachers taught in about 1000 schools in 1866 with a casual enrollment of 90,000 young and old illiterates; by 1867 few Southern towns lacked Negro schools, nicknamed "nig schools" by the objecting whites; by 1869 nearly 10,000 teachers were teaching in the Negro schools. Only half of these were white Northerners and white Southerners. The rest were Northern and Southern Negroes.

The Freedmen's Bureau initially had no congressional mandate to deal with Negro education. But General Howard's second circular, issued on March 19, 1865, stated specifically: "The education and the moral conditions of the people will not be forgotten and the utmost facility will be offered to benevolent and religious organizations and state authorities in the maintenance of good schools for refugees and freedmen until a system of free schools can be supported by the reorganized local governments. It is not my purpose to supersede the benevolent agencies already employed in the work of education but to sympathize with and facilitate them." In his first report to Congress, Howard showed the need for authorization of education as a function of the Bureau.

The second Freedmen's Bureau Bill, passed over Johnson's veto on July 16, 1866, clearly included education as a responsibility of the Bureau. It provided that, while the Freedmen's Bureau was to be discontinued whenever Reconstruction was complete, in no case should its educational work be interfered with until the states had provided for Negro education.

Howard and his associates believed that the sale of crops and abandoned lands, and some local taxation, would finance the Bureau's educational work. But as more and more of the abandoned lands and buildings were reclaimed by their former owners it became apparent that a more definite source of revenue was needed. The Army Appropriation Bill of June 1867 included a $521,000 item for education in its total authorization of $6,944,-450 for the Bureau. All but $21,000 of the educational item was for buildings and asylums; the $21,000 was for salaries of superintendents.

While the Bureau's principal educational purpose was to provide the teachers of the missionary and benevolent societies with school buildings and transportation, it soon developed that the Bureau also had to protect the agents. As J. W. Alvord, its General Superintendent of Schools, put it in 1866, ". . . military force alone can save many of our schools from being broken up, or enable us to organize new schools." In Shelbyville, Tennessee, for instance, John Dunlap, a teacher, was flogged and driven away. When he returned his guard had to fire to break up a mob which clamored for "Dunlap and fried meat." In Charleston, West Virginia, the Ku Klux Klan warned teachers to leave.

Much of the South's opposition to public education for Negroes arose because of the frequently substantiated belief that the schools were also political centers, and of shortcomings in the Bureau and the religious organizations themselves. Too many of the teachers were ill-trained or were more interested in making the Negroes politically conscious than in teaching them the three R's. Sometimes illiterate Negro politicians sat on school boards and parceled out teaching jobs to illiterate or semi-literate black constituents, relying on conniving Freedmen's Bureau clerks to correct or sometimes even to prepare the teachers' progress reports. Too much attention was paid to classical education among a people who needed vocational training.

The white South jibed that instead of teaching the three R's the teachers in the Negro schools were instructing their pupils only in the three P's: Politics, the Pulpit, and the Penitentiary. School graft flourished. In North Carolina only $38,900 out of $138,000 intended for the public schools was turned over to the schools. In Louisiana, in 1872, the Radicals used the proceeds of the sale of a million dollars in state bonds, intended for the state schools, to pay the expenses of the legislature.

But the school programs failed principally because of the white South's opposition during Reconstruction to the education of the Negro by Northerners, or, for that matter, by anyone. Here and there Southern leaders more visionary or more realistic than others did espouse mass education for the Negro while urging that the task be given to white Southerners. South Carolina's Wade Hampton established a Negro schoolhouse on his plantation soon after the war, and a vocal minority of churchmen and a few politicians insisted unsuccessfully that the entire South should follow suit. But although eventually nearly half of the teachers employed by the Freedmen's Bureau were native whites—many of them widows of Confederate soldiers and some of them former Confederate soldiers themselves—the general Southern contempt was destructively lasting.

Retaliation against the Yankee teachers suspected of advocating "social equality" or political activity was sure. Ostracism by the white community was the least punishment that could be expected. Some teachers who were refused board and lodgings in white homes, and some others by choice, lived with Negro families; some women teachers as well as men were driven from the communities in which they taught; a few were mauled. Suspect male teachers were horsewhipped, even murdered. Night riders burned isolated Negro schoolhouses.

Much of the white South's animosity arose from the widespread conviction that the Radicals intended to integrate the public schools, and Reconstruction administrations did attempt to do so in Florida, Mississippi, South Carolina, and Louisiana. They failed because of adamant white opposition that was not confined to the anti-Republican native whites. When Benjamin Butler introduced in Congress in 1875, as an amendment to the Civil Rights Bill, a proposal to force all Southern children to go to school together, Barnas Sears, the New Englander who was a devoted postwar friend of the South and of education, warned President Grant that if such integration were made mandatory, the South's public school systems would be wrecked. At Grant's insistence the amendment was stricken from the bill.

There was another reason for the initial failure of mass Negro education. Perhaps because the freed Negro was a realist of sorts who, after a fling at it, was unable to see how education would do him any good in the cotton field to which he seemed irrevocably shackled, many did not continue after the novelty of the once forbidden fruit had worn off to respond to such educational opportunities as were offered. Not one Southern Negro child in ten attended school in 1870. There would not have been schools for all of them then had they all tried, but there were accommodations of a sort for all who did try, and more. In 1880 more than seventy-five Negroes in every hundred were still illiterate as against ninety-seven in a hundred in 1865.

By 1871 many of the benevolent societies were losing interest in the secondary education of the Southern Negro. All their efforts and all their money had seemed to make little dent on the problem. Moreover, the constitutions of the Southern states, adopted under Radical direction, now called for equal educational opportunities for Negroes at state expense. The Bureau's educational work, which was to be continued only until such educational equality was assumed, had been discontinued. Hopeful that the states would now carry on, the societies turned to other interests.

In 1883 the minutes of the historically pro-Unionist, anti-slavery Holston Conference of the Methodist Church in Tennessee contained one revealing section:

"Whatever aid may be rendered in the near future by the General Government in favor of general education, it cannot at present take the place of the Freedmen's Aid Society. Though it now has 25 institutions of learning among the freedmen—seven chartered, four theological, one medical and fourteen of lower grade—and though it has sixteen schools among the whites which are doing college and seminary work in the same field, the work of this society is but in its infancy. The schools among the freedmen now enroll about 4000 students and 100 teachers. . . . While it is yet true that the freedmen are beginning to help themselves nobly, yet, instead of one hundred thousand dollars, the Freedmen's Aid Society ought to have $250,000 annually to spend in this field. . . . Illiteracy almost all over the South is on the increase, and without more money, the Freedmen's Aid Society cannot equal the work entrusted to it. . . ."

Still available to the cause of Negro education was the Peabody Fund, established to assist both white and Negro education, and administered by the Reverend Barnas Sears. And in 1882 the John F. Slater Fund, the first great permanent fund devoted exclusively to Negro education, was established, to be followed in 1888 by Daniel Hand's million-dollar grant to the American Missionary Association for the same purpose.

With the rout of Radicalism in the South and the ascendancy of the white Conservatives came the near-nullification of the principle and practice of public education for Negroes and the serious crippling of public school education for white children. The economy-minded Redemptionist administrations, motivated in part by the negative Bourbon philosophy regarding mass education and greatly by a general clamor for retrenchment, reduced public educational facilities to the barest of essentials. Their legislatures cut the expenditures for white and Negro education to such an extent that the South would suffer for more than a half century to come.

Virginia's reaction against public education was the most extreme in the South. By 1878 her schools were owed more than a million dollars of their share of tax monies; yet, though the state school commissioner warned that half of the schools could not open in the fall if these funds were not forthcoming, the state auditor refused to honor a legislative act requiring him to pay the amount in cash.

"The state's obligation to its bondholders has precedence," he said.

Leading Virginians declared flatly that it would be better for the state to burn its schools than to readjust its debt upward. Governor F. W. M. Holliday described public schools as a "luxury . . . to be paid for like any other luxury, by the people who wish their benefits"; and a Virginia editor, who was also counsel for protesting bondholders, described free education above the elementary rudiments as a "system imported here by a gang of Carpetbaggers," denounced taxation for the support of public schools as a product of socialist doctrine, and advocated free education for pauper children alone.

To a somewhat less extent the attitudes of other Redemptionist administrations in respect to the Radical educational programs were strikingly uniform. The schools of Mississippi, Alabama, Louisiana, Arkansas, Florida, Texas, and Tennessee were badly crippled by retrenchment policies and by persistently depressed conditions of the agricultural South. During the 1880s the average school term fell off by 20 per cent, and the hundred-days-a-year term, the highest average attained under Radical Reconstruction, was not again achieved until well after 1900. The New Orleans *Times-Democrat* was moved in August of 1890 to protest that "there is an illiterate majority today whereas there was none in 1880" and that "this illiteracy prevails not only among the Negroes alone but among the whites as well." During that decade twenty-five white Southerners in a hundred were illiterate.

The unpleasant prospect of increased taxation for universal public education of the white and Negro child made popular a repeatedly proposed solution—and one that would sound strange coming from Southern politicians today—a program of federal aid for education in the South. Its Southern advocates' argument ran that the provisions in the constitutions of the Southern states for free, universal education were not the South's doing but the nation's, since these provisions had been adopted only after the enfranchisement of the Negro and the domination of the South by an alien coalition. Therefore public education in the South was at least partly the nation's own responsibility.

Not all of the proponents of federal aid were Southerners. In 1883 Senator Henry W. Blair, a visionary New Hampshire humanitarian, introduced a bill providing for ten annual appropriations for public school education, beginning with $15,000,000 and diminishing by $1,000,000 each year, the money to be used among the states in proportion to their illiteracy rates. On this basis the South would have received $11,000,000 of the first $15,000,000.

At the time a huge surplus rested in the Treasury, principally because of revenues derived from the protective tariffs that so greatly handicapped the agricultural South. A considerable number of Southern congressmen balked at the proposals; if the South supported the measure, they argued, she would appear to be approving the high tariffs which had provided the surplus.

The Blair bill, in a variety of forms, was voted upon repeatedly in the Senate, but it never reached a vote in the House of Representatives. On the first Senate vote, in 1884, and on each subsequent vote for the next decade, more than half of the South's senators approved federal aid to education. By 1886 the legislatures of ten Southern states had voted at least once in favor of the bill, some of them several times. The legislature of North Carolina petitioned four times for support of the bill, Louisiana's three times, and the Georgia, Virginia, and Mississippi legislatures twice each. The newspapers of the larger Southern cities almost unanimously supported the measure.

Most of the Southern leaders who favored federal aid were the conservative allies in business and industrial development. They were animated principally by the hope of lower taxes; in the lower South, especially, where the proportion of Negroes was highest, the Blair bill was regarded as the only answer to the vexatious problem of financing the education of the illiterate masses. The agrarian-minded, states'-rights Southerners, on the other hand, argued that it was unconstitutional to spend federal money on schools; that such a proposal undermined the division of powers between federal and state governments; that the inevitable result would be a nationalized system of education; and that Congress should not commit itself to what might mean higher federal taxes when the tariff surplus was spent. Only one senator, James B. Beck of Kentucky, raised the question as to whether federal domination might mean mixed schools.

In 1886, when the treasury surplus had melted away and the danger of tariff reform was over, the Republicans dropped the Blair bill. Its elimination was further and unnecessary proof that the North had abandoned its efforts to rehabilitate the Negro.

However, one source of federal aid was not eliminated with the end of Reconstruction: the funds available to the states from the Land-Grant Act, sponsored by scholarly, self-educated Senator Justin Smith Morrill of Vermont and passed in 1862. The original bill did not require that the funds derived from the sale of public lands for the benefit of agricultural and mechanical arts colleges be divided between white and Negro colleges, since Negro colleges were nonexistent, but a second act made such allocations mandatory. Acting under the first bill, the Radical Reconstruction legislatures in Mississippi, Virginia, and South Carolina set aside funds for Negro land-grant colleges. Mississippi gave the larger part of the $188,928 it received to newly established Alcorn University, a Negro college. Virginia divided $285,000 among the white and Negro institutions which it designated as its land-grant colleges; and in South Carolina the Radical legislature turned over the entire proceeds to the Freedmen's Aid Society's Claflin College.

The sponsors and the teachers failed to make the Southern Negro masses literate. The real and permanent educational achievements under Radical Reconstruction were the establishment of the principles of taxation for public education and of public education regardless of race, and the founding of Negro institutions of higher learning.

In the field of higher education their accomplishments would be notable and lasting. Many of the "colleges" founded in the immediate postwar years were really elementary schools; but most of them grew to be, in fact, colleges worthy of the name rather than classrooms where the students first had to learn the alphabet.

In all the slave states, prior to the war, there had been only one institution of higher learning open to Negroes, Berea, in Kentucky, founded in 1855 under the auspices of the American Missionary Association, with the motto, "God has made of one blood all the nations of men." Because its founder, the Reverend John Gregg Fee, encouraged John Brown to raid Harper's Ferry, faculty and students of the integrated college had to flee from irate neighbors and take sanctuary across the Ohio River. Rechartered after the war, Berea continued to enroll Negro as well as white students until the state legislature prohibited such mingling of the races in 1904.

The establishment of Negro colleges followed fast the end of the war.

The Freedmen's Bureau reported in July 1867 that Howard University had been chartered and opened in Washington, that Fisk was in operation in an old military hospital in Nashville, and that classes were being taught at the Methodist Episcopal Church's Central Tennessee College in an abandoned gun factory in Nashville. The report also said that the troops of the Negro Sixty-second and Sixty-fifth regiments had collected $6325 to help open Lincoln Institute at Jefferson City, Missouri, and that in Raleigh, North Carolina, the Episcopalian St. Augustine's Normal and Collegiate Institute had been incorporated and $50,000 raised in its behalf. Other colleges and normals were in process of development.

Six months later another report revealed the chartering of the National Theological Institute and St. Martin's School in Washington; a normal school in Richmond; Wesleyan College in east Tennessee; Storer College at Harper's Ferry, West Virginia; Atlanta University; Robert College on Lookout Mountain, Tennessee; Marysville College in Tennessee; St. Bridgit's

Parochial School in Pittsburgh; and high schools and normal schools in Alabama and South Carolina. The amount granted these institutions by the Bureau was $168,000.

By 1870 the American Missionary Association had under its patronage Fisk, Atlanta University, and Talladega College in Alabama, as well as the rechartered Berea.

No freedmen's institution so captured the imagination of the American public—and even of Europeans—as did Fisk University, whose Jubilee Singers first won in the early '70s admiration for themselves and, for Fisk University, financial support from the new world and the old with their haunting rendition of slave spirituals.

The American Missionary Association had founded Fisk in 1866 in Nashville as a high school, named for General Clinton B. Fisk, a thirty-eight-year-old, self-educated Michigan man who had risen from private to general during the war and who became, at its close, assistant commissioner of the Freedmen's Bureau in Kentucky and Tennessee. On January 9, 1866, the Fisk School was formally dedicated before an audience of several thousand, most of them Negroes, with Governor Brownlow, General Fisk, and other Republican dignitaries taking part in the ceremonies. Brownlow warned the small faculty of Northern white men and women and the prospective students and their supporters not to antagonize the whites of Nashville, for so many of them were already opposed to education of the Negroes.

The school was first housed in abandoned federal hospital buildings, and instruction was offered to an initial student body of one thousand, most of them Nashville residents and none of them advanced beyond the fifth reader, elementary grammar, and rudimentary arithmetic.

In 1867, after Nashville had opened two free public schools for Negro children, Fisk School raised its status to that of academy and normal school before securing a charter as Fisk University; and, thus legally qualified to receive Freedmen's Bureau funds, it set as its goal the "power to confer all such degrees and honors as are conferred by universities of the United States."

Between goal and reality yawned what must have seemed an unbridgeable chasm. Freedmen's Bureau aid was insufficient for the school's needs. To raise money for spellers and Bibles, students sold, for scrap, rusty handcuffs and fetters gathered from Nashville's onetime slave pens.

But the nation knew little and the world nothing of Fisk until George L. White, business manager and music teacher in the university, began pondering how to raise money to buy musical instruments. White was a New York village blacksmith's son, of limited formal education; self-taught after fourteen, he became a teacher of music before the war, served in the Union Army, and at the war's end became an employee of the Freedmen's Bureau in Nashville. Fisk's first principal, John Ogden, asked White to teach music in the little school. The choice was fortunate, not only because White was a splendid teacher, but because the understanding between him and his young black pupils was immediate and complete.

George White finally hit upon a way to raise a little money. He took a small Fisk chorus, experimentally, on a concert tour of nearby towns and in Nashville. The singers were enthusiastically received. In October 1871 Fisk's original troupe of Jubilee Singers began a tour of the nation.

Ella Shepherd, the student accompanist, would relate one day how the singers began: "Taking every cent he had, all the school treasury could spare and all he could borrow, Mr. White started in God's strength, October 6, 1871, to sing the money out of the hearts and pockets of the people."

The money didn't come easy. Their first paid concert, at Chillicothe, Ohio, brought the singers less than fifty dollars, and this they contributed to a fund for victims of the Chicago fire. A week later the singers canceled another Ohio concert because only twenty people turned up. On they went, singing for the most part familiar songs by white composers, and only now and then presenting old slave songs. At a religious conference at Oberlin, Ohio, where they were reluctantly permitted to perform, they opened with the haunting "Steal away . . . steal away . . . steal away to Jesus." The conference delegates were spellbound; from then on the Jubilee Singers rarely rendered anything but the spirituals.

Not until they reached New York did they begin to earn enough to more than barely make ends meet. There they were welcomed in the homes of members of the American Missionary Association. Henry Ward Beecher and other New York ministers drummed up large audiences. Money for Fisk began to come in. In New England not only cash but furniture, silver, gas fixtures for unbuilt buildings, a school bell which resounds today over the Fisk campus were contributed. The singers earned $3900 in one week in Connecticut. Before they returned to Nashville they sang "Go Down, Moses" for President Grant at the White House. And when they returned to Nashville they brought $20,000 for the university.

This was but the beginning. Twice in the next two years the Jubilee Singers triumphantly toured Europe, performing before Queen Victoria, the Crown Princess of Germany, Prime Minister Gladstone, and the Czarina of Russia, before tenement children and hospital patients and prisoners, before the most demanding of Europe's music critics. The $150,000 they brought back from Europe meant that Fisk would become what it is today, truly a university. And the Jubilee Singers of Fisk have been singing the spirituals of the days of Negro bondage ever since.

The charter for Atlanta University was obtained in October 1867, and a board of trustees was appointed. The college bought sixty acres of high land in Atlanta and completed its first building by September 1869—a "substantial, four-storied brick building, nearly furnished and contains parlors, dining rooms, kitchen, bathrooms, and dormitories for forty lady pupils." A dormitory for sixty men was completed in August 1870 with Bureau aid.

In eastern Alabama a building which had housed a select school for white boys became Talladega College. The Freedmen's Bureau contributed to the purchase of the building and thirty-four acres. The school was in the middle of nine Alabama counties that had no other school for colored children. The college opened in 1867 with three teachers and 140 students.

The counties sent their promising young Negroes from nearby communities, each bearing the bacon, corn, and other necessities he would need. The boys were lodged in nearby Negro cabins, most of them sleeping on the bare floors. After they had gone through the third grade they started teaching more recent arrivals, and during the summers the boys taught in their own communities what they had learned. No college course was offered at Talladega until 1890; the onetime slave carpenter who had helped construct the school building for white students lived to see three of his own children receive diplomas from the college.

No less significant than the work of the American Missionary Association was that of the Freedmen's Aid Society. By 1869 it had established fifty-eight grammar schools, six colleges and normal schools, two biblical institutes, and one orphan asylum. The colleges—at first by courtesy only—were Central Tennessee at Nashville, later called Walden University, Clark University at Atlanta, Claflin at Orangeburg, South Carolina, and Shaw University, now Rust College, at Holly Springs, Mississippi. By 1878 the Freedmen's Aid Society directed the New Orleans Medical College and Meharry Medical College at Nashville, originally the medical department of Central Tennessee College. From Meharry have graduated more than half of the Negro physicians and dentists now practicing in the United States.

The American Baptist Home Mission Society, which had worked among Southern Negroes soon after its founding in 1832, sent teaching missionaries into occupied Southern areas in 1862. By 1870 the Society had in operation Wayland Seminary in Washington, a school at Nashville, later to be named Roger Williams University, one at Raleigh, North Carolina, later Shaw University, one at New Orleans, later Leland College, and schools in Richmond, Virginia, St. Helena, South Carolina, and Augusta, Georgia.

The university most closely identified with the Freedmen's Bureau is that which bears the name of the man who became its first president.

Howard University grew out of the meeting of a small group of men in Washington's First Congregational Church in November 1866. Their intention was to found a college for the preparation of Negro ministers; but a committee deputized to study the needs of the city, whose population was then one-third Negro, recommended that a night school be opened first, with courses in two Bible subjects and in anatomy and physiology. The Freedmen's Bureau was asked to furnish quarters, fuel, and light. By the time Senator Henry Wilson of Massachusetts introduced the act of incorporation in the Senate, on January 23, 1867, the school's name had become "The Howard University." The act of incorporation provided for departments of theology, law, and medicine, and for university privileges.

The university's first location, in a former German dance hall and saloon, could only be temporary. General Howard and General E. Whittlesey, given the assignment of finding a permanent site, chose a location on part of a 150-acre farm on a good, raised elevation in the northern part of the city. The owner refused to sell a part unless he sold the whole. Fired by enthusiasm for the site and the college, General Howard succeeded in getting the board to agree to buy the whole farm, for $147,500, though the members did not know how the money could be raised for such a large purchase.

General Howard transferred $30,000 of Freedmen's Bureau money to the university for the first payment on the land; by 1870 enough lots had been sold to raise $172,000, leaving still four blocks for the use of the college. During its lifetime the Bureau helped Howard University to the extent of some $500,000.

The white South looked mostly with suspicion on such colleges. Entirely different was the attitude toward Hampton Institute, one of the very earliest schools to be established under the protection of the federal soldiers.

In 1861, when Ben Butler was in command of Fortress Monroe, he had declared all slaves "contraband of war," since they could be used by the South in prosecuting the war against the North. Thousands of these Negroes flocked into the vicinity of the fort. In September of that year the American Missionary Association began the first of the "contraband schools" at Hampton, Virginia, near the fort. Five years later, when General Samuel C. Armstrong was placed in charge of the Freedmen's Bureau in that area, he recommended expansion of the Hampton school's program. Two years later Hampton Institute was founded with General Armstrong as its principal and on its permanent site, the Whipple Farm, which he had recommended that the AMA should buy.

General Armstrong, the son of New England missionaries, had been born in Hawaii and educated at Williams College. His educational theories were based on his knowledge of the Hilo Manual Labor School, where the boys did the farm work and the girls the housekeeping, and where both also attended regular classes. Hampton Institute, as it developed under General Armstrong, was dedicated to the industrial arts and teacher training. Not until the 1920s would it give academic degrees.

Hampton was selected as Virginia's land-grant college for Negroes and became the model for the Negro land-grant colleges of the nation. Its influence was further heightened through its illustrious graduate, Booker T. Washington, who continued its policies at Tuskegee Institute. Strong support for this kind of educational institution for Negroes was to continue long after most other assistance from the benevolent societies had disappeared. Hampton Institute was destined to become the most highly endowed school for Negroes in the world.

The white Southerner gave his approval to industrial education while continuing for many years to look askance at classical education for Negroes. And Negro education in general—primary, secondary, and college—would remain suspect to many whites and be crippled by that suspicion and the discriminations it brought about for generations after the principle of separate but equal school systems had been adopted—and ignored—by every Southern state.

CHAPTER 7

The Uses of Violence

The six young Confederate veterans who lounged around the fireplace of Judge Thomas M. Jones's law office in Pulaski that evening in late December 1865 were bored and impatient with life in the sleepy middle-Tennessee community. They wanted to have some fun and maybe a little excitement. One of them came up with the suggestion that they organize a secret society.

The young men talked the suggestion over for a while and decided to meet in the judge's cozy office again the next evening. At the second meeting they went so far as to elect a chairman and a secretary and divided themselves into committees to write an initiation ritual, to formulate rules for the society, and to select its name. Having accomplished this much, Captain John C. Lester, Captain John C. Kennedy, Captain James R. Crowe, Frank O. McCord, Richard R. Reed, and J. Calvin Jones, the judge's son, went home.

The third meeting was held in the residence of a Colonel Thomas Martin, who had asked Captain Kennedy to stay there while he was on a trip. Too many thieving Negroes were abroad to leave a house empty. Quickly enough, they agreed at the third session upon everything but a name. The committee charged with that responsibility had been unable to agree. They would call their meeting place the "Den," and the den's leader would be known as the Grand Cyclops, his first assistant the Grand Magi, the secretary the Grand Scribe, the greeter of initiates the Grand Turk, the Den's two guards the Lictors, and his two messengers the Night Hawks. Non-office-holding members would be known as Ghouls.

Richard Reed, who must have been something of a student of Greek, finally came up with an acceptable suggestion for the club's name: Kuklos, from the Greek word from which the English "circle" is derived. Captain Kennedy suggested adding the word "Klan," and before the evening was over the name had become, for the sake of alliteration, Ku Klux Klan.

The young men must have been pleased with themselves. The Ku Klux Klan might put some life into old Pulaski yet.

The adoption of grotesque Halloween disguises came a little later and as innocently. To celebrate the founding of the society the young men wrapped themselves in sheets and went galloping about Pulaski. As they gallivanted they laughed at the way the home folks stared after them and at the fright of the Negroes upon whom they chanced. Most of the superstitious freedmen took to their heels. And perhaps the Klansmen chased a few of them down country byways just to "teach them a lesson." From that first sally each member was required to wear a long, ghostly robe, together with a mask and cardboard headdress so high it looked like an upturned churn.

No one would have laughed more derisively than the founders themselves had a soothsayer predicted that this creation of a few idle evenings would come to symbolize the South's determination to resist Radical Reconstruction, to keep unruly and lawless Negroes in line, and to negate through terror the South's political domination of the Northern adventurers and their white and Negro allies. But none of them would likely have opposed resort to violence whenever a man's honor, the protection of his family, or the retention of self-government in the hands of themselves and their fellow Southern whites were involved.

This willingness the architects of Reconstruction surely must have known, for the South had demonstrated her unique regional militancy from the Republic's very beginnings; environment, and the tradition which environment creates, had been producing in the South throughout the nineteenth century the closest approximation of a warrior caste that the nation would ever see. The South was the land of the "paterollers," the organized posses whose especial function was to keep the Negro slave on the plantation, to run him down if he escaped, and to subdue him should he revolt. The South was a frontier land, and its men had been taught early to draw a bead, to grip the saddle, to find joy in the turkey shoot, the coon hunt, the flushed covey, and the trailing of the bear.

These were a people animated by a deadly exaggeration of what is required of an honorable man, more ready than were most others in the nation to level the dueling pistol or—and far more frequently—to forget the niceties of the duello, if they ever knew them, and to avenge themselves with the hunter's knife or the gouging thumb or the surprise shotgun blast. The South loved all that was martial—her militia units, by the hundreds, the Fencibles, the Washington Artillery, the Clarendon Horse Guards, the White Plume Riflemen, the Lafayette Guards—parading and frolicking and entertaining admiring young ladies upon parade grounds and in armories from Virginia to Texas; her military academies and institutes and colleges, so disproportionate to her other educational institutions and to those of the nation, and more proficient in teaching the manual of arms than the classics; the defiant gasconades of her fire-eating orators and her hell-for-leather journalists, who defied, with a braggadocio that was almost tribally ritualistic, the moneygrubbing Yankees who were afraid to fight; her hosts of volunteers for the liberation of Texas or the conquest of Latin lands south of the border where, so her dreamers of slave-based empire foresaw, waited glory and the fulfillment of destiny.

In the fullness of time the martial men of the South fought and lost the war that they had entered upon because, aside from issues that were very real, they were spoiling for a fight. They limped home from battle physically chastised but in spirit unrepentant; and it was inevitable that they would meet the new political and social challengers of their order in the old manner from which war had not fully discouraged them.

This is the heady folk tale. The Carpetbaggers and Scalawags and Negroes united to destroy our way of life. The South's men united to preserve it. The Ku Klux Klan became the principal instrument for its preservation, and it was these eerie horsemen of the night who drove the enemy to cover.

But resistance to the Radical Republicans did not begin with the Klan's transformation to an instrument of terror, nor did it end with the Klan's dissolution.

From the surrender most of the white South resisted the Radicals with any weapon and with any means at hand. Aside from the spate of white and Negro killings having nothing to do with the political shaping of the region, the Southern white man was almost always the aggressor. He generally acted deliberately. Violence was a sure means of dissuading the Negro from voting, and so regain political mastery in those states and counties and communities where it had been lost to the Radicals and retain control where it had not been lost, and, through swift and terrible retaliation, to remind the freedmen of the consequences of lawless acts—murder, rapine, arson, assault—committed against a white person. Sometimes the white man struck as an individual or in the hasty concert of a mob inflamed and drawn together with little or no premeditation. Sometimes there raged, almost as spontaneously, naked race war, small, pitched battles in which, all but invariably, the Negro would be the loser. The Ku Klux Klan represented, for a while, a fairly cohesive force, its members protected by disguise and secrecy and having a semblance of region-wide organization. And, at the last, the white Conservatives threw aside the mask and came out into the open light of day and, in the states of North and South Carolina, Louisiana, and Mississippi, functioned as a disciplined soldiery who relied principally upon the threat of their presence but who would, and on occasion did, fight the Radicals who got in their way.

Whatever else the Negro gained from freedom, he lost in great degree the physical safety he had enjoyed as a slave. The Negro bondsman was valuable property; the owner who would kill off a thousand dollars had to be remarkably angry, or remarkably sadistic, or in peril of his own life. And as a deterrent to the brutal owner and to the poor white who lacked economic restraint and whose hatred could be murderous, state laws provided punishment for the abusers and maimers and slayers of slaves.

But when the Negro was no longer capital the story would be different, and soon.

Here is the tale of the former slave, Leonard Allen of Georgia, that reads like an allegory of racial ill will:

"I was scared of Marse Jordan, and all of the grown niggers was too, 'cept Leonard and Burrus Allen. Them niggers wasn't scared of nothing. If the devil hisself had come and shook a stick at them, they'd hit him back. Leonard was a big black buck nigger; he was the biggest nigger I ever seed. And Burrus was near 'bout as big. And they 'spised Marse Jordan worse'n pizen.

"I was sort of scared of Miss Sally too. When Marse Jordan wasn't round she was sweet and kine, but when he was round she was a yes-sir yes-sir woman. Everything he told her to do she done. He made her slap Mammy one time 'cause when she passed his coffee she spilled some in the saucer. Miss Sally hit Mammy easy, but Marse Jordan say: 'Hit her, Sally, hit the black bitch like she 'zerve to be hit.' Then Miss Sally draw back her hand and hit Mammy in the face, pow! then she went back to her place at the table and play like she eating her breakfast. Then when Marse Jordan leave, she come in the kitchen and put her arms round Mammy and cry, and Mammy pat her on the back, and she cry, too. I loved Miss Sally when Marse Jordan wasn't round.

"Marse Jordan's two sons went to the war; they went all dressed up in they fighting clothes. Young Marse Jordan was just like Miss Sally, but Marse Gregory was like Marse Jordan, even to the bully way he walk. Young Marse Jordan never come back from the war, but 'twould take more than a bullet to kill Marse Gregory. He too mean to die anyhow 'cause the devil didn't want him and the Lord wouldn't have him.

"One day Marse Gregory come home on a furlough. He think he look pretty with his sword clanking and his boots shining. He was a colonel, lieutenant, or something. He was strutting round the yard showing off, when Leonard Allen say under his breath, 'Look at that goddam soldier. He fighting to keep us niggers from being free.'

" 'Bout that time Marse Jordan come up. He look at Leonard and say, 'What you mumbling 'bout?'

"That big Leonard wasn't scared. He say, 'I say, "Look at that goddam soldier. He fighting to keep us niggers from being free." ' "

"Marse Jordan's face begun to swell. It turned so red that the blood near 'bout bust out. He turned to Pappy and told him to go and bring him his shotgun. When Pappy come back, Miss Sally come with him. The tears was streaming down her face. She run up to Marse Jordan and caught his arm. Old Marse flung her off and took the gun from Pappy. He leveled it on Leonard and told him to pull his shirt open. Leonard opened his shirt and stood there as a black giant, sneering at Old Marse.

"Then Miss Sally run up again and stood 'tween that gun and Leonard.

"Old Marse yell to Pappy and told him to take that woman out of the way, but nobody ain't moved to touch Miss Sally, and she didn't move neither; she just stood there facing Old Marse. Then Old Marse let down the gun. He reached over and slapped Miss Sally down, then picked up the gun and shot a hole in Leonard's chest big as you fist. Then he took up Miss Sally and toted her in the house. But I was so scared that I run and hid in the stable loft, and even with my eyes shut I could see Leonard laying on the ground with that bloody hole in his chest and that sneer on his black mouth."

What inflamed men would do alone would be done more readily by the tens and the hundreds. There were Negroes who also killed, and Negro ravishers and arsonists and grudge bearers and thieves and "plain uppity" Negroes, and the offenses they committed and the white man's retaliation had nothing or almost nothing to do with political Reconstruction; and long after the end of Reconstruction the lynch mob would remain an almost exclusively Southern phenomenon. No lynching records were kept before 1882, or any listings of the causes for the lynchings; but it is unlikely that there were fewer Negroes lynched between 1865 and 1885 than the nearly two thousand in the twenty years after 1885, certainly no fewer than the lynchings that continued in shameful numbers well into the twentieth century, until a combination of forces and events—the challenge of Southern women, of Southern churches, and of Southern editors, and the slow emergence of state and county and local police capable of and willing to thwart a mob, together with the pressures of national public opinion—would reduce to the nonsymptomatic and near-vanishing point the most bestial of all manifestations of racial animosities.

Lynchings and spasmodic race rioting, of which the New Orleans riot was the bloodiest, marked the earlier days of the Reconstruction period. The pitched battles came later. They were fortunately infrequent but they were usually characterized by unsparing ferocity and by outright racial divisions. In a savage race riot in Vicksburg white Union veterans joined forces with the Southern whites in a battle in which forty Negroes were killed. Three hundred armed Negroes who sought to invade the little town of Camilla, Georgia, were repulsed with high losses. Scores of Negroes died in riots in Jackson County, Florida, and in Eufaula, Alabama.

Among all such affairs one stands out for its no-quarter quality, the strength and discipline shown by the Knights of the White Camellia—the Louisiana counterpart of the Ku Klux Klan—and the significance of a United States Supreme Court decision in the case of nine white men arrested for murder in the wake of the riot. This was the Colfax riot of April 1873 in Grant Parish, Louisiana.

A more unlikely setting for a historic episode could scarcely be imagined. There was a fantastic irony in the very name of the town and the parish. On the petition of a number of white citizens, well after the war, a Radical legislature had carved Grant Parish from two adjoining parishes in north-central Louisiana, Rapides and Winn, whose whites were mostly small farmers of Anglo-Saxon and Scotch-Irish descent. The new parish was thereupon named for the President and the parish seat for Vice-president Colfax.

In April 1873 Colfax was still a hamlet, made up of less than a hundred dwelling houses, two or three stores, and the former stable of William Calhoun, a brick structure which had been converted into a courthouse. Calhoun, a Scalawag in good standing with the state legislature, desiring that his farm be made the site of the parish seat, had cut the signers' names from the original petition, which asked another location, and affixed them to a document of his forging.

The events leading up to the Colfax battle give vivid testimony to the political near-anarchy in Louisiana in the days of the Radical strangle hold. The two opposing candidates in the gubernatorial election of 1872 had alike claimed victory. One of them was John McEnery, the native-born candidate of the Fusion party, a coalition of Louisiana white Conservatives and the supporters of the Liberal Republican party which in May in Cincinnati had nominated, in opposition to President Grant's candidacy for re-election, Horace Greeley.

Louisiana's Radical Republican nominee was William Pitt Kellogg, a Vermont-born lawyer who had been an organizer of the Republican party of Illinois in 1856, a presidential elector on the Lincoln ticket, and Lincoln's appointee in March 1861 as Chief Justice of the Nebraska territory, a post from which he resigned at the war's outbreak to raise a regiment of Illinois cavalry. In one of his last official acts Lincoln had commissioned Kellogg collector of the port of New Orleans, an enviable launching ground for a career as a Carpetbagger politician. He was elected to the United States Senate by the Louisiana legislature in 1868, and in 1872 the Radical Republicans nominated him for the governorship, with C. B. Antoine, a Louisiana Negro of part-French antecedents, as his running mate.

Two rival returning boards canvassed the ballots, two rival legislatures met, and the two "governors" were inaugurated at separate capitols. Kellogg's ally, United States District Judge E. H. Durell, issued a midnight writ ordering the United States marshal in New Orleans to take possession of the Mechanics Institute, of bloody memory, which was used now as the temporary Statehouse, to prevent the "unlawful assemblage" of the legislature elected on the McEnery ticket. For three weeks United States troops held the Statehouse, admitting only Kellogg legislators and other officials. The McEnery legislature held its meetings in the New Orleans City Hall.

The contest was carried to Washington. When Congress refused to decide President Grant recognized Kellogg as Louisiana's governor. For four years Louisiana would have a *de facto* and a *de jure* governor; the farce would end only after an uprising of the whites of New Orleans and the ensuing compromise which would restore self-government to the three Southern states still under Carpetbag rule in 1876 and make Republican Rutherford B. Hayes President of the United States.

But all that lay far ahead of an Easter Sunday morning in 1873.

Four months earlier "Governor" McEnery had commissioned two Fusionist supporters in Grant Parish, Alphonse Cazabat and Christopher Columbus Nash, respectively parish judge and sheriff. The two men assumed their duties without interference. The following March two leading Conservatives of Grant Parish went to New Orleans and there importuned Governor Kellogg, now firmly lodged in the Statehouse, to issue his own commissions to Cazabat and Nash. Kellogg did issue Sheriff Nash's commission, and the appointment was duly announced in the party's official organ, the New Orleans *Republican*. Very soon thereafter Kellogg commissioned two of his own followers, R. C. Register and Daniel Shaw, as judge and sheriff of Grant Parish.

On March 23 four Kellogg men turned up in Colfax: his tax collector, a man named Brantley; his clerk, Railey; a Pennsylvania Negro named Flowers, and a Negro representative in the Kellogg legislature, Captain William Ward, who had formerly been an officer in a Negro militia company in Grant Parish. Register and Shaw uncertainly presented themselves at the courthouse and, to quote from a committee report to the Forty-third Congress on conditions in the South, "that night for reasons best known to themselves, they began to summon armed Negroes into Colfax."

Between March 23 and April 13 from 150 to 400 armed Negroes—the estimates vary greatly—gathered in Colfax undoubtedly to protect the harried Register and Shaw and to repel any attempt by the white Fusionists to take over the courthouse. It must be remembered that most of the whites of the area, as well as most of the Negroes, did not live in Colfax but in the countryside. The principal concentration of whites was in tiny Montgomery, twelve miles north of Colfax; only a quarter of a mile from Colfax was Smithfield Quarters, an all-Negro settlement. Report Number 261 of the House Committee on Conditions of the South, 1874–1875, graphically described their countermeasures:

> . . . Three captains were elected, and lieutenants, sergeants and corporals were appointed; men were regularly enrolled. The Negroes were armed with shotguns and Enfield rifles, and seizing upon an old steam pipe they cut it up, and by plugging one end of each piece and drilling vents, they improvised and mounted three cannons. They constructed a line of earthworks some 300 yards in length and from 2½ to 4 feet high. Drilling was regularly kept up by Ward, Flowers and Levi Allen, all of whom had been soldiers of the United States army. Guards were mounted and pickets posted, while mounted squads scouted the neighboring country. No white citizens were permitted to pass into Colfax.
>
> Meanwhile the white citizens of Grant parish had invited the Negroes to a mass meeting, set for April 1 in Colfax, to discuss a settlement. Accordingly, some 15 residents of Montgomery, unarmed as instructed by their fellow citizens, did proceed to Colfax but were turned away by the angry, arms-brandishing Negroes . . . which might have averted the slaughter that would follow, never took place. On April 5 several armed white men on horseback rode to the outskirts of Colfax and exchanged fire with the estimated 200 Negroes holding the town. In a letter to a friend written the next day, the Negro captain Ward wrote: "I am in command; I had a battle with the whites yesterday and repulsed them; one man was seen to fall, but got off. . . ."

Ward's letter ended with an appeal for Negroes to come to the assistance of his force "as the whites does."

Two days later a delegation of Montgomery whites and the Negroes in Colfax did meet; but during their deliberations news came that Jesse Kenney, an industrious Negro man and the father of several children, had been wantonly slain by some white vigilantes while he was building a fence. The meeting broke up angrily.

The senseless provocations continued. A Judge Rutland, a Grant Parish lawyer and politician, was informed by a friendly Negro of the decision of a Negro mob to kill him, pillage his house, and burn it. He and his family made it to the riverbank where they induced a ferryman and two other poor whites, although leaning to the Radical cause, to ferry them to the other side. From the far bank the judge and his family watched as the pillagers looted their personal belongings, drank themselves into a stupor on the wines in the judge's cellar, and put the torch to their home.

In other incidents a Negro postmaster was forced to close his office and remove the mails to safety; a house of a leading white citizen was fired upon; the life of another was threatened, and a third was "told by three rioters that they intended to go to the country and kill from the cradle to old age." Roving Negroes stole cattle and horses. Many white families fled deep into the woods for safety.

There is no doubt that Governor Kellogg knew, well before the battle, of the situation in Colfax. Judge Rutland made his way by steamboat to New Orleans, bearing a letter to the governor on the state of affairs in Grant Parish, written by Colonel R. A. Hunter, a distinguished resident of nearby Alexandria. On April 9 the judge had an audience with Kellogg and gave him the Hunter letter and a petition from the white citizens of Grant Parish. Kellogg sent Rutland to the office of the adjutant general, General James Longstreet, the onetime Confederate hero. Longstreet told Rutland that he would be willing to go to Colfax with twenty Metropolitan Police and apparently agreed to leave that very evening. But neither Longstreet nor any of his Negro police did embark then for Colfax. The governor had obviously changed his mind. Nor was Rutland able to get any promise of assistance from the commander of the Military Department, though he was received courteously enough.

Meanwhile, on April 8, Ward, Flowers, Register, and Brantley, the principal Radical troublemakers in Colfax, left the community and on April 10 arrived in New Orleans. On Saturday, April 12, the day before the open hostilities, two inspired articles appeared in Kellogg's *Republican*. Said one:

> But there is one thing apparent: the local majority of Grant Parish is prepared to clean out the local minority of Grant in 24 hours or less. In Grant Parish it seems there is a local majority of colored men, not only accustomed to the trade of war but equipped with arms of the most perfect character.

Read the other story in part:

> . . . The colored population seemed to have reached a heighth of exasperation and resolved to obtain a redress of the wrongs they had suffered or believed they had suffered, and not to disband until they had attained guarantees for the future.
>
> According to statements most worthy of belief they are well-armed, well-disciplined and confident of success. The provocation which has driven them to that attitude is not very clear. The Negroes, not even the field hands, are no longer the weak and simple creatures they were before the war. The years of freedom which they have enjoyed have had their effect on them, as well as the military education which many of them received in the United States

Army. The time has passed, if ever it existed, when a handful of whites could frighten a regiment of colored men.

The white men of Grant Parish had other ideas.

After the effort to hold a conciliatory mass meeting failed, Nash, the Fusion-elected sheriff, raised a posse, with headquarters at Summerfield Spring, four miles north of Colfax. The posse was soon strengthened by scores of volunteers from nearby parishes. About April 6 some of the posse-men, searching a steamer at Pineville, a few miles below Colfax, found, hiding in the hold, William Calhoun, the Scalawag whose farm had become the parish seat. They searched Calhoun and found in his boots a letter from Ward, the Negro militia captain, to Governor Kellogg, asking for aid. They turned Calhoun loose after making him swear that he would return to Colfax and try to persuade the Negroes to disband.

By Easter eve the white vigilantes numbered about 150 men, and on Easter Sunday morning they assembled in military formation under command of "Sheriff" Nash on the banks of Bayou Darro near Colfax. One of Nash's lieutenants took down the names of each man and, after telling them that all could probably be prosecuted for treason, asked those who were afraid to fight for white supremacy to step out of line. About twenty-five lukewarm volunteers took advantage of the offer.

The remaining members of the posse then advanced upon Smithfield Quarters, the Negro settlement near Colfax. Nash, accompanied by two of his possemen, rode into the settlement under a flag of truce. They persuaded a Negro man there to go to the Negro stronghold at the nearby courthouse and ask Levi Allen, one of the principal Negro leaders, to parley with the whites. Soon Allen rode out to meet them on a magnificent black horse, so a white participant would later recall, and waving a sword. Nash demanded of Allen that the Negroes surrender the courthouse and disband. In his ultimatum he gave the Negro women and children on the settlement, and all Negro men who did not intend to fight, two hours to quit the battle zone. Allen rode back to his men, who were waiting behind a newly constructed, crescent-shaped breastworks near the courthouse, or in the converted stable itself.

At about noon the whites prepared to attack dismounted. Every fifth posseman held horses, including his own, out of range. The rest of the force advanced first on Smithfield Quarters. The Negroes opened fire with their two makeshift cannon, without effect. The Quarters were occupied without loss of life. The whites then approached the breastworks in skirmish lines. As they approached Negroes stood up on the breastworks, cursing and daring them to come on, and desultory firing began. Soon the Negroes' cannon exploded. During the initial skirmishing some of the whites searched the deserted Smithfield Quarters, eating the food they found in the cleanest cabins. A few others engaged in a game of seven-up just out of range—or so they thought. One of them, W. Lod Tanner, would recall more than fifty years later: ". . . but it seems that there was a nigger up in the top of the [courthouse] building that had a long-range gun and he decided he would break up our little tea party, so he got to shooting at us. The first bullet struck back about fifteen feet from us, and we did not stop. The next one struck about three feet from us, and I says, 'Jim, I don't want to die at a card table, nor in a barroom. Let's quit.' He says, 'Suit yourself,' so we quit. The next thing we knew was, 'Let's go, boys.'"

It was now about two o'clock in the afternoon. The whites had decided upon their strategy. A detachment of some thirty men was to creep along the riverbank, out of sight of the Negroes, and flank the breastworks. The main body would maintain a steady fire upon the Negroes until Nash ordered a concerted charge. In a few minutes the flankers came up from the riverbank and began firing on the Negroes. A number of Negroes, among them Levi Allen, fled on horseback. About a hundred other Negroes retreated into the courthouse, as the whites, shrilling the Rebel yell, advanced on the breastworks. Shortly, and mysteriously, the courthouse roof burst into flames. Some participants said, years later, that a captured Negro was promised his life if he fired the shingled roof with a long torch, made of lashed bamboo poles and kerosene-soaked cotton. Some desperately courageous Negroes tried to knock off the burning shingles under the fire of the besiegers; but in a few minutes flags of truce were waved from several windows and the firing ceased. Thus far the whites had suffered one fatality. The casualties among the Negroes had been heavy.

Inside the burning courthouse the doomed Negroes debated what to do. Probably most of them, knowing their situation to be hopeless, wanted to surrender. A group of whites, among them Captain James Hadnot and Sidney Harris, approached the courthouse with the intention of coming to terms with the Negroes, so that they could quit the burning building and the structure itself could be saved from destruction. As they reached the main door, some Negroes opened fire and Hadnot and Harris fell mortally wounded in the doorway.

What followed was indiscriminate butchery. Many Negroes were shot down as they ran from the burning courthouse; others were ridden down in the open fields. Those who fell wounded in the courthouse square were bayoneted. When the firing ended, at about four o'clock, some forty Negroes remained alive, held prisoners by white men who apparently did not favor a general massacre and had rounded up the survivors and herded them in a garden surrounded by a picket fence. One prisoner didn't last out the afternoon. He was spotted by a white man who, certain that the Negro was the man who had killed his brother two years before, said, "I got you," grasped his coat, and led him about twenty paces away from the others and shot him.

By nightfall most of the more responsible whites had returned to their homes, leaving the Negroes under guard of younger men until they could be placed in jail in Alexandria. Many of those who remained had been drinking heavily all afternoon. When volunteers were asked to escort the captives to Alexandria, Luke Hadnot, brother of the slain man answered, "I can take five."

Five Negroes were ordered to step out. Hadnot opened fire, killing all of them. The rest of the prisoners broke and ran. Most of them were shot down.

The number of Negroes who were killed in the battle itself, died in the burning building, or were among those massacred in flight or as prisoners has been placed at from sixty-odd to three hundred. The families of the dead Negroes were given permission to bury them; but, terrorized by the slaughter, few came to carry away their dead. The unclaimed bodies were thrown into the trenches from which they had intended to defend the courthouse.

The next day the steamboat *Ozark* landed with a heavy detachment of Metropolitan Police from New Orleans. They were followed within the week by United States Regulars. Police and troops began rounding up suspected white participants. Most of the whites had scattered, some fleeing to Texas, others going into hiding nearer their homes. Sheriff Nash swam his horse across the Red River, untouched by the bullets of pursuing Metropolitan Police who fired at him from the bank.

The troops did round up nine white men. They were to become the principals in a very significant decision. Indicted on thirty-two counts each, which added up in essence to the general charge that they had conspired to imprison and murder Negroes and thereby hinder the freedmen in the exercise of rights and privileges granted under the Constitution, they were convicted in the Louisiana District's Federal Circuit Court. An appeal was taken to the United States Supreme Court in the name of William Cruikshank, one of the nine defendants. On March 27, 1876, the Court handed down, unanimously, a decision which the white South, by then almost completely free of Republican rule, and many citizens in the North would hail as a long overdue and positive statement of the rights of the individual states.

The Court's interpretation of the intent of the Fourteenth Amendment would be poles apart from decisions of another Supreme Court three quarters of a century later. There were, so said the Court in 1876, two separate and distinct kinds of citizenship, that of the United States and that of the states. Security against confinement and murder was not one of the rights appertaining to United States citizenship; the citizen must look for such protection not to the federal government but to the government of the state in which he lives. The United States had no more duty or right to punish a conspiracy within a state to imprison falsely or to murder than to punish for false imprisonment or murder itself, the Court found; the offenses for which the nine were charged were punishable only by the state of Louisiana, and the defendants must be released from federal custody. All that the Fourteenth Amendment had done, so said the Court in short, was to prevent the denial of the protection of the laws of the state to any citizen of that state; it had added nothing to the rights of citizenship under the Constitution.

As to what had happened in Colfax and why, the people could make up their minds from reading the majority and the minority reports of the congressional committee which reported to the second session of the Forty-third Congress. Five of the committeemen were Republicans, two were Democrats. In probable indication of the changing attitude in the North as to continued interference in Southern affairs, two of the five Republicans joined the two Democrats in finding for the majority that Kellogg had not been honestly elected, that he had seized the government through the aid of federal troops, and that all that was needed to restore peace in Louisiana was to withdraw the federal troops and thus permit the people to govern themselves. The majority report was a profound rebuke to the Grant administration. Nothing that the three-man minority could say about the "political massacres and barbarities" committed against Negro and white Republicans could change the course of public opinion.

The administration did gain a temporary victory, for, after tumultuous debate, Congress disregarded the majority report. Instead, both houses passed a resolution which recognized Kellogg as governor of Louisiana. But even that was to give but scant and short-lived comfort. In another year other Louisianians, not unorganized backwoods possemen but well disciplined, ably led, and splendidly armed, operating openly, would win in New Orleans a finish fight against Republicanism. The day of the White League was near.

Now to the early and sanguine flowering of the social club so preposterously organized by the young Tennessee skylarkers back in December 1865, the Ku Klux Klan, whose laughable mumbo jumbo and regalia were to become the fearsome trade-marks of the Invisible Empire of fact and legend.

The founders of the Klan, and the friends whom they soon took in as members, had been amused at the dread their sheeted appearance inspired among the superstitious Negroes in and around Pulaski, a fear which their first official meeting place, a storm-ruined "haunted house" on a hilltop just outside Pulaski, did not dispel. Soon, and inevitably, the Klansmen began paying nocturnal visits to the homes of lawless or politically troublesome Negroes to warn them of what might happen if they didn't behave and to impress them with the supernatural nature of the visitors. Such visitations were remarkably effective.

In a few months the Pulaski Klan, now a regulatory body, was initiating interested visitors from nearby counties and from sister states. The initiates returned home to form branches of their own; and a year from its origin Klaverns of an order no longer social were active throughout the deep South, to punish lawlessness and to discourage Negro and Carpetbagger and Scalawag from political activity.

It must not be supposed that there was any hard and fast relationship among the early dens. Their respective members gave nothing more than a token allegiance to the Pulaski fountainhead; rules, costumes, and local programs, if such they could be called, differed according to the decisions of the individual den's members, and no central direction existed. But every den early had in common the over-all purpose of discouraging and punishing objectionable Negroes and whites.

In every Southern state the order was the beneficiary of fantastic and effective publicity. Newspaper notices and handbills circulated extravagant proclamations awesomely decorated with skulls and bones, with moons and stars and coffins. Nor was this abundance of publicity to be unexpected, at least by the members, for almost invariably the editors of the local Democratic newspapers were Klansmen themselves. The fiery little Southern weeklies opened their columns to local Klan notices and reprinted such remarkable imprecations and threats as that one which, in an apparent play upon Thad Stevens's name, apostrophized him and the South's Negroes in a warning doggerel:

> *Thodika, stevika! Radical plan*
> *Must yield to the coming of the Ku Klux Klan.*
> *Niggers and leaguers get out of the way.*
> *We are born of the night and we vanish by day.*
> *No rations have we, but the flesh of man*
> *And love niggers best—the Ku Klux Klan.*
> *We catch them alive and roast them whole*
> *And hand them around with a sharpened pole.*
> *Whole leagues have been eaten, not leaving a man*
> *And went away hungry—the Ku Klux Klan;*
> *Born of the night and vanish by day,*
> *Leaguers and niggers, get out of the way!*

Yet publicity alone does not explain the rapid growth of the Klan. Southern white men who poured into the order by the tens of thousands felt that the organization was more than justified by the activities of the Negro Loyal Leagues. The relationship between the two was recognized as early as April 1868, when the New York *Herald* observed after General George Meade issued an order for the suppression of the Ku Klux:

The order of General Meade providing for the suppression of the Ku Klux Klan will meet with the approval of all who espouse the cause of order and good government. But the General must not exercise this power on that organization alone. He must rigorously suppress the secret "Loyal Leagues"; they are equally, if not more pernicious in their influence than the white men's society. The arrogance of the Negroes and their attempt to reduce the whites of the South to political vassalage by means of their "Loyal Leagues" and the many other outrages that have been committed by these same Leagues are equally as dangerous to the peace and safety of society as other retaliatory actions of the Ku Klux Klan.

Klan retaliation was at first fairly mild. Some Negroes and Radical Republicans escaped with warnings. Others were whipped and run out of the communities in which they were active. Only rarely, in the first year of the Ku Klux Klan, were the victims more severely treated. Of the mutilations and killings which were committed later by Klansmen or in the name of the Klan one of the founders would write: "The danger which the more prudent and thoughtful had apprehended as possible was now a reality. Rash, imprudent and bad men had gotten into the order and as such men began to get out of hand, the more cautious or law-abiding leaders decided to hold a convention in Nashville in the spring of 1867, soon after the passage by Congress of the drastic first Reconstruction Act."

All known dens were requested to send representatives to Nashville in April, the purposes of the unusual convention being "to reorganize the Klan on a plan corresponding to its size and present purposes; to bind the isolated dens together; to secure unity of purpose and concert of action; to hedge the members up by such limitations and regulations as are best adapted to restrain them within proper limits; to distribute the authority among prudent men at local centers and exact from them a close supervision of those under their charge."

The Nashville delegates occupied themselves principally with drawing up and approving a constitution or, in Ku Klux parlance, a Prescript. Its author was General George W. Gordon, a Pulaski attorney and former Confederate officer, and an early initiate into the Pulaski den. Later Pulaski printers who were members of the Klan would secretly print, at night, a number of small twenty-four-page pamphlets containing the Prescript.

The preamble of the Klan's constitution set forth that "We recognize our relations to the United States government and acknowledge the supremacy of its laws." It then listed the titles and duties of the officers—Grand Cyclops, Grand Magi, Grand Monk, Grand Exchequer, Grand Turk, Grand Scribe, Grand Sentinel, and Grand Ensign; provided for the election of officers and the functioning of a tribunal of justice; set forth sources of revenue—principally from fines, fees, and the sale of the Prescript for $10 a copy—and how such funds should be apportioned out to each den and to state and regional divisions.

The Prescript contained the oath and obligations for admission, which its members were to consider so binding that almost never did arrested Klansmen testify truthfully in federal court, and included a Register with ominous code words for the months, the days of the week, and the hours of the day for use in setting meeting dates. Classic Latin phrases scattered throughout the Prescript summed up the high purposes of the order, concluding after the final paragraph with "*Ad unum omnes*—one for all and all for one."

About a year later a revised and far more detailed Prescript replaced the original version. In neither was the Ku Klux Klan named; instead the order was identified only by three asterisks. It described the Ku Klux as "an institution of chivalry, humanity, mercy and patriotism" with these significant objectives:

First: to protect the weak, the innocent and the defenseless from the indignities, wrongs and outrages of the lawless, the violent and the brutal; to relieve the injured and oppressed; to succor the suffering and unfortunate, and especially the widows and orphans of Confederate soldiers.

Second: to protect and defend the Constitution of the United States, and all laws passed in conformity thereto, and to protect the States and the people thereof from all invasion from any source whatever.

Third: to aid and assist in the execution of all constitutional laws, and to protect the people from unlawful seizure and from trial except by their peers in conformity with the laws of the land.

The states making up the empire of the Ku Klux Klan were named. In addition to the eleven states of the former Confederacy, Klan territory also embraced Maryland, Missouri, and Kentucky. And for the first time the pertinent questions to be asked prospective candidates were set down:

First: Have you ever been rejected upon application for membership in the *** or have you ever been expelled from the same?

Second: Are you now, or have you ever been, a member of the Radical Republican party, or either of the organizations known as the "Loyal League" or the Grand Army of the Republic?

Third: Are you opposed to the principles and policy of the Radical party, and to the Loyal League, and the Grand Army of the Republic, so far as you are informed of the character and purposes of these organizations?

Fourth: Did you belong to the Federal Army during the late war, and fight against the South during the existence of the same?

Fifth: Are you opposed to Negro equality, both social and political?

Sixth: Are you in favor of a white man's government in this country?

Seventh: Are you in favor of Constitutional liberty, and a government of equitable laws instead of a government of violence and oppression?

Eighth: Are you in favor of maintaining the Constitutional rights of the South?

Ninth: Are you in favor of the re-enfranchisement and emancipation of the white man of the South, and the restitution to the Southern people of all their rights, alike proprietary, civil and political?

The Invisible Empire meant business.

In time the Ku Klux Klan degenerated, losing almost all semblance of orderly organization; and, inevitably, men who were not Klansmen gave the organization a desperate name by acts of lawlessness not authorized by any den. But at first the members of the dens, while acting outside the law as regulatory and punitive bodies, adhered to prescribed procedures before meting out punishment. A den council would decide upon the courses of action after members, in open meeting, named persons considered to be deserving of the Klan's unloving attention. If the council decreed that punishment was in order the mode of punishment was then agreed upon and members designated to inflict it.

For maximum secrecy and security the dens usually had more than one meeting place, where they gathered about once a week, to which entry was permitted only after identification through secret passwords, grips, and signs of recognition; these varied superficially from den to den, but they were enough alike to enable Klansmen from one community or state to obtain admission to the den of another.

As a further precaution the members attended their regular meetings in civilian attire, costuming themselves only for raids or other public or nocturnal appearances. The costumes themselves varied greatly. The young men of Pulaski originally wore white robes, actually sheets wrapped around their bodies and belted, with part of the sheet scissored for eyeholes and mouth holes. The basic costume was to have many adaptations. Klansmen wore black robes and red robes and striped robes. Some Klansmen wore horns for headdress, others narrow-peaked astrologers' hats. When out raiding Klansmen disguised their horses too, for these might be almost as easily recognized otherwise as an undisguised rider. On more ornate regalia shiny tin buttons profusely decorated the robe; silk scarves were wound about the waist, and the head was covered by a helmet-shaped black cap with a havelock shielding the neck and topped by a luxuriant plume, the color depending upon the rank of the wearer.

The North Carolina uniform, as described by Joseph W. Holden, the son of the Carpetbagger governor of that state at the height of the Klan-Radical Republican struggle, was unusually gaudy and terrifying.

The costume is a long red gown with loose flowing sleeves, with a hood in which the apertures for the eyes, nose and mouth are trimmed with some red material. The hood has three horns, made out of some common cotton-stuff, in shape something like candy-bag stuff, and wrapped with red strings, the horns standing out to the front-and sides of the hood. It is a large, loose gown, covering the whole person quite closely, buttoned close around and reaching from the head clear down to the floor, covering the feet and dragging on the ground. It is made of bleached linen, starched and ironed, and in the night by moonlight it glitters and rattles. Then there is a hood with holes cut in for eyes, and a nose six or eight inches long made of cotton cloth stuffed with cotton and lapped with red braid half an inch wide. The eyes are lined with the braid, and the eyebrows are made of the same. The cloth is lined with red flannel. Then there is a long tongue sticking out about six inches and so fixed that it can be moved about by the man's tongue. Then in the mouth are large teeth, which are very frightful. Then under the tongue is a leather bag placed inside so that when the man calls for water, he pours it inside the bag and not into his mouth at all.

Though the costumes differed from den to den and from state to state there was no such diversity in the conduct of the Klan before its degeneration. When out raiding or demonstrating the Klansmen maintained a silence which accentuated the unearthliness of their appearance; except when hailing each other, which they did only by numbers, what sounds they made were hideous moans or gibberish, or gurgling blasts from the whistles with which orders were given and summonses for aid sounded.

Most Klansmen everywhere at first contented themselves with macabre warnings to Negroes—"We boil Negroes' heads and make soup"—and warnings to Carpetbaggers to leave town or suffer the consequences. When their orders were disobeyed in the early days they rarely resorted to anything more than a severe flogging. In time the regulators resorted in extreme cases to torture, sexual mutilation, even execution—the foreseeable consequences of a finish fight with one side having the support of state and federal governments and the federal bayonets, and the other relying only upon the terror that could be struck in the hearts of the defiant Negro and Yankee or renegade Southern politician.

The Klan's excesses, and the barbarities committed by avengers who only pretended to be Klansmen, waxed as strong hands relinquished the guiding reins.

The strongest such hand was that of General Nathan Bedford Forrest of Tennessee and Mississippi, the legendary cavalry leader, the South's personification of Jehu, who, though he wisely declined to so incriminate himself before a congressional committee of investigation, was almost beyond any shadow of doubt the Grand Wizard of the Invisible Empire at the height of its disciplined power. When the light of battle flamed in his somber eyes Bedford Forrest needed no mask to frighten an adversary. He was forty-seven years old when he probably served as the Klan's Grand Wizard, a steel-muscled horseman, six feet one and a half inches tall, broad-shouldered, thick-chested, and symmetrical of limb. In his bearing and habit of command the handsome, dark-bearded Forrest was the very epitome of what he was not, namely, a born member of the South's planter aristocracy.

Not that his hell-for-leather riders or the Klansmen of Reconstruction or the aristocracy which looked to him for leadership cared whether he was a blue blood or not. What difference if Bedford Forrest was a blacksmith's son and lacking in formal education; that mostly through the ungentlemanly calling of slave dealer he had acquired enough capital to purchase plantations in Arkansas and Mississippi and so become rich? The Forrest they honored was the brilliant cavalry raider who had raised and equipped at his own expense a battalion for mounted service in the first six months of the war; the Forrest, in combat a reincarnate berserker, who had been wounded again and again, had twenty-nine horses shot out from under him, and who was ever to be found where no general should be, in the thick of the fighting. Yet he was a mild, considerate man, save when the battle passion was on him, austere in his personal habits, and a leader who in defeat could quietly tell his horsemen to return home and obey the laws of the nation which had bested them. Who better could inspire Southerners to last-ditch resistance against conditions they considered intolerable?

Assuming that he did in fact direct the night riders, no one knows how Forrest entered the Klan and became its Grand Wizard. One story has it that when Forrest heard of the organization he journeyed from his Memphis home to Nashville and there questioned Captain John W. Morton, his war-time chief of artillery. Morton, so the story goes, took the general driving in his buggy. After reaching the city's outskirts the two strolled through a wooded area. Once they were out of sight of the road Morton swore Forrest in as a Klan member. Another story has it that he was sworn in by General Gordon, the Pulaski attorney who drew up the original Prescript; but the more probable version is that Captain Morton made him a member.

Forrest had a way of turning up throughout Alabama and Tennessee and Georgia and elsewhere in the South just ahead of the establishment of new dens or outbreaks of Klan activity. Perhaps the best circumstantial evidence of his connection was given by Judge William T. Blackford of Greensboro, Alabama, a former Confederate soldier and a Scalawag, whom a Klan delegation had ordered to leave the state. Later Blackford testified that soon after the visitation "a Confederate general, a warm personal friend," visited him, offered his protection, and impressed him with the unwisdom of standing up to the Ku Klux Klan. The general, said Blackford, told him of the Klan's vast membership and some of its techniques—every Southern jury, the general said, for example, had at least one Klansman.

In his appearance before the congressional investigating committee which questioned him with little success about the Klan, Forrest himself made no bones about aiding Judge Blackford. Though he was something less than co-operative in most of his testimony, he readily revealed that Blackford had asked him for protection and that "I did protect him." The trouble with Blackford, Forrest went on, was that he had given bad advice to the Negroes, had allowed Negro political meetings at his house, had drunk heavily, and while drunk had indiscriminately discharged firearms and threatened his opponents. Forrest was at that time engaged in organizing the Memphis-Selma Railroad, and, as a leading Republican, Blackford was helpful. "I tried to excuse Blackford on the ground that he was drunk," Forrest said, adding bluntly, "I wanted the [railroad stock] subscriptions and tried to carry all the votes I could. I set out by saying railroads had no politics."

If Forrest did lead the Klan at the time of its only real cohesiveness, the available evidence indicates that he was also instrumental in its formal disbandment, probably sometime in 1869. Forrest himself told the congressional committee that he had suppressed the organization, but he failed singularly to recall whether the suppression was ordered early in 1868 or sometime that fall. He did issue what could be taken to be a disbandment order late in January 1869. The order directed all uniform and regalia to be destroyed, in a resolution which began, "Whereas, the order of the Ku Klux Klan is in some localities being perverted from its original honorable and patriotic purposes . . ." and forbade any further "demonstrations" unless a Grand Titan or higher officer authorized them.

Whatever orders were issued or when and by whom, Klan activities did not cease overnight. The Ku Klux was active, especially in the Carolinas, for at least two years after the Forrest edict; and undisciplined ruffians, prowling the countryside in disguise, gave to the Klan long after disbandment a far worse name than the original dens deserved.

If many of the regulatory actions of the Klansmen themselves were savage, the political struggle itself was merciless, the white Conservative's danger of virtual disfranchisement very real for a time, and the mood of the people desperate. The Klansmen—and their scattered counterparts: the Knights of the White Camellia, the Pale Faces, the Society of the White Rose, and numerous other lesser secret groups—killed when they thought killing was required, which was rather often, though not as often as the evidence gathered by the Radicals and Southern folklore alike would lead us to believe.

Naturally the Ku Klux Klan became the subject of congressional inquiry and of congressional legislation; but Grant did not move against the order until his first term was nearly half over. Apparently he was moved more by the necessity of trying to save the remaining Republican administrations in the South than by moral indignation.

In a special message to Congress on December 5, 1870, Grant told the nation that the "free exercise of franchise has by violence and intimidation been denied to citizens in several of the states lately in rebellion." His immediate inspiration was Governor Holden of North Carolina, who was on the ropes. Grant followed up his message by submitting to the Senate a list of nearly five thousand offenses in North Carolina and elsewhere, ranging from floggings to homicides. Down to North Carolina went a preponderantly Republican Senate committee; on March 10 the majority reported that "the Ku Klux organization does exist" and that North Carolina citizens were being intimidated, outraged, and murdered; disclosed that the committee had received complaints of Ku Klux crimes from other states, and recommended that there should be a Southwide investigation. The Democratic minority reported that such tales had been "grossly and willfully exaggerated." Taking the ball again, the President sent a message to Congress suggesting legislative action to protect life and property and enforce the nation's laws in every part of the United States, since corrective power was presently beyond the control of state authorities and since the executive power of the executive to act was not clear.

Congress came through with the notorious first Ku Klux law: "An Act to Enforce the Provisions of the 14th Amendment to the Constitution of the United States, and for Other Purposes"—the broad phrase "other purposes" giving the Radicals in the affected states a free hand to do whatever seemed needful. Congress also called for the appointment of a joint select committee to investigate conditions in "the late insurrectionary states."

By mid-April the committee had been appointed. It was made up of seven senators and fourteen representatives, of whom thirteen were Republicans and eight were Democrats. An initial subcommittee of eight was appointed in May to open hearings in Washington to which witnesses would be summoned. The subcommittee was directed to report to the full committee in September, at which time the committee would appoint other subcommittees to visit disturbed localities in the South.

Thenceforth politics dictated the various committees' procedures. A considerable body of fact was assembled; but it was so contaminated with rumor, lies, and hearsay, and so partisan was the committee in accumulating its mass of gory evidence, that the findings were greatly suspect. Many hundreds of witnesses were interrogated, among them Negroes, United States Army officers, and Southerners of every rank and calling. Although some of the witnesses were undoubtedly Klansmen, these partisans—except for a few renegades who had previously confessed and given state's evidence in criminal suits—denied knowing anything about the Ku Klux Klan; and as for General Forrest, he is said to have told a friend after the baffled committee had finished with him that: "I lied like a gentleman."

The legislation which Grant had asked for was soon forthcoming. The original Ku Klux Act of May 1870 imposed heavy penalties for violations of the Fourteenth and Fifteenth amendments. The states still under Radical rule passed similar statutes of their own. The Klan was outlawed in Tennessee, and part of the state went under martial law. In Alabama a county could be fined $5000 if a person had been killed by a mob or anyone in disguise within its limits. Heavy penalties were provided for wearing a mask or engaging in violence or disguise or for being a Klan member. In February 1871 Congress placed congressional elections under the control of the federal authorities; and in the same year another Ku Klux Act gave the President military powers to suppress violence in the Southern states. Throughout the South thousands of suspected Klansmen and other terrorists were arrested. Hundreds went to trial and many of these were convicted. Most of them were sent to the state penitentiary in Albany, New York; all were free again by 1873.

The Klan was disbanded. The Klan was outlawed. Klansmen were jailed. The grotesque uniforms were burned, and the men who had worn them denied they had ever been Ku Kluxes. But no one forgot the Klan, not for a half century and longer. This is what Ben Johnson, who once was a slave in North Carolina, remembered to his dying day:

> I never will forget when they hung Cy Guy. They hung him for a scandalous insult to a white woman, and they comed after him a hundred strong.
>
> They tries him there in the woods, and they scratches Cy's arm to git some blood, and with that blood they writes that he shall hang 'tween heavens and the earth till he am dead, dead, dead, and that any nigger what takes down the body shall be hunged too.
>
> Well, sir, the next morning there he hung, right over the road, and the sentence hanging over his head. Nobody bother with that body for four days and there it hung, swinging in the wind, but the fourth day the sheriff comes and takes it down.
>
> There was Ed and Cindy, who 'fore the war belonged to Mr. Lynch, and after the war he told 'em to move. He gives 'em a month, and they ain't gone, so the Ku Kluxes gits 'em.
>
> It was on a cold night when they comed and drugged the niggers outa bed. They carried 'em down in the woods and whup 'em, then they throws 'em in the pond, the bodies breaking the ice. Ed come out and come to our house, but Cindy ain't been seed since.
>
> Sam Allen in Caswell County was told to move and after a month the hundred Ku Klux come a-toting his casket, and they tells him that his time has come and iffen he want to tell his wife goodbye and say his prayers hurry up.
>
> They set the coffin on two chairs, and Sam kisses his old woman who am a-crying, then he kneels down side of his bed with his head on the pillow and his arms throwed out front of him. He sets there for a minute and when he riz he had a long knife in his hand. 'Fore he could be grabbed he done kill two of the Ku Kluxes with the knife, and he done gone outen the door. They ain't catch him neither, and the next night when they comed back, 'termined to git him, they shot another nigger by accident. . . .

The redemption of the four states still in Republican hands in 1875—Mississippi, South Carolina, Florida, and Louisiana—was not greatly characterized by such sporadic, unguided mass conflict, though these did occur, or by coercion of selected, individual Radicals. Instead, the white Conservatives of these states initiated open and calculated counterattacks, semimilitary in character; and the North's tolerance of their course of action provided a dramatic indication of the Northern people's new sympathy for the South and of the disintegration of Radicalism in a nation which, in 1874, for the first time since the war had sent a majority of Democrats to the United States House of Representatives.

Mississippi was the first of the four states to perfect what would become known as the Shotgun or Mississippi Plan. Up for election in Mississippi in 1874 were candidates for the legislature, state treasurer, and all county and local offices. Mississippi Conservatives, encouraged by Democratic successes elsewhere in the South, and heartened also by a division in the state Republican party which presaged its desertion by many white and even Negro Republicans, embarked upon a do-or-die program.

Although the elections would not be held until fall, the Conservative leaders began planning the campaign early in the year. The core of their strategy was nothing less than open, organized intimidation of white and Negro Republicans. When the state Democratic convention was addressed in August by Senator Lamar, the party's idol and now a nationally renowned political figure, he emphatically advised the white Democrats not to make race a principal issue and urged his fellow Mississippians against any course that would abridge the rights of the Negroes. Accordingly the platform, as adjusted, recognized the civil and political equality of all men, endorsed public education, and roundly arraigned the administration of Governor Adelbert Ames.

But both sides knew that lofty speeches and reasonable appeals would not be enough. The Democrats chose J. Z. George, formerly a Confederate brigadier general and a prominent attorney, to manage the campaign. This he did on military lines. Between August and the November election day the white Democrats paid only passing attention to their personal or business affairs. Throughout the state military companies, mostly mounted riflemen, were organized and drilled often and conspicuously. The Republicans answered in kind, organizing and drilling Negro militiamen in the guise of political clubs, and instructing them how to register, how to go to the polls, and how to vote. But the Negro organizations appeared insignificant beside the monolithic white structure. The whites even displayed cannons in their parades and put on festive barbecues to which Negroes were welcomed. It was soon noticeable that many of the Negroes were attending the Democratic rallies.

In a strikingly different way Democrats began attending the Republican rallies. General George's counterrevolutionary strategy was designed to over-awe the Negro voters, not with force, except in extremity, but by a show of force and by persistent challenge to the Republican candidates. The well-armed and disciplined whites intruded upon Negro political meetings, rising to heckle or debate Republican campaign orators and to confront them with evidence of Radical dishonesty. Rioting sometimes resulted, though not frequently enough to lead to the intervention, so desired by Governor Ames, of United States troops. Several Negroes were killed when armed whites broke up a Negro Fourth of July political celebration at Vicksburg. The disruption of a political meeting in Yazoo City in September almost led to large-scale race war; other clashes took place at Friars Point and Rolling Fork, and at Clinton, where three Conservative whites were killed at a Republican barbecue and where, in retaliation, twenty to thirty Negroes were slain and hundreds of others dispersed by companies of white riflemen who were rushed to Clinton by special train.

Governor Ames issued a proclamation demanding that the white military companies disband. The whites answered with an offer to place at his disposal several companies, made up only of white men but without respect to party, to maintain order where needed. Ames appealed in early September to Grant for federal troops because "domestic violence in its most aggravated form prevails in various parts of the state beyond the power of the authorities to suppress."

General George countered with a telegram to Attorney General Edwards Pierrepont, declaring that "peace prevails throughout the state, and the employment of United States troops would but increase the distrust of the people in the good faith of the present state government." The upshot was that the Attorney General, in the absence of the President, finally wrote Ames a letter of refusal, quoting in it the presidential comment that the public was tired of the "annual autumnal outbreaks in the South," that the majority were ready to condemn any interference on the part of the government, and that Ames must exhaust his own resources before expecting or receiving aid from the United States Government. However, the President did say that unless peace and order prevailed a presidential proclamation calling for dispersal of insurgents would be issued and federal troops already in Mississippi would be sent to Jackson, but only after Ames had done his best.

Ames raised a state militia of his own, mostly Negro volunteers, under a so-called Gatling gun bill enacted by the legislature the previous spring, which authorized him to form two regiments of ten companies each and to purchase four or more Gatling guns. Not until after the Clinton and Yazoo riots did Ames organize his militia, and again he asked for federal troops in their stead. With neither side willing to give ground, and with hundreds of armed and aroused white and black men, in organized and semi-military units abroad in Mississippi, widespread race war seemed inevitable.

It was averted by what became known as the Peace Agreement between the Democrats and the governor, on the heels of a white mass meeting in Jackson for the unannounced but undoubted purpose of demanding the disarmament of Ames's militia with an outright declaration of war upon Ames as the alternative. Cooler heads at this meeting suggested a conference with the governor; a delegation headed by General George waited upon Ames, and the governor, facing almost certain defeat in the absence of federal military intervention, gave in. If the whites would assure him that they would do all they could to maintain peace and secure a fair election, he said, he in turn would disband the militia.

From then until Election Day, November 3, the rival groups fought mostly with words; the whites continued to break up Republican meetings, especially in the heavily populated Negro counties; in one way or another some local Negro and white Republican leaders were prevailed upon to make speeches for the Democrats; an unestimated number of local Republican politicians and club organizers were run out of the state, and some were killed. White farmers and businessmen published pledges that they would not employ laborers who voted the Republican ticket and would discharge those now in their employ who were politically active for the Republicans. Election Day was quiet except in a few of the counties. The most direct action of all was taken in Aberdeen, where the whites kept a cannon trained on the voting place throughout the day while a cavalry company, made up mostly of Alabamians, paraded the streets and other armed whites guarded the fords across the Tombigbee River where the Negroes from the Black Belt to the east had to cross to come into town to vote.

The Democrats won overwhelmingly, carrying the state, a majority of whose registered voters were Negroes, by thirty thousand and electing the state treasurer, all but two congressmen, a majority of both houses of the legislature, and a majority of the local offices.

So triumphed the Shotgun Plan. Facing certain impeachment, Ames resigned on March 28, 1876, in exchange for the withdrawal of the articles of impeachment which by then had been presented against him in the new legislature. A month earlier the Negro lieutenant governor, A. K. Davis, and T. W. Cordoza, the superintendent of schools, were impeached. Davis was convicted by a Senate vote of thirty-two to four, with six Republicans, one of them a Negro, voting for his conviction. Cordoza asked and received permission to resign in exchange for dismissal of the impeachment charges.

Three weeks before resigning Ames had written Charles Carlton, a friend in New York: "Of course a Republican and an ex-Union soldier has no more consideration or justice here under Democratic Winchester rifle rule than the Union prisoner had at Andersonville. Nothing is charged beyond political sin; of course, with them that is a sin which to a Republican is of the highest virtue. The object is to restore the Confederacy and to reduce the colored people to a state of serfdom. I am in their way, consequently they impeach me, which done, Jeff Davis will be restored to his former supremacy in this part of his former kingdom."

Now only Florida, South Carolina, and Louisiana remained under Radical administrations. And in 1876 they admiringly emulated the Shotgun Plan.

The Radicals in none of these three states were to be as easily disposed of as in Mississippi. Florida with her white majority had the easiest time, her Conservatives achieving victory through a finally achieved white solidarity and a more modest employment of the tactics evolved in Mississippi. George F. Drew, the Democratic nominee for governor, indisputably won; and an honest count would certainly have given the state to Samuel Tilden, the Democratic nominee for President. The state board of canvassers, packed with Republicans, gave the nod to the Republican electors, thus helping set the stage for the showdown and the unprecedented trade which would make Rutherford B. Hayes, the Republican nominee, President of the United States, and would return Florida to her white citizens.

The campaign in South Carolina was complicated by the initial willingness of moderate Democratic leaders from the low country to join forces with Daniel Henry Chamberlain, the best of the Radical Reconstruction governors. He was a Massachusetts man, graduate of Yale, and onetime student at Harvard Law School, who had seen service in a Massachusetts regiment of Negro troops and had been mustered out as a captain. A year after the war, visiting South Carolina to settle the estate of a dead classmate, he decided to raise cotton as a means of earning funds to repay the money borrowed for his education.

Like many another newcomer from the North, Chamberlain failed as a cotton planter and turned to politics. Elected attorney general in the election of April 1868, which placed the state entirely in the hands of the Carpetbag-Negro-Scalawag combination, he had earned unique distinction and the grudging admiration of the Democrats themselves by never being accused of personal dishonesty during the four most corrupt years in the state's history. Seeking the governorship as a Reform Republican in 1874, after two years of law practice in Columbia, Chamberlain won the nomination and then the election. His administration revised the assessment and taxation laws, did away with the abuse of the pardoning power, and reduced public spending; and often defying his party, he refused to commission corrupt officials, notably Franklin Moses, Jr., his Scalawag predecessor whom a grateful legislature had elected to the bench. For this service the city of Charleston publicly thanked Chamberlain in 1875. Such was the man whom the low-country moderates, doubting that the Republican majority could be overturned, were willing to support in a coalition movement.

But the upcountry South Carolinians wanted nothing to do with Republicans, good or bad, or with the Negroes in politics. The memory of the six years of debauchery before Chamberlain was too bitter and too strong. Besides what Mississippi had done, and what Florida and Louisiana were now so patently intent upon doing, the Gamecock State assuredly could accomplish.

Already South Carolinians by the thousands had enlisted in companies which would be known as the Redshirts or Rifle Clubs—and sometimes as Mothers' Little Helpers—under a plan modeled after Mississippi's.

A sanguine race riot at Hamburg early in July 1876, coupled with Chamberlain's desperate alignment with the worst elements of his party in his quest for renomination, and the stern measures he took after the Hamburg trouble, ended Conservative white endorsement of a coalition. Moderates and upcountry white supremacists united and nominated as the Democratic candidate the beloved Wade Hampton.

General Hampton, who had believed since the surrender that the moderate whites could regain control through the promise of fair play and the guarantee of the ballot to qualified freedmen, spoke much as had Lamar in Mississippi the year before. He was determined to allay Northern misgivings and to convince the Negro voters of South Carolina that his long-standing belief in equal treatment was genuine, as it was.

But behind this Southern embodiment of the spirit of *noblesse oblige* rode the Redshirts, employing the battle-proved tactics of the Mississippians. That September, in five bloody days in Ellenton, some fifty Negroes were slain. The red-shirted riflemen forced Negro Republican gatherings to listen to white Democratic speakers; they paid personal calls, as in Mississippi; they persuaded many a white and Negro Republican to change either allegiance or residence. On Election Day itself thousands of Negroes were turned away from the polls by the Redshirts, who, routing or bewildering Republican election officials, happily stuffed ballot boxes, sometimes with more Democratic ballots than there were names on the voting lists. Yet beyond cavil is the conclusion that Wade Hampton, by the belief he could inspire in black men or in white, received enough Negro votes to have assured him of victory in the most untroubled election.

General Hampton's majority was not overruled by the state board of canvassers. But that body did gave a majority to the Hayes electors, a division which satisfied neither side. Whereupon two sets of state officials assumed office, one under Hampton and the other under Chamberlain; and two conflicting presidential returns went to Washington, as South Carolina's preliminary contribution to the great swap.

If politics had been a stench in the nostrils of decent men in Mississippi and South Carolina, Reconstruction in Louisiana added up to an eight-year nightmare not only in political pillaging but in the shedding of blood. There was ample reason. For one thing, no other Southern state offered such rich pickings as did Louisiana, with the South's principal city, New Orleans, one of the nation's important ports, and which from its Latin origins had evolved into a politically indifferent society long accustomed to political thievery. For another, Louisiana's Negro leadership was of a higher intellectual caliber than could be found elsewhere in the South. It included a separate caste, the free men of color, proud of their light skins and of their abundantly French or Spanish ancestry and of a long history of freedom; and such men, less inhibited and of good education, were better able to lead their darker fellows and to command the attention, if not always the respect, of white Conservatives and Radicals alike. They gave an especial militancy to Louisiana Radicalism; they also provided an especial challenge to the whites.

The white Louisianians had fought back in such isolated uprisings as that in Colfax, through Louisiana's variant of the Ku Klux Klan, the Knights of the White Camellia, and through terroristic organizations, including one formed independently by Sicilian and Italian immigrants in New Orleans and south Louisiana.

In July 1874, a year before the Mississippi Plan had proved itself, its Louisiana counterpart was founded in Winn Parish. Its creators designated it the White League. One of the first meetings was held only a few miles from where the Grant Parish courthouse at Colfax had been stormed a year before and its Negro defendants slain or scattered. The resolution there adopted was the most straightforward in its racial animus of any similar statement:

WHEREAS, the state of affairs prevailing in Louisiana for the past six years having convinced all unprejudiced men that this State has been given up to plunder to a horde of barbarous negroes incited and led on by the worst white men that ever imposed themselves upon any civilized country; and

WHEREAS, that by their wholesale and rapacious robbery, our people have been reduced to wretchedness and despair and the State brought to shame; and

WHEREAS, already many of our people, male and female, have been atrociously murdered and outraged by them; and that there is now no security for life and property, that masses of negroes are animated by an inexplicable and deadly hatred of the white race and are now organizing with hostile attitude and design to perpetuate their wicked power in the State; and

WHEREAS, all things point unmistakably to the fact that efforts are being made to Africanize the beautiful and magnificent State of Louisiana, to confiscate the property and compel the civilized and Christian white people to abandon the State or live under the rule of the inferior race; therefore,

BE IT RESOLVED, that it is the solemn duty of the white men to unite into one firm compact organization to protect the lives, the honor and the property of our people.

RESOLVED, that we accept without hesitation the issue of race forced upon us by the insolent and barbarous African and that we believe that a perpetuation of his power would destroy the State as it has every other country in which he has held sway.

RESOLVED, that it was the intention of the founders of this government, that this should be a white man's government and as far as our efforts go, *it shall be.*

RESOLVED, that we deeply sympathize with the people of Natchitoches Parish in their efforts to release themselves from the appalling taxes illegally imposed upon them and the official corruption that has long gone unpunished in their midst; and we assure our friends that we are not idle spectators of their noble struggle.

RESOLVED, that we return our heartfelt thanks to the three able and distinguished members of the bar of New Orleans, Messrs. Robert H. Marr, E. John Ellis and W. R. Whittaker, for the distinguished services rendered in defense of our good friends and fellow-citizens, the Grant Parish prisoners, at a sacrifice of almost their entire business, without promise, hope or desire of pecuniary compensation.

RESOLVED, that we recognize Justice Bradley [of the United States Supreme Court], a true man, an able jurist and an uncorruptible judge.

RESOLVED, that we regard the Shreveport *Times,* Natchitoches *Vindicator,* Alexandria *Caucasian* and New Orleans *Bulletin* as able exponents of our principles and contenders for the white people's rights; we heartily commend them to white people's support; and we hereby express our indignation at the recent outrage perpetrated upon a free press by the ring of desperate politicians who sought the suppression of the *Bulletin.*

A month later, in Red River Parish, two white pickets, posted on one of the roads entering the little community of Coushatta in anticipation of a Negro attack in retaliation for the slaying of several Negroes, were shot to death by a white Radical and two of his Negro associates. A Coushatta posse arrested the white man, four other white Radicals, and a number of Negroes whom they considered to be dangerous. The five white prisoners, in fear of their lives, offered to resign their offices and leave the state. Their offer was accepted; they were placed under a guard and the group set out for Shreveport. The prisoners never arrived. Seventeen miles from Shreveport the white guards were joined by another group, reputedly Texas volunteers on the way to Coushatta, and these newcomers promptly murdered the five white men.

In the wake of such fighting and outrages the White League movement spread rapidly. Meanwhile, the more responsible white Conservatives sought, through the medium of the Leagues, to channel white resistance into more purposeful expression. In New Orleans, the seat of Radical government, the Crescent City White League was formed independently of the organizations in the rest of the state. Its members were fated to engage in a close approximation of a resumption of warfare between Southerners and the uniformed authority of the North.

The events which sparked what Louisianians would come to celebrate as the Second Battle of New Orleans testify both to the desperate intent of the white Democrats and to the anarchy of the period. Let us recall that the *de jure* government of Governor John McEnery had been functioning as if it, and not the Kellogg administration, were in power. The McEnery administration had organized a militia, the First Louisiana Regiment, constituted of four companies. Soon the New Orleans White Leaguers also began to assume a military aspect, its members divided into five companies which drilled secretly in remote warehouses and cotton-press yards. The Kellogg government held the State Armory. The White League and McEnery militiamen ordered the best available arms, munitions, and equipment from outside the state. Some of this equipment reached New Orleans in safety, camouflaged as machinery. Most of the consignment, however, was secreted aboard the steamer *Mississippi;* and Kellogg, learning of the threatening shipment, ordered the seizure of the *Mississippi's* military cargo and the search of private homes suspected of harboring the weapons.

In answer to Kellogg's directive, fifty eminent New Orleans Conservatives signed a call to battle. Their proclamation denounced the Radical government for denying "that right so solemnly guaranteed by the very Constitution of the United States which declares that the rights of the people to keep and bear arms shall not be infringed." As their answer, it went on, the white citizens of New Orleans must close their places of business on Monday, September 14, and assemble at 11 o'clock in the morning at the Clay statue on Canal Street, "and in tones loud enough to be heard throughout the breadth of the land, declare that you are of right, ought to be and mean to be free."

Five thousand solemn and determined men gathered at the monument. They listened to a noted jurist, Judge Robert H. Marr, who read a set of resolutions which declared that McEnery and Lieutenant Governor Penn had been elected by a majority of more than ten thousand and which demanded that Kellogg resign. A citizens' committee then called upon Kellogg to present the ultimatum. Kellogg refused to see the delegation but, through a member of his military staff, he told them that he would not abdicate. When the committee reported his refusal to the mass meeting, Judge Marr, his voice almost drowned by the shouts of "Hang Kellogg," requested the citizens to reassemble under arms at two-thirty that afternoon to take over by force what Kellogg had refused to surrender, namely, the government of the state.

Well before the deadline the White Leaguers—five companies under General F. N. Ogden, a former Confederate officer and president of the Crescent City White League—and McEnery's four companies of militia had encamped in the business district, there erecting barricades and posting sentinels. Kellogg by now had taken refuge in the United States Custom House, before which most of the Metropolitan Police and the Kellogg militia were drawn up. Smaller administration forces guarded the Statehouse, the Cabildo, where the Supreme Court met, and the nearby armory, all in the old French Quarter. In command of the Metropolitan Police was General James Longstreet, late of the Confederate Army. Inside the Custom House itself waited a detachment of United States troops whose only duty was to protect the public property or the property of the United States. During the Canal Street melee the bluecoats cheered the White Leaguers from the Custom House windows as, under the ill-directed fire of Longstreet's Gatling guns, the Orleanians charged and scattered the Metropolitans and the Negro militia.

The White Leaguers reported twenty-one dead and forty-two wounded, Kellogg's forces only eleven slain and sixty wounded. Today, in front of the Custom House at the foot of Canal Street, rises Liberty Monument in memory of the White Leaguers who died there.

President Grant commanded the insurgents to disperse within five days. Men-of-war and additional federal troops were ordered to New Orleans. McEnery and Penn announced their submission to the national authority but said defiantly that their armed followers were not rebels but state militiamen who had been called into existence by the state's legal executive.

Two indecisive, chaotic years followed. When the legislature met next, United States troops forcibly ejected a number of Democratic representatives after a Democrat, by parliamentary maneuvering, had himself declared Speaker of the House and had taken possession of the chair before the Republicans knew what was happening. The white Democrats continued to defy both Kellogg and General Philip Sheridan, that most partisan of military Republicans, who after the Canal Street battle had again been put in command of federal troops in Louisiana. But another general, William T. Sherman, now the Commanding General of the United States Army, spoke words which echoed the conviction of much of the nation:

"I have all along tried to save our officers and soldiers from dirty work imposed upon them by city authorities in the South, and may thereby have incurred the suspicion of the President that I did not cordially sustain his forces. . . . I have always thought it wrong to bolster up weak state governments by our troops. We should keep the peace always but not act as bailiff-constable and catch-thieves; that should be beneath a soldier's avocation. I know that our soldiers hate that kind of duty terribly and not one of those officers but would prefer to go on the plains against Indians, rather than encounter street mobs and serve civil processes. But in obedience to our government, it is hard to stand up in the face of what is apparent, that the present government of Louisiana is not the choice of the people, though in strict technical law it is the state government."

The White Leagues in New Orleans and in the country parishes prepared for the election of 1876, much as had their compatriots in Mississippi in 1875 and as their fellow Democrats in South Carolina and Florida were now doing. Confidently the Democrats of Louisiana nominated two beloved veterans: General Francis Tillou Nicholls, a West Pointer who, seceding with his state, had lost an arm at the Battle of Winchester and a foot at the Battle of Chancellorsville; and Louis A. Wiltz, who had enlisted in the Confederate Army before he was eighteen and who was to become, successively, speaker of the state legislature, mayor of New Orleans, lieutenant governor, president of the Constitutional Convention of 1879, and General Nicholls's successor as governor of Louisiana.

On the face of the first returns the Democrats carried the state by about eight thousand votes. But the decision was up to the Kellogg-appointed returning board. In Louisiana, as in Florida and South Carolina, the stage was set for the most notorious political deal in the nation's history.

With political redemption, organized mayhem directed against the Negro in politics would subside. Its use was, above everything else, a statement of political intent. No one, during Reconstruction or afterward, explained that intent with such icy clarity as did Louisiana's General Richard Taylor.

"Doubtless there were many acts of violence," the President's son wrote in his reminiscences. "When ignorant Negroes, instigated by pestilent emissaries, went beyond endurance, the whites killed them; and this was to be expected. The breed to which these whites belonged has for eight centuries been the master of the earth wherever it has planted its foot. A handful conquered and holds in subjection the crowded millions of India. Another and smaller handful bridles the fierce Caffre tribes of South Africa. Place but a score of them on the middle course of the Congo, and they will rule unless exterminated; and all the armies and all the humanitarians cannot change this, until the appointed time arrives for Ham to dominate Japheth.

"Just in proportion as the whites recovered control of their local governments, in that proportion Negroes ceased to be killed; and when it was necessary to Radical success to multiply Negro votes, though no census was taken, formal statistics were published to prove large immigration of Negroes into the very districts of slaughter. Certainty of death could not restrain the colored lambs, impelled by an uncontrollable ardor to vote the Radical ticket, from travelling to the wolves."

This, Richard Taylor believed, and with him the Redshirts of South Carolina and Mississippi's mounted riflemen, the White Leaguers of Louisiana and the Klansmen of Bedford Forrest. They could not be expected to foresee that the history of the century which followed their own would disprove both the efficacy of their methods and their belief that the white man's hold upon the dark-skinned world could not be loosened by other means than his extermination. Even if they had possessed the supernatural gift of divination, they would not have acted other than they did.

BOOK **III**

WHAT MANNER
OF MEN?

CHAPTER 1

Sons of the Land

THE *story is told of a postwar planter who was informed by a townsman friend that Congress was soon to pass a severe anti-Southern law. The planter asked, "Will it keep cotton from growing?"*
The friend answered, "No."
"Will it keep corn from growing?"
Again the friend answered no.
"Then," said the planter, "damn the law."

One asset the South still had in plenty in 1865: the land. Nine Southerners in ten lived on and from the soil of plantation and farm and forest; a few of them, before the war, in splendor, many of them comfortably, some of them in degrading poverty, and nearly three out of eight in forced servitude. Almost all Southerners could be said to live in the land's behalf, and theirs was an almost mystic belief in the ability of the tended fields and pastures and woodlands to sustain them.

In 1865 the slave was slave no longer, but the land remained. The land meant cotton and tobacco and sugar, the commercial crops for which a market was always assured even though high prices were not; the land meant food and fuel and feed for livestock and timber for homes and outbuildings. In the good old days the land could make a planter as wealthy as any Yankee millowner, and, so its resolute owners believed, the land could do so again. Land, to the planter, meant power and position and a degree of personal ease; and, if his inclination ran that way, land meant the means and the time to improve himself and educate his sons and indulge his womenfolk.

Land did not spell these diverse benefits and luxuries for a second group of Southerners of whom too little has been written, the yeoman farmers, owning few or no slaves; but these cultivators of small holdings of from a hundred to two hundred or so acres did achieve independence out of the land, and in so doing they gave to the South the stability it needed in the days when ruin beset the great landowners in the wake of war and the freeing of the slaves.

And the land meant something else again to a third category of white Southerners, the shiftless squatters and wandering backwoodsmen, independent, too, so long as there remained fishing creeks and forests with game and a pine-barren patch that could produce garden sass and corn for meal and for hogs.

The land meant neither luxury nor independence to the largest group of all, the slave Negroes who tilled the plantation fields in supervised labor gangs or worked side by side with the yeoman owners on the small farms, the Negroes who by their employment and their very presence galled the poor whites whose skin color more often than not alone set them apart from the black men. Yet, even to the Negro slave, the land meant a certain subhuman security; and to the free Negro of Reconstruction the land was an unkept promise of the reward that would come with being free.

It is provocative to speculate upon what might have happened to the land—and to the people—of the South if either of two really revolutionary proposals for rehabilitating the Negro had been undertaken. If Lincoln had been able to win Congress to his or similar schemes to resettle Negroes during or after the war in the Caribbean, in Africa, or in racially separate areas upon the American continent, the South's farm lands might have been tilled principally by small farmers, their economy much the same as that which the tide of European immigration had created in the Middle West. If Thaddeus Stevens's proposal to expropriate the slavocracy's immense acreage for distribution among the freedmen had been approved by Congress, almost every freed Negro could have stepped directly from slavery to land ownership, though for how long and at what cost in blood cannot be surmised.

The Negro resettlement schemes ended about as soon as they were attempted. Stevens introduced his outrageous land confiscation bill in 1867, but few of his fellow Radicals could accept it, even though Senator Sumner had written two years earlier: "Can emancipation be carried out without using the lands of the slave-masters? We must see that the freedmen are established on the soil and that they may become proprietors . . . the great plantations, which have been so many nurseries of the rebellion, must be broken up, and the freedmen must have the pieces." The Freedmen's Bureau did distribute some abandoned acreage, but the original owners eventually got almost all of it back. A modified homestead law made available to Negroes 46,000,000 acres of public land in Louisiana, Arkansas, Mississippi, Alabama, and Florida in eighty-acre tracts and for a few cents an acre, and former Confederates were barred for a year from this law's benefits; but only 40,000 tracts were taken up, most of them by white farmers and speculators. Occasionally Negroes resorted, or threatened to resort, to violence to obtain land. In the Ogeechee River ricelands in Georgia federal troops had to be used in 1869 to subdue hundreds of Negroes who had driven away white landowners, occupied the land, and declared that they would hold what they had seized. A year later, in Louisville, Georgia, troops were again employed to suppress rioting Negroes, the followers of a mesmeric Negro fraud, Cudji Fry, who promised members of his "clubs" immunity from arrest and payment of taxes and debts and the appropriation of land owned by whites.

Thousands of Negroes sought land in Kansas and Texas, but most of them either did not find what they wanted or failed to hold it for very long.

Instead the sharecropping system came into being as the readiest means of keeping the Negro in the fields. Sharecropping was condemned almost from its inception as slavery in a superficially different guise and defended as a practical, even considerate, adaptation of Southern agricultural practices to postwar reality.

Whatever else sharecropping was in its beginnings or would become, and whatever its shortcomings, the system was an inevitable alternative to revolutionary resettlement, revolutionary expropriation, or—what occurred to no one—revolutionary federal planning and overseeing of the agricultural South's recovery. In the bankrupt South, tenantry was the only practical accommodation between the landowner who required more labor than his own family could provide and the freedman—and to a lesser but significant extent, the poor white who had no land of his own. This must be understood, as also must be the roles and the relationships of the several groups of Southerners on the land—the planters, the yeoman farmers and cattle grazers, the poor whites and the free Negroes—in the postwar agricultural adjustment; for without such understanding it is impossible to comprehend the rationale of the South's transition from a slave-based to a sharecropper-based farming society.

Socially the nineteenth-century white South was not rigidly stratified. Not many of its landholders were hereditary aristocrats. A hard-working, capable farmer could move swiftly up the social and economic ladder by the acquisition of productive land, and almost as swiftly the improvident could descend that ladder. The white society of the South was frontier-like in its belief that one man was as good as another; but the large-scale, successful planter would and did wield a disproportionate political influence.

The great cotton, sugar, and rice planters, owners of thousands of acres each and as many as a thousand slaves, had sat firmly in the political saddles in their respective states before the war, despite the Jacksonian upheavals. The planter class was the wellspring of the South's political genius, and logically so, for its relative leisure, its education, and its economic interests directed its members to civil and military leadership. These members were determined that this leadership would not be lost to them after the war.

Because they had been slavery's staunchest defenders, they were, to the Radicals, the henchmen of Antichrist. Theirs was the land Thad Stevens intended to expropriate for division among the freedmen. They had suffered the greatest financial loss through emancipation and had the greatest stake in discovering a prompt substitute for slavery.

Many and varied have been the descriptions of the planter class, the Southern gentlemen; but none written contemporaneously with the flowering of the landed aristocracy matches the complimentary likeness set down in 1860 in *Social Relations in Our Southern States* by Daniel R. Hundley, an Alabamian, educated at the University of Virginia and Harvard. It is offered here in contrast to the considerably less flattering characterization of the South's gentry which W. J. Cash gave seventy-five years later.

Hundley was a Unionist and was living in Chicago on the eve of the war; but so deep was his love for the South that he returned to Alabama, helped organize and was elected colonel of the Thirty-first Alabama Infantry, and served with distinction until he was captured in 1864 during Sherman's march on Atlanta. Here are excerpts from Hundley's characterization:

> We think we may attribute the good size and graceful carriage of the Southern Gentleman, to his out-of-doors and a-horseback mode of living. For we might as well here inform our readers, the genuine Southern Gentleman almost invariably lives in the country. But let them not conclude from this circumstance that he is nothing more than the simple-hearted, swearing, hearty, and hospitable old English or Virginia Country Gentleman, of whom we have all heard so repeatedly. The time has been when such a conviction could have been truthfully entertained; but that was long ago. In those good old times the Southern Gentleman had little else to do than fox-hunt, drink, attend the races, fight chicken-cocks, and grievously lament that he was owner of a large horde of savages whom he knew not how to dispose of.
>
> But times change, et nos mutamur in illis. The new order of things which succeeded the innovations of Mr. Jefferson made it necessary for the Gentlemen of the South, for all the old families who had before lived upon their hereditary wealth and influence, to struggle to maintain their position, else to be pushed aside by the thrifty middle classes, who thought it no disgrace to work by the side of their slaves, and who were, in consequence, yearly becoming more wealthy and influential.
>
> Besides, after the repeal of the Law of Primogeniture, the large landed estates, the former pride and boast of the first families, very soon were divided up into smaller freeholds, and the owners of these, of necessity, were frequently forced to lay aside the old manners and customs, the air and arrogance of the grand seignor, and to content themselves with the plain, unostentatious mode of life which at present characterizes most gentlemen in the South. The result of all which has been, that the Southern Gentleman of to-day is less an idler and dreamer than he was in the old days, is more practical, and although not so great a lover of the almighty dollar as his

Northern kinsman, still is far from being as great a spendthrift as his fathers were before him.

But, notwithstanding the old style of Southern Gentlemen has in a measure passed away, the young South is nurtured in pretty much the same school as formerly—at least so far as physical education is concerned—and participates more or less in all those rollicking out-door sports and amusements still common in England to this day. Scarcely has he gotten fairly rid of his bibs and tuckers, therefore, before we find him mounted a-horseback; and this not a hobby-horse either (which the poor little wall-flower of cities is so proud to straddle), but a genuine live pony—sometimes a Canadian, sometimes a Mustang, but always a pony. By the time he is five years of age he rides well; and in a little while thereafter has a fowling-piece put into his hands, and a little black boy of double his age put en croupe behind him, (or in case mamma is particularly cautious, his father's faithful serving-man accompanies him, mounted on another horse) and so accoutred, he sallies forth into the fields and pastures in search of adventures.

At first he bangs away at every thing indiscriminately, and the red-headed woodpeckers more often grace his game-bag than quail or snipe; but by degrees he acquires the art and imbibes the spirit of the genuine sportsman, and ever after keeps his father's hospitable board amply supplied with the choicest viands the woods or fields or floods afford. By floods, the reader will please understand rivers, creeks, and ponds; for our young Southerner is as much of a fisherman as a Nimrod. When he tires of his gun, he takes his fishing-rods and other tackle, and goes angling; and when he tires of angling, provided the weather is favorable, he denudes himself and plunges into the water for a swim, of which he tires not at all. Indeed, he will remain in the watery element until the sun blisters his back, and if thus forced to seek terra firma, he does it "upon compulsion," and under protest. As a general thing, the blue-noses of Nova Scotia, or the natives of South-America, are not greater lovers of the healthy exercise of swimming than the boys of the South, of all classes.

In his every foray, whether by flood or field, our young gentleman has for his constant attendant, Cuffee, junior, who sticks to him like his shadow. At the expiration of five years or so of this manner of living, (provided there is no family tutor, and in that case his mother has already learned him to read) the master is sent to the nearest village, or district, or select school, returning home every night. Sometimes this school is from five to ten miles distant, and so he has to ride from ten to twenty miles every day, Saturdays and Sundays alone excepted.

Again Cuffee is sent with his young master, and morning and evening the two are to be seen cantering to or from the school-house, the negro taking charge of their joint lunch for dinner, (to be eaten during "playtime") and the master carrying on the pommel of his saddle or his arm the bag which contains his books and papers, and maybe a stray apple or peach to exchange with the village urchins for fishing-rods, or to present to some school-boy friend, who has a rosy-cheeked little sister, with a roguish black eye and a silvery laugh.

Among the Southerners who lived directly from the land the slaveholding families numbered only one in four; and among this minority less than eleven thousand slaveowners, representing only 3 per cent of all slaveholders, owned in 1864 nearly one fourth of all the slaves, with an average of about ninety slaves to each of these highest-income families. Half of the South's slave population of three and one half million was owned by fewer than one third of the total number of slaveholders. Nearly three quarters of all slaveholders were the yeoman farmers, the solid backbone of the agricultural South; but they owned only a fourth of the slaves, rarely more than ten to a family and ordinarily only two or three. Most of the yeomen could do without slaves in a pinch, and because their holdings were smaller, their homes less pretentious, and the animosity of the Radicals not primarily directed at them, they were better able from the beginning to adapt themselves to the reversals of defeat; and, less susceptible to the changing fortunes of cotton, the yeoman farmers were better able to hold to and pass on their modest home places to their sons than were the great planters.

The yeoman farmers and cattle raisers, the plain people, made up more than 60 per cent of the white population. They were self-sustaining, self-reliant folk to whom the land was good as long as they were good to the land. Their stock fattened on the wild grasses and the pea vine and the grain of the savannas and the open forest, and their swine roamed the woodlands for wild pecans and acorns and mast. The fish and game of the rivers and woodland that girt their farms seemed inexhaustible. It was well in the latter years of the war and at the onset of peace that this was so; the free-roaming hog, the deer, and the wild turkey and the smaller game and fish were God-sent staples in many a Southern farmhouse.

The importance of the yeomen in the South's background was generally overlooked until the publication of Frank L. Owsley's *Plain Folk of the Old South* in 1949. Of their role in Reconstruction Owsley says:

It was, however, during the Reconstruction period that the plain folk revealed their real vitality and power of survival. Accustomed to every phase of work in any way related to farming and rural life, and often frontier life, they had no such readjustment to make as the planter who had usually little manual skill or experience in manual labor. With an ax, saw, auger, frow, drawing knife, and hammer, which might be assembled by a neighborhood pool, the farmers held their house-raisings and rebuilt with logs their houses and barns that had been burned during the war. With a sledge hammer and anvil they fashioned crude plows and hoes from the worn-out parts of old implements or from scrap iron and steel gathered here and there. They built crude wagons and carts, made horse collars by plaiting shucks, fashioned harness from hickory saplings with ax and drawing knife, and made traces and other parts of the harness from old pieces of chain or home-tanned leather.

Often there would be a shortage of work stock, in which case what few old animals that were left would be passed around from place to place until they were unable to go. In some cases on record, men hitched themselves to the plow. In this way the plain folk by ingenuity, heartbreaking toil, patient endurance, self-denial, and physical toughness were able to survive the Civil War and Reconstruction, and restore their farm economy—a vital portion of Southern economy. This was accomplished when the plantation system was in shambles or severely crippled from the devastation of war and the destruction of the slave-labor system. It is not too much to say that the plain folk thus rescued the South from complete and, perhaps, final ruin with little or no aid or sympathy from any sources whatsoever outside the borders of their own section.

And of the sturdy folk themselves Owsley gives a warm, accurate account, with rightful emphasis upon the family clannishness of the plain people:

The rural environment of the Old South where the whole family worked together, hunted together, went to church and parties together, and expected to be buried together and to come to judgment together on the Last Day, helps explain the closely knit family group. Certainly it helps explain the deference of younger persons to their parents and elders, for daily association demonstrated that "pa" knew the seasons, the habits and peculiarities of the crops; that he was a master of woodcraft, and he knew the stratagems of the chase and many other fascinating matters that only long experience and reflection could teach. "Pa" could also cut a smarter step in the reel and square dance and play the fiddle better than the boys could, and they knew it. As for "ma," it would take a lot of hard apprenticeship for the daughters to learn to cook, quilt, knit, garden, and "manage" like she could. As likely as not, too, she could dance forty different square-dance figures—and call them. In other words pa's and ma's opinions were respected because they demonstrated in their day-long work with their sons and daughters in field and house and in their play that skill and wisdom come from experience.

Religion was also a vital part of Southern folkways. Indeed, it is difficult to conceive of a genuine folk without religion. The same or similar religious beliefs and practices are an important factor in the creation of a folk, for they help bind together both the family group and the community. The Southern people, inland from the coast where the Episcopal and Catholic Churches were strong, adhered generally to the Methodist, Baptist, Presbyterian, and Church of Christ denominations with their evangelical characteristics.

The rural church, whether a small log house or a pretentious structure, was the center of a community. Here gathered rich and poor, slave and master, to hear the uncompromising champion of righteousness proclaim a gospel of eternal reward for the faithful, and for the wicked, one of eternal punishment varying from Milton's outer darkness to lakes of molten lead. To those believing but sinful souls who still had a large acreage to be sown to wild oats, such sermons were too horrible to contemplate; and they did not contemplate them. Such sinners usually stopped short of the church door and spent their time outside. They were the young bucks whom the county grand jury sometimes indicted for disturbing public worship by discharging firearms, profane swearing, and fighting near the church ground. To the saints and to those who had placed their feet upon the path of righteousness—though they might occasionally take a little detour—it was a joyous religion proclaiming a loving and forgiving God, a God who watched over the lives of his poor, earthly creatures with such care that He marked the sparrow's fall. Their happiness not infrequently moved them to loud amens and occasional loud exclamations of joy.

The church house, though reverently called the "House of God," was also a social center, where friends and neighbors met. Many would gather on the church grounds long before services began and many would linger after the preacher had finished. The older men, singly or in small groups, would visit the graveyard. After that they discussed politics, the crops, the prospects for rain if the weather was dry, and their hopes for dry weather if it was rainy; and they laid plans for corn shuckings, logrollings, houseraisings, and other co-operative enterprises that usually combined business and pleasure. Nor was any occasion permitted to come to an end without tall tales and spicy anecdotes going their rounds. The older women, breaking quietly into little groups, would visit the churchyard, where each, perhaps, had laid away one or more children and other close relatives, and where inevitably other children and other members of the family would be buried. The churchyard was a sacred place. But these women were not overwhelmed by death. They were borne up by their religion, which promised the resurrection of the body and which taught that to give way to unrestained grief over the death of a loved one was to question God's wisdom and His love. This sorrowful duty being performed, they chatted about their family, their gardens, flowers, chickens, clothes, and the forthcoming wedding, and planned the dinners and quiltings that accompanied the logrolling, corn shucking, or other co-operative work their menfolk had arranged.

The young men and young ladies were, of course, more preoccupied with jollification and love-making. They usually paired off and strolled to the spring or well. Here they conspired to gather at some neighbor's house in the afternoon to sing, and to meet again at Wednesday-night prayer services. But while plans were made for further pleasure, the pilgrimage to the well or spring was not wasted. Perhaps some couple would become engaged; and certainly each young beau would return triumphantly bearing the spoils of conquest—a rose or a cape jessamine or a bouquet as large as his mother's feather duster pinned on his lapel.

The younger children played games, hunted snakes and lizards in the woods, boasted of the prowess of their dogs or their father's mules and horses, all of which not infrequently and most naturally ended in a fight.

When at last the crowd broke up, it was not unusual for over half the congregation to go home with the others to eat late Sunday dinner. The cakes, pies, and meats—baked ham, turkey, roast pork—were already cooked and waiting in anticipation of this, for word that they were "expected" next Sunday would already have reached the ones to be invited. Only the chicken had to be fried, the biscuits cooked, and the huge pot of coffee boiled. It was not at all against the principles of the most devout for the menfolk to go to the smokehouse and uncork the wine barrel or the brown jug, to put a razor edge on the already sharp appetite in preparation for the meal that was being laid on the table in such quantities that the legs were almost buckling under the load.

For the third group of white Southerners, the poor whites, neither war nor peace, nor emancipation of the Negro, made much difference in their way of life or in the animosity they held for the well-to-do white man and the Negro whom the white man fed and housed. Happily the poor white, the South's hapless bottom rail, was very much in the minority in the prewar and postwar South. But they were more than enough to outrage the sensitive observer. Their numbers, then and later, were exaggerated. No more than a million of the South's white population of 5,500,000 in 1860 fell into the contemptuous categories of cracker and hillbilly, sand-hiller, squatter, white trash, and po'buckra.

No better image of the poor white exists than that evoked by Daniel Hundley in the same volume wherein he described the planter class:

In the settlements wherein they chiefly reside, the Poor Whites rarely live more than a mile or two apart. Each householder, or head of a family, builds him a little hut of round logs; chinks the spaces between these with clay mixed with wheaten straw; builds at one end of the cabin a big wooden chimney with a tapering top, all the interstices being "dobbed" as above; puts down a puncheon floor, and a lot of ordinary boards overhead; fills up the inside of the rude dwelling with a few rickety chairs, a long bench, a dirty bed or two, a spinning-wheel (the loom, if any, is outside under a shed), a skillet, an oven, a frying-pan, a triangular cupboard in one corner, and a rack over the door on which to hang old Silver Heels, the family rifle; and both the cabin and its furniture are considered complete.

The happy owner then "clears" some five acres or so of land immediately surrounding his domicil, and these he pretends to cultivate, planting only corn, pumpkins, and a little garden truck of some kind or other. He next builds a rude kennel for his dog or dogs, a primitive-looking stall for his "nag," ditto for old Beck his cow, and a pole hen-house for his poultry. This last he covers with dirt and weeds, and erects on one side of it a long slim pole, from the upper branches whereof dangle gourds for the martins to build their nests in—martins being generally regarded as useful to drive off all bloody-minded hawks, that look with too hungry an eye upon the rising generation of dunghills.

Indeed, the only source of trouble to the Sand-hillers is the preservation of their yearly "craps" of corn. Owing to the sterileness of their lands, and deficient cultivation, that sometimes fails them, running all to weeds and grass. But they have no lack of meats. Wild hogs, deer, wild turkeys, squirrels, raccoons, opossums—these and many more are at their very doors . . . And should they desire to purchase a little wool for spinning, or cotton ditto, or a little "swat'ning" to put in their coffee and their "sassefack" tea, or a few cups and saucers, or powder and shot, salt, meal, or other household necessaries—a week's successful hunting invariably supplies them with enough venison to procure the wished-for luxuries, which they soon possess themselves of accordingly, from the nearest village or country store. Having obtained what they want, they hasten back again to their barren solitudes; their wives and daughters spin and weave the wool or cotton into such description of cloth as is in most vogue for the time being; while the husbands, fathers, sons, and brothers, betake themselves to their former idle habits—hunting, beef-shooting, gander-pulling, marble-playing, card-playing, and getting drunk.

In physical appearance, the Sand-hillers are far from prepossessing. Lank, lean, angular, and bony, with flaming red, or flaxen, or sandy, or carroty-colored hair, sallow complexion, awkward manners, and a natural stupidity or dullness of intellect that almost surpasses belief; they present in the main a very pitiable sight to the truly benevolent, as well as a ludicrous one to those who are mirthfully disposed. If any thing, after the first freshness of their youth is lost, the women are even more intolerable than the men—owing chiefly to their disgusting habit of snuff-dipping, and even sometimes pipe-smoking.

The vile practice of snuff-dipping prevails sometimes also among the wives and daughters of the Yeomanry, and even occasionally among otherwise intelligent members of the Southern Middle Classes, particularly in South Carolina. The usual mode is to procure a straight wooden toothbrush—one made of the bark of the hickory-nut tree preferred—chew one end of the brush until it becomes soft and pliant, then dab the same while still wet with saliva into the snuff-bottle, and immediately stick it back into the mouth again with the fine particles of snuff adhering; then proceed to mop the gums and teeth adroitly, to suck, and chew, and spit to your heart's content.

Few of them can read, fewer still can write, while the great mass are native, genuine Know-Nothings, though always democratic in their political faith and practice. Indeed, puzzled to comprehend for what other purpose the miserable wretches were ever allowed to obtain a footing in this country, we have come to the honest conclusion, that it was providentially intended, in order that, by their votes, however blindly and ignorantly cast, they should help to support the only political party which has been enabled thus far to maintain a National organization. Nor can they be blamed for voting the democratic ticket, live they in the North or the South; for to the democratic party do they owe the only political privilege which is of any real use to them—the privilege of the elective franchise.

In religion the Poor Whites are mostly of the Hard-Shell persuasion, and their parsons are in the main of the Order of the Whang Doodle.

The Poor White Trash rarely possess energy and self-reliance enough to emigrate singly from the older Southern States to the South-west, but usually migrate by whole neighborhoods; and are thus to be seen nearly every summer or fall plodding along together, each family having its whole stock of worldly goods packed into a little one-horse cart of rudest workmanship, into which likewise are often crowded the women and children, the men walking alongside looking worn and weary. Slowly thus they creep along day by day, camping out at night, and usually carrying their own provisions with them—bacon, beans, corn-meal, dried fruits, and the like simple and unassuming fare.

When they reach a large river whose course leads in the proper direction, they build them a rude kind of flat-bottomed boat, into which, huddling with all their traps, they suffer themselves to drift along with the current down to their place of destination. Having reached which, they proceed immediately to disembark, and to build their inevitable log-cabins, squatting at their free will and pleasure on Uncle Sam's domain; for they seldom care to purchase land, unless they can get it at about a "bit" an acre. Owing to this custom of occupying the public lands without making entry of the same according to law, in most of the new Southern States the Poor Whites are almost invariably known as Squatters.

The Poor Whites of the South seldom come in contact with the slaves at all, and thousands of them never saw a negro; still, almost to a man, they are pro-slavery in sentiment. Unlike the Southern Yeomen, who are proslavery because these dread the consequences to the humbler whites of the emancipation of the negroes, and because also they are intelligent enough to understand what would be the nature of these consequences, the Poor White Trash are pro-slavery from downright envy and hatred of the black man.

The small farmer, sufficient to himself, and the poor white outcast were alike in their relative or absolute independence of Negro labor, but the two extremes of Southern agricultural society, the planter and the former slave, required an immediate substitution for slavery. The alternative for the planter was economic ruin. The slave's very existence was at stake.

In the first delirious days of freedom, when the Army and the Freedmen's Bureau were feeding them, the Negro was reluctant to work. Jubilee soon ended. For a few freedom and the franchise brought political preferment. But the forty acres were a mirage, and neither the Army nor the Freedmen's Bureau itself showed patience for long with the freedmen who would not work. The government's concern was to see that he obtained a fair contract, and in time even that concern was dissipated. The Southern planter and farmer who needed workers to replace the few or the many slaves soon had little trouble in recruiting them. And the Southern landowners, accustoming themselves to the unpleasant business of making contracts with Negro laborers, as prescribed by the Freedmen's Bureau, began to work out terms of their own as soon as the power of the Bureau and the interest of the government waned.

Thus did the sharecropper system come into being; and since neither war nor Radical Reconstruction had changed the white South's concept of the Negro as a political and social inferior and economic chattel, many of the practices and almost all of the prewar attitudes were carried over into the postwar sharecropping substitutes for slavery. The good masters had been kind and fair. The bad masters had been cruel. The onetime good masters were now the fair-minded partners of Negro sharecroppers. The onetime cruel masters remained cruel and dishonest. And in the eyes of the good and the bad white landowners the Negro remained what most of them had always thought him to be: a lesser member of the human race, fortunate to have exchanged his African past for his Southern present and neither fit nor intended by God for anything but labor in the field, except for the intelligent few who could serve as domestics and craftsmen.

Three years before the war the *Texas Almanac* had bluntly and defiantly set down the Southern argument for slavery, and emancipation had not abolished the white South's concept of the Negro. Explained the *Almanac:*

"Every citizen of the United States should be the warm friend, the unceasing advocate and the bold defender of the institution of African slavery, as it exists in the Southern States of the Union. Why?

"*First:* Because the African is an inferior being, differently organized from the white man, with wool instead of hair on his head—with lungs, feet, joints, lips, nose and cranium so distinct as to indicate a different and inferior grade of being. Whether this comes from the curse upon Ham and his descendants forever, or from an original law of God we will not here discuss. But the great fact is as true as that man exists. The negro is incapable of self-government, or self-improvement, as proven by his universal ignorance and barbarism, though ever in contact with civilized nations, for five thousand years. He has never advanced one step, excepting as a slave to white men. And when civilized and Christianized in slavery, and then freed, he invariably relapses, more or less rapidly, into ignorance and barbarism. Three generations of him as a freeman find him, in his offspring, a confirmed barbarian. The exception is only where he remains surrounded by white civilization, as in the United States, and then he becomes a petty thief and loafer. For proof, look to Jamaica, to San Domingo, to Hayti, to his now acknowledged degeneracy in Liberia and to the freed blacks of the United States and Canada.

"He cannot amalgamate with the white race without producing disease and death in the offspring. The mulatto of the fourth degree, unless bred back into the pure white or black, cannot re-produce himself. Hence, the law of God stamps disease and death as the penalty for amalgamation.

"*Second:* As a slave in a mild climate, the negro is contented, cheerful, obedient and a long-lived laborer. He attains his highest civilization in slavery, receives religious instruction—becomes faithful, trustworthy and affectionate to his white master and superior—yields him willing obedience and enjoys his own highest attainable happiness on earth. For proof, look at the negro in his wild native haunts—in his free condition, after having been a slave—and at his past and present happy, contented and healthy condition, as a slave in the Southern States.

"*Third:* As a slave, he produces the great staples of cotton, sugar, rice, hemp, tobacco, coffee, etc., which cannot be grown either by white or free labor to meet the demands of the world. Abolish slavery, and we abolish the production of these great staples. Abolish their production, and we break up the commerce of the civilized world—we destroy the manufactories of Europe and America—we destroy their combined shipping interest—we throw the white man of both continents out of employment, and cause anarchy, revolution and internecine wars to usurp the paths of peaceful commerce, progress and Christian advancement. The Northern States, without manufactures, without commerce, would present one universal scene of waste and desolation in this now great and prosperous confederacy of free and sovereign states. 'Ruin' would become the watchword of every civilized State and nation. Relief would only be found, after the total extinction of the negro and the suppression of anarchy through a military despotism in this now great and prosperous confederacy of free and sovereign states. My space is limited by the publishers of the 'Texas Almanac,' and I can but glance at this great question of questions. But to every citizen of Texas let me say—'These are sober, solemn portentous truths! Look at them! Meet them like men who know their rights!' How to meet them, do you say? By placing in the hands of every man and woman possible one or more of the excellent books written in elucidation and defence of slavery —by convincing every one of the truths herein so briefly stated—and thus, not only rendering the institution a moral Gibraltar, as it is, but convincing every white man of the land that slavery is not only a wise, humane, necessary and glorious institution, in which every one, rich or poor, is vitally interested, and thereby sweeping away, once and forever, the low and unsound misinformed popular feeling of the American people against what is commonly called the 'Slave Trade,' or the transfer of the beastly, savage negroes of Africa from their ghastly, paganistic slavery there, to the Heaven-ordained and Heaven-approved system of Christian slavery in this country. Do this: repeal the law of Congress: import them in good, well-ventilated ships: look to their health and well-being as a dependent but useful race: break up the present inhuman system of clandestine importation: obey the behests of Heaven to make slaves, like Humane Christians, of the heathen: and, in due time, the glorious results will be manifest—for the smiles of Deity will be upon the work."

To this former chattel, who was now a free sharecropper, the postwar planter offered rations of hogback, corn meal and molasses, a cabin in which to live, the tools with which to raise a staple crop, a garden site, and the necessary work stock and feed. To many a Southerner, then and later, the arrangement seemed eminently fair. William Alexander Percy gave, in *Lanterns on the Levee,* a vivid approximation of the bargain of his grandfather to the former Percy slaves. In its essentials it was the offer made to all free, landless Negroes who wanted to stay on the land:

"I have land which you need, and you have muscles which I need; let's put what we've got in the same pot and call it ours. I'll give you all the land you can work, a house to live in, a garden plot and room to raise chickens, hogs, and cows if you can come by them, and all the wood you want to cut for fuel. I'll direct and oversee you. I'll get you a doctor when you are sick. Until the crop comes in I'll try to keep you from going hungry or naked insofar as I am able. I'll pay the taxes and I'll furnish the mules and plows and gear and whatever else is necessary to make a crop. This is what I promise to do. You will plant and cultivate and gather this crop as I direct. This is what you will promise to do. When the crop is picked, half of it will be mine and half of it yours. If I have supplied you with money or food or clothing or anything else during this year, I will charge it against your half of the crop. I shall handle the selling of the cotton and the cottonseed because I know more than you do about their value. But the corn you may sell or eat or use for seed as you like. If the price of cotton is good, we shall both make something. If it is bad, neither of us will make anything, but I shall probably lose the place and you will lose nothing because you have nothing to lose. It's a hard contract in these hard times for both of us, but it's just and self-respecting and if we both do our part and have a little luck we can both prosper under it."

Such arrangements were to characterize large-scale farming in the South until the middle of the twentieth century, when mechanization, wider crop diversification, and federal crop control combined to eliminate the planters' need for great numbers of Negro hoe hands and pickers.

The worst evil of the sharecropping system was that it could be fair to the sharecropper, even in the best years, only if the landlord were honest, and profitable to the landlord only if the sharecropper were diligent, the land productive, and the price of cotton high enough to give planter and sharecropper both a profit. Fair landlords, diligent sharecroppers, and high cotton prices were rare enough as separate phenomena; in conjunction they were extraordinary indeed. But no other solution, save for migration or the expropriation of lands enough to resettle the freed Negro, was offered at the time a solution was most needed. At its best sharecropping gave the croppers a year's living and the hope and sometimes the reality of land ownership, providing that they were thrifty enough, the land productive enough, and the landlord honest enough for them to have something left over at settlement time; and it could work out that way. And, at its worst, even sharecropping on worn land or for a dishonest landlord, the Negro sharecropper was better off, in theory if not in actuality, than he had been, in that he was now a freeman.

The sharecropping system was not the only agricultural end product of war and Reconstruction. Many a Northern farm boy, trudging behind Grant and Sherman, had cast covetous, appraising eyes on the rich lands, the virginal forests, the fruitful, neglected fields of the wartime South. Thousands of Yankee troops remained in the South after their discharge to settle down and send for their families, if they were married, or to find brides in the enemy country. Louisiana alone attracted nearly fifty thousand Union men during and immediately after the war. In general the South was willing to accept these settlers as long as they did not meddle with politics or with the Negroes. Sometimes localities even advertised for them. Linton Stephens, half brother of the Confederacy's vice-president, joined many other Georgians in signing an invitation to "all good people of the North, whether farmers or mechanics, whether Protestants or Catholics, or of no church—all classes—to come and settle among us, for our mutual good; assuring all such, again that they shall have thrown around them, the same law, the same protection, and the same justice in every respect as are 'meted out to us.' "

Needy Southerners sold their acres to anyone who could pay the outrageously low prices for which Southern farms and plantations were advertised in the North's newspapers and journals. Speculative land companies were organized in the North. Widows of dead Confederates and veterans too old or broken to re-engage in agriculture let their farms go for little or nothing. Into the undeveloped South flocked honest and dishonest land speculators and developers, would-be exploiters of the region's natural resources. Not all of them, or even a majority, were successful. Southerners must have been especially pleased over the failure of an Abolitionist group headed by Henry Lee Higginson of Massachusetts which went broke on a Georgia plantation to the tune of $65,000. John Hay, the dead Lincoln's former secretary, fared no better with a Florida orange grove; and the lowlands of South Carolina were inhospitable to Benjamin Wade and Simon Cameron, when those two political scavengers tried to add to their fortunes through the acquisition of Southern farm land.

The increase in the number of small farms in the twenty-year period between 1860 and 1880 was marked and generally beneficial. They doubled in Alabama, Arkansas, Georgia, Mississippi, North Carolina, and Tennessee, trebled in South Carolina, Louisiana, and Florida, and multiplied four times in wide-open Texas. In South Carolina farms smaller than a hundred acres rose from 352 in 1860 to 10,286 in 1870. A notable increase also was made in the number of smaller plantations of a thousand acres or less. And, since the South's capital, such as it was, no longer had to be so greatly invested in slaves, planters and farmers began to experiment with new agricultural methods, either independently or in emulation of Yankee newcomers. The use of commercial fertilizers became widespread. This, however, was not an unmixed blessing; while fertilizer did increase cotton yield and built up the land, its use led to abandonment of crop rotation, the most sensible of all means of soil restoration. A host of such new and generally impractical mechanical devices as steam plows and mechanical cotton-picking machines appeared and were in turn heralded as foolproof, only to prove futile. The examples set by the Northern farmers, the realization of Northern manufacturers that the South could become a passable market for new farm implements, and the willingness of Southern farmers to experiment, led to introduction or wider use of such newfangled instruments as corn shellers and reapers, corn planters, grain rakes, threshers and separators, hay cutters and cultivators.

For a while Southern farmers turned to untried new crops as substitutes for or supplements to the old staples of cotton and rice and tobacco. They planted oranges and strawberries, watermelons and peaches. They experimented with growing okra as a raw material for papermaking and with even such exotics as tea, cinchona, flax, and castor beans. Ramie, a fiber plant, was introduced, and lespedeza, the great soil builder, appeared.

But the Reconstruction South's agricultural recovery, if recovery it was at all, was slow. Not until 1880 did the production of cotton and oats match the yields of 1860. Only in Texas was there more livestock in 1880 than in the last year before the war. Rice and sugar, the staples which had helped balance the cotton economy, disappeared in Georgia and North and South Carolina. Even in Louisiana the sugar plantations which were worth $200,000,000 in 1861 could have been bought for less than $10,000,000 in the late 1860s.

The South, which could have become a diversified agricultural paradise, a region whose water power, forests, and minerals could have been translated into industrial wealth, clung willy-nilly to cotton raising. As a way of life it was the best its people had known. Cotton was a hardy, long-lived commodity and one always in demand. Cotton could make use of the South's Negroes. Conceivably a man could again get rich from growing cotton. But King Cotton played the postwar South false because he was the pawn of greater powers than he: the industrial North, and the Republican party which Northern industrialism so firmly controlled.

Throughout the rest of the century and long afterward the cotton growers of the South, selling in an open market and buying their necessities behind the tariff walls that New England's manufacturers demanded, paid what was most certainly the longest lasting penalty of Southern defeat; and the Southerners who paid the highest price of all were the black folk whom Northern victory had, after a fashion, set free.

CHAPTER 2

Children of Jubilee

THE *immutable fact in 1865 was that 3,500,000 human beings who had been enslaved were now free. The inescapable problem was what to do with them.*

Long before the fact of freedom Thomas Jefferson had given his own considered and pessimistic answer to the problem of the black man freed.

"Nothing is more certainly written in the Book of Fate," said the author of the Declaration of Independence, "than that these people ought to be free; nor is it less certain that the two races, equally free, cannot live in the same government."

Abraham Lincoln, in historic debate with divided Democracy's Stephen A. Douglas, had echoed and expanded upon Jefferson's solution. Said Lincoln at Peoria:

"If all the earthly power were given me, I should not know what to do as to the existing institution. My first impulse would be to free all the slaves and send them to Liberia—to their own native land. But a moment's reflection would convince me that, whatever of high hope (as I think there is) there may be in this, in the long run its sudden execution is impossible. If they were all landed there in a day, they would all perish in the next ten days. What then? Free them all and keep them among us as underlings? Is it quite certain that this betters their condition? I think that I would not hold one in slavery at any rate, yet the point is not clear enough for me to denounce people upon. What next? Free them and make them politically and socially our equals? Our own feelings will not admit of it, and if mine would, we well know that those of the great mass of whites will not."

The problem plagued Lincoln even as the Union fought for its very life. Time after time during the war the President and his Cabinet discussed deportation of the Negroes as a way out. Mr. Lincoln espoused a non-compulsory colonization program to resettle Negroes in Panama and the West Indies; a promoter did ship four hundred Negroes, the vanguard of five thousand he intended to transport, to an island leased for the purpose from Haiti. The unprepared, sickened survivors among these volunteer migrants had to be brought home. Lincoln also thought of using the Navy, once the war had been won, to bear at least 150,000 Negro men to distant climes. And there were men in Congress and in his Cabinet who agreed with the President's "first impulse." As early as 1862 resettlement advocates in the House of Representatives sought approval of an appropriation of $20,000,000 for the resettlement of freed slaves and prewar free Negroes and another for $180,000,000 to purchase 600,000 slaves owned by loyalists in the border states.

A favorable congressional report on the 1862 colonization proposal contained some ominous predictions:

"The most formidable difficulty which lies in the way of emancipation in most if not all the slave states is the belief which obtains especially among those who own no slaves that if the negro shall become free, he must still continue in our midst and . . . in some measure be made equal to the Anglo-Saxon race . . . The belief [in the inferiority of the Negro race] . . . is indelibly fixed upon the public mind. The differences of the races separate them as with a wall of fire; there is no instance in history where liberated slaves have lived in harmony with their former masters when denied equal rights—but the Anglo-Saxon will never give his consent to negro equality, and the recollections of the former relations of master and slave will be perpetuated by the changeless color of the Ethiopian. The emancipation, therefore, without colonization could offer little to the negro race. A revolution of the blacks might result, but only to their undoing . . ."

Congress rejected the resettlement proposal, and eventually its advocates gave up. Senator Sumner, among others, denounced the scheme; the nation at war, he said, needed labor; and General Butler told the President, sardonically, that it would be impossible for the Navy to ship the Negroes to the nearest possible Caribbean island "half as fast as negro children will be born here." On July 2, 1864, all legislation relating to future colonization of the Negro was repealed.

Meanwhile the President's Emancipation Proclamation of January 1, 1863, had promised freedom to some three million slaves in those seceded states which had not yet been overrun by the Union armies. The proclamation was more political in its inspiration than humane. Emancipation was not granted to about 450,000 slaves in the border states, which had not seceded, or in safe Tennessee or in those areas of Virginia and Louisiana which had also been conquered by the Union and were under federal administration. But it was a telling political and military stroke.

The wartime congressional resolution authorizing the submission of the Thirteenth Amendment, the instrument which would formally abolish slavery, had a rough time. Especially did the border congressmen oppose it. Not until January 31, 1865, would eleven Union Democrats in the House of Representatives, deserting their party's leadership in the wake of an

Abolitionist upsurge in the border states, give the resolution the necessary two-thirds majority in the House of Representatives. Eleven months later, the Thirteenth Amendment having been ratified by twenty-seven states, the Negro was constitutionally a free man. The United States, or a victorious majority thereof, had accomplished its most revolutionary undertaking, the unshackling of three and one half million human beings with a going value of more than $2,000,000,000, and without compensation for their former masters.

The day of rejoicing had dawned.

Hand in hand, the children of Jubilee pranced down the freedom road where no patrollers pursued. Yankee rations and the Yankee promised land waited just around the bend. The roaming freedmen were mostly plantation field hands; few freed house servants or artisans or long-time-free Negroes, secure and even contented in their occupations, were among them.

Not since the Children's Crusade had Christendom witnessed such a childlike, aimless, tragic meandering. The freedmen roved in search of food and out of sheer delight at being able to wander; young plantation hands overran the towns, complicating the task of the occupying forces. Young plantation wenches, freed from a bondage in which their virtue was of no account, offered their bodies in the camps of the liberators until they were driven away by military order. Behind the wanderers wailed the children who could not keep up with the grown-ups or who had been left behind. The luckier abandoned waifs and untended elders were cared for by the Army and the missionaries and the church societies and the Freedmen's Bureau; but the bodies of many, the too young, the too weak, the too aged, lay unidentified in forsaken cabins and in the ditches alongside freedom's road.

The roaming multitudes paid a high price at the beginnings of their freedom. The standard of living even for most of those who remained on the plantations or soon returned to them was considerably worse than before the war. The death rate from tuberculosis, malaria, malnutrition, venereal disease, from all the consequences of inadequate diet and lack of supervision, soared. Before the war the Negro population had been increasing faster than the white. The birth rate had been greater and the death rate little higher than that of the whites; in Charleston, South Carolina, for example, the Negro death rate in 1860 was 26.45 per thousand as against 26.60 for the whites. The Negro death rate in that city after the war rose abnormally to 43.33 per thousand, while the white death rate fell slightly to 24.4. In no year since 1865 has the death rate for Negroes approached its low ante-bellum ratio to white deaths.

Where the vagrant freedmen passed, fields and outbuildings and pens were left barren of vegetables, chickens and hogs, cattle, horses, even cotton. They stole all that they could lay their hands upon, some in vengeance but most of them because they were hungry. The crimes committed by the free Negroes, from petty thievery to murder, far outran those of the whites; and Negroes were the victims of Negro violence far more than were the whites. An astounded Northern visitor reported in 1865 that "a young colored gentleman seems to think he is not fully dressed unless he has a pistol buckled to him or hid away in his pocket, and when in company he uses the most trivial pretext to draw it out." The absence of a sexual code under slavery encouraged sexual license among the free. Bigamy, desertion, and adultery were far more commonplace in every state in the South than were Negro weddings. The rape of white women by Negro men, rare before and during the war, increased measurably in the more isolated regions of the South.

And the towns and the countryside of the Southern states were unwilling hosts to a new kind of Negro. Two hundred thousand already free or escaped Negro men had served in the Union Army. About twenty thousand of these soldiers were deployed in the South after the war, as garrison troops. They were not kindly disposed toward the former Confederates, for the Southerners had been merciless when they fought Negro soldiers, and many of these Negroes in uniform were arrogant, provocative, trouble seeking, and undisciplined. Their presence created such resentment in the South that melees between Negro troops and white citizens were frequent; and at General Grant's urging, and despite the opposition of the Radicals, Negro troops were withdrawn from the South less than a year and a half after Appomattox. They were to be used again when Radical Reconstruction was undertaken in earnest.

The freedmen would have been other than human had not their first reactions to liberty included a disinclination to do anything at all or as little as was needed to keep body and soul together. In time Army orders, the supervision of the Freedmen's Bureau, and necessity combined to return most of the freedmen to the plantations. A lucky, foresighted or politically favored minority became landowners themselves; by 1874 Negroes owned 338,769 acres of farm lands in the South, but they were a minority. The landless Negro had to return to the land for there was nowhere else for him to go, and the white man needed him.

If it was natural that a freedman would initially react to the memory of his days of serfdom by taking life easy, it is equally understandable that he should imitate as a freedman the white society which was his only guide. In most respects this was fortunate; in some respects it was not. Few of the South's Negroes sought social identification with the whites. Indulging instead in a generally lighthearted imitation of white social behavior, they evolved a caste system which was more rigid then than prevails today. The Negro who had been free, educated, and a property owner before the war looked down from the peak of Negro society. Only slightly below him rested the political officeholders of Reconstruction. The teacher lorded it over the artisan, the artisan over the house servants of the white gentility, the mulatto over the full-blooded black man. And all of them looked down upon the field hand. The least educated and the worst off indulged the most avidly in a seemingly endless succession of revivals, all-day picnics, and political rallies. Fanciful secret organizations glorying in such names as the Sisters of Sympathy and the Young Men Never Lies Society, band led and brightly uniformed, vied with each other at important funerals and on national holidays. A people whose links with the ancestral African past had long since been severed appropriated the surnames of old American heroes and of the liberators who had set them free or, sometimes with blood right, the names of the families which had owned them.

Would the white South have held out a helping hand to the Negro had he expressed his freedom only through minor lawlessness, sloth, and social mummery or in a worthy hunger for education and ownership?

Some would have answered then, as others would answer now, with an emphatic no. Some would have said then, as others would say now, probably or possibly. The question was not to be put to a test. Instead the development of the freedmen in the South was to be impeded by the resistance of Southern whites to what they considered a premature, retaliatory projection of the Negro masses into the political life of the region. Out of that resistance came the lasting legacies of Reconstruction: the white South's eventual consignment of the Negro to political oblivion, and the white South's acceptance, in so doing, of the thesis that, for the restoration and the maintenance of white political supremacy, the end justified any means.

The concern of literate, ambitious Negroes in the South with enfranchisement, especially the free Negroes, considerably antedated the ratification of the Thirteenth, Fourteenth, and Fifteenth amendments. In November 1863 Louisiana's free men of color, who occupied a separate and generally respected position between the slave and the white master, proposed Negro suffrage in New Orleans and in the other regions of Louisiana which were occupied by Union forces. These free men of color were, as a group, much better off than the free Negroes elsewhere in the South and even in the North. They were often men of property; in 1860 Louisiana Negroes of mixed blood owned real property and slaves valued at $50,000,000. But their request for the voting privilege went unanswered. Louisiana's provisional governor was not happy over the probability that, if the request were complied with, more Negroes would vote than whites.

In March 1864 a perplexed Lincoln, unready to propose wholesale suffrage for Negroes after the now-anticipated victorious conclusion of the war, privately suggested a compromise to Michael Hahn, the newly elected

Loyalist governor of Louisiana: " . . . now that you are about to have a convention, which among other things will probably define the elective franchise, I barely suggest, for your private consideration, whether some of the colored people may not be let in, as, for instance, the very intelligent and especially those who have fought gallantly in our ranks. They would probably help in some trying time in the future to keep the jewel of liberty in the family of freedom. But this is only a suggestion, not to the public, but to you alone. Truly yours, A. Lincoln."

This was, in substance, the same proposal which moderate Southern white leaders would later recommend, and unsuccessfully, to the extremists of the North and the South.

When the Louisiana constitutional convention met on April 6, 1864, principally the issue of Negro suffrage mired it down for seventy-eight days, though the questions of compensation for loyal former slaveholders and the education of freedmen at the state's expense also contributed to the drawn-out session. By a vote of seventy-two to thirteen the convention abolished slavery. It appealed to Congress for compensation for the owners of freed slaves. But the Loyalist delegates were initially adamant in opposing Negro suffrage. The convention even adopted a resolution that the legislature should never authorize the vote for the freed Negroes.

General Banks and Governor Hahn induced forty delegates to change their minds and substitute a resolution, denounced by most of the former slaveholders in the convention as a "nigger resolution," which would give the legislature "the power to pass laws extending the rights of suffrage to such persons, citizens of the United States, as by military service, by taxation to support the government, or by intellectual fitness may be deemed entitled thereto." Neither the Louisiana legislators nor the President of the United States believed the free Negro was entitled to the ballot without qualifications or restrictions. But the Radicals in Washington had other thoughts; and the seed of universal political equality which they planted and nurtured germinated fast.

On October 18, 1864, a convention of free Negroes assembled in Syracuse, New York. The delegates demanded the complete and immediate abolition of slavery in the United States. Coupled with this ultimatum was a memorial to Congress demanding voting rights which went far beyond Lincoln's private proposal. "Your fathers laid down the principle, long ago, that universal suffrage is the best foundation of government," the memorial read in part. "We believe as your fathers believed and as they practiced; for, in eleven states out of the original thirteen, colored men exercised the right to vote at the time of the adoption of the federal constitution . . ."

The memorial then struck what to the professional politicians of the Republican party must have been a warning chord: "You are sure of the enmity of the masters—make sure of the friendship of the slaves; for, depend upon it, the government cannot afford to encounter the enmity of both."

The agitation for universal suffrage did not originate with the Negro masses themselves. The overwhelmingly uneducated freedmen of the South —at least ninety-five in a hundred—did not know what suffrage meant, some even believing the ballot to be a waiting gift that could be eaten or worn. What the ordinary freedman apparently wanted and what he needed above everything else were land and education. Instead he was shepherded into what would turn out to be almost uninterrupted political warfare with the white South; the unprepared, gullible field hands were to be the victims of a political conflict which they had no part in precipitating. Even in the ascendancy of Negro suffrage only a few Negroes would profit politically, either directly or indirectly, from the right to vote. The white shepherds would see to that.

What must be emphasized is that with few exceptions the South's Negroes were the pawns, and not the gainers, in a political upheaval such as the world had never seen before. The unsavory behavior of the average Negro politicians, the ignorance of the average Negro voters, and their almost solid racial unity have been well enough documented to go unchallenged. What has not been sufficiently dwelt upon is the fact that the Negro officeholder and voter alike got the short end of the stick.

The objections of the white South to universal enfranchisement could have been dismissed by its proponents as an expected prejudice; but there were misgivings in the North as well. General Sherman recommended a training period prior to the granting of the franchise to the freedmen. Political equality, said Henry Ward Beecher, could not be "bought nor bequeathed nor gained by sleight of hand. It will come with sobriety, virtue, industry, and frugality." Louis Agassiz warned in 1863: "I cannot therefore think it just or safe to grant at once to the Negro all the privileges which we ourselves have acquired by long struggles. History teaches us what terrible reactions have followed too extensive and too rapid changes." And in 1873, after seven years of the South's involuntary experiment in universal suffrage, a Northern newspaperman who had earlier been sympathetic to the Radical program of Reconstruction gave a disillusioned—and perhaps overly anti-Negro—report of what he found in the South Carolina legislature. He was Northern-born James Shepherd Pike, before the war an anti-slavery Whig and later a Republican, and from 1852 to 1860 an associate editor of Horace Greeley's New York *Tribune*.

Pike's *The Prostrate State: South Carolina Under Negro Government*, an indictment of Carpetbag and Negro rule, contains a description of the behavior of the South Carolina House of Representatives which is the classic account of the legislative functioning of Radical Reconstruction at its worst.

In the place of this old aristocratic society stands the rude form of the most ignorant democracy that mankind ever saw, invested with the functions of government. It is the dregs of the population habilitated in the robes of their intelligent predecessors, and asserting over them the rule of ignorance and corruption, through the inexorable machinery of a majority of numbers. It is barbarism overwhelming civilization by physical force. It is the slave rioting in the halls of his master, and putting their master under his feet. And, though it is done without malice and without vengeance, it is nevertheless none the less completely and absolutely done.

Let us approach nearer and take a closer view. We will enter the House of Representatives. Here sit one hundred and twenty-four members. Of these twenty-three are white men, representing the remains of the old civilization. These are good-looking, substantial citizens. They are men of weight and standing in the communities they represent. They are all from the hill country. The frosts of sixty and seventy winters whiten the heads of some among them. There they sit, grim and silent. They feel themselves to be but loose stones, thrown in to partially obstruct a current they are powerless to resist. They say little and do little as the days go by. They simply watch the rising tide, and mark the progressive steps of the inundation. They hold their places reluctantly. They feel themselves to be in some sort martyrs, bound stoically to suffer in behalf of that still great element in the State whose prostrate fortunes are becoming the sport of an unpitying Fate.

Grouped in a corner of the commodious and well-furnished chamber, they stolidly survey the noisy riot that goes on in the great black Left and Centre, where the business and debates of the House are conducted, and where sit the strange and extraordinary guides of the fortunes of a once proud and haughty State. In this crucial trial of his pride, his manhood, his prejudices, his spirit, it must be said of the Southern Bourbon of the Legislature that he comports himself with a dignity, a reserve, and a decorum, that command admiration. He feels that the iron hand of Destiny is upon him. He is gloomy, disconsolate, hopeless. The gray heads of this generation openly profess that they look for no relief. They see no way of escape. The recovery of influence, of position, of control in the State, is felt by them to be impossible.

They accept their position with a stoicism that promises no reward here or hereafter. They are the types of a conquered race. They staked all and lost all. Their lives remain, their property and their children do not. War, emancipation and grinding taxation have consumed them. Their struggle now is against complete confiscation. They endure, and wait for the night.

This dense negro crowd they confront do the debating, the squabbling, the law-making, and create all the clamor and disorder of the body. These twenty-three white men are but the observers, the enforced auditors of the dull and clumsy imitation of a deliberative body, whose appearance in their present capacity is at once a wonder and a shame to modern civilization.

Deducting the twenty-three members referred to, who comprise the entire strength of the opposition, we find one hundred and one remaining. Of this one hundred and one, ninety-four are colored, and seven are their white allies. Thus the blacks outnumber the whole body of whites in the House more than three to one. . . . As things stand, the body is almost literally a Black Parliament, and it is the only one on the face of the earth which is the representative of a white constituency and the professed exponent of an advanced type of modern civilization.

But the reader will find almost any portraiture inadequate to give a vivid idea of the body, and enable him to comprehend the complete metamorphosis of the South Carolina Legislature, without observing its details. The Speaker is black, the Clerk is black, the door-keepers are black, the little pages are black, the chairman of the Ways and Means is black, and the chaplain is coal-black. At some of the desks sit colored men whose types it would be hard to find outside of Congo; whose costume, visages, attitudes, and expression, only befit the forecastle of a buccaneer.

It must be remembered, also, that these men, with not more than half a dozen exceptions, have been themselves slaves, and that their ancestors were slaves for generations. Recollecting the report of the famous schooner Wanderer, fitted out by a Southern slave-holder twelve or fifteen years ago, in ostentatious defiance of the laws against the slave-trade, and whose owner and master boasted of having brought a cargo of slaves from Africa and safely landed them in South Carolina and Georgia, one thinks it must be true, and that some of these representatives are the very men then stolen from their African homes. If this be so, we will not now quarrel over their presence. It would be one of those extraordinary coincidences that would of itself almost seem to justify the belief of the direct interference of the hand of Providence in the affairs of men. . . .

The old stagers admit that the colored brethren have a wonderful aptness at legislative proceedings. They are "quick as lightning" at detecting points of order, and they certainly make incessant and extraordinary use of their knowledge. No one is allowed to talk five minutes without interruption, and one interruption is the signal for another and another, until the original speaker is smothered under an avalanche of them. Forty questions of privilege will be raised in a day. At times, nothing goes on but alternating questions of order and of privilege. The inefficient colored friend who sits in the Speaker's chair cannot suppress this extraordinary element of the debate.

Some of the blackest members exhibit a pertinacity of intrusion in raising these points of order and questions of privilege that few white men can equal. Their struggles to get the floor, their bellowings and physical contortions, baffle description. The Speaker's hammer plays a perpetual tattoo all to no purpose. The talking and the interruptions from all quarters go on with the utmost license. Every one esteems himself as good as his neighbor, and puts in his oar, apparently as often for love of riot and confusion as for any thing else. It is easy to imagine what are his ideas of propriety and dignity among a crowd of his own color, and these are illustrated without reserve. The Speaker orders a member whom he has discovered to be particularly unruly to take his seat. The member obeys, and with the same motion that he sits down, throws his feet on to his desk, hiding himself from the Speaker by the soles of his boots. In an instant he appears again on the floor. After a few experiences of this sort, the Speaker threatens, in a laugh, to call "the gemman" to order. This is considered a capital joke, and a guffaw follows. The laugh goes round, and then the peanuts are cracked and munched faster than ever; one hand being employed in fortifying the inner man with nutriment of universal use, while the other enforces the views of the orator. This laughing propensity of the sable crowd is a great cause of disorder. They laugh as hens cackle—one begins and all follow.

But underneath all this shocking burlesque upon legislative proceedings, we must not forget that there is something very real to this uncouth and untutored multitude. It is not all sham, nor all burlesque. They have a genuine interest and a genuine earnestness in the business of the assembly which we are bound to recognize and respect, unless we would be accounted shallow critics. They have an earnest purpose, born of a conviction that their position and condition are not fully assured, which lends a sort of dignity to their proceedings. The barbarous, animated jargon in which they so often indulge is on occasion seen to be so transparently sincere and weighty in their own minds that sympathy supplants disgust.

The whole thing is a wonderful novelty to them as well as to observers. Seven years ago these men were raising corn and cotton under the whip of the overseer. To-day they are raising points of order and questions of privilege. They find they can raise one as well as the other. They prefer the latter. It is easier, and better paid. Then, it is the evidence of an accomplished result. It means escape and defense from the old oppressors. It means liberty. It means the destruction of prison-walls only too real to them. It is the sunshine of their lives. It is their day of jubilee. It is their long-promised vision of the Lord God Almighty.

The Negro would have been less human than his worst detractors believed him to be had he not listened to the promises and succumbed to the blandishments of the friends who came down from the North to tell him of the wondrous benefits which would be his if he would vote Republican now and forevermore. What he actually got for his vote was something else.

Only a few Negroes, some capable and honest and educated, others ignorant or dishonest or both, held major state or federal offices in the South during Reconstruction. The voting masses received through enfranchisement only the vote itself—which could have been reward enough—and the free liquor and barbecues and small change and promises with which their votes were wooed. When the showdown came the white political invaders who had used the Negro left him to the untender mercies of the white South.

Not even in the states where the Negro's political strength was greatest —in Louisiana, Mississippi, South Carolina, and Florida—would any Negro be elected governor, though Mississippi, Louisiana, and South Carolina did elect Negro lieutenant governors—Louisiana's serving briefly as governor— and Mississippi sent two Negroes to the United States Senate. In South

Carolina a Negro was a member of the Supreme Court, and, between 1868 and 1870, seven Southern states sent altogether twenty-six Negroes to the United States House of Representatives—not much reward for the three and a half million who held the political balance of power in the nation itself.

So incapable or dishonest was a majority of the Negro officeholders and voters that before Reconstruction had run its full course even some of the old-line Radicals, North and South, had turned against them. In 1868 when white Radicals and Conservatives in the Georgia legislature united to expel the Negro membership, it required the joint power of the United States Congress and the United States Army to reinstate them. And what the white South was to remember principally and to resent the most was not the state and federal officeholders but the unfit Negro constables and sheriffs, the superintendents of education and justices of the peace, who did hold a majority of these and other lesser county and local offices in the Black Belts of the South.

The policy of immediate enfranchisement of the Negro, without any qualifications, was wrong as a political concept and woeful in its consequences. Because of their mobility, political adroitness, and racial identification with their white opponents, most of the Carpetbaggers and Scalawags eventually escaped from or outlived individual if not group stigmatization. Not so fortunate were the freedmen politicians who had been the white politicians' cat's-paws far more often than their cosharers of political plums. Their punishment, almost total disfranchisement, was to outlast the lifetime of the youngest of those who cast their first vote beneath the reassuring bayonet.

And in Reconstruction's wake the unforgiving white South created a stereotype of the Negro voter which lumped all Negroes into a single and repugnant caricature of ignorance, dishonesty, and vengefulness. The stereotype was unfair. The marvel was not that the Negroes produced so few able political leaders in Reconstruction but that they produced as many as did appear; but the capable few were swept away with the unready many. Among the able were Jonathan Jasper Wright and Joseph Hayne Rainey of South Carolina, and B. K. Bruce, and Hiram Rhodes Revels of Mississippi, all of them estimable citizens, and P. B. S. Pinchback of Louisiana, not estimable but politically astute. They deserve at least passing recognition.

Jonathan Jasper Wright, a full-blooded Negro born in Pennsylvania of free parents and self-educated in the law while teaching school there, came to South Carolina in 1865 to organize Negro schools for the American Missionary Association. He returned North a year later to become the first Negro admitted to the Pennsylvania bar and subsequently served again in South Carolina as a Freedmen's Bureau legal adviser to freedmen and refugees. From 1868 until the restoration of white supremacy Wright was variously a member of the state constitutional convention, a legislator, and a justice of the state Supreme Court, to which he was elected by the legislature.

A judicious and conciliatory man, Wright joined in February 1877 in signing the legal order that made General Wade Hampton governor of South Carolina after the disputed election of 1876. He resigned from the Supreme Court in December 1877 and died of tuberculosis only eight years later at forty-five, an impoverished and forgotten man. His political and judicial career in South Carolina was marked by a manifest desire to bring Negro and white together in common respect and understanding.

Joseph Hayne Rainey, the son of a South Carolina mulatto barber who had bought his family's freedom, had little book learning and was himself a barber in Charleston at the outbreak of the Civil War. He served as a steward on a Confederate blockade-runner in 1861. After he was drafted in 1862 to work on the Charleston fortifications he escaped to the West Indies. Returning after the war, he became politically prominent in the Republican party, was a member of the Radical state constitutional convention, and was later elected to the state senate. In 1870 he resigned from the senate to go to the United States House of Representatives, to fill a vacancy occasioned by the House's refusal to accept the credentials of B. F. Whittemore, and thus became the first Negro to be a member of the House. An able spokesman for his own race and for the Republican party, he showed no ill will toward the Southern whites; but he did champion legislation for the enforcement of the Fourteenth Amendment and the Ku Klux Act and the Civil Rights Bill, and so strongly did he believe that Negroes should be admitted to all public places that he once refused to leave the dining room of a white hotel in Virginia until he was forcibly ejected. It is revealing that after he had lost health and fortune while in the banking and brokerage business in Washington, he returned in 1886 to his birthplace, Georgetown, South Carolina, to live out the last year of his life.

Quaker-educated Hiram Rhodes Revels, born of free, mixed Negro and Indian parentage, was also a barber, as freemen of color so frequently were. He became a Methodist minister and a wartime chaplain who served as provost marshal of Vicksburg after the city's fall. Later he organized Negro churches in Jackson, occupied pulpits in Kentucky and Kansas, and in 1866 moved to Natchez, where in 1868 he was elected an alderman. A moderate Republican, he was elected by the Radical-dominated Mississippi legislature to the United States Senate as Jefferson Davis's successor. Retiring from the Senate in 1871, he served ably as president of Mississippi's newly founded Alcorn College for Negroes. So disgusted did Revels become with Radical Republicanism that in 1875 he joined the Democrats in overthrowing the Carpetbag-Scalawag-Negro government; and in an open letter to

President Grant he declared that the good men of Mississippi, regardless of party or race, had been forced to combine to defeat the graft-ridden Republican organization.

Politically a Conservative, and a dedicated minister, Hiram Revels was liked by the whites of Mississippi; and in Mississippi he remained after his retirement from the presidency of Alcorn, to engage in church work until his death in 1901 at the age of seventy-nine.

Blanche K. Bruce, the second and last Negro United States senator from Mississippi, was a Virginia-born and Missouri-bred freedman who was educated at Oberlin College. Coming to Mississippi soon after the war, he prospered as a planter before he entered politics. He served successively as sergeant of arms in the state senate, assessor and later sheriff of Bolivar County, and in 1872 was a member of the Board of Mississippi River Levee Commissioners. In all of these posts Bruce showed himself both able and honest. As a senator he energetically attacked white Southern election frauds and violence and sought the implementation of civil rights legislation; but he also supported the removal of the political disabilities imposed upon the Confederate leadership by Radical Republicanism. And in a day when most Negro political leaders were single-mindedly seeking rights for their own people, Bruce was active in his opposition to the Chinese exclusion policy and fought for better treatment for the American Indian. More visionary than most of his contemporaries, he strove also for flood control and navigation improvements of the Mississippi so as to make the river attractive for interstate and foreign commerce. The Republican party would reward his fidelity and ability after the victory of Mississippi's white Democrats made it impossible for him to hold any elective office. He served as Register of the Treasury under President Garfield, Recorder of Deeds in the District of Columbia under President Harrison, and again Register of the Treasury under McKinley, a post he held until his death in 1898.

And there was another and celebrated Negro politician, though not in the honest mold of Bruce, Revels, Rainey, and Wright. He was Pinckney Benton Stewart Pinchback, reputedly the son of a white Mississippi planter and a light-skinned, onetime slave who had been emancipated by her children's father and sent with them to Ohio so that they could be educated.

A man so white as to be able to make his choice of race, Pinchback remained a Negro. Before the war he was a cabin boy and then a river-boat steward; after the surrender of New Orleans in 1862 he ran a Confederate blockade on the river, enlisted in the Union Army, and raised and commanded a company of colored troops who were known as the Corps d'Afrique. Forced to resign later because he was not a white, after white officers were prescribed, he then raised a company of colored cavalry.

Pinchback was for a time the dominant political figure in postwar Louisiana: a member of the constitutional convention in 1868, state senator and president pro tempore of the Senate, and lieutenant governor of Louisiana when the mulatto incumbent, Oscar J. Dunn, died in 1871; temporary governor of Louisiana for less than five weeks, December 9, 1872, to January 13, 1873, when the elected Carpetbagger governor, Henry Clay Warmoth, was debarred from serving because of impeachment proceedings; and in time a congressman-elect and United States senator-elect, though he never filled either seat because of successful Democratic contests.

As did Senator Bruce of Mississippi, Pinchback quit the Republican party to support the Democrats in 1877. A shrewd, highly intelligent man, if not an idealistic one, Pinchback approximated the popular concept of the Negro in Reconstruction politics because Louisiana, under Radical Republicanism, was the most graft-ridden of the Southern states; but the principal political offense that damned him in Louisiana was that he was not white.

Had the race—and the politics—of these men been different at least some of them might have been remembered by the white South as at least minor statesmen. As it is, the white South, save for those few historians and students interested in such matters, identifies them either not at all or as one with the stereotype of the Reconstruction "nigger politician."

What are recalled instead are the rampaging buck Negroes, reeling drunkenly down Freedom's Road, and the truculent Negro soldiers who could not get Petersburg's Crater or the plantation whipping post or Fort Pillow out of their minds; remembered are the gullible field hands toting buckets and saucepans and sacks to the polling places so as to carry home a mess of ballots for supper, or proudly displaying the red, white, and blue certificates that entitled them, so the hoaxers who took their dimes and dollars told them, to forty acres and a mule; and the black sheriffs and state legislators and assessors and justices of the peace who stole what they could, which was not nearly as much as many of their white mentors were stealing. The South would remember the illiterate Negro teacher and the indifferent pupil and the high-stepping burlesquers of white society and the moaning of the hysterical deviationists from supervised Christianity. They would remember the scavengers and the land squatters and the cotton-field shirkers, and, terribly, the lustful, murderous handful who courted the noose and the crackling pine knot and the castrating knife.

But, by the grace of God, the white South and the black South would remember something else too: the persistent reality of decent personal relationships which existed and endured and may yet prevail. Had affection and trust and respect not existed between white man and Negro in the South during the war and afterward, the nation might have suffered in Reconstruction a blood bath from which it would not yet have recovered. The genesis of the higher sentiments was the simple fact of human decency; it cannot be laughed or frowned away as an enforced amity between Uncle Tom and the master.

John R. Lynch, a notable Negro Reconstruction leader, was to look back many years afterward on "the bond of sympathy between the two races at the South—a bond that the institution of slavery with all its horrors could not destroy, the rebellion could not wipe out, Reconstruction could not efface, and subsequent events have been unable to change." And John T. Trowbridge, a Massachusetts journalist and novelist who inspected the South in 1866, put his finger on a peculiar and lasting aspect of Negro-white relationships in the region when he noted that "every man who curses the black race and prays for its removal or extermination, makes exception in favor of Negroes he has raised or owned, until I am beginning to think that these exceptions constitute a majority of the colored population."

Nor were these exceptions made only by the whites. The bodies of almost all of Jubilee's black celebrants now lie moldering in their graves, but in the 1930s there survived hundreds of onetime slaves whose rheumy eyes could light with the fires of memory; and in those years of depression, when the Federal Writers' Project collected slave narratives, they added greatly to the American story. Let them talk to us across the years, first, some from among those who remembered in hate, and then those who remembered with affection.

Here speak the haters:

"My old master mean to us. We used to watch for him to come in the big gate, then we run and hide. He used to come to the quarters and make us children sing. He make us sing 'Dixie.' Sometimes he make us sing half a day. Seems like 'Dixie' his main song. I tell you I don't like it now. But have mercy. He make us sing it. Seems like all the white folks like 'Dixie.' I's glad when he went away to war."

—Eda Harper, slave in Mississippi

"They stands me up on a block of wood and a man bid me in. I felt mad. You see I was young then, too young to know better. I don't know what they sold me for, but the man what bought me made me open my mouth while he look at my teeth. They done all us that-a-way, sells us like you sell a hoss. Then my old master bids me good-bye and tries to give me a dog, but I 'members what Miss Nancy done say and I sassed him and slapped the dog out of his hand. So the man what bought me say, 'When one o'clock come, you got to sell her 'gain, she's sassy. If she done me that way I'd kill her.' So they sells me twice the same day."

—Mintie Maria Miller, slave in Texas

". . . Lots of old people like me say that they was happy in slavery and they had the worst tribulations after freedom, but I knows they didn't have no white master and overseer like we all had in our place. They both dead now, I reckon, and they no use talking 'bout the dead, but I know I been gone long ago iffen that white man Saunders didn't lose his hold on me.

"It was the fourth day of June in 1865 I begins to live, and I gwine take the picture of that old man in the big black hat and long whiskers (the freedom man) setting on the gallery and talking kind to us, clean into my grave with me.

"No, bless God, I ain't never seen no more black boys bleeding all up and down the back under a cat-o'-nine-tails, and I never go by no cabin door and hear no poor nigger groaning, all wrapped up in a lardy sheet no more!

"I hear my children read about General Lee, and I know he was a good man. I didn't know nothing about him then, but I know now he wasn't fighting for that kind of white folks.

"Maybe they that kind still yet, but they don't show it up no more, and I got lots of white friends too. All my children and grandchildren been to school and they git along good, and I know we living in a better world, where they ain't nobody cussing fire to my black heart.

"I sure thank the good Lord I got to see it."

—Katie Rowe, slave in Arkansas

"My papa was strong. He never had a licking in his life. He helped the master, but one day the master says, 'Si, you got to have a whopping,' and my papa says, 'I never had a whopping and you can't whop me.' And the master says, 'But I can kill you,' and he shot my papa down. My mama took him in the cabin and put him on a pallet. He died."

—Anne Clark, slave in Louisiana

"Slavery was the worst days was ever seed in the world. They was things past telling, but I got the scars on my old body to show to this day. I seed worse than what happened to me: I seed them put the men and the women in the stock with they hands screwed down through holes in the board and they feets tied together and they naked behinds to the world. Solomon the overseer beat them with a big whip and Massa look on. The niggers better not stop in the fields when they hear them yelling. They cut the flesh 'most to the bones, and some they was when they taken them out of stock and put them on the beds they never got up again.

". . . Once my maw and paw taken me and Katherine after night to slip to 'nother place to a praying singing. A nigger man with white beard told us a day am coming when niggers only be slaves of God. We prays for the end of tribulation and the end of beatings and for shoes that fit our feet. We prayed that us niggers could have all we wanted to eat and special for fresh meat. Some the old ones say we have to bear all 'cause that all we can do. Some say they was glad to the time they's dead, 'cause they'd rather rot in the ground than have the beatings. What I hated most was when they'd beat me and I didn't know what they beat me for, and I hated them stripping me naked as the day I was born."

—Mary Reynolds, slave in Louisiana

"I's hear tell of them good slave days, but I ain't never seen no good times then. My mother's name was Lisa, and when I was a very small child I hear that driver going from cabin to cabin early as 3 o'clock in the morning, and when he comes to our cabin, he say 'Lisa, Lisa, git up from there and git that breakfast.' . . . We had old ragged huts made out of poles and some of the cracks chinked up with mud and moss and some of them wasn't. . . . I tended the children when I was a little gal and tried to clean the house just like Old Miss tells me to. Then soon as I was ten years old, Old Master, he say, 'Git this here nigger to that cotton patch.' . . . Then she [mistress] grab that broom and start to beating me over the head with it and calling me low-down nigger [stealing a biscuit] and I guess I just clean lost my head 'cause I knowed better than to fight her if I knowed anything 't all, but I start to fight her, and the driver, he comes in and he grabs me and starts beating me with that cat-o'-nine-tails, and he beats me till I fall to the floor nearly dead. He cut my back all to pieces, then they rubs salt in the cuts for more punishment. Lord, Lord, honey! Them was awful days. When Old Master come to the house, he say, 'What you beat that nigger like that for?' And the driver tells him why, and he say, 'She can't work now for a week. She pay for several biscuits in that time.' He sure was mad. . . . I still got them scars on my old back right now, just like my grandmother have when she die, and I's carrying mine right on to the grave just like she did."

—Jenny Proctor, slave in Alabama

And here speak others of friendship:

"When Miss Sarah come back and found it out [that the overseer had whipped mammy], she was the maddest white lady I ever seed. She sont for the overseer, and she say: 'Allen, what you mean by whipping Mammy? You know I don't allow you to touch my house servants.' She jerk her dress down and stand there looking like a soldier with her white shoulders shining and she say: 'I'd rather see them marks on my own shoulders than to see 'em on Mammy's. They wouldn't hurt me no worse.' Then she say: 'Allen, take your family and git offen my place. Don't you let sundown catch you here.' So he left. He wasn't nothing but white trash nohow."

—Ma Eppes, slave in Alabama

". . . She [mistress] wouldn't let one of her slaves hit a tap on Sunday. They must rest and go to church. They had preaching at the cabin of some one of the slaves, and in the summertime sometimes they had it out in the shade under the trees . . . Colonel Chaney had lots and lots of slaves, and all their houses were in a row, all one-room cabins. Everything happened in that one room—birth, sickness, death, and everything, but in them days niggers kept their houses clean and their door yards too. These houses where they lived was called the 'quarters.' I used to love to walk down by that row of houses. It looked like a town, and late of an evening as you'd go by the doors you could smell meat a-frying, coffee making, and good things cooking. We were fed good and had plenty clothes to keep us warm and dry.

". . . If all slaves had belonged to white folks like ours, there wouldn't been any freedom wanted."

—Harriet Payne, slave in Arkansas

"We children never didn't know nothing 'bout no hard times in that day and time. Seems like the Lord had just opened up and fix the way for us to have everything we want. Oh, honey, we children never been harness up in no little bit of place to play like these children 'bout here these days. We had all the big fields and the pretty woods to wander round and 'bout and make us playhouse in. Seems like the Lord had made the little streams just right for we children to play in and all kind of the prettiest flowers to come up right down 'side the paths us little feet had made there. . . . That how come we been so satisfy. I here to tell you my old missus was a dear old soul, and we children sure had a fine time coming up. She didn't never have her niggers cut up and slashed up no time. She was good to us, and we stuck to her."

—Mom Hester Hunter, slave in South Carolina

"Master always wanted to help his colored folks live right, and my folks always said the best time of they lives was on the old plantation. He always 'ranged for parties and such. Yes, sir, he wanted them to have a good time, but no foolishment, just good clean fun. There am dancing and singing mostest every Saturday night. He had a little platform built for the jiggling contests. Colored folks comes from all around, to see who could jig the best. Sometimes two niggers each put a cup of water on the head and see who could jig the hardest without spilling any. It was lots of fun."

—James Smith, slave in Texas

". . . I tells you that Marse William am the greatest man what ever walk this earth. That's the truth. I can't lie on him when the poor man's in his grave . . . Nobody ever hit me a lick. Marse always say being mean to the young ones make them mean when they grows up and nobody gwine to buy a mean nigger.

"One day a little man come riding by on a little dun hoss so fast you couldn't see dat hoss's tail a-switching. He whooping and hollering. Us niggers 'gun whoop and holler too. Then first thing you know the Yanks and the Democrats 'gun to fight right there. They a high old mountain front Marse's house and the Yanks' gun pepper cannon ball down from the top that hill. The war met right there, and them Yanks and Democrats fit for twenty-four hours straight running.

"When the bullets starts raining down, Marse calls us and slip us way back into the woods, there it so black and deep. Next day, when the fight over, Marse come out with great big wagons piled full of mess-poke for us to eat. What us call hog meat. Us sure glad to 'scape from the Yankees."

—Ellen Betts, slave in Louisiana

". . . Yes, honey, the Lord done put it on record that there is sure a burn-ing place for torment, and didn't my master and mistress larn me the same thing? I sure does thank 'em to this day for the pains they took with the little nigger gal that growed up to be me, trying to show her the right road to travel. Oh! if I could just see 'em one more time! But they can look down from the glory land and see I's still trying to follow the road that leads to where they is, and when I gits to that good and better world I just knows the Good Lord will let this aged woman be with her dear master and mistress all through the time to come . . ."

—Nicey Kinney, slave in Georgia

For the haters and the friendly the political ending was the same. In Reconstruction's wake the white South would plant one simple sign of politi-cal warning to the Negro. It read: "Keep Out." The warning would be ob-served and enforced until almost the last of the remembering former slaves had died.

CHAPTER 3

The Whys of the Scalawag

AMONG *the rough-tongued Shetland Islanders, a Scalloway was an unkempt, filthy cow or hog or sheep; or, derisively applied to humans, a Scalloway was a scamp. The Scots-Irish who settled so thickly in the South brought the epithet with them and their sons corrupted it in time to Scalawag. It was a fighting word; but no political significance was attached to it until Reconstruction, when its meaning became explicit and restricted, stigmatiz-ing the native Southerners who, for one reason or another, made common political cause with the white and Negro Republicans.*

The word spat hate. "Our Scalawag is the local leper of the community," explained the *Independent Monitor* of Tuscaloosa, Alabama, in 1867. "Un-like the Carpetbagger, he is a native, which is so much the worse. Once he was respected in his circle; his head was level, and he would look his neigh-bor in the face. Now, possessed of the itch of office and the rheum of Radicalism, he is a mangy dog, slinking through the alleys, haunting the governor's office, defiling with tobacco juice the steps of the capitol, stretch-ing his lazy carcass in the sun on the square, or the benches of the mayor's court."

As with all caricatures, this portrait is an oversimplification. The Scala-wags were not always so basely driven or so different in their characteristics and appearance, their education and social status, from the white Southern majority which refused to truck with the Republican party. They were animated by a variety of motives and by combinations of them: by class hatred, by lust for power, by simple greed, by expediency or despair, by political opportunism; by honestly espoused, long-time loyalty to the Union; by a belief that they could aid their states by joining forces with the late enemy, or by the zeal of the reformer.

The Scalawags of the South included former generals of the Confederacy and wartime Southern governors; planters and poor whites; onetime Whigs, ministers and businessmen and lawyers; men of principle and men lacking principle. For one reason or another such assorted Southerners were willing to subject themselves to the scorn, the enmity, and the ostracism of other men who had been their friends and their wartime comrades. They were manifestly more complex than is indicated by the all-embracing myth of traitorous cupidity which grew in their wake and which persists so strongly even today that the word Scalawag remains the most abhorrent one in the Southern vernacular.

For the dissipation of that myth it may be helpful to meet six variously impelled Southern men who moved boldly across the Reconstruction stage as Scalawags. They are Franklin J. Moses, Jr., of South Carolina, William Gannaway Brownlow of Tennessee, William W. Holden of North Carolina, Joe E. Brown of Georgia, General James Longstreet, Georgia-born and a Louisianian during Reconstruction, and General James Lusk Alcorn of Mississippi.

Some were corrupt, dissolute men. . . .

Had Franklin J. Moses, Jr., lived a century earlier he could have been Hogarth's inspiration for "The Rake's Progress"; a century later a producer of soap opera would have rejected as grossly implausible a script relating the inexplicable degeneration of a pleasant, promising, socially acceptable young South Carolinian to an extravagantly evil renegade to tradition and race. Frank Moses, an odious enigma, came to represent and to be remembered in the South as the typical turncoat. He was not, but there were enough lesser men like him to make the identification stick.

There is no evidence that he or his distinguished father was handicapped because of their Jewish blood and only one small indication that this lineage disturbed them. When the boy was born in 1838, in Sumter District, South Carolina, he was named Franklin Israel, after his father; later each would drop the middle name and substitute, without giving reason, simply the initial J.

The elder Moses was a successful attorney, a state senator for twenty years, a secessionist, and, from 1868 to 1877, a Chief Justice whose impartiality and wisdom were admired despite his postwar desertion to the Republican party. Young Frank Moses married a Gentile, as had his father, the daughter of a brilliant lawyer and member of a leading South Carolina family. He was only twenty-two and one year married when, in December 1860, he began a short but influential career as private secretary to Governor Francis W. Pickens. As violent a rebel as any other South Carolina hothead, young Frank raised the Confederate flag over Fort Sumter after its surrender. Soon thereafter he entered military service as enrolling officer with the rank, thanks to his political standing, of colonel.

His wartime career was satisfactory enough and his immediate postwar behavior exemplary. In the autumn of 1866 he was admitted to the South Carolina bar, and in the following April he was elected a vestryman of the Sumter Episcopal Church. Meanwhile, during the first two postwar years, he was editor of the Sumter *News* and persuasively endorsed President Johnson's Reconstruction program.

And then, in 1867, that which was evil in Frank Moses seized the whole man. Control of the enfranchised Negro was the key to political mastery of the state. Moses allied himself with the Loyal Leagues. He turned savagely upon his Democratic fellow citizens and began wooing the Negro voters. Before the year was out he was dismissed from his editorship. The Negro majority from his district sent him to the constitutional convention of 1868, and there his surrender to Radical Republicanism at its worst became complete. His rewards in the debauched administration that followed were ample: Speaker of the House of Representatives, adjutant and inspector general of the state militia, and trustee of the state militia and trustee of the state university.

No other Reconstruction figure rivaled him in progressive degeneracy. As Speaker of the House he turned bribetaker and dealer in bogus state pay certificates; as adjutant general, a thief who diverted to his own use money intended for the purchase of arms for the militia. After he was overwhelmingly elected governor by the adoring Negro voting majority in 1872, defeating a reform Republican candidate, he sold pardons, political appointments, and gubernatorial approval of legislation. Backed by his Black-and-Tan militia, he defied the state courts. Foremost among the few Scalawags or Carpetbaggers of prominence who mingled socially with Negroes, Moses dined and wined and wenched with the best and worst of them, spending his stolen dollars almost as fast as he could milk them from the public treasury and arousing even some of his most corrupt associates to protest his public and private conduct.

At the end of his two-year term he was penniless, deserted by his fellow pilferers, a financial and moral bankrupt without hope of again being a party leader. Daniel Chamberlain, the new Republican governor and a man of vastly different caliber, refused in 1875 to issue Moses a commission as circuit judge, a position to which the Carpetbag-Negro-Scalawag legislative majority had elected him; soon he escaped prison only by testifying against some of his fellow looters.

Not until 1878 did his brokenhearted wife divorce him, taking with her the children whom she never told of their father's ruin; eventually some of the members of his family were to change their name to escape identification as his kinsmen. From 1878 until 1906, when he died in Winthrop, Massachusetts, Frank Moses was an impoverished wanderer, a drug addict, a petty thief, and confidence man who served a number of short prison terms. Only in Winthrop near the end of his days did he salvage anything from the wreckage of his life. There, strangely, he was briefly moderator of the town meeting and editor of a newspaper; and there he died in December 1906, of accidental asphyxiation.

Frank Moses was the South's Scalawag caricature come true; but it is unfair to make him synonymous with Scalawagism or the Scalawag synonymous with Frank Moses. He was a moral weakling who in any society and in any time would have given way to temptation. But more than any other his career was made to order in his own time and now for all for whom the issues of Reconstruction were drawn in the blackest of blacks and the whitest of whites.

Some were Scalawags through conviction. . . .

A considerable body of Union sentiment had existed in the prewar South and had persisted during the conflict itself. Though Southern Whigs were its chief representatives, this spirit was not confined to the Whigs or to any one group in the population. Not gladly did Robert E. Lee of Virginia follow his state out of the Union; nor was there any joy over secession in the hearts of thousands of his fellow Southerners, men who had hoped with Lee until the last that calmer advice would prevail and that the South and North could adjust their differences within the Union.

Unionism persisted in the South during the war in political enclaves ranging from a few counties, as in Alabama and Mississippi and Arkansas, to large segments of the seceded states, as in western Virginia, western North Carolina, and eastern Tennessee. The loyal Virginia mountaineers were to be rewarded with independent statehood. It was the fate of Tennessee to become not only a battleground between opposing armies but to be torn by a small civil war of its own; and, as the third state—after Louisiana and Arkansas—to be overrun by the Union armies, Tennessee was the first to be returned forcibly to the Union and to be ruled by the mountain folk who had paid cruelly for their loyalty until the Union victory and who would not themselves thereafter be forgiving.

From these native Unionists came William Gannaway Brownlow, whom we have already encountered in his clerical guise; an itinerant Methodist minister and coarsely vituperative editor of *Brownlow's Knoxville Whig,* Tennessee's principal Unionist journal, a man who would become the harshly retaliatory yet personally honest governor of Tennessee.

Whatever else the enemies of Parson Brownlow might and did say of him, which was plenty, neither his courage nor his gift of vivid speech were open to challenge. Preachers of other denominations were "pigpen orators and whisky-shop saints"; Andrew Johnson, a hated Democrat, "an unmitigated liar . . . and a villainous coward." Long before his election as governor of Tennessee in 1865 he had been a powerful, tireless, and pungent advocate of the Union's preservation no matter the cost. As early as 1832, in a pamphleteering controversy, he predicted that the slavery question would shake the nation to its foundation, and that when that time came he, though then no opponent of slavery, would stand by the government. Under his editorship *Brownlow's Whig* thundered against secession so vigorously that it was read by the largest number of subscribers to any pro-Union political journal in the South. It was the *Whig* which in November 1860 declared that although the presidential vote had been, tragically, a sectional one, Abraham Lincoln "is chosen president, and whether with or without the consent and participation of the South, will be and ought to be inaugurated on the fourth of March, 1861."

The *Whig* was the last Union newspaper to be published in the South and the indomitable parson's home the last in Knoxville over which waved after secession the Stars and Stripes. Defiant and raging editorially against the secessionists until a mob destroyed the *Whig's* press and type, Parson Brownlow refused to swear allegiance to the Confederacy and fled to the Great Smokies. There Confederate scouts ferreted him out and returned him to Knoxville, where he was promised a passport into Kentucky. Instead, on December 6, 1861, Parson Brownlow was jailed on a charge of committing treason against the Confederacy in his final *Whig* editorial and also on suspicion of helping other Unionists to burn railroad bridges in the state.

Desperately stricken with typhoid fever while in prison, the fifty-six-year-old Unionist was permitted to go to his home, where he remained under guard for eight weeks. The Confederate government then passed him through their lines into Kentucky in March 1862. From Kentucky he went to Ohio to recuperate. In Ohio he wrote the provocative and violent *Sketches of the Rise, Progress and Decline of Secession; With a Narrative of Personal Adventures Among the Rebels* and began lecturing to Northern audiences. "This war must be pursued with a vim and vengeance until the rebellion is put down," he told listeners in New York, "if it exterminates from God's green earth every man, woman, and child South of Mason and Dixon's Line!" Hitherto indifferent to the slavery issue itself, he endorsed

Lincoln's emancipation policy, though not nearly as fervently as he had demanded allegiance to the Union.

Parson Brownlow accompanied General Burnside and his army when they entered eastern Tennessee in the autumn of 1863, and again he set up shop in Knoxville. Soon he was again foremost among the Unionist leaders in the conquered state. His reborn paper he named *Brownlow's Whig and Rebel Ventilator*. In it he incited loyalists to commit physical violence against Confederate sympathizers. He participated in the calling of the nominating convention of loyalists, required under the Lincoln program for the restoration of civil government, and that convention, by carefully rigged acclamation, made him governor.

Now it was the unforgiving Parson's turn. He made the most of it. He demanded and won a severe disfranchisement law to punish all who had borne arms against the Union. He secured absolute control of the election machinery. His legislature also created a state militia to keep defeated Tennessee's Confederates in subjection. He rammed ratification of the Fourteenth Amendment through a divided legislature in July 1866, and Tennessee, last of the states to quit the Union, thereby became the first to be readmitted. When the Ku Klux Klan burgeoned after passage of the disfranchisement statute, and the government in Washington denied Brownlow's subsequent request for federal troops, he called up 1600 state militiamen, proclaimed martial law in nine counties, and dealt highhanded justice to the rebel, fractious Klansmen.

Brownlow's militia assured Unionist domination of Tennessee until 1870, though Grant's poor showing in Tennessee as a presidential candidate in 1868, the Parson's own unwary ambition, and the cumulative effects of Klan intimidation foreshadowed the end of Brownlow Reconstruction. The ambitious Parson had given up the governorship in 1869 to go to the United States Senate, and a factional fight between the Republicans over the vacant governorship gave the Democrats their chance. They supported the more conservative Republican candidate and elected him. A year later a coalition-dominated constitutional convention granted universal suffrage. Thousands of previously disfranchised Democrats, now permitted to go to the polls again, meant the end of Brownlow's domination; a sick man, he served in the Senate ineffectively for a full term and died soon afterward, in April 1877.

Some became Scalawags through class hatred or opportunism or both. . . .

Obscured by the titanic American division over slavery and the right of secession was another schism, nonsectional in nature and less widespread and rigid in the United States than elsewhere in the Western world. This was, in essence, class warfare, tempered by the fluid nature of American society; in the South it principally arrayed spokesmen for the landless poor white, the precariously small farmer, and the artisan, with some allies among tradesmen and professional men, against the larger landowners, its lawyer-politicians, and assorted financiers—this line-up being drawn only as a generality to which there were numerous intergroup and intragroup exceptions.

The evidence of this struggle in the South is abundant. It is notable that in Louisiana's convention for reunion in 1864 control was vested, for the first time in the state's history, in white men from the lower economic levels; that a year later Louisiana's white and Negro artisans joined in a common labor movement; and that a longer lasting, foredoomed alliance twenty years later between economically submerged whites and Negroes would frighten the Bourbon South and lead to countermeasures which would shape the region's behavior for still continuing generations.

From the resentful ranks of the insecure came William W. Holden, of North Carolina, a man as empty of fixed political principle as of purse, but rich in the political arts. Self-taught as a printer's devil in his native Orange County, North Carolina, he was only nineteen when he became in 1837 a political writer for the Raleigh *Star,* the state's leading Whig paper, reading law in his spare time. He readily turned from the solid Whig gentry when ne was offered the editorship of the *North Carolina Standard,* the principal Democratic organ, on condition that he become a Democrat himself. A powerful writer, a shrewd politician, and a personally courageous man, the young turncoat—and there were many others like him in the South—made the *Standard* the state's most influential newspaper; and, breaking completely with his Whig past, he became an advocate of secession.

Holden's brilliance and pugnacity made him a leader of his adopted party, but in 1858, after seeking and losing the Democratic gubernatorial nomination, principally through the opposition of other former Whigs who had also become Democrats, he all but parted company with the party. Wavering between Unionism and secession, after Lincoln's election, he was a delegate to the state's secession convention and made a stirring speech in behalf of withdrawal from the Union, although he had earlier been a Union delegate to an initial state convention whose decision to remain in the Union the North Carolinians had rejected.

The war was not a year old when Holden changed his tack again. He took part in the establishment of a conservative splinter party and, after its success, plotted to control the new state administration and to engineer a break with the Confederate government and seek peace with the United States. But the new governor, Zebulon B. Vance, was no peacemaker. Holden parted company with him and became the open leader of the peace movement which in 1863, after the Battle of Gettysburg and the fall of Vicksburg, won strong minority support in the state. Georgia soldiers wrecked the *Standard's* printing plant, and in retaliation some of Holden's followers destroyed the Vance administration's newspaper plant.

In May 1864 he again sought the governorship. It was generally known that should he be elected he would either call a convention to secede from the Confederacy or open direct peace negotiations with the United States; he was defeated, and thereafter, until a month after the surrender, he stayed in the background. President Johnson appointed him provisional governor of North Carolina. In November 1865, after a brief and unprincipled administration as Johnson's interim appointee, Holden was defeated in the first postwar gubernatorial election.

The political changeling then swung to the Radicals, urging adoption of the Fourteenth Amendment, punishment for the late leaders of the Confederacy, and the enfranchisement of the Negro, although as provisional governor he had advocated in the preceding spring the colonization of the free Negroes because "the two races could not live in harmony together as free races." He became president of the Loyal Leagues of North Carolina and turned savagely on Johnson. By now the Holden pendulum had swung from one extreme to the other—from Whig to Union Democrat, to Secessionist, to Unionist and Johnson supporter, and finally to Radical Republican ally of the Negro.

With the backing of the Carpetbaggers who now dominated him, and the Negro electorate, Holden was elected governor in 1868. In all probability he did not profit personally from office; but he protected the looters, and North Carolina learned what it meant to be ruled by corrupt and extravagant men. North Carolina's white Conservatives turned to the Ku Klux Klan and to the terrorizing of Negro, Carpetbag, and Scalawag officeholders and voters.

In 1870 the legislature, at Holden's insistence, enacted several statutes intended to destroy the Klan. One such act gave Holden the authority to proclaim a state of insurrection in any county and to use the militia to suppress uprisings. His abuse of this authority boomeranged. The Conservatives, employing every useful method from fraud and intimidation to murder itself, one-sidedly carried the state in a violence-ridden election. Holden was impeached, removed from the governorship, and disqualified from holding office ever again in North Carolina.

Strangely, he cherished the state which he had dishonored and which in turn had punished him. President Grant offered him the post of minister to Peru in 1872. He declined the appointment. Instead he accepted the postmastership at Raleigh, became an active Methodist, and lived out his life there. Before the old man died he had won back some old friends and made new ones, and he defended himself to the end of his days against charges of wrongdoing or personal gain.

Some had the Midas touch. . . .

Of all the Scalawags who held high office during Radical Reconstruction only one survived politically the odium of apostasy after the tumbling of their dynasties. He was Joseph Emerson Brown, a South Carolina-born, Georgia hillman of undistinguished antecedents, who worked as a day laborer on his father's small farm until he was nineteen and yet, five years later, after prior admission to the Georgia bar, was graduated from the Yale Law School. So sensitive was Joe E. Brown to shifting political winds, so dominant was his personality, so persuasive, and so adroit a financier was he that, after ranging himself in turn with secessionism, Radical Republicanism, and the Bourbon-led Democratic restoration, he ended his unprincipled career not only a rich man but a political master more powerful as a post-Reconstruction Democrat than he had ever been as a passing ally of Radicalism.

Joe Brown's political career was fabulous. After eight vigorous years in state politics, as senator, and circuit judge, the thirty-six-year-old politician won in 1857 the Democratic nomination for governor of Georgia, as a compromise candidate in a deadlocked convention. He defeated the celebrated Benjamin H. Hill, the Unionist and Know-Nothing candidate, and, re-elected in 1859, 1861, and 1863, served throughout the war as Georgia's governor. As an extreme States' rights man he tangled time and again with Jefferson Davis to the detriment of the Confederacy's prosecution of the war. Paroled after Lee's surrender, his parole was soon revoked and he was briefly imprisoned in Washington. Granted a presidential pardon by Johnson, he returned to Georgia. With the state under military administration, he resigned his governorship in June 1865.

When the Radical Congress refused the following December to seat Southerners elected to Congress under the Johnson Reconstruction program and required instead that the Southern states adopt the Fourteenth Amendment in order to be readmitted, Joe Brown made a dramatic political decision for motives which are still debated. Almost alone among the wartime political leaders of Georgia, he advocated acceptance of the hateful conditions for re-entry on the grounds that Georgia could not resist the victors and that the alternative would be prolonged military occupation, even more drastic Radical demands, and political chaos. He was reviled and discredited by his former friends and party associates. The Democratic press labeled him a renegade. So Joe Brown quit the Democratic party and joined up with the Republicans to put through the hated congressional requirements for readmission. In the subsequent election the Radicals won handsomely and the new legislature was dominated by the usual triumvirate of Carpetbagger, Scalawag, and Negro. Rufus B. Bullock, the transplanted

New Yorker who had come to Georgia as a communications expert, defeated General John B. Gordon, the state's foremost Confederate, for the governorship. Bullock was destined to go down as the worst governor in the state's history.

Brown offered himself as a candidate for the United States Senate before the Radical legislature. He was defeated, in his first and only political setback. Governor Bullock appointed him chief justice of the supreme court of Georgia that same year.

For two years Brown presided as chief justice, resigning in 1870 to become president of an inside-track corporation formed to lease the state-owned railroad. Among the directors of the company were his old antagonist, Ben Hill, and also the former vice-president of the Confederacy, Alexander H. Stephens, united under the soiled intersectional banner of the rampant locomotives. That same year a legislature largely hostile to Bullock was elected, and in the face of certain impeachment, or worse, that worthy fled the state.

After this turn of events Joe Brown returned to the Democratic fold, and in a special gubernatorial election held early in 1871 to replace Bullock he aided greatly in the election of a Conservative Democrat, James S. Smith. The triumphant Democrats forgave him. The Georgia historian, C. Mildred Thompson, was to write that Brown "was first in secession, first in Reconstruction and very nearly first in the restoration of Democratic home rule. Consequently he came up on top with every revolution of the wheel of destiny."

For the next ten years Joe Brown devoted most of his time to making a fortune out of coal and iron mining, investments in Atlanta real estate, and railroading. He was not squeamish as to how; it is revealing that the onetime Radical Republican leased convict labor, mostly Negro, from the state for about seven cents a day.

A wealthy man, he returned to political life. The beloved General Gordon, whom the state had rewarded with a United States senatorship for his part in throwing out the Radicals, resigned suddenly under highly questionable circumstances, just three weeks before the end of his Senate term. Governor Alfred H. Colquitt, another onetime Confederate major general and unswerving secessionist, and an enemy of Brown during Reconstruction, appointed his old foeman to Gordon's vacant Senate seat. There seems to be no doubt that General Gordon resigned to accept the presidency of the Brown-dominated Western and Atlantic Railroad and that Colquitt had then appointed Brown to his place in exchange for the wealthy former governor's political support.

If such was the agreement, Brown lived up to it handsomely. His financial and political backing of Colquitt when the governor sought re-election was a principal factor in Colquitt's victory. Brown then offered himself to the new legislature for re-election, and that body obliged. He served as a United States senator for two terms, in rather astonishing proof that unswerving loyalty to a principle or party is not necessarily a prerequisite for political achievement or approbation, and, more pertinently, in evidence that a man could be a Scalawag in Georgia and live it down. No other Reconstruction Southerner—or any other for that matter—ever outshone him in the ability to use political power to further his business enterprises and to use his financial power to influence politics. And Georgia seemed to like it.

Some were expedient or confused or hopeless. . . .

Had another than General James Longstreet commanded the Confederate First Corps at Gettysburg, the course of American history might have been decisively changed. It also may be that the characteristics to which most historians ascribe Longstreet's singular performance at Gettysburg are responsible for his desertion of his fellow Southerners soon after the end of hostilities.

Longstreet was a stubborn man and slow-moving, a good fighter·whose troops went where he told them to go, but a subordinate who could be uncertain to the point of despair, even to insubordination. Controversial in his military behavior, taciturn and unyielding, he was not the kind of man in Reconstruction to win many converts to his policy of joining up with the recent enemy; and he was alone among the ranking Confederate officers in going over to the Radical Republicans, lock, stock, and barrel. It is more difficult to determine what motivated him than is the case with any other of the leaders among the Carpetbaggers, for much of what Longstreet was remains hidden in the shadows of a life that has not yet been sufficiently examined and recorded.

South Carolina born, of New Jersey ancestry, and raised in Georgia and Alabama, Longstreet was a widow's son when he was admitted to West Point in 1838. He did not distinguish himself there, graduating fifty-fourth in a class of sixty-two. In 1861, a major with a battle wound to remind him of the Mexican campaign, he resigned from the paymaster's department of the United States Army to serve the Confederacy in the same department. Sixteen days after his resignation he was commissioned a Confederate brigadier general. In his subsequent career as a chieftain in the Confederate forces he excelled as a leader of men in combat, but under General Lee he was effective as a subordinate only when Lee's plans met his approval. Rarely has military history revealed a high-ranking subordinate as reluctant to follow orders when he thought they were ill-advised. His courage was unchallengeable. His judgment and self-discipline were not. He was not among the generals whom the South revered in defeat.

Even so, the stocky, hard-of-hearing veteran did well enough in the early months after the surrender, as the president of an insurance company and as a New Orleans cotton factor. But in 1867 something, or a combination of somethings—his several biographers differ so widely that his behavior is described all the way from near simple-mindedness to overwhelming hunger for fame and money—happened to him; the old yielding to hopelessness, the disbelief in the efficacy of Southern resistance to Radical Reconstruction, a professional soldier's full acceptance of the terms and the consequences of surrender, a conviction that any other course save collaboration meant lasting disaster, even personal ambition, though never marked before—these, and who knows what other considerations, prompted one of the foremost of Lee's lieutenants to join the foe. And he was to make his living as a Republican political appointee until the day of his death in 1904 —as surveyor of customs in New Orleans, detested adjutant general of the Louisiana militia, railroad commissioner, minister to Turkey, United States marshal for Georgia, postmaster of Gainesville, Georgia.

Perhaps his prewar friendship with General Grant—he was best man in Grant's wedding, and Grant had also written personally to President Johnson in behalf of a pardon for his old friend—led him to believe, before and after Grant became President, that he and Grant could work together to end the South's travail. Perhaps his own explanation of his decision, in a letter to the New Orleans *Times* on June 3, 1867, reveals his real motivation:

"There is only one route left open, which practical men cannot fail to see. The serious difficulty arises from want of that wisdom so important for the great work in hand. Still, I will be happy to work in any harness that promises relief to our discomfited people and harmony to the nation, whether bearing the mantle of Mr. Davis, or Mr. Sumner.

". . . It is fair to assume that the strongest laws are those established by the sword. The ideas that divided political parties before the war—upon the rights of the state—were thoroughly discussed by our wisest statesmen and eventually appealed to the arbitrament of the sword. The decision was in favor of the North, so that her construction becomes the law and should be accepted.

"The military bill and amendments are the only peace offerings they have for us, and should be accepted as a starting point for future issues."

From the day the letter appeared Longstreet would be an outcast, scorned by his closest former friends. For a year after his published declaration he lived in near poverty. Then Grant appointed him surveyor of customs. As commander of the Negro Metropolitan Police in New Orleans, his degradation in the eyes of his fellow whites was completed when, in 1875, he was present on the side of these armed, uniformed Negroes when they and New Orleans' White League did battle.

Though opprobrium was to be his punishment at the hands of his fellow

Southerners, he had his defenders. One, naturally, was his second wife, Helen, who in 1904 wrote *Lee and Longstreet at High Tide*. The loyal wife defended his military record, his telltale letter, and his subsequent behavior: "The very head and font of his offending consisted in his belief that it was better for the South to accept the situation then presented; better for the high class men of the South to hold the offices than to have the Negroes and Scalawags hold them; better for the South to keep faith with its Appomattox parole, which promised obedience to constituted authority. It was a few years after this letter [to the New Orleans *Times*] that President Grant appointed him surveyor of the port at New Orleans. He never asked for this appointment, and was not consulted about it. President Grant, in the generosity of his heart, voluntarily sent his name to the Senate, and the first news General Longstreet had of it came through the press."

No one could really know then and no one knows now what moved Dutch Longstreet. Perhaps his decision did come, as he himself said, as the result "of my meditations and His Divine aid" and "from the duty that I felt that I owed to God above all others."

And some Scalawags were coldly logical men of affairs.

Probably more than any of his Scalawag contemporaries, James Lusk Alcorn of Mississippi was driven by logic. He was a wealthy man before the war and even at its close. Class envy could not have animated him. Although he was a self-made newcomer among the landed gentry of Mississippi he was accepted with respect and as an equal. If his wartime business dealings were questionable, and his political ambitions great, he was not unique in either. He was not a turncoat, for he remained throughout his life an orderly conservative. He had no illusions about the newly freed Negro as a citizen. He was unsympathetic toward the Northern reformer. He believed implicitly that he could serve Mississippi in Reconstruction better than could any other of her citizens.

Kentucky-born James Lusk Alcorn came of ordinary people. His first American ancestor was a North-Irish last maker who set up shop in Philadelphia in 1721; he was the grandson of a hard-working millwright in Georgia and son of a Mississippi River boatman. He studied one year at Cumberland College, Kentucky, then taught school, served as a deputy sheriff of Livingston County, Kentucky, and read law until he was admitted in 1843 to the bar. As ardent a Whig as was Henry Clay, he served in the Kentucky legislature for a term and soon thereafter migrated to Coahoma County, Mississippi, where he invested his small savings in a farm which in time would expand to holdings of twelve thousand acres. These cotton lands would make him wealthy.

Two years after Alcorn came to Mississippi he was elected to the state legislature. An outspoken anti-secessionist, he soon became Mississippi's foremost Whig. In 1851 he led the fight against secession in the state convention called by the governor to sound out state sentiment, and in 1852 he was the presidential elector-at-large on the Winfield Scott ticket, the defeat of which meant the end of national Whiggery. Five years later he declined the combined Whig and Know-Nothing nomination for governor but accepted a nomination for United States representative. In a spirited race he was defeated by L. Q. C. Lamar. Temporarily abandoning politics, he spent the next four years augmenting his already considerable fortune.

As a Unionist delegate to the Mississippi secession convention Alcorn was defeated by a secessionist for president of the convention. Lamar again worsted him in a debate before the convention's committee of fifteen when he sought the defeat of Lamar's ordinance of secession. By an eleven to four division the committee voted to secede. The convention approved its decision.

"I have thought that a different course . . . should have been adopted and to that end I have labored and spoken," Alcorn told the convention. "But the die is cast—the Rubicon is crossed—and I enlist in the army that marches to Rome."

The Unionist still commanded the respect of his rebellious fellow citizens. He was offered a seat in the Southern Congress which would assemble in Montgomery, Alabama. To his wife, Amelia, he wrote in January 1861: "I have told my friends that I had rather be placed in the army; to the battlefields, my dear wife, I must go, if war ensues, which I have no doubt. I think I will be elected a brigadier-general."

And elected he was, as one of the four original brigadiers in command of Mississippi's state troops. The other three were veterans of the Mexican War. For eighteen months General Alcorn served grudgingly and inconspicuously in the conflict which he had foreseen, for a cause in which he did not believe, and under a commander in chief whom he detested. Probably because the Confederate government doubted his loyalty, he did not receive a commission in the regular Army. In the autumn of 1862, when on duty in Kentucky, he requested General Simon B. Buckner to relieve him of his duties.

"This post is an important one, and should not be commanded by one who has not the confidence . . . [of] the government in Richmond," he wrote Buckner. "If the Confederate government wishes me, I would be appointed [a regular brigadier general]. This not being done, I am an intruder."

Buckner obliged him. Alcorn returned to Mississippi to take command of sixty-day volunteers. From camp in Grenada he wrote Amelia, "I am away from my family, fighting a war brought on the country by the corruption of a party, which long since secured my deepest hatred, this in itself is calculated to irritate me, and I have no patience to trifle with drunken, lounging vagabonds. . . ."

In common with almost all Southern Whigs and many Democrats as well, he had an abhorrence of Jefferson Davis and a suspicion of the Democratic party which in part explains his willingness to become a Republican after the war. To Amelia he wrote from camp, "I detest Jeff Davis for his stupidity, he sits at Richmond with his servile congress and defends that city of brick and mortar and permits . . . the life blood of his government to be poured out . . . It is not so much on account of the act of secession . . . but I blame him for his stupid policy: his egotism, arrogance and superciliousness have ruined the South, a brave people have been sacrificed on the altar of Jeff Davis' egotism. The capacity of his mind may be judged by his surrender of the Mississippi River."

And again on March 16, 1863:

"Our Negroes will soon be ashes in our hands, our land valueless without them. Oh curse the Democratic party for the ruin they have brought me, and give me, Oh God, as a solace in my poverty, the pleasure of witnessing their tears of lamentation. They doubtless boast where you are yet but they will smell sulphur before another year rolls by, then they can sing paeans of praise to their demagogue Jeff Davis—the miserable, stupid one-eyed dyspeptic arrogant tyrant who now occupies the cushioned seat at Richmond, draws his $25,000 a year, and boasts of the future grandeur of the country which he has ruined . . . O, let me live to see him damned! and sunk into the lowest hell. . . ."

Meanwhile, and later, he was doing his best to escape financial ruin. His questionable trafficking with the enemy can be explained only by the assumption that he had never been loyal to the Confederacy and was, indeed, a Unionist. He sent Amelia gold and federal greenbacks. As did many another planter, he sold his cotton, without compunction, to Yankee traders on the river. He reminded Amelia that he should save from the wreck whatever he could.

"I have sold 80 bales of cotton which brought me $12,000 and something over," he wrote her as early as November of 1862. "I hope to be able to sell 100 bales more which will bring me should I succeed $15,000 more. I sell my cotton at 35¢ per pound and am paid in 'greenbacks' such as I send you and with this I can buy in Memphis, Confederate money by the sacksfull less than 30 to 40¢ on the dollar. I have thought about buying $10,000 or $15,000 worth and investing it in a good piece of land in . . . [Alabama]. Do you think it would pay? I think I'll also smuggle out $3,000 or $5,000 more in gold. This will do to keep, but all paper money is bound to depreciate, and I had rather invest it, if I could do so wisely retaining enough to pay me through the war . . . I have hauled my cotton mostly at night, and I suppose I have slept a dozen nights on the open banks of the Mississippi River . . . The smuggling business has now become popular and people are beginning openly to trade . . . I was at Delta a few nights since when near 400 bales of cotton were openly sold and full 50 men were on the bank participating. There is scarcely an exception in the county—Carnes and Perry, Pettit, Simms, Dr. Hull, John Miller, John Jones and old Billy Atkinson and Stanfield Boyd, and Lownes Bridges. . . . You remember how they once talked. It would astonish you to witness the reaction. The authorities out in the hills, I am told, are furious. A company of [Confederate] soldiers came one night as far as Simms to burn our cotton there on the bank—we were all at the river. Mrs. Simms addressed us a note giving us the information. We had just weighed our cotton . . ."

And the next month:

"I have been very busy hiding and selling my cotton. I sold in all 111 bales. I have now here $10,000 in paper (greenbacks) and $1,000 in gold. I still have some 50 bales of old cotton and about 40 bales of new cotton picked but not ginned, if I escape the burners I will be able to realize $20,000 more . . . Among the Feds, I have made many agreeable acquaintances. I don't think they will disturb me. All appear to like me, and it is said I have great influence with them; they treat me with every respect . . . I will send you everything I can and should I dispose of my cotton in time will come myself. I wish, however, to fill my pockets—and should the war continue, we will spend our summer in New York—and leave them to fight who made the fight. . . ."

The federals must have found him agreeable. Provisional Governor J. H. Wilson of Arkansas, presumably relaying military information, wrote to Lieutenant Colonel John A. Rawlins, Grant's most trusted staff officer, on February 4, 1863—Vicksburg was to fall on July 4 of that year: ". . . a prominent Rebel living near Helena, General Alcorn, says there will be no difficulty in reaching the Yazoo River with boats of medium size." One of Grant's schemes to capture Vicksburg was to approach the city from the rear, by way of the Yazoo, which would be reached by a man-made pass.

A month after the Confederacy fell James Alcorn, Whig, Unionist, sometime general of the Mississippi state troops, trader in cotton with, and possibly counselor to, the enemy, met with other prewar Mississippi political leaders to chart the state's course. Soon thereafter the legislature, convening under Johnson's Reconstruction plan, selected as United States senators its fellow legislator, James Alcorn, and another prewar Whig, William L. Sharkey.

The subsequent refusal of Congress to seat the Southern senators and congressmen most probably prompted Alcorn to join forces with the Radical Republicans in Mississippi. The logical Delta planter must have believed that Mississippi could salvage nothing from the wreckage unless some of

its leaders, and especially the former Whigs and Unionists, would ally themselves with and then control the Radicals.

When Mississippi elected the Confederate brigadier, Benjamin G. Humphreys, as her first postwar governor and enacted the Black Codes, Alcorn
predicted accurately that the state's behavior would alienate the Republican moderates and insure Radical retaliation. And after Congress
divided the South into military districts subject to martial law and demanded
unconditional surrender to its terms for statehood, Alcorn urged acceptance of congressional reconstruction. The Negro, he pointed out, could
outvote the qualified Mississippi whites. Only if the whites recognized the
Negro as a fully equal citizen before the law could a destructive division of
political parties based on color be averted. In alliance the whites and Negroes
of Mississippi could demand of the Northern Republicans the abolition of
the almost confiscatory cotton tax, the restoration of political rights to proscribed white citizens, and the rebuilding of the Mississippi River levees so
largely in ruins.

As for the Negro, "I propose to vote with him; to discuss political affairs
with him; to sit, if need be, in political counsel with him; and from a platform
acceptable alike to him, to me, and to you, to pluck our common liberty
and our common prosperity out of the jaws of inevitable ruin."

Alcorn's own land lay behind those levees. As a planter he suffered from
the exorbitant cotton tax. Accustomed to managing Negro slaves, he believed that he could likewise direct the free Negroes and, with their votes,
become governor. If his proposals were in part selfish, they were also
logical. They would be acceptable, he was certain, to reasonable Mississippians, especially those of his own planter class.

But not many white Mississippians were rational people just then. Almost
unanimously the state's Democratic leadership and even many of his old
Whig and Unionist friends and associates turned against him.

They were further outraged when Alcorn sided with the Negro-Carpetbag-
Scalawag majority in the constitutional convention in 1868, the first political
gathering in Mississippi in which Negroes took part. The convention was
made up of seventeen Negro delegates, twenty-six Carpetbaggers, most of
them former Union soldiers, twenty-nine native Scalawags, and nineteen
Conservatives, former Whigs and Democrats who hoped to thwart the
majority. The convention was in general a bickering, demagogic affair, lasting for 115 costly days.

When, after much unruly debate, a guarantee of universal suffrage was
embodied in the new constitution, most of the white Conservatives resigned
and went home. The constitution as finally adopted contained a number of
punitive measures. Applicants would be required to take the test oath of
loyalty and to swear that they acknowledged the civil and political equality
of all men. No person could hold office who, as a member of the legislature,

had voted for the call of the secession convention, or who, as a delegate to such a convention, had voted for or signed the secession ordinance; or who had accepted or attempted to exercise the functions of any office, civil or military, under any authority or pretended government, hostile to the United States, except all persons who had aided Reconstruction by voting for the present convention or who had continuously advocated the assembling of it.

Other ordinances forbade the adoption of property qualification for office or any property or educational qualification for suffrage. Slavery or involuntary servitude other than for punishment for crime was forbidden, as was the right of the state to withdraw from the Union on any account. Also prohibited was any abridgment of the right of every citizen to travel on public conveyances.

Alcorn opposed the proscriptive clauses but campaigned for popular approval of the constitution itself. Mississippians were going to have none of it. In July 1868 Governor Humphreys was re-elected and, by a vote of 63,860 to 56,231, the constitution was turned down. Four of five members elected to Congress were Democrats, as were 66 of the 138 members of the legislature. Fraud and intimidation contributed to the victory. But the election was supervised by the military with federal troops stationed at some sixty voting places in the state. Many of the Negro voters joined with the almost solid mass of whites to defeat the constitution.

The victory was to be an empty one. A five-man committee, which the convention had appointed to canvass the election returns, declared that the constitution had been ratified and adopted by a majority of the legal votes cast at the election and that the Republican state ticket had also been victorious. The committee asked Congress to approve its audacious ruling.

In November the Republican state convention also memorialized Congress to declare the constitution ratified; and a committee of sixteen Republicans, among them Alcorn, was sent to Washington to lobby for readmission. Conservative Mississippi Republicans joined with Democratic delegations in Washington in protest to such tactics. The result, after months of wrangling, was that Mississippi remained under military rule. Congress authorized the newly elected President Grant to make his own decisions as to when Mississippi could again seek to enter the Union.

In July 1869 Grant set November 30 as the day on which the constitution should be resubmitted to the electorate. This time the voters had a choice of voting for the constitution in its entirety or voting for it with the exception of the proscriptive clauses. By now the Republicans had split into a moderate and a radical faction with the Democrats and former Whigs aligned with the Conservative Republicans and the Negroes almost entirely with the Radicals. Twenty days before Grant's proclamation for the new election the Conservatives met at Jackson, organized themselves as the National Union

Republican party, and, in an open invitation to the native white Democrats to join them, denounced proscription and deplored the imposition of any disabilities other than the Constitution and the laws of the nation provided. The Democrats, who had decided not to put a ticket in the field, thereupon aligned themselves with the Conservatives.

The Radical Republicans, convening in July, recommended, at Alcorn's insistence, the removal of political disabilities and declared for universal amnesty, universal suffrage, and a free school system.

Then came one of the oddest quirks in American political history. The Conservative Republican-Democratic coalition selected as their gubernatorial candidate Judge Lewis Dent, who, when he was so honored, was a guest of his brother-in-law, President Grant, in the White House. He had come to Mississippi near the end of the war as a lessor of abandoned lands in Coahoma County, where Alcorn lived. The Radical Republicans chose conservative James Alcorn, the onetime slaveowner. Seeking the lieutenant governorship on his ticket was a former Union soldier, R. C. Powers. The Reverend James Lynch, an Illinois mulatto, was nominated for secretary of state. The Conservative coalition also chose a Negro, Thomas Sinclair, as candidate for secretary of state and divided the rest of its ticket among three former Union soldiers and two native Democrats.

The Conservatives hoped for Grant's endorsement of his brother-in-law. But the President lost no time in writing Judge Dent that the success of his group in Mississippi would result "in the defeat of what I believe to be the best interests of the state and country"—a comment that was an augury of the hardening attitude of the man who, as commander of the Union Army, had been sympathetic with the South and even outspoken in his antagonism to the unrestricted participation of the Negro in the nation's political life.

Without Grant's blessing the Conservatives had no chance. Judge Dent was an amiable man with a gift for sarcastic debate, but he was no match for Alcorn, who denounced the Conservatives as violators of the laws and abusers of the Negro. The Negro voters responded to his racial appeal. He was supported also by General Adelbert Ames, the then military governor and a man who, as the last Reconstruction governor of Mississippi, would be the most hated figure in the state. Not a few white Mississippi Democrats, caught between the devil and the deep blue sea, decided that, despite his fiery speeches, James Alcorn, a lifelong Conservative whose interests were completely bound up with Mississippi, was a more suitable candidate than was the judge who had come into Mississippi only after the invading wave had submerged the state. Alcorn won easily by a vote of 76,143 to 38,133.

As governor, James Alcorn astonished and sometimes outraged supporters and opponents alike.

One Radical wrote: "In some of his appointments he has put in his style of Whig d—mn Rebels as you are well aware of and I suppose you can further see that he is fixing up a party of his own (Whig) and using the Negro for a blind . . ." Of his three appointees to the state supreme court, two were old and honored citizens of the state and no Radicals. The third was a New York Carpetbagger but an honest and hard-working jurist, though not well versed in Mississippi jurisprudence. Most of his other appointments met with nonpartisan approval.

His policies during the first year of his administration reassured many of his foes. He embarked upon a levee-rebuilding program and sought reduction of land taxes and state aid to railroad building. Reluctantly he agreed to the leasing of convicts, with the explanation that the state was not itself prepared to put its prisoners to work. He recommended restrictive legislation to protect the citizens and the state from the activities of the hordes of railroad and insurance and other promoters who were swarming into Mississippi. Though he urged economy and did hold down expenditures, he warned that increases in the costs of government were unavoidable because of the need to spend far larger sums on public education than before the war. He was responsible for the establishment of the state's first normal school and for the Negro college which bears his name.

Alcorn enraged the whites of Mississippi in 1870 and again in 1871 by asking and obtaining legislation intended to suppress the Ku Klux Klan. The legislature gave him a contingent fund of $60,000, the accounting to be left up to him, for use in a personally directed secret service. He employed this body of agents to obtain evidence against Klansmen and other lawbreakers. He also offered a reward of $5000, under an anti-Ku Klux law enacted in 1870, for the arrest and conviction of anyone found guilty of committing crimes of violence in disguise and asked the legislature to create a state cavalry regiment to put down rioting. But when Klan violence mounted he refused a Radical demand that he ask President Grant for federal troops. Not a single Klansman was ever convicted in Mississippi; and Alcorn's enemies within the Republican party cited the Klan's apparent immunity as proof of his secret sympathy with white lawlessness.

Alcorn's next political adventure, in November of 1871, may have been of his own making, or it may have resulted from Radical Republican strategy to get him out of Mississippi. In January 1870 the Radical-dominated legislature had selected two interim United States senators to fill the seats left vacant during and since the war. That which had been occupied by Jefferson Davis went to Hiram R. Revels, the Southern-born Negro Methodist minister who had come to Mississippi as an official in the Freedmen's Bureau. The other seat went to General Ames. Revels's term was to expire in March 1871 and that of Ames in March 1875.

In November 1871 Alcorn resigned his governorship to replace Revels. In the Senate he became a spokesman for the white Mississippians. He debated with Senator Ames over the extent of violence in Mississippi; he opposed integrated public schools; he urged an end to civil and political disabilities. He asked that Mississippians be given more time to accept the new order and warned that a public school system directed from Washington would have to be upheld by federal bayonets. He also opposed a proposed income tax, supported railroad land-grant laws, and denounced the federal cotton tax as robbery. Persistently he challenged Ames on state issues.

By 1873 most Mississippi Conservatives had swung to him, and in that year he and Ames carried their feud to the people. The Republicans chose the Maine Yankee as their candidate for governor. Alcorn's followers in the party bolted and, meeting at the state capitol, nominated him as their candidate. The Democrats, with no slate of their own, and believing that Alcorn could split the Negro vote and so defeat Ames, decided to espouse his candidacy. But their efforts were feeble. Many Democrats would not support wholeheartedly the Coahoma planter who had advocated legal and political equality for the Negro. And despite Alcorn's reminders to the Negro voters of his efforts in their behalf, they turned from him. He was defeated by a vote of 69,870 to 50,490. Adelbert Ames, the Maine adventurer who was not even a citizen of the state and had never paid any state taxes, entered upon a rapacious, highhanded administration which would end with his own eventual disgrace.

Alcorn's defeat meant the end of his political career. But in his personal feud with Ames he emerged, in a sense, victorious; for when the governor, facing almost certain civil uprising in 1875, sought military aid from Grant, the President refused. His refusal was based in part upon the advice of James Alcorn, to whom, among others in Mississippi, the President turned.

In that same violent year Alcorn led a force of whites in Coahoma County against a group of Negroes, after white Republicans and Democrats in the county had united to overthrow a corrupt ring of Carpetbaggers and Negro partisans of Ames. In a pitched battle at the hamlet of Friars Point six Negroes and two white men were killed and the Negroes dispersed.

Alcorn emerged from political retirement in 1890 long enough to represent Coahoma County in the new state constitutional convention, at which mass disfranchisement of the Negro was accomplished. Disclaiming membership in any party and listing himself, quite accurately, as a conservative in politics, Alcorn was appointed to the vital Election Franchise, Apportionment and Elections Committee and to the Militia Committee. In the debate of the new constitution he spoke and worked in behalf of property and literacy qualifications for the franchise, as well as for the more restrictive tests designed almost wholly to reduce the Negro vote to nothing.

Four years later he died at seventy-eight, a still controversial symbol of the multiple, conflicting impulses that drew native white Southerners to the Republican ranks during Reconstruction. Lechers, thieves, turncoats, men of conviction and cupidity, they would in time share a common onus. But they were not animated by any single, common impulse, and some among them were uncommon men indeed.

CHAPTER 4

Albert Morgan, Carpetbagger

OF THE *Yankees who came South by the tens of thousands after the war, only a memorable minority earned lasting enmity. These were the political adventurers who were ridiculed as Carpetbaggers, a nickname derived from the popular Southern belief that to the land of Radical opportunity they carried all their belongings in a single piece of hand luggage known as the carpetbag.*

Sometime early in 1884 a $1600-a-year minor employee of the Pension Office in Washington, a man not always obscure, completed a singularly defiant apologia.

Aside from the vindication his recollections might win, the proceeds from their sale, however meager, would be welcome. In this year of Democratic resurgence the unforgiving foes of Albert T. Morgan, sometime brevet lieutenant colonel of the Second Wisconsin Volunteers, and more lately sheriff and tax collector of Yazoo County, Mississippi, would soon catch up with him. A year later, on the heels of Grover Cleveland's presidential victory, he would be jobless—Mississippi's Senator Lamar would see to that—and heading west with the wife who had contributed to his fall and their six children.

Already Mississippi had heard about Colonel Morgan's forthcoming book, for provocative circulars had been mailed both to friends and enemies. Albert Morgan's old political opponents, and they included most of Mississippi's native white citizens, did not relish its title, *Yazoo, or On the Picket Line of Freedom*. They would like its contents much less.

The author had reserved for the last chapter his defense of the one lapse which those Mississippians would not forgive. The error was not that Oberlin-educated Albert Morgan and his older brother, Captain Charles Morgan, sons of a prosperous Wisconsin farmer, had come in 1865 as Yankee settlers, eager to raise cotton in the state whose good earth they had first admired as invading Union officers. Many another Yankee had done likewise and won acceptance. The error was not so much that, failing as a cotton planter, the twenty-three-year-old Albert had entered state politics as a Republican. Reasonable Southerners would admit that an honestly Republican Yankee was not as bad as a home-grown, nigger-loving Scalawag and that some of them were decent fellows. Eventually many such Yankees would become one with their Southern neighbors. Since the Mississippians were violent folk themselves, they might even have forgiven the two gunfights in which Albert Morgan had shot and killed one man and probably another, for he apparently had not been the aggressor in either instance. In his personal habits he was exemplary. He neither drank nor smoked, and competent Southern historians would later vouch for his honesty in public life. And Mississippians could have winked at his fathering of children more dark-skinned than he, had he been a conventional miscegenationist, for in the Yazoo River country there were few men who could cast the first stone; some before the war had felt enough affection or responsibility or pity for their bastards to free and educate them, but almost never did they publicly recognize them.

In this regard Albert Morgan was different. The Yankee colonel had knowingly married a beautiful quadroon, the New York-born daughter of a mulatto freedman and a Northern white mother. Carolyn Victoria Highgate was a college-educated schoolteacher who had come from Syracuse, New York, to teach in a Freedmen's Bureau school in Mississippi; but she was, under state law, a Negro woman none the less. In marrying her Morgan was to earn in the state from which he would later be driven a notoriety that set him apart. He had compounded the forgivable and commonplace Southern sin of miscegenation with an unpardonable deviation which gave the legitimacy and security of his name to his mate and his children. And Albert Morgan not only violated the taboo; he was unashamed of the violation.

Colonel Morgan's story of his life in Mississippi affords insight into far more than his own combative personality. From 1868 to 1875 he exercised considerable political power in the state. He was forceful, unafraid, and honest in his expenditures of public funds. Politically and in his social life he cast his lot almost entirely with the Negroes. He was imbued with the raging fervor of Abolitionism. He was not typical of the political adventurers from the North who were to be lumped together and uniformly hated as Carpetbaggers. But he came to be remembered as typical, for the Reconstruction legend dwells upon Carpetbagger approval of and indulgence in mixed marriages, even though the legend is almost entirely without foundations. His story is salient in its evidence of the essentially racial nature of the Reconstruction conflict and in its frank, if jaundiced, disclosure of what white Southerners thought of Carpetbag politicians and what the Radical Carpetbagger of convictions thought of white Southerners.

What follows is mostly Albert Morgan's own story, much as he told it himself. It is supported in outline by less partisan historians, Southerners among them.

Soon after the Morgan brothers landed by steamboat at Vicksburg in the autumn of 1865 they rented Tokeba Plantation in Yazoo County, one of the hundreds available in the broken state. The brothers were at first fairly cordially received and even were the house guests of their landlords, a Colonel and Mrs. Black; but Albert was disturbed and aroused, at least in retrospect, by the treatment of the plantation Negroes and by his host's social boast that before the war he had used a young Negro slave girl as bait among the county voters and thus won election to the state legislature as a Whig.

Like many another Northerner's experiment in cotton raising, the Tokeba venture was to fail, even though the Morgans were able to hire Negroes—so he recalled—when they would not work for their former masters; and in the light of his later career this is likely.

At first the young Yankee planter tried to identify himself with the interests of his Southern neighbors, but soon came the inevitable parting. Attending a meeting of armed white men who believed, he relates sarcastically, that there existed "a deep, damnable conspiracy by the Negroes to rise and kill all the white people from the cradle up," Morgan challenged the possibility of such a plot and declared that he doubted the Negroes would throw away their many gains by such behavior. He was not applauded; neither did the rising occur.

Soon thereafter he went to Vicksburg to hire farm workers in the freedmen's camp there. Among these derelicts were a number of Colonel Black's former slaves, who began telling tales which he was at first "unwilling to accept" about the cruelty of their former owners:

"What shocked me most was the unanimous opinion of these people that Mrs. Black was more cruel and tyrannical than the colonel, and their accounts of cruel floggings, brandings and starvings inflicted on them by the order of Mrs. Black were simply incredible. My estimate of that lady, [was] based upon what I had seen in her own home . . . and I secretly attributed them the habit of recounting their wrongs to Federal soldiers, until they had learned to exaggerate them in order to gain sympathy for themselves."

He soon quarreled also with the Blacks when they and some friends spoke vehemently against the Radical leaders whom he revered, while extolling as patriots, noblemen, and statesmen and leaders of the South. Secretary Seward was "the traitor"; General Ben Butler "the beast, the wretch, the reviler of women"; Charles Sumner "the miscegenationist"; Stanton "the tyrant." Morgan kept silent, he says, until he was asked to express an opinion, whereupon he told the gathering that he believed the freedmen should and eventually would enjoy all the rights of citizens; that Grant was an able general and a merciful conqueror, Ben Butler a patriot and "the right man in the right place"; that the men who followed Grant were not hirelings and that those who followed Sherman were not barbarians; that Lincoln was a great man, Sumner a scholar and statesman with a spotlessly pure character, and that all the rest deserved the thanks of their country. Whatever else he might have been, young Colonel Morgan was no diplomat.

Mrs. Black tried to smooth things over after his retort, saying she "wouldn't be surprised if Mr. Sumner was a real gentleman"; but Albert Morgan was no longer welcome in the Blacks' home or in any other homes of the upper-class white families of the county.

Soon afterward brother Charles Morgan returned from up North where he had gone to buy plantation supplies, and the Tokeba operation got under way. The brothers were especially successful, at first, with a sawmill. They were able to sell as much lumber as they could cut and mill, theirs being the only sawmill in the area, and they became popular with the merchants, for they bought from the tradesmen with "good cypress lumber which was as good coin as big greenbacks."

Young Morgan must have been naïve. He tells that he soon noticed that a number of Negro women were frequent visitors to his leased plantation and that many of them were of light complexion and some very pretty.

"I never suspected what their frequent visits meant. To me they were freed people. All poor, all needy—needing land, money, clothes, bread, meat no more than the dignity of self-respect . . . I had no other idea than that these people would look to the Yankees for light, as they had done for liberty, and while it was neither my business, nor my inclination at that time to be their instructor, I could not so far humiliate and degrade myself as to fail of trying to be an example to them in my private life and habits."

Soon two of these visitors made suggestions that he could not mistake, thereby much embarrassing him. The pair, so he learned, were mistresses, respectively, of a prominent county planter and a Yazoo City merchant. Shortly thereafter the mother of a fourteen-year-old light-skinned girl suggested that he take charge of her daughter.

"I found myself asking myself: Well——! What kind of a country is this anyway? . . . The level of morality was low indeed, and it was clear to me that new influences must be introduced . . . They must be taught to think, I said."

Then came the lasting schism. Colonel Black met Morgan on the street in Yazoo City and told him that it was rumored throughout the county that a Northerner had said "a Negro wench was as good as a white lady." Was it he? At first Morgan refused to answer. The colonel continued haranguing him, declaring that "the peace of this Union depends on we all being left to manage ouah Nigros in ouah own way, by God, sir-r-r-r." The colonel then denounced Morgan for having been seen putting up a fence alongside some Negroes and his brother for talking to Mrs. Black in his shirt sleeves. Further, said the colonel, Morgan had permitted the Negroes to call him Colonel Morgan instead of Master, and himself had called the Negro blacksmith's wife Mrs. Smith. Colonel Black heatedly suggested that Morgan publish a card retracting the statement that a Negro was as good as a white. In this case, he said, he would do all he could to repair the damage to Morgan's reputation. Morgan refused.

" 'Colonel Black, you say that Negroes are free?'

" 'Yes, by God, sir,' he exclaimed excitedly.

" 'Well, you'll grant that I'm a free man too, will you not?'

" 'Well, sir, by God, sir, what do you mean, sir?'

"But I kept cool, saying only:

" 'We hold the lease on Tokeba for three years. . . . We believe that we can get more and better labor for the same money out of our hands by treating them as though they too had rights . . . than if we cheated them as though they were brutes.' "

As Colonel Black fumed Morgan continued:

" 'We had not dreamed that it would be considered revolutionary nor even thought of it in that light. But we may as well understand each other. . . . I am assured no member of our firm is sorry for what we have done in this regard . . . We shall make no display of our views or examples; at the same time we shall not hide our light under a bushel. We shall continue to treat our people as though they were worthy of their hire. . . . We shall never forget that Mrs. Smith is a member of our community, nor can I understand why we should be disturbed in our lawful and peaceful pursuit by reason thereof.' "

By now, Morgan wrote, Colonel Black was completely beside himself, as is more than likely, red of face, trembling, leaning on his cane to support himself. As he turned to leave he taunted: " 'Well, by God, sir . . . I took you for a gentleman.' " From then on Charles Morgan, who apparently got along much better with the Southerners than did Albert, conducted what business was necessary with the Blacks.

Not long afterward, when Morgan sought to collect a bill for lumber from a former Confederate captain, the Southerner, after first treating him courteously, followed him down the street and accosted him with "What in the hell do you mean, you Yankee son of a bitch, [Morgan uses dashes] by God, sir, I'll have you to bear in mind that I pay my debts; I'm a gentleman, by God, sir, and if you don't know it I'll teach you how to conduct yourself toward one, damn you."

At this point in his memoirs the former colonel of Wisconsin Volunteers observes that he was by inclination a noncombatant, having been brought up by parents who believed in the law of love. Never before had he raised his hand against any human being, he declares, overlooking his war experiences; and besides, he was weakened by a prolonged spell of ague and was no match for the powerfully built captain. He answered that a gentleman would "hardly assault one in my condition in such a manner as this." The captain then knocked him down and continued beating him while the bystanders shouted, "Kill the damn Yankee, kill him," until a Union Army officer and two former Yankee officers broke up the fight. His compatriots then told the beaten man that he should never go out unarmed.

Morgan recalled that "of the 19 ex-federal officers and soldiers in that county engaged, some in manufacturing, some in planting, and some in merchandising, there was not one who had not been the victim of such outrages or witness of them, so that as a class we were a unit in opinion and feeling as to the purposes of the late Rebels respecting their former slaves."

From that day on Albert Morgan openly threw his lot in with the Negroes, as he had perhaps intended all along. He encouraged the activities of the Freedmen's Bureau and, with his brother, determined to build a combination Negro church and school. This further aroused the Yazoo countians. When he appeared on the streets he was greeted with shouts of "Hi, old polecat" and other taunts. Eventually a squad of white federal troops was sent to Yazoo City to prevent interference with the building of the school-church; but these soldiers, says Morgan, were won over by the citizens. They described him to the commanding officer as a Yankee adventurer who sought to gain the confidence of the Negroes in order to fleece them. The troops were eventually withdrawn, but not before the school had been completed and a teacher sent to it by the Freedmen's Bureau.

In all probability Morgan was now ready to enter into politics. Nature hastened his decision. The army worms took the brothers' crop for the second year. The sawmill could have saved them. But before another crop could be made Colonel Black seized the mill, its fixtures, and the sawed lumber, claiming that the Morgans intended to defraud him of the rent on Tokeba. If the colonel had allowed the mill to operate, Morgan says, he could have paid out.

The property was sold out from under them and they lost $50,000, but the stubborn Morgans didn't leave. Instead Albert decided in 1867 to seek election as a Radical Republican as one of the county's three delegates to the fateful constitutional convention of 1868. Three other former Union officers were running on the Conservative Republican ticket, backed by the white Democrats. Morgan's running mates, after he failed to persuade any native white Mississippians to run with him, were a Negro freedman and another former Union officer.

On the first day of the three-day balloting Morgan gathered up a large number of freedmen and escorted them to the polls. There he discovered that the white citizens were abstaining from voting in the hope that if a majority of qualified voters did not vote the results of the election would not be sustained by Congress or by the Supreme Court. Not a single Yazoo County native white man did vote, although, so Morgan claims, there were more than two hundred native whites who had sympathized with the Union cause. These, he says, were frightened into staying away from the polls.

The Negroes elected Morgan over his white Yankee opponent. In immediate consequence the brothers faced physical danger. While Albert was attending the constitutional convention Charles and a Northern friend, a former Union general, identified only as General Greenleaf, were guarded by freedmen in Yazoo City. Negro women brought them food. No one would openly trade with them. The apartment was a fortress, its occupants equipped with Spencer rifles, double-barreled shotguns, and two revolvers. Later Charles told his brother that for several days they received warnings through Negro friends that the whites were going to try to provoke violence and then arrest and lynch them.

One such warning came from a girl named Rarety, a mistress of one of the conspirators, others from servants in white homes or white places of business. These Negroes told Charles Morgan and his friend that if they were to draw a weapon against any assailant they would be arrested and placed in jail, from whence the Ku Klux would take them at night and hang them. Charles and the general determined to make no resistance to any affront except in the last extremity. While walking from their apartment to the post office they were insulted and the general was struck in the face; but they reached their apartment in safety, followed by a mob, whose members banged on their doors and threw stones at the windows. "It's so long since they've been allowed to whip a darky here in town in the good old fashioned way," the general observed, "that they have all gone stark mad."

Following the constitutional convention, there was, for a while, relative quiet in Yazoo County. More than two hundred Negro children were now attending the school which the Morgans had founded. Neither teachers nor pupils were harmed, although white teen-agers consistently heckled them during school hours. But the organization of a Loyal League led to a resumption of violence. The complete unity of the Negroes convinced the white people that their own destruction was sought.

Charles Morgan was an early victim of their retaliation. A group of white boys accosted him at a ferry. Fearing that they intended to push him in the river, he drew his pistol. For this he was arrested, found guilty for drawing a lethal weapon, and fined sixty dollars. Mocked the Yazoo *Banner,* "Toward the close of the trial [Morgan] seemed to have become a coward, and cringed like a poor cur. It was difficult to repress a feeling of sympathy for the depraved creature, as he realized that all his arts and devices had failed, and felt the iron grasp of justice tightening around him. . . ."

After the trial General Greenleaf was again insulted, apparently to provoke him into drawing a pistol; and shortly thereafter Charles was re-arrested on the former charge on the grounds that he should not have been tried before the mayor but bound instead to the grand jury. Neither Charles Morgan nor his friends could raise the $300 bail, so Charles was lodged in jail. Widespread disorder might have followed, for a mob of Negroes, armed principally with bludgeons, and convinced that the Klan would lynch Charles Morgan that night, gathered in the vicinity of the jail. The general sought out the agent of the Freedmen's Bureau and begged him to intervene. The agent at first advised him that the Morgans should not continue their struggle. By dusk the situation had become desperate. Klansmen from other communities were rumored to be converging upon Yazoo City to lynch Charles Morgan. Sullen freedmen, their numbers mounting hourly, swarmed through the town, orderly at first, except for some defiant shouting. Then, apparently, they began moving on the jail to liberate Charles Morgan. One of the town's more prominent businessmen rushed to the jail, shouting, "Turn him out! Turn Captain Morgan out of there!" meanwhile calling for the sheriff and the mayor. The freedmen fell in step behind him, echoing his demand.

At the same time a group of Northern men went to the Freedmen's Bureau agent and persuaded him that unless he acted quickly blood would be shed. The agent sought out the white ringleaders, among them Colonel Black, and told them that if Charles Morgan were harmed they would suffer serious consequences. He also warned them that he would join Morgan in the jail and that they would have at least two men to hang. In half an hour Charles Morgan, a free man, walked into the Bureau agent's office to thank him.

The brothers must have had amazing tenacity. Their father, mother, and sisters in Wisconsin were writing letters begging them to leave. Charles vented to Albert the anger both felt against the uncomprehending folks back home.

"Don't understand it at all! No; they don't any of them understand. They couldn't understand dear old 'Pap' Thomas, nor Grant, nor Sherman; they couldn't understand Stanton nor Lincoln; they can't understand us! During the war they were so wrapped up in big prices for their wheat and in buying and selling, they couldn't find time to keep up with current history. Now they are so tamed by their fears that these poor, half-starved, half-naked unarmed Negroes *may* rise and slaughter their old masters and mistresses for what they have done to them . . . and so full of tenderness and pity for whiskey-drinking, tobacco-smoking, swine-eating, scrofulous, lecherous, cowardly rebels, that they have forgotten our wounds; forgotten our generosity to these same rebels when our bayonets were at their throats, and today if one of us should be shot down like a dog, or hung to a lamp-post, so that it were done in the *common* jail, or while under some foul charge, these same kind people would never be able to understand it, and would go down to their graves feeling that, somehow, we were in the wrong. I tell you, Albert, we must fight this thing out, if it takes our lives. The country don't understand it at all, and they won't understand it until we have furnished them proof upon proof, and they have come to see with their own eyes that the last state of the sick man of the South is worse than the first. Think of it! The Negroes' only refuge is the Bureau, and you know how feeble, uncertain and treacherous are the means of protection that affords them. But here we are, without even so much as that—unless by a subterfuge, when the agent happens to be a man with some little of the milk of human kindness in his breast, and enough sand in his gizzard to support his backbone in a game of bluff. These same poor, despised Negroes, after all, are our only protection, and they have proved their courage and fidelity to my entire satisfaction."

Yazoo never let up on Albert Morgan.

A mocking song to the tune of "If You Belong to Gideon's Band" was printed in the Yazoo *Banner* in 1869, during the gubernatorial fight between the Conservative and the Radical Republican factions.

> *Old Morgan came to the Southern land* (three times)
> *With a little carpet-bag in his hand.*
>
> *Chorus: If you belong to the Ku Klux Klan*
> *Here's my heart and here's my hand,*
> *If you belong to the Ku Klux Klan*
> *We are marching for a home.*
>
> *Old Morgan thought he would get bigger* (three times)
> *By running a saw-mill with a nigger.*
>
> *Chorus*
>
> *The crop it failed and the saw-mill busted,* (three times)
> *And the nigger got very badly wusted.*
>
> *Chorus*

And so on for many, many verses.

In his naturally prejudiced recollections Morgan had nothing but praise for the Radical and Negro-dominated constitutional convention of 1868. He was especially pleased with the provisions which hit at concubinage, prohibited lotteries, and forbade the pledging of county, city, or town credit to any company without the sanction of two thirds of the qualified voters— all of them salutary acts. He noted proudly that, except for those provisions affecting Negroes' rights, the constitution would have been accepted anywhere in the United States: "Yet the people of Yazoo dived upon it so bitterly that one portion of the whites became savages in their efforts to defeat it while another lent themselves to all manner of devices, by cajolery, by bribery and by intimidation to the same purpose. Opposed to them were Charles, the general, five other Northerners, a handful of Unionists, the freed people—the Republican party of Yazoo!"

His account of the campaign to ratify the constitution of 1868, which the white citizenry succeeded in defeating, is dramatic if one-sided: "Merchants deliberately rolled out of their warehouses barrels of flour, huge sides of bacon, or pork, or tossed out pairs of shoes, boots, pants . . . Money . . . was freely and openly tendered to the freed people in consideration of their consent to be led to the polls by one of their former masters and there voted for what they called the people's ticket."

In Yazoo County a pitched battle between hundreds of whites and Negroes was barely averted. The Radical Republicans carried Yazoo.

In his account of this campaign Albert Morgan quoted a native white on the concubinage clause: ". . . all the damn Negro wenches in the county will believe they are just as good as the finest lady in the land; and they'll think themselves too good for thar place, and ouah young men'll be driven back upon the white ladies and we'll have prostitution like you all have in the North. . . . The end of it will sho'ly be the degradation of ouah own ladies to the level of ouah wenches—the brutes!"

Morgan was an indefatigable collector of critical newspaper comments, such as the one from the Meridian *Mercury* which gloated in July of 1868 over the defeat of the Radical constitution: ". . . Thank God it is over! And pray his Holy Name to remove the sin-created and creating thing, Negro Suffrage, the most abominable of abominations . . . from the land, and sink the hell-deserving authors of it to everlasting perdition! . . ."

As for the freedmen: "Alas!" Albert mourned. "The slave's dream of freedom had disappeared . . . He could not answer his old master's criticism of the Yankees . . . But he never failed to resent in some manner, if in no other than a sullen silence, any criticism upon General Greenleaf, Captain Morgan or 'Kunnel' [himself]. He knew he had never been promised land nor mules by the Yankees, certainly not by the general, my brother nor by myself. He had never expected to acquire land in that way . . . [But the failure of ratification of the constitution and other indications throughout the land] made it clear . . . that the thing we sought in Yazoo [justice and universal suffrage] . . . had little support anywhere, North as well as South, except among the Negroes and a baker's dozen of fanatical leaders in Congress, whose strength with the Northern people would be found to lie with that dim and uncertain margin which existed between downright lunatics and shrewd, farseeing money-making Yankees . . . The white race in Yazoo solidified."

By now Morgan and his brother were broke. But the election of General Grant to the presidency buoyed the small band of Northerners in Yazoo. Morgan rejoiced that Colonel Black "was unable to secure labor to work Tokeba himself, had lost a year's rent and a year's crop, and was trying to drown his sorrows in whiskey." Charles Morgan moved to Washington County, Mississippi, where he would be accepted as a good citizen and eventually die of yellow fever. For a while after the constitutional election Yazoo was again quiet.

But the peace was broken one night when Albert Morgan and General Greenleaf, who were still living in the Yazoo City apartment, were aroused by the sound of shuffling feet and martial orders. Peering through their windows, they made out between thirty and forty men in black hoods and gowns, armed with guns and pistols. They barricaded the door and prepared to defend themselves. The Klansmen had to approach the apartment by way of a narrow, outside stairs. After a brief argument among themselves the Klansmen dispersed. Upon their departure a freedman, a shoemaker who lived near by, knocked on the door. He told the defenders that he had been awakened by the Ku Klux and had armed himself and come to help them. His wife was summoning a guard of freedmen. The Klan did not return.

When the night riders rode again in Yazoo, six years later, Morgan recalled, they "marched in solid column, 900 strong, armed with Winchester rifles, needle guns, double-barrel shotguns and with ropes over the pommels of their saddles, and pistols and knives in their belts." That was in 1875, when the Mississippi whites overthrew in Yazoo City and elsewhere the Negro-Carpetbag governments.

In his memoirs Morgan pokes fun at the white Southern emissaries who went to Washington and elsewhere in the North on the heels of Grant's victory to spread what he ridiculed as unwarranted stories of Negro uprisings, Negro domination, Negro threats against the lives of white men, and Negro determination to marry white girls. He also set down his protests about the low taxes paid by the Mississippi landowners under the laws passed by the short-lived white Democratic legislature in 1865–66.

Under those laws, he says, the landowner was himself permitted to assess his land for taxation at a rate under 1/10 of 1 per cent—and 1/4 of 1 per cent upon all personal property—while high privilege taxes all but excluded freedmen from trade and professions. County and municipal governments were given the power to increase the poll tax almost without limit, and black-smiths, bakers, butchers, bricklayers, carriage makers, carpenters, timber dealers, printers, gunsmiths, sawmill operators, shoemakers, tailors, canners, watchmakers, painters, and milliners were required to pay twenty-five cents on every hundred dollars' worth of their gross earnings, the tax to be based upon gross receipts. But in Warren County in 1869, Morgan notes, the owner of 8506 acres of good cotton land paid only $99 in taxes; the heirs of General John A. Quitman paid on 6810 improved acres only $188.64, while a liveryman paid $671.03, a butcher $243.70, and a Negro drayman $33.82 on his dray and two mules.

"The greatest hardship was from the poll tax," he wrote. "In many instances in Yazoo City and County, freedmen, after working hard in the cotton field, or in the shop, the entire year without other pay than food and clothes, except an occasional mite for spending money, were arrested, 'tried,' and convicted for a failure to pay five dollars, sometimes ten dollars, upon their poll, and put at work in a chain gang, or sold, to satisfy the amount."

Morgan was as denunciatory of the Black Codes, charging that they nullified the Civil Rights Bill and in actuality reinstituted slavery. ". . . this conspiracy," he raged, "under the guise of conferring civil rights upon the freed people, involved them in a more terrible servitude than that which all agreed had been destroyed by the war; for it exalted the white man above the position of owner, by taking away the responsibilities of ownership." He charged that the only recourse of the freedmen, when Mississippi was presided over by a military commander "whose sympathies were known to be with the conspirators," was the Freedmen's Bureau, "and this recourse was effective only when the subaltern at the Bureau chanced to have influence at headquarters in Washington, or clandestinely performed his duty, or when General Grant or General O. O. Howard, or the heroic Mr. Stanton ventured to brave the wrath of the conspirators or the whole Democratic party of the nation . . . And in the county of Yazoo, under these provisions, men and women were cheated, swindled, robbed, whipped, hunted with bloodhounds, shot, killed; nay, more, men were robbed of their wives, their children; fathers, brothers, sons saw their mothers, wives, sisters seduced, betrayed, raped, and if Yazoo law afforded them any promise of the hope of redress, Yazoo practice gave them no remedy whatever. . . ."

The Black and Tans, as Morgan described his group, believed that nine out of every ten white anti-Reconstructionists were determined to win by superior sagacity and statesmanship what they had failed to accomplish on the battlefield. "We could have purchased smiles, praise, even rich rewards in the shape of gifts from the enemy had we been so craven as to be willing to treat with them. Not being so, we bared our heads to the pitiless storm. Some died under the terrors of it, others were shot, others hung and at least one burned. But now Grant was president, the knowledge of that fact literally suppressed the enemy. At the same time it filled the blood of every loyalist in Mississippi with iron. . . . The men who had garrisoned that Yazoo stronghold were not tyrants. They bore the enemy no malice. . . . So I became an enthusiastic advocate of universal Amnesty."

When the more conservative Republicans and the white Democrats joined forces to put forward the Conservative National Republican ticket led by Grant's brother-in-law, Lewis Dent, Morgan joined the regular, or Radical Republican, ticket headed by General James Alcorn. As a member of the Radical faction Morgan ran for state senator on a county ticket nearly half of which was made up of native whites. His opponent on the Conservative ticket was Major W. D. Gibbs, member of a distinguished Mississippi family. Also on the Conservative ticket as candidate for the House of Representatives was a former slave whom Morgan mocked as a "White folk's nigger, a cat's-paw dominated by the white former slaveholders and resented and reviled by the Negroes."

His account of a joint debate between himself and Major Gibbs, and its aftermath, is revealing both as to the politics and the tempers of the time. Morgan spoke first. He told his freedmen listeners that when the state was controlled by the postwar Democrats, the ruling party had connived in a bank swindle in which the state, having chartered two banks, had endorsed their bonds to the extent of several million dollars. The bonds were sold in Europe and the proceeds divided among the financial conspirators. Then, said Morgan, the state had repudiated its obligation as endorser and left the creditors without any remedy.

It is doubtful that his freedmen listeners were much impressed by this denunciation. They were more influenced by his reminder that never before had they had free schools. The nation's effort to aid in their schooling through generous land grants had been aborted, he told them, by the conversion of the proceeds of those lands to private uses. Furthermore, his opponent's party had taxed heavily new and feeble industries; before the war the Democratic party had passed the secession ordinance in convention and had dragged the state into war without the vote of even the white people of the state. This same party, he said, in an appeal to the poor white voters, had passed a wartime law providing that all who owned as many as twenty Negroes should be exempt from conscription and had even provided their conscript officers with bloodhounds to hunt down the poor whites who refused to be conscripted.

In rebuttal Major Gibbs told the Negroes that only the Yankees held prejudice against the freed people because of their color. Even Frederick Douglass, he said, "the greatest black man that ever lived, the man who made the Radical party," had been refused a seat in a hotel restaurant in the North, which was where Colonel Morgan came from. As for himself, said the major, he had no prejudice "against the color which God gave the Negro, and which they could no more help than they could fly. . . ."

The Confederate major reminded his listeners that "his black mammy, Aunt Sally . . . had suckled him and he loved her to that day as much as his own dear mother almost." The Yankees had gone to war not to free the slaves but because of the tariff. The Yankees wanted the Southerners to pay a bonus for making machinery and goods which the South was compelled to buy from them. As for the Negro rights, said the major, there was no difference between Morgan's platform and his own. After all, the Conservatives did have a colored man on their ticket, and General Alcorn, the Radical candidate for governor, had been one of the most cruel masters in the state.

The debate was not destined to run its course. A white Democratic heckler became more and more violent in his interruptions and, after engaging in an altercation with a Negro adherent of Morgan, shot and killed the Negro and was himself wounded in the exchange of fire. Morgan and Major Gibbs hastily agreed to quit speaking and to deny that either of them had fomented the trouble.

In the wake of the shooting rumor spread of a Negro uprising. The sheriff swore in some extra deputies. "But insurrection ended where it began. . . . And that was thereafter the most peaceful, good natured campaign ever held in the county, and the election was the most quiet, orderly affair ever held before or since in Yazoo County . . . the new constitution was ratified unanimously and the Republican [Alcorn] ticket was elected by an overwhelming majority, and there was perfect peace in Yazoo."

Now Albert Morgan was senator from Yazoo County. With the position came financial security he had not known since migrating to Mississippi. He had failed in business; he had alienated most of the native white leadership of the county; he had completely identified himself with the Negroes' aspirations. But he was well on his way in politics. It was high time to take a wife.

Before Morgan makes autobiographically the outwardly casual disclosure that his bride-to-be is a quadroon schoolteacher from the North, he sets up his defense with a lengthy discussion of the undeniable practice among Mississippi white men of keeping Negro concubines. He describes the anti-concubinage clause of the new constitution as the section most widely resented by the whites. Every Negro woman had previously been at the mercy of every white man with no recourse whatever, he says, and the white men resented the law as a protection for so many potential mistresses. Concubinage, Morgan argues, was one of the greatest evils of slavery, for it was not possible under such conditions for the Negro man to maintain a stable family life or for the Negro woman to gain a respected place in society. Now it would be possible "to rear a generation of colored women who could neither be purchased by the blandishments of a system which made household pets of concubines and prostitutes, nor bulldozed into subjection by the libidinous demands of dissolute master, as mistresses . . . a generation of colored men, whose manhood would as quickly resent all overtures for the possession, for such evil practices, of their mothers, wives, sisters and sweethearts," as would the manhood of "the best white man who ever lived."

The tide had turned in other ways too, Morgan notes, for on the heels of the Radical Republican victory, the native whites of Yazoo were beginning to change their attitude toward the Carpetbagger leaders and were making social overtures toward them. Some of his fellow Radicals succumbed to the blandishments of the native whites. But Morgan says that he remained aloof.

He must have already met the young woman whom he intended to marry and thus to separate himself completely from the county's established white society.

These are the ponderous, strangely sincere reasons that twenty-six-year-old Senator Albert Morgan gave for deciding that he was ready to marry a girl who legally was a Negro and thus ineligible in most of the nation to marry a white man. President Grant was in sympathy with the Radicals; the anti-concubinage section of the Mississippi constitution had been unanimously ratified; the onetime "polecats" were Yazoo's lawmakers, freed Negroes sat on juries, the poll tax had been reduced, and the Negro was no more liable to arrest for failure to pay it than was his former master; the Negro now had the right to buy and to bear arms and buy land; the rape of a Negro girl by a white man was a rape.

But racial intermarriage was illegal in Mississippi. Senator Morgan introduced a bill to repeal the proscription, and the measure passed with few objections. Hard upon its approval he married Carolyn Victoria Highgate, whom even white Mississippi Conservatives in the legislature had admiringly described as "the beauteous Miss Carrie Highgate."

To mock his marriage, Morgan says, "some of the white people sent two of the most notorious Negro prostitutes" to make a formal call on his wife when they returned to Yazoo City. Mrs. Morgan apparently was equal to the occasion. She welcomed her visitors kindly and offered them chairs, but only on the porch, and asked them to be seated. Because they were not invited into the house the Negro whores "promptly lifted their skirts and indignantly withdrew."

Not again does Morgan mention the humiliations and ostracism which his marriage must have inspired. But if his social position in Yazoo County was something less than secure, his political power was not. The Radical Reconstructionists were riding high in Mississippi, as elsewhere, and Senator Morgan with them. So solidly and idolatrously were the Negroes behind him that when a Northern newcomer, attempting to organize the freedmen in a bloc apart from both parties, denounced Morgan as a fraud and no true friend of the colored people, the Negroes ran him out of the county. Because of hard times and unrest among small farmers the Radicals won recruits among lower-income whites, resentful of the Bourbons and undoubtedly influenced by the social reforms achieved or sought by the Carpetbagger-Negro lawmakers. So, when Morgan ran in 1873 for the office of sheriff, the most powerful and lucrative post in any Mississippi county then and now, his lopsided victory was achieved in considerable part through white votes.

Very probably much of Morgan's support among the whites came from their conclusion that he was the lesser of two evils. Morgan frankly reveals that, in seeking the sheriffship, he was asking for justifiable reward for five years' service in the cause of Radical Reconstruction. He was still in debt. His opponent was the incumbent sheriff, a man named Hilliard, who had been as closely identified with the Radical Republicans as had Morgan himself, and who had held that office since 1869. They had then supported each other. But, according to Morgan, Hilliard's record had been an unsavory one. The freedmen and the old Carpetbagger guard were resentful of Hilliard's present identification with the native white leaders. There was no Democratic candidate for sheriff. The principal Democratic leaders supported Hilliard. Morgan defeated him, 2365 votes to 431.

Since there were 1500 registered white voters it is obvious that Morgan received a majority of those votes. He says that the Grange, the protesting, eventually powerful organization of small farmers, gave him considerable support.

"Morgan Men" won every office. The chancery clerk was an all but illiterate Negro, the circuit clerk a Negro of considerably more intelligence, the county treasurer a Negro who could write passably. Two of the three men elected to the state legislature were Negroes, one of them from Ohio. The third was a white Carpetbagger. The white circuit judge was from Pennsylvania, the chancellor from New Hampshire. On the county board of supervisors were three unschooled Negroes, a Northern white man, and a native white Republican. In the governor's chair sat General Adelbert Ames, West Point graduate and a man who would believe almost nothing bad of the Mississippi Negro and almost nothing good of the Mississippi white Democrats.

Even a relatively honest sheriff, whose compensation was swelled by fees as tax collector, and who could deal in depreciated state warrants, could lay aside a tidy sum in four years. The sheriff's power in the Mississippi counties was nearly absolute. He controlled the selection of trial juries. He collected the state and county taxes and he appointed one of the three election registrars.

But Albert Morgan's victory was to have tragic consequences. Sheriff Hilliard and his irreconcilable white supporters were determined that Morgan should not take office. First they tried to prevent owners of real property, who alone could qualify as bondsmen, to go his bonds of $20,000 as sheriff and $105,000 as tax collector. The bonds were raised by a combination of freedmen, local merchants, and, he says, even some planters. Morgan then gave the required notice to Hilliard to vacate the office. Hilliard replied that he did not intend to surrender his post. The board of supervisors was, at the time, the only court in session in the county. The sheriff was required by law to be in attendance on it. Morgan thereupon presented his credentials to the board. Hilliard petitioned that he not be recognized, arguing that Morgan had threatened that if the office were not turned over to him he would round up his Negro followers in the county and take the sheriff's office by force.

Probably the Negroes would have done just that; but Morgan assured the board that he had never thought of using violence. The board recognized him as sheriff. Hilliard withdrew from the meeting of the board. That evening he placed three men on guard at the sheriff's office to prevent Morgan from taking over. The next day Morgan appointed his deputies, all of them Negroes, and stayed in attendance at the board of supervisors.

That night, he says, Hilliard sent a friend to him with an offer of $5000 if he would allow Hilliard to remain in office thirty days more. Morgan refused. Early the next morning he went to the sheriff's office in the courthouse. Only one man, a young nephew of Hilliard, was there. Morgan told him that he had come to take possession of the office and asked him to notify Hilliard to remove his personal effects.

Less than two hours later Hilliard was dead and one of Morgan's deputies badly wounded. A mulatto partisan of Hilliard, W. H. Foote, who once had been and would again become a Morgan man, precipitated the fatal clash. Discovering Morgan and some of his deputies in the sheriff's office soon after Hilliard's nephew had vacated it, Foote cursed them roundly until they shut the door against him. Then he rang the courthouse bell. Soon thereafter Hilliard and some of his adherents, all of them armed, began converging on the courthouse. With Morgan were six friends and deputies, including a newly arrived brother, William Morgan.

The sheriff-elect ordered his followers to close and bolt the door and to remain in the sheriff's office after he left, no matter what happened. Then he went out on the street to confront Hilliard. There he said to his challenger that he was the sheriff of Yazoo County and had possession of the office.

"Mr. Hilliard not only saw me, but he must have heard me for I was almost in front of him . . . some of his followers hesitated . . . but Mr. Hilliard turned and shouted to them to follow him, which they did. . . . They all passed by me. It was now impossible for me to regain the courthouse ahead of them. . . . So I followed . . . Mr. Hilliard and some of his friends violently forced open the door [of the sheriff's office] breaking the panel and one of them fired into the room. The shot was returned from inside. At that moment I reached the steps leading into the main part of the building . . . saw [Hilliard] reeling away from the now open office and was met with a blinding flash and crushing noise."

Morgan himself then began firing. Within a few minutes the courthouse was cleared of all of Hilliard's group save Hilliard himself, who lay dead on the floor near the front door of the sheriff's office. Inside the office one of Morgan's Negro deputies lay badly wounded.

Even before a doctor reached the scene a charge of murder had been filed against Albert Morgan. The rumors swelled. The county Negroes were coming again to Morgan's rescue; the whites were going to lynch him; he had foully murdered Hilliard when the already wounded man was trying to escape.

Morgan retained three lawyers, two of them native Yazoo countians and onetime slaveowners, and the third the county's Republican state senator. The mayor had decided that Morgan need not be placed in jail prior to the hearing; but after protests were made by Morgan's enemies Morgan himself asked the mayor to lock him up. He and the deputies who were with him during the shooting were jailed.

While the accused rested there the county chancellor, whose appointment had not yet been confirmed by the state senate, bowed to the anti-Morgan group and appointed a new sheriff, although, under the law, a coroner should have taken over. The chancellor also refused bail.

Once again the Negroes swarmed into Yazoo City to stand by their leader. Whether to avoid a racial clash or to save Morgan himself, the chancellor ordered him removed to Jackson. There Governor Ames, a close friend of Morgan, got busy. Angry at the chancellor's appointment of a successor to Morgan and his refusal to grant bail, Governor Ames revoked his appointment, removed the newly appointed sheriff, and placed Morgan's brother William in his place "to continue during the disability of the lawful sheriff," and ordered the deputies released.

The new chancellor freed Morgan. Two years later, after the white Democrats had assumed control, that act would provide one of the specifications in the governor's impeachment trial, for the Democrats charged that Ames had exacted a promise from the chancellor to release Morgan in exchange for the appointment. Morgan's version is that the chancellor released him on bail in order to save his life.

Actually the new chancellor was an able native jurist who had for years been head of the state university's law department. He held that Morgan had been *de facto* and also *de jure* sheriff of the county at the time of the shooting scrape and that he was attempting to fulfill the duties of his office and restrain the mob at the time of Hilliard's death. A few of the Democratic newspapers also supported Morgan, the *Clarion Ledger* of Jackson editorializing that "having read the testimony and the statement of both sides, we have never been able to reach the conclusion that Morgan was not entitled to bail, even if he did the killing, about which there seems to be some doubt." Within two months Morgan was back in office.

For six years now Albert Morgan, the Midwest farmer's son, had been in Mississippi politics. In addition to being a state senator he had also served concurrently, ever since 1869, on the decisive county board of supervisors, first by appointment of General Ames when that Maine martinet was military commander, and later by election. Now, as sheriff, he was the absolute political boss of Yazoo County. As a close friend of the governor he was a man to be reckoned with in state politics. He would always recall, perhaps too pridefully, the record of what he termed his stewardship throughout the six years of Radical Republican domination of Yazoo County. Whatever else his political foes and the incredulous critics of his marriage were to say of him, impartial historians would afterward admit his efficiency and doubt that his personal conduct in office had been corrupt.

During Albert Morgan's tenure on the board, county property assessments were increased to what he considered equitable figures and the county millage raised. New cells were built in the county jail; the county's roads and bridges were overhauled and several new ones built; a $70,000 courthouse was constructed and paid for in full upon completion, and the poor farm was improved and made nearly self-supporting through cultivation of its land. By 1875 the county could count forty-five free white schools and sixty-three free colored schools; sixty of them were housed in buildings erected during Morgan's period of domination. Before 1869, he says, there were no free schools in the county, almost every public building was a hovel, much of the sixteenth-section school lands had been stolen, and the total indebtedness of the county could not be ascertained because of the lack of records. All of his improvements, Morgan claimed, had been accomplished by a tax levy which never exceeded 2½ per cent and a county indebtedness which at no time exceeded the annual levy for current expenses. During that period Yazoo City itself bought a new fire engine, installed new sidewalks and pavements and gutters, tried its best to get a railroad and lost out only because of the national depression of 1873.

Morgan gives almost entire credit for this material reconstruction to a board of supervisors' majority made up of himself and two Negroes. Another Northern Republican and one former slaveholder, the other two members of the board, usually opposed his proposals. When the superintendent of schools, described by Morgan as a conscientious man but too desirous of having the good opinion of Southerners, established more public schools for white children than for Negroes, despite the two-to-one majority of Negro children of school age, Morgan had him thrown out and replaced by his brother William.

Life in Yazoo again became superficially quiet after the Radical victory of 1873. The lot of the freedmen in Yazoo was vastly different from what it had been in 1865. More than three hundred Negroes owned real estate in the county, and it was among these that outcast Sheriff Morgan passed many visits of "solid enjoyment," after his ostracism from Yazoo's white society. But the white Democrats of Mississippi were determined to regain political mastery. Had Morgan's administration been twice as honest and efficient, ten times as economical and visionary and creative, it would not have been approved.

But, so Morgan recalls, his relations with the community were good. Only his more implacable enemies refused to support him. The leader among these was a Captain Henry Dickson, whom Morgan described throughout his narrative as the "Human Hornet." Dickson would play a lethal part in Morgan's abrupt departure from the county. Dickson's reason for hating the Carpetbag leader, so Morgan believed, was that Morgan had testified against him in 1872 when he was tried for killing a Negro who worked on his plantation.

By the end of 1874 the Democrats of Mississippi were ready for a showdown. The whites were organizing their own independent military companies which drilled nightly, patrolling Negro neighborhoods, disarming Negroes, and embarking upon a campaign of intimidation which would be the principal factor in their eventual victory. And everywhere in the state the whites were being aroused to fury by rumors, politically advantageous and almost entirely unfounded, of threats of Negro uprisings and by such publications as the book *Your Sister Sally,* which luridly related what would happen to Sally if the Negroes ruled the state.

The Negroes and the Radicals were neither ready nor psychologically prepared for an armed showdown. When Morgan remonstrated with a white Yazoo countain who had voted for him in the previous election and who was complaining that the country was "tired of free love, Beecher, Credit Mobilier, and Radical corruption," the white man warned him that he'd better leave because the white Mississippians intended to carry the county next time, peaceably if they could, forcibly if they must.

Governor Ames recommended the calling out and arming of the principally Negro militia; but the Republicans, in legislative caucus, opposed the recommendation because such action would further arouse racial antagonism. Moreover, says Morgan, the Republicans believed that General Grant would back them up. And so came the showdown in Mississippi. For Albert Morgan defeat would be accompanied, as was his biggest victory, by gunfire and death.

During the summer Democratic newspapers printed stories of a planned Negro uprising in Yazoo County, where, they asserted, sixteen hundred military rifles had been cached. Morgan counted less than sixteen. He was certain that the Human Hornet had been chosen to assassinate him. But he and the Republican freedmen went ahead with their plans for a political rally of the Yazoo City Republican Club, set for September 1, 1875.

In the meeting hall on the night of the rally Morgan, three or four white Radical officeholders, and about a hundred Negroes turned up. Except for the speaker's platform, which was illumined by a lamp and several candles, the hall was dimly lighted by small tallow dips.

As Colonel Morgan began to speak seven or eight of "the most substantial white men of the town" filed in and sat down silently in the front of the hall. They were followed by Captain Dickson. Almost immediately the newcomers began their interruptions. Dickson withdrew but soon returned. He had with him a companion whom Morgan describes as "a reckless, worthless colored man, whose property had been levied on by the delinquent tax collector for unpaid taxes." At about this time a Morgan adherent objected to the interruptions. Morgan asked the visitors to state their questions and then let him answer them. The newly arrived Negro rose with Dickson, his pistol drawn, and, proclaiming his right to speak, began denouncing Morgan. For perhaps half an hour the wrangling continued.

At length when Morgan mentioned the name of the chairman of the board of supervisors, Dickson cried out, "He's a thief!" To this charge someone in the audience either cried out, "No, no," as Morgan relates, or what is more probable, "That's a lie."

Pistol in hand, Dickson advanced upon his challenger.

"I did not run," Morgan writes. "On the contrary, observing the violent movement of the Hornet, I turned toward him and commanded peace. At that instant, the first shot was fired, and before I could take two steps toward them, the volley. I stood, confronting them, in the full glare of the lights upon the platform. That volley was fired directly at me, and each bullet was aimed to kill. . . . The window facing the wall at the back of the platform was literally peppered with bullet marks. The day following, when asked by his admiring associates, 'why in hell he allowed Morgan to escape,' the Hornet, puzzled and confused by his failure to kill me, declared: 'I stood just so . . . not twenty feet distance and emptied every barrel of my two navies. . . .'" To Morgan's way of thinking the hand of God had intervened.

Morgan says that he fired twice, and then, unable to see who was firing or what was going on, since the tallow dips had either been extinguished or were obscured by the smoke of pistol fire, he climbed out the window at the rear of the platform and was descending a ladder when it gave way with him. He fell twelve feet to the pavement. Recovering after being momentarily dazed, he climbed back into the hall. In the nearby market place the market-house bell was tolling. It was the signal for the white citizens to gather.

The hall, when Morgan re-entered, was all but empty. Some frightened Negroes were still trying to push through a rear door. A white man named Dick Mitchell, a Morgan adherent, lay dying. Of him the Yazoo *Banner* wrote: "We regret the death of Dick Mitchell. He was a brave man but forfeited his life by joining Morgan and our enemies and drawing his sword in their defense."

Foote, the Negro circuit clerk, who had opposed Morgan in his fight with Hilliard and was now once again his ally, was seriously wounded but was able to make his escape. Several other Negroes were slain.

As Morgan leaned over his dying associate a Negro rushed in to tell him that some white men were looking for him. A multitude of Negroes had congregated outside, some armed with pistols and rifles, some only with hardwood sticks. The whites were converging on the market house.

The Negroes wanted to stand and fight. But he told them to return to their homes and stay there. He remained at his own residence. Shortly thereafter the Dickson men knocked on his door and asked Morgan's hostler where Morgan had gone. Believing that he had ridden away on horseback, they did not enter the house.

For eleven days Albert remained in his house. Then, disguised in old clothes, he quitted Yazoo forever, making his way by horseback to Jackson, the state capital. Behind him the Yazoo City *Banner* gloated: "Morgan the murderer, by aid of some of his white Radicals here, skipped out of town last Monday night. Young man, your action of last Monday night is noted. Better keep your optics well open. A word to the wise, realign." The individual warning was intended for Charles Thorn, a Northerner who had helped Morgan escape. He was shot to death a few days later.

Of the 4046 votes cast in the county, only two were counted for Morgan. The Yazoo County grand jury re-examined the slaying of Hilliard and indicted Morgan for murder. No effort was made to arrest him on the murder charge. It was obviously a device further to discourage him from ever returning to Yazoo County.

In Jackson he conferred with his harried friend, Governor Ames, who was also on the way out. Ames offered three hundred Negro militia to escort him to Yazoo City and reinstate him as sheriff. News of the offer soon became public, and into Yazoo City rode hundreds of heavily armed white vigilantes, well-disciplined and eager to give battle. Morgan wisely decided not to return to Yazoo.

Albert Morgan was one of the first of the Carpetbaggers to leave Mississippi in the wake of the Democratic revolution. Of the Northerners who were prominent in the state's Reconstruction politics no more than five or six remained as citizens after 1876, and these were men about whose integrity and good conduct in office there had been common agreement. But no matter how incorrupt, how efficient and evenhanded Albert Morgan might have been, he would not have been acceptable to white Mississippi, even after the fires of Reconstruction conflict had died, for he had violated the lasting taboo. He had committed the unforgivable sin of giving legitimacy to miscegenation.

Nor was he to have a happy later life. After moving to Lawrence, Kansas, in 1886 with his wife and their four daughters and two sons, he failed in several business ventures. He then emigrated to Colorado to try his luck at silver mining, leaving Carrie and the girls in Topeka. Albert never saw Carrie again. He spent the remaining thirty-two years of his life in Colorado where he prospected for gold and silver and conducted a "School for Money" in Denver.

The four girls, all of them beautiful, became actresses. Carrie herself became a Christian Science lecturer and a dramatic reader, and when daughter Angela went to England on a theatrical tour Carrie accompanied her. From England she applied for a pension as a widow of a Union veteran, and there she apparently lived out her life.

CHAPTER 5

General Wilder and the Yankee Dollar

WILLIAM WARNER, *an Ohioan who acquired an Alabama plantation in 1866, said this: "A Northern man who is not a natural fool or foolish fanatic may live pleasantly anywhere in Alabama without abating one jot of his self-respect or independence."*

The story of General John Thomas Wilder can be commended as a surprising lesson for all who believe that every Yankee who came South during Reconstruction was a predatory, unwelcome rascal. His is a pleasant tale, and its principal instructiveness lies in the obscure fact that it is unique only in degree.

John Wilder was a handsome giant of a man whose life makes the rags-to-riches saga of a Horatio Alger hero appear not only completely unbelievable but even humdrum. He was a Catskill mountaineer by birth and came of fighting folk. His great-grandfather had lost a leg at Bunker Hill; his grandfather had also fought, as a sixteen-year-old lad, in the Revolution, and his father had raised and commanded a company of light horsemen to ride against the British in the War of 1812. Restless, penniless, and with only a fair public school education, young John turned westward at nineteen. That was in 1849, the year of the California Gold Rush; but John traveled only as far as Columbus, Ohio, where he went to work as a foundry apprentice. His industriousness and skill so pleased his employer that in a few years the foundryman offered the business jointly to his own son and John.

Instead of accepting, the twenty-seven-year-old craftsman moved to

Greensburg, Indiana, and there in 1857 opened his own foundry and mill-wright establishment. A year later, already a successful businessman, he married Martha Stewart, a Greensburg girl. Well before the war began John Wilder had won a nationwide reputation as a hydraulics expert. He had erected mills and hydraulic works in Virginia and Kentucky and Tennessee and throughout the Middle West, even as far away as Wisconsin. As with many another Hoosier, he was a Democrat, but he was no secessionist. When the fighting started John Wilder cast two six-pound cannons in his own foundry and raised a company of light artillerymen who were incorporated into the 17th Indiana Volunteer Infantry. His men elected him captain, as might have been expected; less than two months later Governor Oliver P. Morton appointed him a lieutenant colonel in the regiment. He became its colonel and later a brigade commander and ended his army career as a brevet brigadier general.

Although John Wilder was a good tactician and inspired his men with confidence, his military reputation was built upon his remarkable innovations. Contrary to established military practice, he moved his men by horseback and fought them dismounted; and the rapidity of his brigade's movements earned it the name of Wilder's Lightning Brigade. He armed his troops with the then unauthorized Spencer eight-shot repeating rifle, advancing the men the purchase money on condition that they repay him, after he could not persuade the Army to supply the rifles. He and his riflemen acquitted themselves brilliantly in the fighting in middle Tennessee.

The restless brigadier commander found time while fighting near Chattanooga to collect mineral specimens which convinced him that here were regional resources crying for development. Poor health caused him to resign from the Army in October 1864, and because of his enthusiasm over Tennessee's potentialities he moved to Chattanooga in 1865 and began mining iron, coal, and limestone.

Two years later John Wilder formed the Roane Iron Company, in partnership with two fellow veterans, Major W. A. Rockwood and Captain H. S. Chamberlain. The partners laid out the town of Rockwood, imported skilled Pennsylvania foremen, and set up a blast furnace there, using coke for the first time in the South. Soon thereafter they set up a second furnace and established the Roane Rolling Mills in Chattanooga to manufacture rails for railroads.

These enterprises gave Chattanooga's postwar economy a desperately needed lift and probably laid the groundwork for the city's future role as a principal industrial center of the middle South. One successful venture followed another: Wilder's Machine Works, which produced a turbine of his own invention; the Dayton Coal and Iron Company; the Durham Coal Company, and the Southern Car and Foundry Company. Well before Reconstruction's end General Wilder was probably the most notable citizen of

Chattanooga and one of the foremost in the state. His best friends were former Confederates. Of the Roane Rolling Mills, Robert Sommers wrote contemporaneously in his *Southern States Since the War:* "The Rolling Mills of Chattanooga . . . have now entered upon a new and prosperous career . . . General Wilder, whose campaigns had revealed to him the mineral resources of this section of the country, is the active spirit in this enterprise. He has joined with him a partnership of capitalists, and is displaying a natural sagacity and aptitude in mining coal and iron, as well as in the mechanical operation of the Rolling Mills . . . They have built a new mill in line with the old one, and are fitting up the necessary power and machinery, including twelve of Dank's Patent Puddling apparatus—a new invention of which confident hopes are entertained. This is the first mill in which it is to be put to actual working test, and if it proves successful, the saving will be about $9 per ton. . . .

"The company calculates that it will be able to make the iron rails and lay them down in Pittsburgh cheaper than they can be produced in that great center of the Pennsylvania coal and iron fields; and if this should be demonstrated, the mineral resources of east Tennessee, Georgia and Alabama will command immediate attention."

Honor after honor came General Wilder's way. He was Tennessee's commissioner to the Vienna Exposition in 1873 and put together the state's challenging exhibition of minerals at the Philadelphia Centennial in 1876. He served briefly as mayor of Chattanooga, resigning after eight months because of his disinterest in politics. He was made an honorary member of the Iron and Steel Institute of Great Britain and a member of the American Institute of Mining Engineers. At Johnson City, Tennessee, he organized the Carnegie Land Company and set up another blast furnace and a hotel and office building. An indefatigable organizer and promoter, he acquired for himself and his associates about a half million acres of iron ore, and coal lands in North Carolina, Virginia, Kentucky, and Tennessee, built the Cloudland Hotel on Roane Mountain as a resort for hay-fever sufferers, and was active in the promotion and the partial construction of the Charleston, Cincinnati, and Chicago Railroad.

Even more spectacular than his financial talents—and more lasting, too, since his fortune was all but wiped out in the Baring Brothers' panic of 1893—was his popularity among former Confederates. His old enemies had liked him from the very beginning of his residence in Chattanooga, respecting him as a soldier and grateful to him for his industrial activity. And he became completely one of them when, during Grant's first administration, he visited the President in behalf of Nathan Bedford Forrest, when that unreconstructed Confederate cavalryman was threatened with prosecution as the suspected leader of the Ku Klux Klan.

Before making the trip General Wilder had called upon Forrest, who, apparently admitting his role, had convinced Wilder that the Klan had been necessary for the South's protection. Wilder's intervention led to what was possibly the most singular act ever taken by any veterans' organization. The Nathan Bedford Forrest Post of the United Confederate Veterans elected the former Union general an honorary member. In 1898 Tennessee gave his name to the camp occupied by the 6th Tennessee Regiment during the Spanish-American War; and when the Wilder Brigade monument was dedicated in Indiana, in 1903, the surviving members of the Forrest Post attended the ceremony in a body.

At the dedication Colonel Tomlinson Fort eulogized the Yankee general in behalf of the post: "His name is a household word in the South; particularly in all east Tennessee where he has lived continuously since the close of the war; and no man has done more than General Wilder in bringing order out of chaos. . . . No commander in either army with five regiments and a battery accomplished as much. No brigade in either army stands with the record for efficiency, courage, brains and patriotism beyond that displayed by General Wilder's Lightning Brigade. . . ."

Such a marked affinity between former foes was unusual; but it would have been more unusual, even unnatural, if normal social and business intercourse had not been resumed, extensively and soon, between the South's financial and professional leaders and their Northern counterparts who came South, as long as the newcomers did not enter politics as Republican allies of the Negro. The legend of universal Yankee chicanery in the South and of unrelenting Southern hostility to all Yankee interlopers simply does not hold water. There were many good reasons for resumption of old ties, and some bad ones: prewar friendships and business relationships; the admiration of professional soldiers who had been classmates and comrades in arms before they had opposed each other in battle; the uninterrupted unity of the Protestant Episcopal and the Roman Catholic churches; the sympathy which political moderates in the North held for the South, especially among the upper classes; the re-established bonds between Northern and Southern Democrats; a common desire for financial gain; racial consanguinity and racial aversions, and the eventual widespread antagonism in the North toward Radical Reconstruction in the South—all these contributed, save among the purposeful Radicals, to reconciliation between North and South and to Southern individual and group acceptance of the Northern settler.

And more immediately important than any other consideration was the Yankee dollar. Friendly John Wilder would have been accepted by the citizens of Chattanooga even had he contributed little to its material welfare. His personality, his war record, his sympathy for the South would have made him all the friends he needed. But his role as an industrial savior in a ravaged land made him doubly welcome, and with him many others. The number of Northerners who settled in the South after the war is unknown, but there were many thousands of them, the majority of them farmers and most of the rest merchants. The smallest group, but one whose imprint was long-lasting, was made up of speculators and industrialists not generally as honest as John Wilder, who, often in concert with Southern associates, built or promised to build railroads and cotton mills, and dug mines and cut away the forests, and, it should be added, usually had little compunction about the wasting of resources or the purchase of public officials.

The dollar-bringing and dollar-seeking Yankees turned their hands and their cash to almost anything that looked good. The results were not always beneficial either to themselves or to the region. The Yankees who came as farmers were frequently disillusioned. The times were against them. They were better off than the Southern farmer, for they brought some capital; but they found it difficult to adapt themselves to Negro tenants and Negro hired hands. The Negroes didn't work like Northern farm laborers, said the Yankee farmers with feeling; they didn't think like Northern farm laborers, and they didn't take pains like Northern farm laborers. The letters home, the diaries, and the account books of the newcomers were filled with such protests. Before long the transplanted Northern farmer would outdo his Southern neighbors in his scorn of the Negro cropper, and he would end by making common cause with that white neighbor to thwart the aspirations of the black worker for political equality or economic reform. Or he would until, near the century's close, the economic degradation of the small farmer, west and north and south, brought many such landowners and tenants and hired hands everywhere into a brief and dramatic interracial and intersectional alliance which for a time menaced, though it could not conquer, the likewise intersectional alliance of railroaders and industrialists and bankers and assorted Bourbons and their political lieges. But that lay ahead. Long before then many a hopeful dirt farmer from the North would have become, as did his Southern compatriot, a victim of a one-crop, colonial economy and of high tariffs, of nature's unpredictability and of the curse of too few acres for himself and his family.

If the Northern agriculturalist with too little cash and too little knowledge of the pitfalls of cotton farming frequently fared ill, the South as a whole suffered as frequently from the speculative activities of the few Northerners with many dollars who sent their dollars down to do their bidding, and who, unlike the General Wilders, did not accompany their investments themselves.

These dishonest financial adventurers were no more unscrupulous as individuals than were the thieves who were flourishing everywhere else in the America of rampant industrial expansion; but even the best ones often devastated the land more lastingly than had General Sherman himself. Especially was this true of the Yankee lumbermen, who bought up vast timber tracts, at no more than fifty cents an acre, sawed off fortunes in timber, and left the ruined land to its doubly ruined people. They did make the South more conscious, in one way or another, of its resources in coal and iron, petroleum and sulphur and timber, and of its woeful lack of industry. The Yankee industrialists and manufacturers organized and operated cotton mills, winning the pathetic gratitude of Confederate widows and orphans for the underpaid mill jobs that kept them alive. They went into railroading and mining, as did General Wilder; into naval stores, since resin and tar and turpentine were essential items for the Navy and for a variety of other uses; into odd, exotic enterprises ranging from the making of artificial ice, with which they could greatly undersell their New England kinsmen's lake ice, to patent-medicine manufacture; and, by anonymous thousands, into every aspect of Southern trade and commerce.

Not every Yankee dollar was brought into or sent to the South for personal profit. Individual Northern philanthropists and many thousands of small donors sent their charitable dollars to the destitute enemy almost as soon as the conflict had ended. More than $3,000,000 went to the South in the first two hungry years after Appomattox, the collective gift of Northern and border benevolent organizations. The New York Southern Famine Relief Commission gave needy Southerners $200,000 in the famine year of 1867. Philadelphia's Southern Famine Relief Fund contributed as much and also sought unsuccessfully a congressional appropriation of a million dollars for the South. St. Louis raised $126,000 in 1867 and Baltimore $100,000 at one Southern Relief Fair alone; a Californian contributed $45,000 in gold, and these are but random examples.

The South has largely forgotten George Peabody, the English-born Massachusetts financier and philanthropist who gave two million dollars in cash and another million in Mississippi state bonds for the advancement of education among white Southerners. It has largely forgotten Barnas Sears, who administered George Peabody's Southern charities, a reasonable man who lived in the South and loved it. It has largely forgotten Paul Tulane of New Jersey, who brought back to life in New Orleans the all but abandoned University of Louisiana which now bears his name; and accomplished Edward Atkinson of Massachusetts, an economics pamphleteer, inventor of the Aladdin cooking stove, and wise counselor to Southern agriculture and industry. It has largely forgotten the thousands upon thousands who gave to the South throughout Reconstruction and afterward, and never more generously than in 1878 when the lower Mississippi Valley counted its yellow fever dead by the thousands in the worst of the century's fever epidemics. And the South has forgotten a poem written in 1878 by a hitherto unreconstructed Southern priest, Father Abraham Joseph Ryan. In

Reunited Father Ryan, in love and gratitude and Christian humility, made his own peace with the North:

> *Purer than thy own white snow,*
> *Nobler than thy mountains' height;*
> *Deeper than the ocean's flow,*
> *Stronger than thy own proud might;*
> *O Northland! to thy sister land,*
> *Was late thy mercy's generous deed and grand.*
>
> *Nigh twice ten years the sword was sheathed:*
> *Its mist of green o'er battle plain*
> *For nigh two decades Spring had breathed;*
> *And yet the crimson life-blood stain*
> *From passive swards had never paled,*
> *Nor fields, where all were brave and some had failed.*
>
> *Between the Northland, bride of snow,*
> *And Southland, brightest sun's fair bride,*
> *Swept, deepening ever in its flow,*
> *The stormy wake, in war's dark tide:*
> *No hand might clasp across the tears*
> *And blood and anguish of four deathless years.*
>
> *When Summer, like a rose in bloom,*
> *Had blossomed from the bud of Spring,*
> *Oh! who could deem the dews of doom*
> *Upon the blushing lips could cling?*
> *And who could believe its fragrant light*
> *Would e'er be freighted with the breath of blight?*
>
> *Yet o'er the Southland crept the spell,*
> *That e'en from out its brightness spread,*
> *And prostrate, powerless, she fell,*
> *Rachel-like, amid her dead.*
> *Her bravest, fairest, purest, best,*
> *The waiting grave would welcome as its guest.*
>
> *The Northland, strong in love, and great,*
> *Forgot the stormy days of strife;*
> *Forgot that souls with dreams of hate*
> *Or unforgiveness e'er were rife.*
> *Forgotten was each thought and hushed;*
> *Save—she was generous and her foe was crushed.*
>
> *No hand might clasp, from land to land;*
> *Yea! there was one to bridge the tide;*
> *For at the touch of Mercy's hand*
> *The North and South stood side by side:*
> *The Bride of Snow, the Bride of Sun,*
> *In Charity's espousals are made one.*

"Thou givest back my sons again,"
The Southland to the Northland cries;
"For all my dead, on battle plain,
Thou biddest my dying now uprise:
I still my sobs, I cease my tears,
And thou hast recompensed my anguished years.

"Blessings on thine every wave,
Blessings on thine every shore,
Blessings that from sorrow save,
Blessings giving more and more,
For all thou gavest thy sister land,
O Northland! in thy generous deed and grand."

This much is as certain as any generality can be. Only those Yankees who were active in Radical Reconstruction's program for Negro political equality were universally unacceptable to the Conservatives. The South's own Bourbons, her great landowners, her bankers and promoters, and embryo industrialists, her restless, out-of-pocket generals readily joined with the Yankee in money-making schemes. In Reconstruction, as now, one hand was extended gladly to the outsider with investment and speculative capital or the offer of a business partnership; the other was clenched into a hard fist for the Yankee with dangerous political and social notions.

Despite their romantic coloration, these post-bellum Bourbons were practical men with an affinity for the economic leaders of the North. They knew that the South could offer much to the Northern industrialist and, not entirely incidentally, to themselves and to all of the South's peoples; its water power, its raw materials, its labor and climate were advantages which were forcefully advanced. The Reconstruction South needed industry, a modern transportation system, and a revitalized and expanded commerce. Her rivers and railroads and seaports required development. Railroad promotion schemes in the South would afford proof of the common corruptibility of man without respect to nativity or residence or political leanings or old loyalties.

The South's "Redeemers," her heroes who led the fight for white political self-determination in local and state affairs, included men who were prominent before and after political victory as partners of Northern investors, and sometimes not to their own credit. Throughout their colorful and courageous lives these doughty but practical-minded warriors would thunder their everlasting defiance of the Yankee reformer; but they were not so ill-disposed toward the Yankee speculator who often needed reforming of a different sort. Save for a few who could not forgive, like General Jubal Early, who would have no truck with Yankees at all, the Confederacy's aristocracy was willing to identify itself with Northern financiers, Northern development of Southern railroads and industries, and Northern business-men in the South in general.

Gallant former Confederates became presidents and vice-presidents and lobbyists for railroad companies of doubtful virtue, congressional interces-sors for Yankee-owned Southern corporations, respected counsels for coal and iron companies and cotton mills, and other enterprises most of whose profits were being siphoned off to the North. They manifested, in short, a nonsectional, American admiration for the making and the makers of a fast buck. Most of them were primarily animated, of course, by desire for personal wealth and power, which, after the Redemption, were the dominant motivations of their day as in most days. Yet many were driven concurrently by a patriotic, regional dream of the attainment in the South of a self-sufficient prosperity, and a hoped-for economic balance, which, had it been achieved before the war which they had fought and lost, might have made that war's outcome a different one.

It was for the more high-minded—and practical-minded—Bourbon Re-deemers that Henry W. Grady became perhaps the most persuasive spokes-man in the later postwar, changing South. The sincere, sentimental Georgia editor's address before the New England Society of the City of New York, "The New South," proclaimed somewhat overoptimistically to the nation in 1886 that there was indeed a new and hopeful South and that North and South alike should forget the animosities of the Civil War and of Re-construction. Said Grady, in part:

". . . The South found her jewel in the toad's head of defeat. The shackles that had held her in narrow limitations fell forever when the shackles of the negro slave were broken. Under the old *regime* the negroes were slaves to the South, the South was a slave to the system. The old plantation, with its simple police regulation and its feudal habit, was the only type possible under slavery. Thus was gathered in the hands of a splendid and chivalric oligarchy the substance that should have been diffused among the people, as the rich blood, under certain artificial conditions, is gathered at the heart, filling that with affluent rapture, but leaving the body chill and colorless.

"The old South rested everything on slavery and agriculture, unconscious that these could neither give nor maintain healthy growth. The new South presents a perfect Democracy, the oligarchs leading in the popular move-ment—a social system compact and closely knitted, less splendid on the sur-face but stronger at the core—a hundred farms for every plantation, fifty homes for every palace, and a diversified industry that meets the complex needs of this complex age.

"The new South is enamored of her new work. Her soul is stirred with the breath of a new life. The light of a grander day is falling fair on her face. She is thrilling with the consciousness of growing power and pros-perity. As she stands upright, full-statured and equal among the people of the earth, breathing the keen air and looking out upon the expanding horizon, she understands that her emancipation came because, in the inscrutable wisdom of God, her honest purpose was crossed and her brave armies were beaten."

Not all of the Yankees came as farmers or politicians or bona-fide investors or philanthropists or get-rich-quick speculators. Still another group contributed possibly as much as did any of these to the new South to which they flocked. These were the Yankee tradesmen, founders of what were at the beginning mostly insignificant mercantile ventures, and professional men who saw the opportunity that was implicit in the rebuilding or the building of the South's communities. They too were readily accepted and absorbed.

Theirs was a needful contribution to the resurgence of the war-scourged Southern communities, whose recoveries make up in the aggregate a great and yet unwritten American business saga. Such unyielding communities as Charleston and Beaufort, South Carolina, would disdain to catch up with the unwelcome times. To most purposes Charleston remained apart from the Union even after the surrender and lived by preference in her past; and Beaufort, abandoned early in the war by her principal white citizens, whose homes were then taken over by Negroes, long remained only a tomblike reminder of glory. Other cities, too, were sadly slow in recovering. Much of Mobile had been destroyed in an ammunition explosion soon after the war, and it had fewer people in 1880 than its 1860 population of 29,000. Though Memphis had grown to 40,000 by 1870 and could claim to be the South's biggest inland cotton port, it was to be severely handicapped by the visitations of yellow jack, which in 1878 took 5000 lives and made of it such a ghost town that the state legislature abolished its corporate existence so that the city could not be sold for its public debt. By 1870 siege-battered Vicksburg had trebled from 4500 to 12,400, only to lose population for the next ten years.

But Atlanta, the South's Phoenix-like symbol of recovery, and the least Southern of its post-bellum centers, rose from its literal ashes to become the center of Southern land-centered commerce. Most of the rest of the South's larger cities likewise grew after the war, and with their population growth their civic problems mounted also. Animated greatly by Northern capital, the mill towns began to thrive, Wilmington and Fayetteville in North Carolina, Macon and Savannah in Georgia, Montgomery in Alabama. Tobacco gave life to Durham, North Carolina, the little town to which Washington Duke, an upcountry boy, had wandered after Appomattox with a fifty-cent piece which a Yankee had swapped him for a five-dollar Confederate bill. The population of New Orleans, the largest city in the South, its port handling a third of all the South's cotton exports, rose from 168,000 in 1860 to 216,000 in 1880, with a gross commerce of more than a half billion dollars a year. In and near New Orleans were established cottonseed and rice mills, sugar refineries and foundries; and although these were pygmies in comparison with New England's industries, and although political corruption and the fear of yellow fever had retarded her growth, the city gave backing to the Southern claims that the South had entered upon an overdue industrial revolution. In middle Tennessee, Nashville's expansion was second, relatively, only to Atlanta's, her population rising from 17,000 in 1860 to 43,000 by 1880, a community teeming with such generally Yankee-inspired industries as flour mills, carriage, wagon, and furniture manufacturies, foundries, machine shops, lumber mills, and publishing houses.

The South was not destined to have a truly urban stamp for nearly three quarters of a century; even so, between 1860 and 1870 the urban population rose in unforeseen degree, though not nearly as greatly as in the rest of the nation, where between 1860 and 1870 the urban population increased 50 per cent while the national population had grown only 20 per cent. As late as 1880 the state of Massachusetts included more towns of 4000 and counted a combined city population greater by 300,000 than the entire South together.

Every Southern community, the prosperous and the backward, the booming and the resisters of change and progress, was alike burdened with the same problems. The principal ones arose from the continued and excessive migration of the Negro from country to town. It is hardly an exaggeration to say that slums were unknown even in the larger Southern communities until Reconstruction; by the end of the period many of these same communities, where few Negroes save domestics and craftsmen had lived before the war—among them Savannah, Montgomery, Selma, Shreveport, Macon, Columbia, and Charleston—had more Negro residents than white. Most of the other Southern towns and cities had onerously large Negro minorities, almost all of them segregated in the more undesirable dwelling areas, in the back alleys and on the far side of the railroad tracks and in dank, low-lying, and swampy grounds; whole families crammed into a single room, breeders, involuntarily, of crime and disease as their inheritors would also be. They lived, as accurately described in South Carolina in 1873, "in huts and hovels so poor that their total destruction from one end of the state to the other would not diminish the taxable value of the state by one tenth of 1% . . . They were no better than dog kennels or pigstys. Crime abounded in these areas. Murder, fighting, theft, drunkenness, public disturbances and vagrancy . . ."

Few whites, whether Northern newcomer or Southern standpatter, were seriously disturbed over the Negro's slums except when disease overran the segregated borders and smote impartially the white man with the black. The recurrent yellow fever epidemics prompted the South's cities to organize sanitary associations and boards of health. Even though they were unaware of the relationship of the mosquito to yellow jack, the South began to drain her swamps and clear out ditches and burn refuse; and none were more ardent apostles of municipal cleanliness than were the migrants from New England and the Middle West. The Yankees, in general more insistent upon urban sanitation than were the citizens of the swelling Southern communities, gave direction to many a campaign—some of them as Reconstruction officeholders and many others as private citizens—for sewers and waterworks, paved streets and street railways, improved police and fire departments, and gaslights; and with such good effect that by the late '70s, and in places even earlier, the more progressive Southern cities were proudly indistinguishable in their municipal facilities from their Northern sister cities.

It is certain that had the John Wilders not come as enterprising investors to the South's cities and countryside the region's recovery, such as it was, would have been long delayed. Few Radicals had a mind to help the South; nor, for that matter, had the South ever received its proportionate share of federal expenditures since the founding of the nation. The total of federal expenditures to aid in the development of railroads, roads, and canals, from 1789 to 1873, had been $104,705,173. Only $4,430,192 of this sum was spent in the South; $83,000,000 of the total had been expended on the Union Pacific and the Central Pacific Railroads from appropriations made while the South was out of the Union.

The Yankee dollar that helped lift the South out of the mire of its despond was the dollar of the individual Yankee. And the story of John Thomas Wilder, the coming of the Yankee farmers and investors and philanthropists and mill owners, poses a question that may be answered in more than one way: What if the Yankee had not, after the war, come South at all?

BOOK IV

AFTERMATH

CHAPTER 1

Sam Tilden Gets Swapped

BOTH presidential nominees in 1876, Governor Rutherford B. Hayes of Ohio, the Republican, and Governor Samuel J. Tilden of New York, the Democrat, reflected the nation's dissatisfaction with Grantism— the Grantism of corruption in high places and the Grantism of the repressive Southern policy which was still effective only in South Carolina, Louisiana, and Florida.

The parties themselves no longer had more than outward unity. The Republicans were divided into three factions: Grant's own clique, bound by self-interest or personal loyalty to the President; the remnants of the ideological Radicals, still doggedly determined that the Negro's political equality must be achieved and maintained; and the practical reformers, sick of the racial issue and sicker still of the seemingly endless scandals that had rocked Grant's second administration even more than his first.

The Democrats, too, were far from being of one mind. There was little love lost between the Southern and Northern wings, the Southerners especially resenting the frequent refusal of Northern congressmen to support legislation that would bring primary economic benefits to the late Confederacy. Moreover, the prewar differences between Southern Whig and Southern Democrat had come into the open again in the eight states already restored to the whites.

Hayes, a fifty-three-year-old Midwesterner, was a conciliatory, essentially moderate man. He had been a Whig until 1855 and was more sympathetic to the Conservative leaders of the postwar South than to Radical Republicanism. His military career had not been brilliant, but neither was it mediocre. Slightly wounded in 1862, he was commissioned a brigadier in 1864 and, toward the war's end, a major general of volunteers. Elected to Congress in 1864, while still in service, he expressed himself, though suspicious of "the Rebel influences . . . ruling the White House," as critical of Thaddeus Stevens's Radical program; he recommended educational requirements for the new Negro voters.

From Congress Hayes went to the governorship of Ohio in 1867 and was re-elected in 1869. In four years he effected a number of reforms: in the state prison system, in the supervision of charities, in the care of the insane, and in behalf of the merit principle, even appointing some Democrats to office. He also opposed higher taxes, criticized abuses in railroad management, and gained a certain national prestige as a reformer and an able administrator. But he did not join in the Liberal Republican movement in 1872; as a good party man, he campaigned for Grant. Having shrewdly decided not to seek a third gubernatorial term, he ran instead for Congress. He was defeated because of a Republican split and retired to the practice of law and to his real estate business.

In 1873 his Republican successor was beaten by the Democratic candidate for governor, and in 1874 the Democrats elected thirteen of twenty Ohio congressmen. Back to the hustings Hayes went in 1875 and defeated the Democratic governor, William Allen, by less than six thousand votes. His victory heartened the Republicans, almost everywhere on the defensive in those ominous years of depression; and Rutherford B. Hayes, of Ohio, moderately liberal and a loyal party man with a satisfactory war record, became the logical candidate for the presidency.

In St. Louis the Democrats quickly settled on Samuel J. Tilden as their candidate. A slight, personally unimpressive yet brilliant corporation lawyer and financier, Tilden had a solid reputation as a reformer whose zeal could and did lead him to turn upon his own party's Augean stables, New York City's infamous Tweed Ring.

A Democrat by family tradition and by conviction, Tilden had engaged in private practice, not in politics, after graduating from the Law School of the City of New York in 1841 at the age of twenty-seven. Many of the principal railroads were his clients, a connection which contributed no little to his eventual amassing of one of the greatest personal fortunes in the United States.

Opposing Lincoln in 1860, the New York Democrat predicted that Republican victory would mean the practical disfranchisement of the South, with terrible consequences to the nation; yet soon after war was declared Tilden advised Secretary of War Stanton to attempt to crush the South immediately, by one devastating stroke with superior numbers. He took little part in wartime activities, exerting himself instead in encouraging "constitutional opposition" to the potential tyranny of a highly centralized wartime federal government. At the war's end he endorsed the Lincoln-Johnson Reconstruction program and supported Johnson in his struggle against the Radical Republicans.

For eight years after 1866 Tilden served as chairman of the Democratic State Committee, and in that office he worked tirelessly and successfully to rid New York City of the thieving dominance of William M. Tweed. In 1874 he defeated the Republican governor of New York, John A. Dix, by a fifty thousand plurality. As governor, Tilden effected reductions in state taxes and expenditures principally through the elimination of frauds. He destroyed the notorious "Canal Ring," a combination of Republican and Democratic politicians having in common their complete dishonesty and the wealth they had gained through corrupting the state canal system. He advocated resumption of specie payments by the national government—as did President Grant—and vigorously protested, in a special message to the New York legislature, General Philip Sheridan's usurpation of civil government in Louisiana.

By 1876 the millionaire bachelor, through his honest if overly intellectual and detached leadership, had made himself the all but inevitable choice of the Democrats for the presidency.

The presidential opponents were worthier than their times.

The United States has never witnessed a clean presidential campaign. The campaign of 1876 was dirtier than most. More importantly, it was the first since 1860 in which the outcome was seriously in doubt. The Republicans pulled out the old reliable bloody shirt, labeled the Democrats as rebels at heart and Tilden a tool of the railroads and a tax-evading millionaire whose poor health added to his unfitness. The Democrats whaled away at the hard times, the domination of the Republican party by urban, financial, and industrial interests, at the evil-doing among the remaining Carpetbag governments, and the waste and venality of Grantism.

When the votes came in on the night of November 7, 1876, Republicans and Democrats alike were convinced that Samuel Tilden was the President-elect. The Democrats had carried the doubtful states of Connecticut, Indiana, and New Jersey, as well as New York. Almost everyone believed—all but knew—that every Southern state would go Democratic. Every Southern state was reported solidly Democratic except Florida, South Carolina, and Louisiana, where the balloting was close. Tilden had obtained 184 electoral votes, without any from the three possibly debatable states, Hayes only 166; Tilden, on later official returns, actually led Hayes by more than a quarter of a million popular votes. That night the national Republican chairman, wealthy Zachariah Chandler, Republican boss of Michigan, former senator, and Grant's Secretary of the Interior, and his cohorts in the New York headquarters went to bed believing that their man had lost.

But early the next morning John C. Reid, managing editor of the Republican New York *Times,* and William E. Chandler of New Hampshire, Republican national committeeman and later Secretary of the Navy and United States senator, had a long-shot inspiration. They asked and received permission from Zach Chandler to telegraph Republican officials in the three uncertain states asking if they could bring those states into the Republican column. The device they proposed to change Democratic votes into Republican ones was brazenly simple. In each state there functioned so-called returning boards, made up of four or five men of whom all or a majority were Republican, whose duty it was to canvass election returns and certify as to their accuracy.

Louisiana's board was made up of a Negro undertaker, a Negro saloon keeper, and two flagrantly dishonest white political hangers-on. Three of South Carolina's five members were Republican candidates for office in the very election on which they were to pass judgment. The Florida board, made up of two Republicans and one Democrat, was almost as partisan. All that had to be done was for these boards to reverse the returns in the three states and give their total of 19 electoral votes to Hayes, who would then have 185 votes—a majority of 1.

Zach Chandler wasted no time. As soon as the telegram's import dawned on him he announced to the nation that "Hayes has 185 electoral votes and is elected." The Republicans then set about turning the audacious claim into reality.

Close on the heels of Chandler's statement Abram S. Hewitt, New York congressman and the Democratic chairman, sent committees into the three states to keep an eye on the canvassing of the returns. Behind the Democratic investigators went Republican delegations, on Grant's orders.

Even the most honest investigators would have found evidence on both sides of violence, fraud, and intimidation; no one can say for certain, to this day, what the results would have been had the elections been completely fair. Since Negroes were in the majority in Louisiana and South Carolina, the Republicans had grounds for claiming a majority of the votes in each of these two states, although a considerable number of Negroes had themselves turned against the Carpetbaggers. But a majority of Florida's population was white, and now all but completely united, and there the Republicans were badly split. In the considered judgment of some latter-day historians a fair count would possibly have given Hayes the electoral votes of Louisiana and South Carolina, but Tilden should have received Florida's four electoral votes, which would have given him the presidency by an electoral college vote of 188 to 181.

It didn't turn out that way. Meeting secretly, Louisiana's five election canvassers disallowed 13,000 Democratic votes and 2000 Republican votes, thereby awarding Louisiana to Hayes. The South Carolina board's canvass gave Hayes the presidential electors but the governorship to Wade Hampton and a legislative majority to the Democrats. Through similarly arbitrary decisions the Florida board turned the electoral votes over to Hayes and the state to the Democrats.

When the Democratic majority in the House learned of the conflicting electoral counts it appointed committees to investigate the situation in the contested states. The Republican-dominated Senate dispatched its own committees.

Even sober men talked of the possibility of fighting between the regular Army, now small and scattered, but under the command of the Republican President, and the National Guard, commanded in a majority of the states by Democratic governors. Some senators and congressmen began to carry sidearms to congressional sessions.

Before March 4, when Grant's term would expire, something had to give.

For many years most historians and the general public—or that part of the public which remained interested—accepted and set down as fact a vastly oversimplified account of the secret negotiations which were suppposed, only a week before the end of Grant's term, to have ended in what was known variously as the "Compromise of 1877," the "Bargain of 1877," or the "Great Swap."

The long-accepted version was a simplified one. Republican and Southern Democratic negotiators met in February 1877 at the Wormley Hotel in Washington to effect a last-minute solution. The Republicans agreed, by withdrawing the troops which alone supported them, to run out on the Carpetbag administrations in Louisiana and South Carolina—there was no question about the Democrats' sweep of state offices in Florida—in return for Southern aid in completing the electoral count for President, thus permitting Hayes to be inaugurated. The South's conferees agreed to respect the Negroes' civil rights and to refrain from physical reprisals against the deposed Carpetbaggers, Scalawags, and Negro politicians. The Republicans all but guaranteed that President Grant would withdraw the troops from the South as soon as the votes were counted and promised that if Grant did not come through, Hayes would act as soon as he was inaugurated. So on the eve of national anarchy the House filibusterers gave up, the presidential results as returned by the Republican boards of the three states were accepted, and Rutherford Hayes was declared elected.

So goes the usual tale of the fantastic Compromise. It falls far short of the whole truth.

Through a half century one painstaking delver after another has uncovered parts of the missing whole, and some have tried to piece the entire puzzle together. None has succeeded as brilliantly as the most recent chronicler of the compromise, C. Vann Woodward, perhaps the most eminent historian of the post-bellum South, whose *Reunion and Reaction* is a myth-dispelling revelation of the multiple and sometimes less than honorable aspects of the agreement. We follow his account here.

Before the time of the Wormley Conference enough Southerners had already committed themselves to a deal. Furthermore, the congressional Democrats had already figured a sure way to get rid of the troops regardless of Hayes's promises. At a Democratic caucus on February 19 a majority of the Democratic House members approved a resolution to incorporate in the not yet authorized Army appropriations bill a clause outlawing the use of federal troops to uphold any Southern state government until that government should receive congressional recognition. Stringent penalties were provided for violations. The Republican Senate would not accept the clause. The House, refusing to appropriate any funds whatsoever for the Army, therewith adjourned. The result was that the Army went without pay until the end of November 1877.

So low was the Army's morale during the payless period that Mrs. Hayes, later discussing the President's willingness to scuttle the Republican administrations of Louisiana and South Carolina, said revealingly: "Why, what could Mr. Hayes do but what he did? He had no Army."

Grant himself had in the last year of his administration recognized the popular revulsion against the continued use of military force to support the Carpetbag governments in the South. White Republicans of the North were ready—had been ready a long time—to discard the Negro. In his last three months as President, Grant had acted as an almost neutral observer of the struggle between Redeemers and Carpetbaggers in Louisiana and South Carolina.

As Vann Woodward so succinctly put it: "In effect, Hayes' friends at the Wormley Conference were giving up something they no longer really possessed in exchange for something that had already been secured by other means. While on the other hand, the Southerners were solemnly accepting something that had been secured by other means in exchange for adherence to a course to which, by that time, they were already committed."

The Compromise was no two-day haggle in February. The bargaining had been going on for months. Nor were the issues restricted to the restitution of home rule in Louisiana and South Carolina. Instead the negotiators also concerned themselves with other and more lasting aspects of the American scene: the South's need for federally financed improvements; the politically natural orientation of Southern and Northern prewar Whigs; the possible breaking up of the white solid South so that the conservative Whigs would find allies above the Mason-Dixon line; and, above all, the conflicting plans of the railroad magnates.

Congressman James A. Garfield of Ohio, who in 1881 would succeed Hayes as President of the United States, wrote on December 12 an optimistic letter to Governor Hayes. The nation's Democratic businessmen were more anxious for quiet, he said, than for Tilden; the leading Southern Democrats in Congress did not want to carry the presidential contest to the ultimate of civil strife. Southern senators and representatives in Washington were making it plain that even though their constituents were convinced that Tilden had been lawfully elected and should be inaugurated, they would not truckle with violence. If the Southerners could be convinced that they would be well treated by the Republicans, Garfield thought, they might desert the national Democratic party in the matter of the presidency.

Hayes was receptive. He had for years been sympathetic with the predicament of the conservative white Southerners and privately critical of Republican Reconstruction policies. A onetime Whig himself, like many of the postwar Southern leaders, the Ohio governor believed that the conservatives of the North and the South could break down the sectional barriers that unnaturally divided men of similar economic and social views. Shortly after the election he had told the managing editor of the New York *Times* that if he became President he would consult leading Southern conservatives on the region's affairs. He had also expressed the conviction that the influential Southern whites would see to it that the Negro received justice and fair play under the Redeemer administrations.

The two men who opened actual negotiations for a compromise were not politicians but newspapermen. Soon after the election the Western Associated Press's general agent, William Henry Smith of Chicago, who was Hayes's closest friend and who had been instrumental in securing his nomination, opened a correspondence with Colonel Andrew J. Kellar, editor of the Memphis *Avalanche,* "to find a path of safety out of our great troubles." Kellar, who had opposed secession, had commanded a Confederate regiment in the war and was now a leader of the Whig-industrialist wing of the Democratic party in Tennessee as opposed to the unreconstructed States' rights-planter group. In mid-December, Kellar and Smith, together with the editors of the Cincinnati *Commercial* and the Cincinnati *Gazette,* Murat Halstead and Richard Smith, met to discuss the possibility of dividing Northern and Southern Democrats on the presidential issue.

When a course of action had been agreed upon Colonel Kellar journeyed to Washington. There he met, by prearrangement, General Henry Van Ness Boynton, a Union war hero and a dedicated muckraker who had helped expose the scandals of the Grant administration and who now represented the Western Associated Press newspapers in Washington.

The negotiators believed that the time was opportune for a new intersectional alignment. Most of the Southerners in Congress and in the Southern state administrations were conservatives. The Republican party was now conservative also. And conservatism, North and South, was threatened by the agricultural rebels of the West, the labor rebels of the East, and the rumblings of belated agrarian revolt in the South. The businessmen and industrialists who dominated the Redemption governments in the South had little love for the hell-raising Northern branch of the Democratic party, which had failed singularly to support the internal improvements they sought. Most certainly it was time for all good men to come to the aid of each other.

The treasuries of the redeemed state governments were nearly empty.

Clearly the South's only present hope for rebuilding lay in federal funds. And Southern conservatives, animated variously by patriotic and personal considerations, were ready to make almost any trade to get financial government support for flood control in the Lower Mississippi Valley, for levees and canals and harbors and highways and railroads. It seemed to the Southerners that the abstemious Yankee Democrats were overly squeamish and far less co-operative than were many Republicans.

The Southern congressional delegations which gathered in Washington in 1876 for the last session of the Forty-fourth Congress were less interested in who became President than in the redemption of South Carolina, Louisiana, and Florida and in presidential and congressional support for such cherished projects as flood control and a Southern transcontinental railroad. If a conservative, friendly man like Rutherford Hayes would agree to the recall of the federal troops remaining in the South and would also look benignly upon the matter of internal improvements—well . . .

Within a week the former Yankee general, Boynton, and the Southern colonel, Kellar, got together on a spectacular deal. The deal involved the cross-purposes of the two most powerful railroad men in the nation, Thomas L. Scott, president of the Pennsylvania Railroad, the world's largest freight carrier, as well as of the Texas and Pacific, and onetime president of the Union Pacific and the Atlantic and Pacific railways, and Collis P. Huntington, president of the Southern Pacific and general agent and vice-president of the Central Pacific. Tom Scott, as assistant Secretary of War during the war years, had supervised all government railway transportation lines; he was a dynamic and affable man. Like Huntington, he was also a purchaser of men and political aggregations of men. It was his ambitious dream to expand the Pennsylvania Railroad into a transcontinental, nationwide transportation monopoly; and he was now well on his way to making that dream a reality. Only the gigantic combine, the Central Pacific and the Union Pacific, dominated by Collis Huntington, which presently monopolized transcontinental railroad travel, stood in his way.

Congress had chartered the Texas and Pacific Railway Company in 1871 to build a railroad to the Pacific by way of Texas and the Southwest and had presented the new line with the last of the munificent land grants ever to be given, at fantastic public loss. For a quarter of a century financial adventurers had tried or pretended to try to build a Southern road to California. None had succeeded; the unfinished road was a memorial to dubious transactions, bankruptcies, and assorted big-time stealing.

It is neither possible nor necessary here to trace the tortuous, unsavory progress of Tom Scott and the Texas and Pacific from the time he became president of the line until the winter of 1876–77. It is enough to say that Scott wanted and needed a subsidy, and Collis Huntington wanted neither a federal subsidy for his foeman nor a competitor for his monopoly.

The panic of 1873 and the failure of Jay Cooke all but ruined Scott and those few intimates who stood to make millions if the road could be completed. The financial crisis made a subsidy imperative. General Grenville Dodge, Tom Scott's head lobbyist, and his aides soon discovered that Congress was more than a little unnerved by public reaction to the continuing inordinate demands and curious activities of the railroad moguls. The upstart Grangers were the loudest in protesting, but they were not alone. So persistent was the public opposition becoming that General Dodge commented darkly that "every convention in the Northwest is putting resolutions in their platforms against that class of legislation [railroad subsidies and grants] so that our fight has got to be made by the combined South and what votes we can get from the middle and eastern states . . . The west, northwest and southwest under this raid of the Grangers will be solid against us . . . We should combine the South and bring it up solid under the leadership of Alexander H. Stephens." Stephens, it will be remembered, had been the vice-president of the Confederacy.

So began the meshing of the ambitions of Tom Scott, the political fate of Rutherford B. Hayes, the maneuvering of Boynton and Kellar, and the requirements of the South. Hayes needed the South. Scott needed the South. The South needed railroads, other public improvements, and an end to Radicalism in any guise.

Enthusiastically the newspapers of the South, the Southwest, and Southern California demanded state and federal assistance for the Texas and Pacific, though few went so far as did the *Methodist Recorder,* which envisioned the Texas and Pacific as "the direct Gospel Line to Mexico," adding that "nothing will better prepare the way of the Lord toward that country than a well equipped railway." Moved by a human combination of personal cupidity and regional concern, and spurred by the endorsement of the T&P by many an old Confederate chieftain, among them Jefferson Davis, the transportation-hungry Southern legislatures passed one joint resolution after another "instructing the Senators and requesting the Representatives" of their states in Washington to vote for a subsidy for the Texas and Pacific. By 1876 only the Virginia and Carpetbagger-dominated Louisiana legislatures, where Scott's rivals had the upper hand, had failed to come out for the subsidy. Everywhere in the South civic and trade organizations were on the T&P band wagon. Only that blessed line, they persuaded themselves, could break the Northern monopoly and direct traffic to the West through the South.

But across the path stood influential men, in and out of Congress, who were opposed to a subsidy for Tom Scott. The most determined man among them was the Californian, Collis Huntington. If there were to be a Southern route, Huntington intended to build it, or at least part of it.

Scott's men warned the Southerners to abjure the Southern Pacific and the Central Pacific as a monstrous monopoly which had no love for the South. Huntington's spokesmen answered that the Texas and Pacific was but the child of the Pennsylvania Railroad and that Scott really intended to bypass their region by going to St. Louis and westerly by a more northern route. The Pennsylvanian, they said, was just another Carpetbagger intent on milking the Southern states.

In November 1875, delegations from Arkansas, Mississippi, Tennessee, Louisiana, South Carolina, Alabama, and Missouri met in Memphis with but a single objective in mind: to make sure that the Texas and Pacific lived up to its promise of a Southern road if it received the subsidy. To a resolution asking Congress to aid the Texas and Pacific was appended a request for the construction of branch railroads to connect the eastern terminus of the T&P in Texas with Memphis, Vicksburg, New Orleans, and St. Louis. The proposals for each of these lines were, in Vann Woodward's words, "unabashed jobbery."

That same November hundreds of Southern state and municipal office-holders, Grangers and business leaders, burning with a nigh-holy fire for the Texas and Pacific, attended a Scott-inspired National Railroad Convention in St. Louis. Jefferson Davis was there as the chairman of the Mississippi delegation. The Confederate general Joseph T. Johnson and the Yankee general William T. Sherman shook hands. Fervidly the convention endorsed Texas and Pacific requests for federal subsidies, not only for the main line but for the outrageous branches. The Texas and Pacific would mean, so the speakers predicted, a trade of $60,000,000 a year with Mexico. It would be a road to India, carrying Christian civilization in freight cars. Its construction would solve the national depression. It would mean true reconstruction for the South.

It was against such a background that the observant General Boynton wrote a significant letter on December 20 to William Henry Smith:

> What we want for *practical* success [the seating of Hayes] is thirty or thirty-six votes. West Tennessee, Arkansas, a large Kentucky element, Louisiana, Texas, Mississippi, and *Tom Scott* want help for the Texas & Pacific Road.
>
> These are strong arguments for making that project an exception to the republican policy of opposition to subsidies—provided the aid is within proper bounds, & properly secured.
>
> The argument may be briefly stated in some such form as this.
>
> 1. It is fair that the South should have a road at the hands of the government as the North has received aid for one.
>
> 2. The country needs a competing line.
>
> 3. The Texas line is below the snow line, has much better grades than the upper route, & has better country for a longer distance from its western terminii [sic].

4. The government needs it to supply its southwestern posts, and to help solve the Indian question.

5. It has important international bearings running along the border of and topping the richest mineral regions of Mexico.

If such arguments and views commend themselves to Governor Hayes, and Tom Scott, and the prominent representatives of the States I have named could *know* this, Scott with his whole force would come here, and get those votes in spite of all human power, and all the howlings which blusterers North and South could put up. I have never had the least relations with the Texas Pacific lobby. But I know its power here, and see or think I see a way of using it to the best material interests of the country.

If Governor H. feels disposed toward this enterprise as many of the best and most honest men of the republican party do—there would certainly be no impropriety for some recognized friend of his giving *Scott* to understand it. He would go to work without any suggestion whatever.

This was practical politics. A presidency was at stake; and if the national crisis was to be compromised, so also might be a conscience or two. In guarded approval Hayes wrote to Smith that "it is so desirable to restore peace and prosperity to the South that I have given a good deal of thought to it. The two things I would be exceptionally liberal about are education and internal improvements of a national character. . . ."

Hayes's Washington strategists urged him to come to the capital early in January. He arrived on January 2 to find that a Republican division seemed as likely as a Democratic one. Even more alarming were the reports that extremists among Northern Democrats were willing to resort to armed force in Sam Tilden's behalf. Some of their firebrands were saying as much, even in open mass meetings. Joseph Pulitzer, the crusading immigrant editor of the New York *World,* offered "to bare his breast to the bullets of the tyrant and rush headlong upon his glittering steel." To a cheering Indiana crowd George W. Julian, the onetime Abolitionist who was now a reform Democrat, declared that "millions of men will be found ready to offer their lives as hostages to the sacredness of the ballot as a palladium of our liberties."

And then the unexpected happened. Tom Scott had been confident that he could handle the House Committee on Pacific Railroads. Unexpectedly, and with Representative Garfield leading the opposition, the Scott men on the committee failed to send a favorable report on the bill. Whereupon late in December Huntington and Scott got together, agreeing, as Huntington phrased it, "on a bill nothing like what we want but as good as we can get." Their bargain was barefaced. Huntington would end his opposition to a subsidy for Scott and Scott would support a subsidy for Huntington. If their agreement made the politicians look silly, neither Huntington nor Scott cared. The House committee made the best of it. On January 11 Chairman Lamar was instructed to report favorably to the House a compromise bill granting federal aid for the completion of the Southern route to the Pacific.

Now it was politically easier for Hayes to endorse "internal improvements for the South." He made no open commitments, but the Republican chieftains worked away assiduously at the projected swap. General Boynton and Tom Scott got together, and on January 14 Boynton wrote Smith: "Colonel Scott feels sure that the attitude of Governor H. toward the South and his willingness to help them in their material interest can be so used here among prominent Southern Democrats as to effectively kill all measures looking toward revolution. He will go to work in the matter personally and with the skill and directness for which he is justly celebrated . . . From today there will be no lack of help, for Scott's whole powerful machinery will be set in motion at once, and I am sure you will be able to detect the influence of it in votes within ten days."

Near the end of January, in what must have seemed to the Republicans a heaven-sent gift, the divisions between the Northern and Southern wings of the Democratic party became an open and acrimonious rift. On January 24 Chairman Lamar reported two more bills from the Committee on the Pacific Railroad. One was a compromise Texas and Pacific bill, jointly approved by Huntington and Scott. The other, which he reported first, would give the Northern Pacific Railroad eight more years to complete its main line to Puget Sound and thus receive a mammoth federal land grant of 36,000,000 acres.

The Northern Democrats objected as strongly to the Texas and Pacific as to the Northern Pacific bill. Representative Franklin Landers, also an Indiana Democrat, introduced a substitute measure for Lamar's Texas and Pacific bill, eliminating the branch roads and the Huntington subsidies and requiring much more security for the government. The bill was then placed at the bottom of the calendar of the Committee of the Whole, behind thirty-four others; its passage before the end of the Forty-fourth Congress was all but impossible.

On January 29 the Texas and Pacific lobbyists sought to secure the two-thirds vote necessary to suspend the House rules in order to call up the Lamar bill. Cocksure lobbyists even crowded onto the House floor itself, openly prodding doubtful congressmen. Ironically they were seeking precedence for the new subsidy bill ahead of several bills to force the old Texas and Pacific road to pay off what it owed the government. Only a parliamentary maneuver postponed a vote on the measure that would have put the Democratic division into the record.

But Congress was concerned with much more than railroad subsidies. On January 18 bipartisan Senate and House committees had jointly brought out a bill for an Electoral Commission. This body would be made up of fifteen members, five from the Senate, five from the House, and five from the Supreme Court. Three of the Senate members would be Republicans and two Democrats; two of the members of the House of Representatives would be Republicans and three Democrats. The bill named two Democratic members of the Supreme Court and two Republicans, leaving the choice of the fifth justice to the four justices selected. The commission's decision on the election returns would be final save for the improbable chance that an objection would be upheld by both houses.

The Democrats one-sidedly supported the Electoral Commission bill. The Republicans were fairly evenly divided in the Senate, but they opposed the bill by more than two to one in the House. Rutherford B. Hayes also was opposed to the creation of an Electoral Commission. After all, the returns had given the three Southern states to Hayes; and since a Republican was president of the Senate, it was only sensible for the party to insist that his was the right to count the electoral votes.

The fifth Supreme Court member of the commission was all important; honest men on both sides believed and hoped that the fifth member would be the politically independent Judge David Davis of Illinois.

But on January 25 Washington learned that the Illinois legislature had just elected Judge Davis to the United States Senate and that the judge had announced that he could not properly serve on the Electoral Commission. This meant that the fifth and deciding member must be chosen from among one of the remaining four Supreme Court justices, all Republicans. The Tildenites cursed their luck, but their hopes rose somewhat when the four justices already selected picked Justice Joseph P. Bradley as the fifth. Bradley was a Grant appointee who had written a decision against the constitutionality of the Enforcement Act and who, before his appointment, had been fairly popular as a circuit judge in the South. Moreover, after the commissioners had been appointed, further all but incontrovertible evidence of the venality of the Louisiana Returning Board had been received. A United States Treasury agent testified before a House committee that Republican Governor J. Madison Wells of Louisiana had authorized him to sell Louisiana's votes in Washington. "He said he wanted at least $200,000 apiece for himself and Anderson," the agent said, "and a smaller amount for the niggers."

Not the Louisiana but the Florida vote came first under the scrutiny of the commission. Justice Bradley voted with his fellow Republicans, giving Florida to Hayes. The Tilden men howled that Bradley had been reached. They made much of reported visits to Bradley's home, throughout the night before the decision, of carriage loads of Republican politicians and Texas Pacific lobbyists who, so the Tilden men alleged, persuaded the justice to change his mind "between midnight and sunrise." Bradley, of course, denied every charge.

The more optimistic Democrats still believed that the commission would throw out the Louisiana returns. Two of the Republican electors in Louisiana were federal job holders and thus constitutionally ineligible to serve. The returns had been forged. The Democrats had actually received a majority of the votes. The Returning Board was not made up of five persons of different parties but of four persons from the Republican party. So the Tilden men argued, but they were whistling in the dark. The commission turned down every Democratic claim by an eight-to-seven vote. The Tilden men raged that it would be better to start another civil war than to submit to the conscienceless decisions of "The Eight."

Again the political atmosphere was filled with the ominous sound of saber rattling. A bullet was fired into the Hayes residence in Columbus while the family dined at night. Ostentatiously President Grant reviewed regular troops. Stephen B. Packard, the Republican claimant to the disputed Louisiana governorship, was shot and wounded. In state after state Democratic war veterans were reported to be drilling under arms.

On February 10, the day that the Electoral Commission's report on the findings in the Florida case was officially announced, the Democrats in Congress began a series of recesses, actually thinly disguised filibusters, to slow down the electoral count. In the first recess vote the Southern Democrats lined up solidly with the Northern members of their party. If the two wings could hold together the count would not be concluded before the inauguration date. General Boynton was little concerned. He wrote to Smith that he hoped the Democrats would go ahead with their filibuster efforts. He was certain that the deal which he, Colonel Kellar, Tom Scott, and the other plotters had worked out was not in danger. "Of course it will be a splendid thing to have the Democrats submit quietly," he commented, "but it would be a much better thing to have them start a filibustering themselves and have 35 or 40 of their party refuse to carry it on—as I am now convinced they will refuse after a little, the moment it begins to appear that the real object is to defeat the working of the bill [the Texas and Pacific subsidy measure] through filibustering."

Hayes kept quiet, but his backers insisted that their man would be a friend of the South, a supporter of internal improvements and of the return of home rule in Louisiana, Florida, and South Carolina.

Some of his advisers were recommending that he appoint two Southerners, one Republican and one Democrat, to his Cabinet. Colonel Kellar suggested Senator Davis M. Key of Tennessee, who like himself had been anti-secessionist but had fought for the Confederacy and was a close friend of the state's Redeemer Governor John C. Brown. Key was eventually appointed to the postmaster-generalship, where he dispensed patronage lavishly to good Southern Democrats as well as to old-line Whigs and Unionists, turning down many a Republican applicant in the process.

If what the Southern Democrats were asking appeared high, it was not out of line with what they could pay in turn. The conspiring Southerners would work with the Republicans to complete the electoral count in Hayes's favor and to organize the new House of Representatives with Garfield as speaker. Some of them could also assist in a rebirth of the Republican party, notably in Tennessee, under native white Conservative leaders.

On February 17 the Democrats voted a two-day recess, again delaying completion of the count of Louisiana electoral votes. That night the party met in a caucus at which the Tilden men sought intersectional approval of their filibustering tactics. They introduced resolutions denouncing the Electoral Commission and favoring the defeat of the counting procedure by any possible means so as to prevent Hayes's inauguration. The Southerners, almost to a man, turned deaf ears to their recommendations. Instead Representative John Reagan of Texas introduced a separate resolution to end the filibuster and complete the count. The caucus passed the substitute motion sixty-eight to forty-nine, with a considerable number of Democrats absent or not voting; only one Southerner voted against the substitute.

The North-South break was complete. On February 19 the New York *Times* quoted Northern Democrats as asserting that "the Southern representatives have deserted them in a body, so as to make fair weather with the Republican party." The Democratic Cincinnati *Enquirer* commented acidly that "last night's caucus settled beyond peradventure that they [the Southern representatives] have made terms. Two cabinet places are claimed, and the mess of pottage also includes other favors." In his Memphis *Avalanche,* Colonel Kellar wrote that "at last the conservative members from the South have openly cut loose from the Northern Democrats." In another of his many letters to William Henry Smith, General Boynton elatedly and impartially praised the spadework of Colonel Kellar and of Tom Scott's men.

By February 22 the Hayes strategists were certain of his inauguration. The Northern Republican press fulsomely praised the Southern Democrats who had acted as "honorable, patriotic statesmen," and who, as the Washington *National Republican* put it, "bade farewell to the tricky, scheming, filibustering, dough-faced faction composing the Northern Democracy, and boldly put themselves on record as being against any attempt to evade the decision of the judicial tribunal or thwart its result. It is the bravest and wisest act that has been recorded in the annals of political history for half a century." Understandably the Tilden Democrats of the North thought otherwise.

It was after all this that the Wormley Conference took place. Far from having an important effect on the outcome of the contest, it contributed very little to the ending of the crisis.

Hayes's closest advisers, who had developed the formula which the Southerners found acceptable, did not participate directly in it. Neither did the inner coterie of Southerners who had been going along with the Republicans. Instead the principals were mainly Louisiana Democrats and Ohio Republi-

cans, and their discussions concerned almost entirely the recognition of
the Democratic state governments in Louisiana and, secondarily, in South
Carolina, not through vague Republican promises but by absolute guarantees. The Louisianians, led by Major E. A. Burke, a bizarre adventurer,
threatened that unless the Republicans surrendered Louisiana and South
Carolina the Louisianians' many friends in Congress would join in the filibusters. Major Burke insisted that the Republican leaders forthrightly commit
themselves.

On Monday, the twenty-sixth, Major Burke met with President Grant. At
the conclusion of their interview the President approved a news dispatch
which indirectly quoted him as saying "unequivocally that he is satisfied that
the Nicholls [Louisiana Democratic] government is the government which
should stand," that the Republicans there were helpless without the protection of federal troops, and that public opinion in the nation was "clearly
opposed to the further use of troops in upholding a State government."
Grant also promised that there would be no further interference by federal
authorities in Louisiana unless there were violent excesses. Burke then conferred with Senator John Sherman, at Sherman's request. Two months earlier
Sherman had reported to Hayes that the Louisiana Democrats had taken
control of the state through terrorism and intimidation. Now Sherman had
just accepted, on a trip to Columbus, a place in Hayes's Cabinet. And Hayes
was ready to pull the rug out from under the Louisiana and South Carolina
Republicans. When Burke told Sherman he wanted him to tell Grant that the
withdrawal of troops would not be embarrassing to Hayes, Sherman exclaimed that there was no use to try to approach Grant. The major then
produced the dispatch which Grant had just approved. Sherman, and Stanley Matthews of Cincinnati, a relative of Hayes and counsel to Tom Scott,
and former Governor William Dennison of Ohio, who were with him, thereupon agreed to call on the President. They also assured Burke that when
Hayes became President he would follow Grant's recommended policy for
Louisiana. Sherman asked for and received assurances in turn that the Democratic governor of Louisiana would not mistreat Negroes and other Republicans when the troops were withdrawn, and that the Democratic Louisiana
legislature would delay electing a Democratic United States senator for a
week after the inauguration so that the Republicans might not be tempted
to turn against their President in retaliation and refuse to confirm his cabinet
nominations.

That evening the so-called Wormley Conference was held.

At the gathering Sherman, Matthews, Dennison, and Garfield repeated
the set Republican promises to Major Burke, two other Louisiana politicians, and to Henry Watterson, editor of the Louisville *Courier Journal* and
a representative from Kentucky. Garfield, who as a member of the Electoral
Commission had been voting with the Republican majority and who had

been aware of Kellar's and Boynton's maneuverings from the beginning, noted piously in his diary that "the whole nation would honor those Southern men who are resisting anarchy—and thus are preventing civil war; but neither they nor we could afford to do anything that would be or appear to be a political bargain."

The next day the Associated Press carried so much of the story of the Wormley Conference as Burke had seen fit to give out, namely, that Hayes would recognize the Democratic government in Louisiana and that the Democratic state administration in turn would deal fairly with the Negroes and the other deserted Republicans. Burke also tendered to Matthews a guarantee, drawn up at a caucus of the Louisiana Democratic legislature, of political and civil equality for the Negroes and absolution of Republicans for their past political misdeeds. Simultaneously Henry Watterson read into the Congressional Record Grant's dispatch in favor of the Democratic government in Louisiana. The Democratic majority of the House then approved a resolution that Congress recognize both the Nicholls government in Louisiana and the Hampton government in South Carolina.

The Tilden diehards fought tenaciously to the end. On March 1, in perhaps the wildest session of the House of Representatives, the chamber lost almost all semblance of order, with the members shrieking, yelling, demonstrating against each other, and with the floor packed with lobbyists working against the filibusterers. At one point the Tildenites mustered 116 votes to refuse to proceed with the count.

After hours of pandemonium Representative William M. Levy of Louisiana announced from the floor that he had received solemn and truthful assurances from Grant and from the friends of Hayes that the troops would be withdrawn and that a policy of conciliation toward the Southern states was certain. He besought all members "who have been influenced in their actions . . . by a desire to protect Louisiana and South Carolina" to help in having the count completed.

At four o'clock in the morning the Electoral Commission declared Hayes elected President by a majority of one electoral vote.

The rest was anticlimactic. President Grant told Major Burke that he had telegraphed Packard, the Republican claimant to the governorship of Louisiana, that federal troops would no longer be at his back and that he had also instructed the commanding general in New Orleans to remove the troops from the vicinity of the Statehouse in New Orleans. Somehow the order did not reach the general, but it made little difference. Packard continued to occupy the Statehouse until Hayes himself acted, but the Democrats ran the state government.

Hayes arrived in Washington on March 2 in a private car. It had been furnished by Tom Scott's Pennsylvania Railroad. He was privately inaugurated at the White House on March 3. That same day the House Democrats rammed through a resolution declaring that Sam Tilden had been "duly elected president of the United States for the term of four years, commencing on the 4th day of March, A.D., 1877." Nevertheless on March 5 Hayes was publicly inaugurated President of the United States.

The South did get its railroad to the West, but it wasn't Tom Scott's Texas and Pacific. President Hayes balked at the subsidy bill; and, outgeneraled by Huntington, who went ahead with his own line without benefit of subsidies, Scott sold his Texas and Pacific holdings to Jay Gould. Huntington and Gould made peace in November 1881. The next year the two lines met just east of El Paso.

Nor did Southern Democratic support for the Republicans or Republican backing for Southern internal improvements last long. But the troops were withdrawn, as promised, and the Redeemers ruled in every state in the South.

The comment of Vann Woodward on the morality of the horse trading which he bares in detail in his *Reunion and Reaction* is restrained and, in all likelihood, fair:

"To account for the action of the Southerners without reference to patriotism and the more statesmanlike motives would be to adopt a deplorably cynical interpretation of human conduct. On the other hand, to offer such motives as the complete explanation would be to advance a questionable theory regarding the sectional distribution of the more admirable virtues. The charitable supposition would be that while patriotism was equitably distributed between Northern and Southern Democrats, the patriotic course of resisting violence and complying with the Electoral Commission law happened to coincide more nearly with the interests of the Southern than of the Northern Democrats—as they understood their interests."

CHAPTER 2

The Bourbon Ascendancy

EVEN had not purposeful intimidation, the political double-dealing that cast Sam Tilden into the outer darkness, and the yearnings of honest and dishonest men for material benefits combined to assure Radicalism's debacle, its disintegration should have been predictable almost from the beginning. The ingredients needful for its perpetuation could not have long survived its inception. What was required was unrelaxed party discipline and unity, unswerving honesty of purpose and of behavior, and the maintenance of an artificially contrived division of the numerically and economically dominant, race-conscious American whites for the benefit of a racial minority and a single political party.

Instead the Radical cause foundered upon the internecine warfare between Liberal Republicanism and Grantism; the divisions within the Southern Radical administrations which preceded, accompanied, and followed the national party's schism of 1872; the Negro's own disillusion as to Republican intent, so apparent in the party's disinclination to welcome his people in politics elsewhere than in the captive South; and the near imperative intersectional compulsion toward white solidarity. Surely had the North been sufficiently impelled by political discipline or ideological zeal, the political equality which Reconstruction gave to the Negro would not have been forfeited after a single decade, no matter how heroic the efforts of the South's Redeemers.

Apparent from Reconstruction's beginning was the inclination of the divided cells of a political, economic, and racial organism, the white body politic, to reunite.

The evidence of this inclination is abundant. Gerrit Smith, the wealthy New York reformer and philanthropist who had given John Brown his approval and money, declared in 1867 that "the United States should buy the Southern heart, worth more to us than a thousand Alaskas," and that the only way to purchase it was "by proving to the South that the North loves her—that the North has a heart to give in exchange for her heart." That same year Horace Greeley signed Jefferson Davis's bond, and Charles O'Conor, the brilliant Irish-American Democrat of New York, tendered Davis his legal services.

James Russell Lowell, one of the angriest of New England's fulminators against the South before and during the war, wrote in 1868 to Edwin Godkin, editor of *The Nation,* who now was one of the foremost apostles of forgiveness for the South: "We can never reconstruct the South except through its own leading men, nor ever hope to have them on our side till we make it for their interest and compatible with their honor to be so. At this moment in Virginia, the oath required by the new constitution makes it impossible to get a decent magistrate."

Eight years later, during the presidential campaign of 1876, Lowell wrote: "We are deliberately trying to make an Ireland of the South, by perpetuating misgovernment there."

In January 1868 Gilbert H. Bates, late sergeant in the 1st Wisconsin Heavy Artillery, bet some Wisconsin friends that, without money and alone, and carrying the United States flag, he could travel through the heart of the South unharmed. The sergeant won his wager; he was cheered, housed, and fed by Southerners throughout his travels, and the South offered his adventureless tour as proof that no animosity toward the Union remained.

As the years of Reconstruction dragged on the acts of good will increased. Though the pension-minded Union veterans' organization, the Grand Army of the Republic, clung to the bloody shirt, individual G.A.R. chapters and unorganized groups of veterans and federal regulars extended their hands in friendship time and again. Southerners began decorating graves of Yankee boys buried on Dixie's battlefields, and Northerners tended the resting places of Confederates who had died in Northern prisons.

The first instance of remembrance of the fallen foe was recorded in Columbus, Mississippi, only a year after the end of hostilities, when the "ladies of the community" decorated the graves of Yankees who had died there in a Union hospital. The G.A.R. post of Rome, New York, invited Admiral Raphael Semmes, the once-proscribed Confederate sea raider, to speak, with the stipulation that the proceeds would buy tombstones for federal graves. Admiral Semmes was unable to go. In the same year United States troops stationed in Mobile sent a wreath, and lent Admiral Semmes a cannon to fire the salute, on the occasion of the decoration of Confederate graves in the city.

When Senator Sumner died in 1874 Lamar of Mississippi, secessionist by passionate conviction, who had lost his two brothers in Civil War battles, eulogized him in the House of Representatives; and even calculating politicians wept as he spoke of the man who had embodied more than most of his contemporaries, all that the South hated in the North:

". . . I see on both sides only the seeming of a constraint, which each apparently hesitates to dismiss. The South—prostrated, exhausted, drained of her life blood, as well as of her material resources, yet still honorable and true—accepts the bitter award of the bloody arbitrament without reservations, resolutely determined to abide the result with chivalrous fidelity; yet, as if struck dumb by the magnitude of her reverses, she suffers on in silence. The North, exultant in her triumph, and elated by its success, still cherishes, as we are assured, a heart full of magnanimous emotion for her disarmed and discomfited antagonist; and yet, as if mastered by some mysterious spell, silencing her better impulses, her words and acts are the words and acts of suspicion and distress.

"Would that the spirit of the illustrious dead whom we lament today could speak from the grave to both parties to this deplorable discord in tones which should reach each and every year throughout this broad territory: 'My countrymen! *Know* one another and you will *love* one another!' "

In 1875 and 1876, as Americans celebrated the events leading to the Declaration of Independence and the centennial of the Revolution—a rising in which rebels of the North and rebels of the South had fought a common foe—popular demonstrations of intersectional amity multiplied. When Massachusetts celebrated the Battle of Lexington, a delegation of Confederate veterans from Charleston presented to Massachusetts the battle flag which Boston's Colonel Robert Gould Shaw and his Negro regiment had lost in an attack on a Confederate redoubt during the siege of Charleston twelve years before.

At Boston's celebration of the Battle of Bunker Hill, Charleston's Washington Light Artillery and Norfolk Blues paraded under General Fitzhugh Lee, Robert E. Lee's nephew. And the Greenville, South Carolina, *Enterprise and Mountaineer* put into words in the fall of 1875 what must have been in the minds of many: "This centennial glorification of the Rebels of '76 cannot fail to teach the Northern mind to look with more leniency on Confederate Rebels who only attempted to do in the late Civil War what the ancestors of the Northern people did do in the American Revolution. . . . It shows a want of sense as well as a want of principle, and a want of truth, to call the Rebels of '76 patriots and heroes, and the Rebels of 1861 traitors."

To the centennial in Philadelphia the South sent orators and paraders and exhibits and spectators by the thousands, and as Hayes's policy of conciliation became clear, friendly gesture met friendly gesture, North and South; only the party liners of the Grand Army of the Republic in the North and a comparatively few unreconstructed Southern Rebels were unwilling to forgive and to try to forget.

The nation was ready for the conciliatory policy of President Hayes. When he toured the South with some of his cabinet members a few months after his inauguration he was hailed in Virginia, Georgia, Tennessee, in all of the major Southern cities which he visited; and the friendly receptions prompted *The Nation* to observe joyfully "that the president whom this campaign produced should be traveling triumphantly through the South, pleading before joyous multitudes for union and conciliation, has all the looks of a special providence, and must fill the souls of those who supported him as a vessel of wrath with strange confusion."

The President's hand of friendship was sincerely extended; but behind the Republican rightabout-face lay two illusions. One was a belief that the Conservative Democrats would live up to their promises to safeguard the Negroes' civil rights. Northern concern over that guarantee would decrease, before the end of the nineteenth century, nearly to the vanishing point. The other illusion was that, with the Negro issue relegated to the background, the proper source of Republican strength in the South would and should be the Conservative element, the legatees of the propertied classes which had unavailingly opposed Jacksonian Democracy. Hayes himself, who had once been a Whig, represented the new Republican party so out of tune with its founders, the party of economic privilege, high tariffs, and a hard dollar. These latter-day Republicans dreamed of their kind of Republicanism in the South, led by white Southerners whose economic interests and political philosophy were generally similar to their own.

The Southern Conservative leaders whom the Republican strategists saw as eventual political allies held two equally illusory ideas. One was that under their administrations an end would be made to dishonesty in state government. Their second illusion was that the purposeful unity inspired by the common white determination to regain political supremacy could be preserved under Bourbon direction. They were wrong. Political corruption decreased but did not disappear with the Carpetbaggers' departure; and the small farmers and other low-income Southerners were to show that they wanted something else from their elected officials besides penny-pinching honesty. Even before Conservative Democratic rule had been established in the last of the former Confederate states that had rid themselves of the Radicals, white rebellion against Bourbon leadership had begun in others. A long, ruinous struggle, between the haves and the have-nots of the white South, between conservative and liberal political ideology, between the poor whites who were derided as "rednecks" and the upper- and middle-class coalitions, was in the making.

Out of that intermittent contest would emerge the monolithic Southern Democratic party, a massive, entombing structure wherein the white men of the South might fight out their personal, factional, or economic differences, but beyond which no combatant could carry his quarrel on pain of becoming an outcast who had imperiled white unity and therefore white supremacy.

The derisive description of "Bourbon" had first been applied to unreconstructed Southerners who regarded any compromise with the Yankees as utter treason; in employing it the New York *Herald* had likened them to the doomed French kings who had never learned anything or forgotten anything. Now the name was generally, if unfairly, applied to almost all Southerners of substance. Many of these landed, business or professional gentry had been Whigs and opponents of secession, some even critics of slavery. But most of the Whig leadership had chosen to fight for state and region. The South's aristocrats, and her well-to-do, whether aristocrats or not, had led into battle the yeoman farmers, the small town artisans and mechanics, and the poor whites who made up the Confederacy's independent, unruly, magnificent soldiery. Even in defeat the unrepentant white citizenry had turned to the old leaders in those few months during which, under the Lincoln-Johnson program, they had free choice.

These Bourbons had been the principal architects of Redemption. They had no intention now of vacating the driver's seat.

The Bourbons do not fit into a common mold. A wide moral chasm separated Wade Hampton from Georgia's war hero, John B. Gordon, more admirable on the field of battle than in the field of finance. But in their motivations, their philosophies, and their achievements the Bourbons of the post-Reconstruction South were a distinct economic and social grouping.

Most of them shared the habit of command and a mistrust of the political mass, a misgiving which antedated their Reconstruction experience but which was immeasurably sharpened thereby. They believed that political direction belonged properly to an elect selected from themselves. They were determined that what had happened before would not happen again. They had no intention of permitting the white South to divide politically again as it had been divided before the war; nor did they intend to permit a resumption of the later division by race. The Negro would vote under their direction and at their will or not at all. The white independent who tempted him would not be tolerated. Whether their wealth was great or small, whether it was derived from the land, from business or industry, or from the professions, they were the South's principal taxpayers; and fresh and fearsome in their memories were the Carpetbaggers' expansion of public services and the increase in taxes which were needful for the creation and maintenance of those services for which the Bourbons principally paid.

The Bourbons could be brilliantly Machiavellian during Redemption and throughout the later contest between themselves and the rebellious Independents. They so adapted their tactics to place and time that in one county or section of a state they might hold a majority of poor whites by recalling the days of Negro domination, while in another county they would employ the Negro vote to overcome white majorities. Nor did they forget the stratagems to which they had resorted in the twilight of Reconstruction.

This is not to say that the Bourbons bulldozed or bought their way to the top after the native white Southerners came again into power after Reconstruction. They were already on top.

The Bourbons—some called them the Confederate Brigadiers—concentrated on programs of niggardly economy and a rewriting of state constitutions. In the new state constitutions the Bourbons tightened up on voting qualifications and gave expression of their mistrust of the legislative branch. Of the Texas constitution, in which half of the sections dealing with the legislature severely limited its power, the Houston *Daily Telegraph* commented in 1876: "The harness is so small, the straps drawn so tight, the check rein pulled up to the last buckle hole, and the load to draw so heavy that the legislative horse will be galled from collar to crupper and the state wagon will go creaking along the highway of progress in the rear of the procession."

In the legislatures thus restrained the Redeemers set about economizing; their financial slogan, in the words of Governor Drew of Florida, was "Spend nothing unless absolutely necessary."

Most of the Bourbon administrations did better—or worse—than that.

They drastically reduced salaries of officeholders and abolished many offices, and with them the services they rendered. Four states paid their Redemption governors only $3000 a year; only two Southern states paid their governors as much as $5000. While they did not do away with universal education—the Carpetbagger plant had taken too firm root—the Bourbon administrations failed to provide adequate funds for colleges and higher education.

Their most remarkable retrenchments were accomplished through the repudiation of a part of the state debts.

Most of these debts had accumulated during Reconstruction, though varying amounts had been carried over from the prewar and war years. Only Texas and Mississippi did not arbitrarily reduce their obligations; the other states, constitutionally immune from suits by individuals, hacked away at a combined indebtedness for the eleven states of $140,000,000. North Carolina repudiated her obligations to the extent of $22,000,000, Louisiana $38,000,000, Georgia $9,000,000, Arkansas and Alabama about $13,000,-000 each, and Virginia more than $30,000,000, all protesting their inability to pay.

In moral justification they could well claim that the repudiated portions were the work of alien lawmakers, saddled upon them at bayonet point; and they could plead that they could not repay on the scale set by the Radical administrations. As Allan Nevins commented in *The Emergence of Modern America, 1865–1878:* "No other part of the Union was half so poor as the South, yet the South groaned under levies which were unapproached elsewhere. When computed according to wealth, it was a more destructive taxation, in all probability, than has ever been borne before or since in the United States."

Though state governments under the Bourbons were in general akin, they were not uniform.

In Tennessee, whose warring, divided white citizens were least disturbed by Negro political intrusion during Reconstruction, Redemption had at first the nature of a private vendetta between the hill folk and the lowlanders. "I have nothing to conceal in the matter," said the chairman of a Tennessee Senate committee, in proposing a redistricting bill soon after the Radical collapse. "One main object was [so] to redistrict the state that for the next ten years not a Republican can be elected to the legislature. . . . I believe in the law of revenge. The Radicals disfranchised us, and now we intend to disfranchise them."

But once the party revenge was accomplished, Tennessee's Bourbons became almost indistinguishable from their Northern counterparts.

General John C. Brown, Tennessee's first Democratic governor, was a former Whig, a wartime Confederate officer, and brother of a prewar Whig governor. Governor Brown was close to the fabulous railroader, Tom

Scott; eventually he served as vice-president of the Scott-projected Texas and Pacific Company and was president, at the time of his death, of what was to become the dominant financial-political force in Tennessee, the Tennessee Coal, Iron and Railroad Company. He was succeeded by James D. Porter, another former Whig and Confederate veteran, who became, after two gubernatorial terms, president of the Nashville, Chattanooga and St. Louis Railroad and, among other industrial directorates, a director of the Tennessee Coal, Iron and Railroad Company.

Governor Porter's successor was Albert S. Marks, kinsman and onetime law partner of Colonel Arthur S. Colyar, the most neanderthal of Tennessee's Whigs-turned-Democrat. Marks controlled the Nashville *American,* one of the three principal newspapers of Tennessee, all of which were pronouncedly Republican in their economic policies. The *American* opposed the railroad investigation commissions. Marks was a high-tariff man and a ready defender of the Tennessee Coal, Iron and Railroad Company of which Colyar was general counsel and director. He was also an ardent champion of the leasing of state convicts to the highest or the most favored bidder; the T.C.I. and R. had the privilege of working the felons of Tennessee to death for an annual payment of $101,000.

Yet among the postwar Conservatives of Tennessee were dissenters who warred with the industrial wing; foremost among them was Senator Isham G. Harris, a wholehearted secessionist and wartime Confederate leader, a principal representative of the planter faction which continued to give battle long after total Redemption in the South to Tennessee's industrial Bourbons. Harris's faction effected in 1882 the repudiation of some Radical-issued, fraudulent Tennessee bonds and the creation of a regulatory railroad commission.

Florida's Redemption leader, Governor Drew, was a Whig of Whigs and a loyal Unionist who had refused to take any part in the war. "Millionaire Drew" he was called, because of his multiple, profitable holdings in land, timber, and merchandise which contributed no little to his philosophy of thrift in government.

North Carolina, like Tennessee, experienced a Reconstruction program imposed not by a Negro majority or near-majority but by wide white participation in Radical Reconstruction. North Carolina had been a Whig-minded state. Her Conservatives had been unfriendly to the trouble-making Democrats; some of them had even stayed aloof from the fight against Radical Republicanism until they were convinced that no other course save union with the Democrats could defeat the Radicals. Even after the success of the coalition many of them disliked it. North Carolina's Conservative party did not accept the name Democrat until eight years after the war; in 1884 the Raleigh *News and Observer* would recall that, since the war, the Democratic nominees for governor "had been Worth, a Whig; Ashe, a Whig; Merrimon, a Whig; Vance, a Whig; and Jarvis, who was too young before the war to have had much political leaning one way or the other." North Carolina went along with the Bourbons.

Wade Hampton faithfully carried out his pledges to the Negroes of just treatment and free participation in the state's political life, despite the resentment of the upcountry "All-Outs" who wanted to remove the Negro completely from the political scene. Yet, as everywhere else, the Conservatives failed to perceive the needs and aspirations of the small farmer and the other low-income population. The South Carolina Redeemers now linked themselves to those emerging interests witn which they were mostly already identified, to the textile mill operators and industrialists, to the railroaders, the corporation lawyers, the supply merchants, whenever these came into conflict with the little people.

In Texas the Redeemers soon fell out. Her agrarians, under John H. Reagan, the Confederacy's postmaster general, unsuccessfully sought federal and state regulation of the railroads. The Bourbons had their way. They did away with many public services introduced by the Radicals and sharply reduced taxes and school funds. Governor Oran M. Roberts vetoed the state public school appropriation in 1879, while advocating a ten-year tax exemption for manufacturers, and flagrantly favored the railroads and utilities. By 1885 the state's great public domain had been all but exhausted; the public schools had been defrauded of most of the land holdings dedicated in 1875 to public education; and twelve railroad companies had snatched 32,400,000 acres, an aggrandizement larger than the states of New Hampshire, Vermont, Massachusetts, Rhode Island, and Connecticut together.

Arkansas' Redeemers first fell out over debts. The proponents of full payment, many of them bondholders themselves, were in the ascendancy in the early years of Redemption; by 1885 the Democratic party had all but destroyed itself over the issue. But the repudiationists finally won out after the revelation that many railroad and levee bonds were fraudulent and that they had been parceled out among Democratic and Republican politicians in order to insure full payment of the bonds.

Of the other Southern states Georgia and Alabama would most readily accept the industrial autocracy and the individual opportunism of the men she trusted; South Carolina and Louisiana would provide the best examples of dedicated leadership, Mississippi, the evil results of degenerative conflict between small hill farmers and the planters of the lowlands; and Virginia, the least affected by Reconstruction of all the Southern states, the most unchallengeable evidence of the complexity and the inconsistency of political man. And across all of them fell impartially the dominating shadows of the railroaders.

Nowhere did the Bourbon leadership put to better personal use than in

Georgia the issue of white supremacy and the public clamor for railroad construction and industrial development. A celebrated and colorful triumvirate dominated Georgia, though not without opposition, until the small farmers whom they disregarded at last revolted. They were Governor—later United States Senator—Joe E. Brown, whose political qualities and business acumen we have already noted; the militarily distinguished General John B. Gordon, courtly incarnation of the Lost Cause and a less comforting reminder that the chivalry of the battlefield is not necessarily carried over into the world of business; and gentlemanly, calculating Alfred H. Colquitt, whose business and industrial interests dwarfed his agricultural holdings although he was one of the largest of Southern planters and landowners; he was an investor in such varied businesses as New England textile mills, Tennessee fertilizer factories, and Southern coal mines and speculated heavily in two Southern railroads.

A Conservative first disputed their domination. He was General Robert Toombs, lately a member of the Confederate Cabinet, who secured in Georgia's constitutional convention of 1877, despite Joe Brown's opposition, constitutional prohibitions against railroad monopolies, state subsidies to railroads, and irrevocable franchises.

More than any other state, post-Reconstruction Alabama offers evidence of the continuity of the influence of the railroad lobbyists under Radical and Restoration administrations. The railroads were the catalyst which brought together ambitious, adventurous men of every political complexion; they were so at home with Radical and Redeemer alike that many of the same figures kept turning up throughout the twenty years beginning with the 1850s and continuing on to and after Redemption: such Alabamians as Josiah Morris, member of the legislature before the war and still politically active even in the 1880s; James W. Sloss, onetime storekeeper, who as a farsighted coal and steel and railroad developer and speculator was, before and after Reconstruction, influential with Radicals and Bourbons alike; and Robert Patton, who had been Andrew Johnson's provisional governor of Alabama, and in that capacity had validated state bonds which provided $12,000 a mile for Sloss's railroad, and who became, under the Radicals, vice-president of a Sloss line, the state grant for which the legislature considerately increased to $16,000 a mile.

The principal beneficiaries of fast and loose railroad politicking in Alabama were the Louisville and Nashville empire and the Alabama and Chattanooga Railroad, rivals in the struggle for access to the northern Alabama mineral area. Both roads were the recipients of extravagant state aid under the Radicals; the liabilities which the state assumed in endorsed bonds totaled $17,000,000 of the state's Reconstruction debt of some $25,000,000. And it was George S. Houston, Alabama's Redeemer governor and a man closely identified with the L&N, who engineered, in 1876, a settlement between the bondholders and the railroads which was especially advantageous to the L&N. When Governor Houston went to the United States Senate, after two terms as governor, his successor was an L&N attorney and president of an L&N-operated ironworks.

As in Georgia, a Bourbon triumvirate controlled Mississippi's political destinies. Its members were Senator Lamar, General E. C. Walthall, and General James Z. George, the man who had been the principal strategist in the campaign of 1875 which restored white Conservative rule. They, and Mississippi's governors for the twenty years after Redemption, were corporation and railroad lawyers.

The Mississippi Bourbons had a harder time than their fellow Conservatives; Mississippi's immediate post-Reconstruction history was the most turbulent of the Southern states.

A newspaper editor, Ethelbert Barksdale of Jackson, symbolized for years the challenge of liberal Democrats to Bourbon control of the party. Barksdale espoused the abolishment of the convict lease system, morally the most indefensible of Bourbon institutions, regulation of the railroads, cheap currency and free coinage of silver, and the Farmers' Alliance. Though he never gained political ascendancy, he did threaten and even check Bourbon domination of the state; and the planter-corporation lawyer dynasty was disturbed enough by the threat and actuality of political insurrection to resort to shameless stratagems. They entered into cynical and successful alliances with Negro Republicans, whose leaders they persuaded to support the regular Democrats in state and local elections in exchange for Democratic aid in securing patronage for Mississippi's Negro Republicans. The strategy was double-barreled; with federal patronage in the hands of Negroes more Negro recruits would be drawn to the Republican party and thus give the Bourbons an argument to hold white voters who might otherwise desert the Conservative party.

So involved did state politics become that when James R. Chalmers, a Bourbon leader in the overthrow of the Radicals in 1875, having been successfully challenged on grounds of fraud by the Negro congressional incumbent, John R. Lynch, after his election to Congress as a Democrat in 1880, sought and failed to receive Senator Lamar's support, he turned Republican and, with the backing of a number of influential politicians including the practical James L. Alcorn, again ran unsuccessfully for Congress in a contest in which a majority of Negro as well as white Democrats opposed him.

The Mississippi Bourbon deals with the Negroes from 1876 on were open and purposeful. In the heavily Negro counties of the Yazoo-Mississippi Delta, Negroes were consistently included on the Democratic tickets, though generally for minor offices, although in 1877 a Negro, John D. Webster, was nominated at the Democratic convention for Secretary of

State. The Democrats insisted on a Negro Republican member on each local election commission; they formed Democrat-Negro Republican fusion tickets in the Delta counties and permitted minority Negro representation on the county governing bodies, the boards of supervisors. As late as 1883 Negro Republicans held the offices of county assessor and coroner in Hinds County, in which Jackson, the state capital, is located, shared magistrate and constable posts, and sent one representative to the state legislature and one supervisor to the county board of supervisors, all by prearrangement with the outnumbered Democrats, who filled the more important offices themselves. The job-sharing plan was not without its critics. Some of the lesser Democratic politicians coveted the offices given to the Negroes; others feared that job distribution and participation in politics with Democratic co-operation only encouraged the Negro to greater political activity.

Except for the cynicism with which the arrangements were made, there was nothing reprehensible in giving the Negro a share of the political plums. But the Bourbons did not stop with job distribution. More than anywhere else Mississippi's Democrats practiced the ungentle art of "bulldozing," as violence or the threat of violence was nicknamed. Independents and upstart white Republicans were waited upon by delegations which usually convinced them of the error of their ways.

The state's most tragically celebrated incident of bulldozing in the early post-Reconstruction years grew out of a political and personal enmity between two Kemper countians, John Gully, a Democrat, and Judge W. W. Chisholm, an Independent and former Republican. Gully was ambushed and shot to death; Judge Chisholm, suspected of having a hand in the murder, was imprisoned in the county jail on charges of having conspired with a Negro who confessed to the actual shooting. Fearing for his family's safety while he was in jail, Chisholm asked and received permission for them to stay in the jail with him. On the Sunday morning after his imprisonment, from a hundred to three hundred armed men rode to the jailhouse at daybreak and ordered the jailer to surrender the judge. The jailer and his deputy promptly fled. Arming themselves from the jail's small arsenal, Chisholm and two loyal friends, who had also joined him in jail, killed several of the mob before the attackers set fire to the jail and forced the beleaguered group into the open. As they ran from the burning building, Judge Chisholm, his fourteen-year-old son, his fifteen-year-old daughter, and one of his defenders, a British citizen, were shot to death. Shamefully the Meridian *Mercury,* the Jackson *Clarion,* and the Vicksburg *Herald* gloated over the killing; a Republican newspaper, the Jackson *Daily Times,* best summed up the situation: "The judges are Democrats, the prosecuting attorney is a Democrat, and all have to be re-elected next fall. The white liners . . . run the state, its courts, governors and all." Nor did the governor himself take any action, a lapse which did not prevent his renomination and probably helped it.

The Redemptionists of Virginia behaved with restraint, that being the nature of her more sedate and secure white society. The principal achievement of her Redeemers, who were challenged and, for a time, hamstrung by an upstart former Confederate general, was the perfection, through county nuclei which ungenteel folk were to call the courthouse gangs, of the smoothest functioning, the most respectable, and one of the most ruthless of the nation's political machines.

Virginia's political and economic conflicts and meanderings well illustrate the contradictions, the compromises with conscience, the conflicting concepts of the state's social responsibilities, and the personal ambitions which make impossible any interpretation of Bourbon rule in simple terms of good and evil.

Her early restoration to the Union in 1870 was accomplished without the experience of Radical Reconstruction. Instead the state passed from military Reconstruction to the restoration of civil rule under an unlikely Conservative coalition of secessionist former Confederates, conservative Republicans whose faction was known as "True Republicans," prewar Whigs, and a mass of Negroes, better educated on the whole than members of their race anywhere else in the South and more inclined to follow their former masters than the Radical newcomers.

The governor this coalition elected was Gilbert C. Walker, a banker and director of the Norfolk and Petersburg Railroad and a Hamiltonian sound-money man. Though he was also a Republican and a Carpetbagger, he was regarded by most of Virginia's gentry as a respectable citizen.

The Virginia Conservatives wasted no time in showing whose interests most concerned them. The General Assembly of 1870–71 passed two telling bills. One bill, the Railroad Act, provided for the sale, at great sacrifice, of the state's stockholdings in its own railroad. These sales continued until most of the state's railroads were privately owned, most of the owners being Northern railroad systems or the men who dominated them; and, accommodatingly, when the privately owned railroads went out from under state regulations, they retained the exemptions and other privileges which had been theirs under state ownership.

The other gravely consequential bill was the Funding Act, under the terms of which the annual interest on the state's funded debt approached its entire revenues. The sponsors of the Funding Act were an assortment of state bondholders, railroads, bankers, brokers, and speculators, and a handful whom Pendleton describes in his *Political History of Appalachian Virginia* as "a few excellent men who were influenced by a desire to protect what they believed to be the essential credit and unsullied honor of the Commonwealth."

For the rest of the century the Conservatives remained almost uninterruptedly in control of the state; and so closely were they identified with the railroad interests that almost every state chairman of the party was a president or a director of a railroad.

The only man who successfully challenged the Conservatives and so disturbed the state that his very name would become a part of the Virginia vocabulary was General William Mahone, himself a railroad developer and speculator, whose unusual story may be used to conflicting purpose, depending upon the teller's point of view.

Billy Mahone was a tavern keeper's son. As a boy he rode the mails in Southampton County, a region of plantation blue bloods, and added greatly to his income through his skill as a card player. Family friends helped him through the Virginia Military Institute, from which he was graduated in 1847; then, after four years of teaching in a military academy and continuing his engineering studies on the side, self-made Billy Mahone became engineer on a railroad project and, in 1851, engineer of the well-constructed Norfolk and Petersburg Railroad. By 1861 he was its president, chief engineer, and superintendent.

Though then no politician, upon Virginia's secession he was appointed quartermaster general of state troops; soon he went into the field and served ably in a succession of engagements and campaigns, especially distinguishing himself in the Wilderness. He became a Southern hero after his brilliant repulse of federal troops in the Crater at Petersburg after the explosion of the murderous mine. He was alert to the needs of his men, and Mahone's Brigade had as high an *esprit de corps* as any Confederate unit.

The war over, Billy Mahone went back to railroading and, unobtrusively at first, into the politics which successful railroad promotion required. By 1870, through two legislative authorizations, he had created and dominated the privately owned Atlantic, Mississippi and Ohio Railroad, formed of three small, formerly principally state-owned lines, and as president of what was probably the best railroad in the South—it later became the Norfolk and Western—Billy Mahone drew a salary "as big as the President's." He worked powerfully in the background for the election of his fellow railroad associate, the respectable Carpetbagger, Gilbert Walker.

From that time on Mahone was in politics to the hilt. Until 1877 he sought political power within the Conservative ranks. Through railroad patronage he built up a powerful following in the legislature and came to dominate the Richmond *Whig,* but during those six years his enemies were more powerful than he.

The man whom those opponents rebuffed as "the Railroad Ishmael" and

"King of the Lobby" lost his railroad in the disastrous '70s to an unfriendly receivership; and in 1877, seeking the Conservative nomination for governor, he was defeated at the party convention.

Thereafter Billy Mahone had no more to do with the Conservatives. In 1879 he organized the Readjuster party, which advocated the reduction of the state's tremendous debt to a liability within the provable means of the state to pay, as well as social and economic reforms which appealed to the common man, white and Negro, but from which the Bourbon leadership, including most of the Confederate hierarchy, shrank.

Mahone's Readjuster movement swept Virginia in 1879 and again in 1881, first winning control of the legislature, which obligingly sent him to the United States Senate, and two years later putting Mahone's candidate, William E. Cameron, in the governor's chair. In 1882 Governor Cameron signed a bill readjusting the state debt on the principle that Virginia's creditors should share in the state's losses from war and Reconstruction.

The Readjusters did much else besides. Mahone's men went far beyond Bourbon intent in aiding the public schools; they repealed the poll tax, increased taxes on corporations and reduced them on realty, made mechanics' wages secure, abolished the whipping post, appropriated generously for colleges and other state institutions, and enacted a variety of laws intended to serve "the interest of the masses and to break the power of wealth and established privilege."

But hand in hand with these worthy objectives and accomplishments went Mahone's own overweening political ambition. He manipulated the Negro vote, distributed railroad, state, and federal patronage to his own immense advantage, and so completely dictated all Readjuster policies that the term "Mahoneism" began to be used even by rebels within the Readjuster party, as well as by the Conservatives, to describe all that was politically disreputable.

In the almost evenly divided United States Senate, where his vote could often be the decisive one, Billy Mahone traded his leverage for committee assignments and offices, winning Northern Republican applause for his "anti-Bourbonism"—meaning his protection in Virginia of the Negro's right to vote—and incurring the lasting wrath of Southern Democrats for his "treason" to the South. Within two years Billy Mahone and his Republicans and Readjusters bossed Virginia.

The desperate Conservatives turned to more liberal leaders and to some of Mahone's own social programs. The anti-Mahone Virginia press discovered that public schools were worthy institutions and that readjustment of the state debt had some merit. Progressive Conservatives took control at the party's state convention in 1883; the welcome sign was hung out for insurgent Readjusters; and, to appeal to ordinary folk, the name of the party was changed from the Conservative to the Democratic party.

Above both parties towered the omnipresent railroads. The mastermind and principal director of the Conservative Democrats in the 1883 campaign was John S. Barbour, an elderly but vigorous Virginia aristocrat who was the party's state chairman. Barbour was an implacable foe of Mahone, not only in politics but because of their conflicting railroad interests. He was a brilliant organizer, a board member of three railroads identified with the far-flung Baltimore and Ohio, and a man destined to fashion the underdog Conservatives into an irresistible political juggernaut.

The Virginia election of 1883 might have turned out differently had it not been for a race riot in Danville two days before the election. Danville's white citizens, outnumbered by the Negroes, and paying most of the taxes, chafed under a Negro-controlled town government. Incendiary speeches by Mahone-Republican campaigners to Negro audiences brought on general fighting in which Negroes and whites were killed.

Such an outcome of Mahoneism had been predicted by the Democrats; the white citizenry of Virginia, angry and apprehensive, made of the election a racial conflict and repudiated what the Lynchburg *Virginian* characterized as the "vice, venality, corruption and unscrupulous rapacity of Mahoneism."

The still apprehensive Democrats then adopted the same improper techniques that Billy Mahone had used in his rise to political power. The governor's appointive power was taken away; the election machinery was so redesigned as to put it in the hands of the Democrats; congressional districts were gerrymandered, and town charters were amended to require new voter registrations in which thousands of Mahone supporters could be and were disqualified.

Billy Mahone fought back, in 1884, as an outright Republican, but Virginia went for Grover Cleveland. In that same year a new election law made the Democrats, as a New York *Times* correspondent put it, "the receivers, the custodians and the judges of the election."

The tavern keeper's son picked a decent enough candidate at the Republican convention, John S. Wise, a Confederate veteran who, as a Virginia Military Institute cadet, had been wounded in the celebrated fight with Union regulars at New Market. Wise, a lawyer and later a novelist, was a sincere Readjuster with a strong social conscience; but his deviation, and especially his affiliation with Mahone and the Republicans, caused Virginians who ordinarily would have been his familiars to turn against him, so that his legal genius eventually found outlet and success not in his home state but in New York City. Against John Wise the Democrats pitted a candidate who would have been unbeatable in almost any circumstance. He was Fitzhugh Lee, late major general in the Confederate Army, nephew of Robert E. Lee, and a highly principled man. With Barbour adroitly directing the campaign the Democrats regaled the white voters with barbecues and with martial processions which Fitzhugh Lee led on horseback, ensconced in a saddle that had belonged to Uncle Robert.

Each party stole as best it could, but the Conservative Democrats were unbeatable; they had the heroes, the election machinery, and Mahone's own assailable record, and they could yell "nigger" more loudly and effectively. The Democrats won a legislative majority as well as the governorship. Each side was as tainted with election fraud as the other. Mahone, who knew the techniques of the victor, was undoubtedly right when he said that "the Democrats have carried the state and legislative tickets by unscrupulous use of election machinery, over which they have absolute control, and which was provided by their recent usurping legislation with this end in view." The staid old Dominion had written a chapter of which it could not have been proud.

Billy Mahone kept on fighting. He lost again in 1887, when the Democrats swept the elections and entrenched themselves seemingly for all time to come. Mahone's Republicans split because of his dictatorial tactics; they united again, to no avail, in behalf of Harrison. Cleveland carried Virginia. In 1889 the aging upstart was the Republican candidate for governor, with organized Negro support as his principal hope. Again he lost. Behind the Conservative Democrats were the New South's businessmen and railroad promoters; the Democrats favored what would then have passed for big business. Behind Mahone were only the miscast Republican party and Virginia's white and Negro rebels. The hands of neither side were clean.

As the discerning historian of the period, Dr. Alan W. Mogere, put it: "Both . . . parties advanced good arguments for justifying their methods. Although Mahone's motives in leading the Readjuster movement were mixed, he would have been unsuccessful had he not emphasized liberalism in government and the interest of the people against the speculators and Bourbons . . . for the extremes of Mahoneism, the uncompromising attitudes of the backward looking Conservatives . . . were responsible. Had they possessed the vision and the will to recognize that the issues involved more than a question of honor, Mahone would have had little excuse for his movements. . . . He [Mahone] succeeded because his issues were more realistic and his methods more businesslike than those which had been developed by politicians to win battles in the pre-war period. But his success meant the ousting of the natural leaders of Virginia. If given reasonable justice and consideration, the masses would follow their leaders who emphasized white rule, honor, pride and ancestry. Mahone's union with the Negro elements and the Republicans sealed his doom. His dictatorial management and unnecessarily acrimonious treatment of both enemies and those who desired to be friends hastened his downfall. By his activities he induced the Conservative-Democrats to become more liberal and realistic. But once this was accomplished, they were too skillful and clever to permit themselves to be defeated. To break the Mahone machine, which had gone further than even the Conservatives in prostituting the offices of state for partisan and personal purposes, and to destroy what they considered a blot on Virginia's political record, the Democrats ignored conscience and custom. Not only did they use nearly every trick and method of the general, but they discovered new and clever methods of their own."

And so Billy Mahone, the Republican party, Virginia's small farmers, and the racial untouchables went down to permanent political defeat. Virginia's traditional adherence to her traditional leaders, the allegiance of almost every Confederate hero—Billy Mahone to the contrary—to the Democratic party, the usefulness of the racial issue, and, most important of all, the rigged election procedures which put the machinery of the democratic process in the hands of the Democrats, spelled an end to any challenge of Bourbon rule in Virginia.

Mahone's principal historic contribution was the impact of the Readjuster policies upon the Bourbon tradition. The Virginia gentlemen at least became aware of the common man.

But, unfortunately, they became more aware of the value of foolproof political organization. Out of the turmoil was born an all but indestructible system of self-perpetuation, an integrated oligarchy closely bound to urban and railroad interests which, in the considered opinion of the Richmond *Times*, meant "a tyranny and corrupt domination of us no whit inferior to that which Mahone imposed on the state." From the defeat of Mahoneism on until the present the Democrats of Virginia were to take no chances. The courthouse clique, answerable through the county chairman to the party's state chairman, would put into effect what his superiors wished to be carried out. With such an organization the conservative gentlemen of Virginia would thenceforth direct her destinies.

It must not be thought that the Redeemers of easy conscience restricted themselves, any more than did their Radical Republican counterparts, to gainful participation in the legal but morally questionable promotion of railroad lines which would never pay anyone save the speculators. Louisiana added a Latin fillip of its own, the Louisiana Lottery, which for a quarter of a century after the war impartially bought Radical and Democratic legislators so as to keep secure its fabulously remunerative position as a state-chartered monopoly.

The Louisiana Lottery's founders and principal owners were John A. Morris, an already rich and socially impeccable Philadelphia financier and sportsman who before the war had married the sister of the Anna Maria Jennings whose presidential pardon we have scanned earlier, and Charles Howard, a young Confederate veteran and lottery ticket vendor from Alabama.

So far as its awards and drawings were concerned, the lottery was scrupulously honest; it did not need be otherwise, for the company's percentage of the take was so great that the lottery was able to donate huge and politically protective sums to schools and churches and flood control and other worthy institutions and undertakings, and other large, less publicized sums to win the support of politicians, with residual profits which would make its creators millionaires several times over. Its grand prizes were fantastically big. For some years the dignity of the drawings was enhanced by the presence, as masters of the ceremonial selection of the winning tickets from the wheel of chance, of two distinguished former Confederate generals, Pierre Gustave Toutant Beauregard and Jubal Early, both fallen on evil days and more than willing to lend their names and their reputations as guarantee of the honesty—never disputed—of the drawings. Though Louisiana's magnificent postwar governor, General Francis T. Nicholls, had no truck with the lottery people and would eventually return to the governor's chair as its nemesis, the lottery monopoly apparently had little more difficulty for more than a decade in maintaining itself under Democratic than it had experienced under Radical regimes.

The Bourbon administrations, scarcely less than the Radical regimes though with considerably more finesse and individual honesty, showed their willingness to serve a multiplicity of interests which could not by any stretch of the imagination be identified with the cause of white supremacy or the needs of the common man: the wholesale merchants, the liquor and tobacco interests, the land-grabbers, the bond speculators, and the railroad promoters. There were also independents among the tempted. No fewer than seven post-Reconstruction Southern Democratic treasurers absconded spectacularly. Some were convicted and sent to jail; some were not. All of them might have pleaded the parsimony of the administrations they served. Their salaries were so small as to make some extra outside income, however come by, almost mandatory if their families were to be properly fed and clothed and housed.

In 1883 Marshall T. Polk, Democratic treasurer of Tennessee since 1877, a nephew and adopted son of the late President, decamped. Investigators found that, as treasurer, he had stolen more than $400,000—a simple enough defalcation inasmuch as his office had not been audited for some years— and that he had been investing the stolen state funds in silver mines in Mexico, iron mines in Alabama, Tennessee state bonds, and Louisville and Nashville railroad stock. All the while he had been high among those Democrats who unsuccessfully opposed any readjustment of the state debt in the name of Tennessee's sacred honor. He was arrested, convicted of embezzlement, fined $366,540, and sentenced to twenty years in prison.

Shortages in the accounts of two other state treasurers were discovered soon after Polk's defalcation was exposed. Alabama's Isaiah H. Vincent, Redemptionist governor from 1874 to 1878 and a Confederate veteran so respected that when he entered upon his second term as treasurer no one had demanded the requisite $250,000 bond, had defaulted in the amount of $232,980.79 and for five years had been using public funds to gamble on cotton futures. In time he too was arrested and convicted and sentenced to a fifteen-year term.

Within a month after Vincent took to the woods investigators for the Arkansas legislature reported that T. J. Churchill, the state's former treasurer and later its governor, was short $294,876. The State Supreme Court eventually set the amount of his shortage at $80,522. The contention of the widely popular Churchill that he was a victim of lax records was generally accepted. He pleaded bad bookkeeping and was exonerated; his successor, Major William E. Woodruff, left a shortage of $138,789 after serving as state treasurer for ten years.

Mississippi's William L. Hemingway was unique in that he stayed home to face trial on charges of embezzling $315,612. He too was found guilty and sentenced to a five-year term. Georgia had been plagued even earlier, in 1879, by scandals which brought about the impeachment and resignation of the state treasurer, the impeachment and conviction of the comptroller general, the resignation of the commissioner of agriculture, and the implication of leading Redeemers in the abuse of the convict lease system. In 1873 Virginia's Conservative state treasurer was indicted for defalcation and embezzlement but escaped trial on a plea of insanity.

Flamboyant Louisiana contributed the most colorful thief of them all. He was the same Major E. A. Burke who participated in the Wormley Conference. His military title, whether legitimately acquired or not, accompanied him out of Texas where he had taken some obscure part in the war—and less is known about his antecedents and his career prior to his arrival in New Orleans than of any other contemporary piratical figure. It is believed that he was somehow involved in a whisky-revenue scandal in Texas and that he worked as a day laborer in a stonecutter's yard after he arrived in New Orleans in 1870, when the Radicals were yet strongly entrenched. Yet two years later Burke was a ranking official in a small railroad and chairman of the state Democratic campaign committee.

When the White Leaguers rose in New Orleans in 1874 the major contributed to the enemy's discomfiture by sidetracking a federal troop train en route to New Orleans on his railroad. After the Hayes-Tilden crisis was resolved Burke, having endeared himself to Louisiana's democracy, was elected state treasurer, an office which he held for ten years; and so adroit was his politicking that he was the only state official to escape removal at the hands of the lottery-dominated Constitutional Convention of 1879.

From then until his exposure as a treasury looter Burke was one of the most powerful men in Louisiana politics. The very day that the convention of 1879 opened the New Orleans *Democrat*, until then the foremost foe of the lottery, came into the hands of Major Burke and the co-owner of the lottery, Charles Howard. Two days later the partners acquired the New Orleans *Times;* and the two papers were consolidated, with Burke as editor of the Democratic party's most potent organ.

Whatever the major's past, he was now a powerful and popular figure, a director general in 1884 of New Orleans' World Exposition and a free-spending and convivial man about town. President Louis Bogram of Honduras met Burke at the exposition and, after inexplicably becoming financially indebted to the major, gave him concessions in Honduras that, so reported the New York *Herald* in the fall of 1889, made him "the dictator, practically, of the mining as well as the fruit shipping interest of Honduras."

In January of that year Burke had gone to London to form syndicates to exploit his new Honduranian holdings; his successor as Louisiana's treasurer discovered in his absence that hundreds of thousands of dollars' worth of state bonds, which had been believed to have been destroyed as ordered, were still on the market and that their coupons had been paid at required intervals. The fabulous Major Burke, so a grand jury determined, had begun robbing the state of its bonds in 1880, his second year in office.

By the time his operations were discovered Burke had stolen $1,777,000 of state bonds, not counting interest. The recovery of bonds from Burke's bank box reduced the loss to $793,000. While Louisiana futilely sought to extradite her most successful rascal, Burke had formed his syndicates and soon became, though a fugitive from Louisiana justice, the overlord of Honduras.

If such tales—and they could be spun almost endlessly—provided the sole insight into the character of the Bourbon administrations, or demonstrated only that personal integrity does not necessarily go hand in hand with personal courage, regional loyalty, or pride of race and caste, the stories of the Bourbons themselves would scarcely be worth the telling. They would prove only what has long been known—that no race or caste has been immune to temptation anywhere or any time. The Bourbons, in their period of early post-Reconstruction ascendancy which, save in Virginia, was virtually unchallengeable, had other identifying characteristics which had nothing to do with the presence among them, as in every grouping, of lions and foxes and jackals: identification with the new, urban dynamic of which the cozening, warring, expanding railroad empires were the most evident but not the only symbol; an accompanying lack of concern for the needs of and a disregard for the latent political power of the South's small farmers and mechanics and poor whites; a sincere conviction that government was safest when entrusted to them, and an accompanying distrust of the political mass; an unswerving determination that the Negro should not again become a menace to white political supremacy; a cynical willingness to use the Negro to perpetuate their own political mastery; and an ancestral conviction that the lower the taxes the better off the citizenry.

And in more personal ways they were a breed to themselves; they were mannerly aristocrats or pretenders to aristocracy who had proved their mettle in war and Reconstruction. They believed themselves to be, and many of them were, men of honor, though the definition could be oddly elastic for, as a class, they failed to recognize the shared guilt of the bribegiver, the bribetaker, and the scheming, ultimate beneficiary of each. Yet in this blindness they were no different from their ambitious familiars throughout a seam-busting nation.

And if they willingly debased and perverted the democratic processes to maintain their own adaptations of them, they did so with a hot recollection of indignities and with a no less incendiary conviction that the alternative meant the doom of region and caste, an end to a social order founded upon the superior-inferior relationship between the white master and the Negro subordinate.

The Bourbons failed because they offered to the white majority, which could not feed and clothe and house itself upon the past, only the tender of a leadership which in that past had proved courageous and trustworthy. So, inevitably, Southern Bourbon and redneck came to grips. Neither destroyed the other. Their strife continues. Instead it was the political Negro who was swept away.

CHAPTER 3

The Rise of the Rednecks

A MAN *does not walk erect behind a plow. Instead he leans to the plow handles, his shoulders hunched and his head inclined to the stubborn earth. In time, if the man is white, his neck becomes etched with a deep crisscrossing of many lines and burned to a dull, leathery red. Long before this happens he is already a redneck to those Southern men whose plowing is done by others or who make no use of the plow at all.*

The hot winds of agrarian revolt were sweeping plain and prairie, bottom land and hillside corn patches, west to east and east to west, in the years after the peace; but in the white South the heat of the Reconstruction struggle was at first hotter still. The redneck revolt came late, and though it had its links with agrarian uprising of the Middle West and other sections, there were significant differences.

The postwar distress of the nation's farmers was almost endemic. Whatever his crop—wheat or cotton or corn or tobacco or cattle or hogs—the farmer was in a fix. The Republican party's generally laissez-faire attitude gave the middlemen and the railroads almost absolute control over the prices the farmer received for his produce and those he paid for his necessities. The currency system was weighted in favor of the holders of bonds and mortgages. Recurrent natural disasters snatched away the better harvests. In the South the ruin and dislocations of the war bore heavily upon the farmer, whose credit was determined by the size and fertility of his farm, and who was burdened with an ad valorem system of taxation which levied inequitably upon the land because there was so little else to squeeze.

Three years after the war the Patrons of Husbandry, better known as the Grange, was organized by Oliver H. Kelley, a clerk in the Bureau of Agriculture who had become especially aroused by the condition of the South's farmers. By 1873 the Grange had seven thousand chapters in forty-four states, among them 210,000 white farmers in the former Confederate states. Negroes were not permitted to join. And that year the farmers of Illinois demonstrated that aroused and organized farmers could elect candidates to public office and affect public policy. A farmer-backed candidate won the governorship of Kansas. And if the Grange, ill led, soon fell apart, farmer unrest continued.

A Greenback Labor party had been organized in Toledo in 1878, capitalizing alike on rural and urban discontent, and elected fourteen candidates to Congress. In the 1880s C. W. Macune, a Texan, organized the National Farmers' Alliance and Co-operative Union of America, commonly called the Farmers' Alliance, principally in Texas, Arkansas, and Louisiana, and an effort was made to merge it with other agrarian organizations. A national convention was held at St. Louis in 1889; a year later these groups met in joint convention, at Ocala, Florida, with the Farmers' Mutual Benefit Association and a Negro group it sponsored, the Colored Farmers' Alliance. They demanded that the federal government construct warehouses to store farm products and pay the farmers 80 per cent of the market value in greenbacks. The specter of the Negro voter impelled most of the Southern Alliancemen to oppose those who sought to organize a third party, but the tide was rising. In 1891 the People's Party of the U.S.A., or Populists, held its first meeting in St. Louis and soon became, even in the South, a force which to some appeared as fearful, and to be destroyed as ruthlessly, as the Yankee radicals of a quarter of a century earlier.

The Populists nominated for President James B. Weaver of Iowa, who had been the Greenbackers' presidential candidate in 1880, and James G. Field of Virginia for Vice-President, and offered a platform few of whose planks appear as startling now as they did then to the Democratic and Republican conservatives: a national currency without the use of banking corporations; government ownership and operation of all transportation and communication facilities; unlimited coinage of silver at the ratio of sixteen to one and an increase of money in circulation of not less than fifty dollars per capita; a graduated income tax; direct election of United States senators; a postal-savings system; the secret ballot, the initiative and the referendum; a shorter day for the industrial worker; immigration restriction and prohibition of alien ownership of land.

Weaver and Field received 22 electoral votes to Grover Cleveland's 277 and Benjamin Harrison's 145. Party regularity was a habit hard to break and the Populist prescription yet too strong a medicine for the majority to stomach. But many of the goals and reforms which the idealists and demagogues had espoused in its name would again be championed in another era of discontent and depression, and with notable success, by the Democratic party's New Deal that was so greatly a synthesis of much that was old but unrealized.

Nowhere in the nation was the plight of the farmer as desperate or as unrelieved or as complicated by political exigencies as in the South of Reconstruction. But invasion and defeat, Radical Reconstruction, and Negro political activity had combined to hold for a generation the disaffected small farmers of the South in unnatural political alliance with and subservience to the Bourbons.

In the first twelve years after Redemption victories of the agricultural rebels were neither many nor impressive. The advent of the Alliancemen who, eschewing third-party tactics, chose to fight it out within the Democratic party made a different story. Beginning in 1890, the farmers of the South won victory after victory. In South Carolina raging Benjamin R. Tillman led the agrarian revolutionaries to a succession of triumphs so complete that Wade Hampton himself was eventually retired from the United States Senate and Tillman became the long-time political boss of the state. Georgia's Alliancemen elected the governor, a majority of the legislators, and six of the state's ten congressmen in 1890. That year the Alliancemen of North Carolina took over the Democratic party; Alliance candidates in Texas and Tennessee were elected governors, and the Alliance dominated the legislatures of Alabama, Florida, Tennessee, and Mississippi. In 1892 Alliance candidates, handicapped by the desertion of key Alliancemen to the Populist party in protest against the Democratic party's conservatism, lost their races for state and federal offices almost everywhere to the regular Democratic nominees.

But the redneck revolution did not end with the disintegration of the Alliance and the Populist party. The rank and file of the South's farmers remained in the Democratic party but accepted Alliance doctrines. In conjunction with Western rebels, they made, in 1896, Bryan, the hypnotic apostle of free coinage of silver, their party's nominee. And the rednecks and peckerwoods, the hillbillies and poor whites and wool-hat boys would continue to wage within the Democratic party organizations of every Southern state an unending ideological struggle with their Bourbon rivals.

The Southern agrarian rebel was a good hater. He hated high-tariff Republicans and the nearby mill owners who bought his cotton so cheap and sold their bolts of cloth so dear and paid so little to the mill hands recruited from the farm homes. He hated the unbridled railroads which provided almost the only outlets to his markets. If he were a tenant he hated the landlords. He hated the local bankers and merchants for whose exclusive benefit the crop lien laws and chattel mortgages were seemingly devised, and who preyed indiscriminately on large and small landowner alike. The lien laws had been originally intended to provide security to the planter for the supplies which he furnished his tenants throughout the year, by giving him liens on the crops to be planted. But since even the large-scale cotton farmer rarely had sufficient capital to finance his tenants, he was compelled to borrow either from the banks or from the merchants from whom he purchased supplies for himself and his tenants. The "furnish merchant" charged the farmer 25 to 50 per cent above the cash price on the supplies he provided on credit. The farmer mortgaged to the merchant his future crop and stock and implements; and the merchant or banker who made the advances generally insisted that the farmer put most of his land in cotton. As the price of cotton declined, the furnish merchants became planters as well as businessmen by foreclosing upon thousands of distressed farmers. Thus did William Faulkner's tribe of Snopses so greatly replace the Sartorises and bring to its logical end whatever remained of the onetime spirit of noblesse oblige which had made more human the debilitating relationship of master and slave and landowner and tenant.

But most of all the redneck hated the Negro as a civil equal, as an economic bedfellow and rival, and as a political balance of power. And, save during Populism's short, furious period of interracial appeal, and its brief demonstration that the Bourbon was no match for a coalition of white and Negro agrarians, that hatred would long postpone the day of the redneck. It would dawn only after the Negro as citizen had been eliminated.

Among the conglomeration of charlatans and reformers whom the rednecks hailed as their champions, none better exemplified the frustration of Southern liberalism because of the racial dilemma than did Thomas Edward Watson of Georgia, master criminal lawyer and politician, a brilliant, tormented Lucifer flaming across the Southern sky.

Red-haired, skinny Tom Watson was a sensitive and poetically inclined zealot, proud of his forebears, vengefully resentful of the poverty to which his twice-wounded father sank after the war; and he was also an ambitious and dogmatically assertive political rebel whose voice and ideas wrought magic for the poor.

Tom Watson was twenty when, after two years at Mercer University and two more as an ill-paid rural schoolteacher who studied law on the side, he began a meteoric career as a criminal lawyer; and he was only twenty-three when, at the Georgia Democratic convention in 1880, he led a wild agrarian uprising against the party bosses. He didn't win that fight with Georgia's highhanded Bourbon tiumvirate: Joseph E. Brown, General John B. Gordon, and Alfred H. Colquitt, the trio who, in the name of white supremacy, held the state captive from 1872 to 1890. But the young agrarian and his followers gave the Bourbons an indication then of what was to come. In a rambunctious speech in opposition to Colquitt's renomination as governor, Watson called upon the Georgians to turn upon their rulers even if the party of the white man were thereby rent asunder. The campaign was as bloody and as dishonest as any in the state's history. The Bourbons won, but only by manipulating the herded Negro vote to overcome what was undoubtedly a majority of the white voters of the state.

For the next ten years insurgent Tom Watson built his political fences while the Bourbons continued to dominate Georgia and the rest of the South. Their most articulate and respected regional spokesman was Henry W. Grady, the brilliant and persuasive Atlanta editor, who believed that all white men were morally obliged to vote together without regard to class, and in the retention of the reins of government in the hands of the businessmen and the industrialists of the New South. A majority of Georgia's white voters went along with Grady's philosophy until 1890, though Tom Watson, an out-and-out Allianceman from the organization's inception, ranged the state in burning advocacy of a new alignment in which not race but class and economic interests would be the political determinants. Co-operation between the races in the established parties he considered to be impossible, for "the Republican party represented everything which was hateful to the whites; the Democratic party everything which was hateful to the blacks."

In 1890, a year after the death of Grady, whom Watson had said would "betray the South with a Judas kiss," the Georgia farmers revolted and elected to state and national office candidates who were pledged to the reform platform of the Farmers' Alliance. Running as a Democrat on the Farmers' Alliance platform and declaring that the agrarian South and West were natural allies, Watson was overwhelmingly elected to Congress from Georgia's Tenth District. Once in Congress, he broke immediately with the Democrats and declined to participate in the party's congressional caucuses. Deciding to stand by his pledges of reform instead of adhering to the Conservative-dominated Democratic party, he announced himself a Populist, participated in the organization of the new party, became its Southern spokesman in Congress, and formulated its policy of co-operation with the Negro.

The Farmers' Alliance had prepared the way for Watson's experiment in interracial political action when it organized more than a million Negroes in the Colored Farmers' Alliance. With loyal white and Negro Alliancemen and whatever other Negroes he could win over from the Bourbons, Tom Watson earnestly set out to create a new political grouping in the South, which would recruit its members from the farmers and urban workers of both races.

In Congress Watson sponsored many of the more advanced agricultural and labor reform bills sought by the Alliance and the Populists. In 1891 he founded the *People's Party Paper,* and in 1892 he wrote and published the *People's Party Campaign Book,* its subtitle being *Not a Revolt; It Is a Revolution.* For his apostasy he paid a ruinous price. Not only the Bourbons were now after his scalp; his determination to unite white and Negro agrarians had earned him the hatred of many a thousand white men who had no use for Bourbonism but who feared and hated the Negro more. It wasn't safe to have in Congress or anywhere else in public life a man who had said: "Now the People's Party says to these two men [white man and Negro] 'you are kept apart that you may be separately fleeced of your earnings. You are made to hate each other because upon that hatred is rested the keystone of the arch of financial despotism which enslaves you both. You are deceived and blinded that you may not see how this race antagonism perpetuates a monetary system which beggars both.'"

Courageously he denounced lynch law in a state which had the distinction of lynching more Negroes than did any other; he hammered away at the Democratic Conservatives, at the eastern trusts and the railroads, at the Ku Klux and convict leasing, and at the necessity for the small people to stick together.

"In the long run self-interest always controls," he would write. "Let it once appear plainly that it is to the interest of a colored man to vote with a white man and he will do it . . . The People's Party will settle the race question. First, by enacting the Australian ballot system. Second, by offering to white and black a rallying point which is free from the odium of former discord and strife. Third, by presenting a platform immensely beneficial to both races and injurious to neither. Fourth, by making it to the interest of both races to act together for the success of the platform."

His inflamed enemies went to lengths not surpassed during Reconstruction to defeat him in 1892. The Democrats gerrymandered his district. Fifteen Negro Populists were murdered. One Negro leader was luckier than many another. He was H. S. Doyle, a young preacher who had made sixty-three speeches for Watson and who hid in Watson's home when a mob sought to lynch him. At Watson's call hundreds of armed white Populists surrounded his house for two nights to save the Negro, provoking by their response the accusation that the South, and especially Watson's district, was threatened with anarchy and communism; yet in the end it was the rednecks' hatred of the Negro which brought about Watson's moral decay more than did any other factor.

In the sanguinary, openly fraudulent congressional election of 1892 Watson's Democratic opponent was declared the victor. Tom Watson held to his convictions though he knew what he was up against. Later he would write in recollection: "No matter what direction progress would like to take in the South, she is held back by the never failing cry of 'nigger.'" And again: "It sickens me to the very soul to witness the unscrupulous skill, on the one hand, and the childlike ignorance and prejudice, on the other, which make the Negro question the invincible weapon of Bourbon democracy in the South." And again: "You might beseech a Southern white tenant to listen to you upon questions of finance, taxation, and transportation; you might demonstrate with precision that herein lay his way out of poverty into comfort; you might have him almost persuaded to the truth; but if the merchant who furnished his farm supplies at tremendous usury or the town politician who never spoke to him excepting at election time came along and cried 'Negro rule!' the entire fabric of reason and common sense which you had patiently constructed would fall, and the poor tenant would joyously hug the chain of an actual wretchedness rather than do any experimenting on a question of mere sentiment . . . The Negro has been as valuable a portion of the stock and trade of a Democrat as he was of a Republican."

Tom Watson was counted out again in 1894 in an election even more murderous and corrupt than before. At the Populist party's state convention that year Watson seconded the nomination of a Negro for the executive committee, asking as he did so: "Tell me the use of educating these people as citizens if they are never to exercise the rights of citizens?" To the Democratic charge that he believed in "social equality" he answered, "This is a thing each citizen decides for himself," but "when it comes to matters of law and justice, I despise the Anglo-Saxon who is such an infernal coward as to deny legal rights to any man on account of his color, for fear of Negro domination. . . . Away with such contemptible timidity counsel."

The regard of the Negroes for this white Southern apostle of civil equality was all but idolatrous. Doyle, the young Negro preacher whom Watson's white farmers had saved from lynching in 1892, testified in the ensuing contested-election case that "Mr. Watson was held almost as a savior by the Negroes. The poor ignorant men and women, who had been so long oppressed, were anxious even to touch Mr. Watson's hand, and were often a source of inconvenience to him in their anxiety to see him and shake hands with him and even to touch him." Negro Populists by the thousands rallied to him at the risk of their very lives, and many paid with those lives for their daring. Negro and white Populist speakers occupied the same platforms in his campaigns, speaking to ranked white and Negro audiences. For the first time a considerable minority of Southern white people came to look upon the Negro as a political ally joined to them by common economic exploitation and common needs. Never had it happened before, nor has it happened again.

In 1896 the Populists endorsed William Jennings Bryan, the Democratic candidate for President, and chose Watson for their vice-presidential candidate. His vote was minuscule; and with the Populist debacle at the polls began Watson's disintegration into a bigot whose attacks upon an assortment of enemies—Catholics and Jews, Socialists and railroad builders and foreign missions and, especially, Negroes—were the most indiscriminately rabid of any ever made by an American demagogue.

But that demoralization did not come immediately.

After his stunning defeat in 1896 he wrote, "Politically I was ruined. Financially I was flat on my back. How close I came to loss of mind only God who made me knows—but I was as near distraction, perhaps, as any mortal could safely be. If ever a poor devil had been outlawed and vilified and persecuted and misrepresented and howled down and mobbed and hooted and threatened until he was well nigh mad, I was he."

In bitterness and despair he retired from public life for eight years to practice law, at which he was to make a modest fortune, and to write. During these years he wrote *The Story of France,* a two-volume popular history which strongly reflected his Populist philosophy, two biographies, *Napoleon: A Sketch of His Life* and *The Life and Times of Thomas Jefferson,* and *Bethany,* a novel of little if any merit. In 1907 he published the tediously subjective *The Life and Times of Andrew Jackson.*

When the Democrats nominated the ultra conservative Alton B. Parker for President in 1904 Tom Watson again entered the lists as the Populist nominee for the presidency. He made a nationwide campaign; but he received only 117,183 votes and was all but completely ignored in the South. It is probable that this final crushing defeat as a Populist candidate convinced him that the Negro as an ally and a political equal had been Populism's insurmountable handicap in the South all the while.

In 1905 he began publication, in New York, of *Tom Watson's Magazine.* Its initial and primary targets were special privilege in all its forms; among its contributors were Clarence Darrow, Theodore Dreiser, Maxim Gorky, and Edgar Lee Masters, and its circulation quickly reached one hundred thousand. Watson hoped, by muckraking, to revive and widen public support for the Populists. In unmeasured terms *Tom Watson's Magazine* berated the railroads, especially those of the South, as being nothing less than Northern-owned plunder rings, contemptuous of law and the safety of crews and passengers. He railed at the tariff structure, the oil, sugar, steel, and tobacco trusts, and subsidies to business. He blamed the political dominance of both parties by the moneyed interests for the unending plight of agriculture. Child labor in the South, he wrote, was the product of connivance between Northern capitalists and Southern politicians. The Northern capitalist owned the Southern mills, but "it is the Southern politician, officeholder, editor or stockholder who rushes to the legislature saying that child slavery must continue because it is good for the child."

In 1906 the publication's name was changed to *Watson's Magazine;* and when he returned to Georgia in 1906, after a quarrel with his publishers, he established the *Weekly Jeffersonian* and *Watson's Jeffersonian Magazine* and set about to dominate Georgia politics and to indulge the canker in his soul.

His principal political theme became the disfranchisement of the Negro in order that white men of divergent opinions would be free to divide politically. "The white people dare not revolt as long as they can be intimidated by the fear of the Negro vote," he wrote in 1906. He pledged the support of his hard core of Populists to any anti-machine Democratic candidate in Georgia whose platform was acceptable to him and who would pledge support for constitutional revisions which would perpetuate white supremacy in the state and nation. He turned viciously upon the Negro, identifying him with all the vices, and demanding a repressive policy for his now politically impotent and friendless onetime ally which must be so complete that "the great mass of the Negroes would gradually reconcile themselves to the condition of a recognized peasantry—a laboring class." He professed to see "the superiority of the Aryan" menaced by "the hideous, ominous, national menace" of Negro domination. Booker T. Washington, he wrote, was "imitative as an ape; bestial as a gorilla." All Negro men were ravishers from whose bestiality "the very animals in the stables are not safe." And he defended lynching because "lynch law is a good sign; it shows that a sense of justice yet lives among the people."

And most white Georgians, a majority of whom had repudiated Populist Tom Watson when he walked with the Negro, loved every word of it. Cynically shifting his support from one Democratic faction to the other, Watson became Georgia's political boss. To the Negro he added as whipping boys Catholics and Socialists and Jews; indisputably the savagery of his denunciations of Leo M. Frank, a Georgia Jew whose death sentence for the murder of a young woman mill hand had been commuted, had much to do with Frank's subsequent lynching. In 1917, with a spark of his old-time, off-beat idealism, he attacked American intervention in World War I as "ravenous commercialism." He fought conscription until his publications were excluded from the mails. In 1918 he was defeated in a congressional race and in 1920 narrowly lost in the state presidential primary. That same year he was elected one-sidedly to the United States Senate on a platform which called for the restoration of civil liberties and the defeat of the League of Nations. And as a senator he died in 1922, a tough old champion of the workingman and of the oppressed everywhere so long as they were not black or Catholic or Jewish.

So fell Lucifer into the outer dark.

Late in his career Tom Watson wrote what could be the epitaph of any Southern liberal who might dare to preach and practice civil equality and be rendered politically impotent thereby: "Consider the advantage of position that Bryan had over me. His field of work was the plastic, restless and growing West; mine was the hide-bound, rock-ribbed Bourbon South. *Besides, Bryan had no everlasting and overshadowing Negro Question to hamper and handicap his progress; I HAD.*"

CHAPTER 4

Enter Jim Crow

IN THE *latter years of tumultuous nineteenth-century America a purposeful figure began to be limned against the Southern horizon. The figure, which disturbed some, and in which others found a promise of security, was not human; but it was sired and shaped by humans. The name that was given to the figure, for reasons now disputed and obscure, was Jim Crow. And, as the figure swelled until it dwarfed all else in the region of its creation, the ghost of General Pierre Gustave Toutant Beauregard of Louisiana may have permitted itself the Gallic shrug that expresses futility.*

A respectable minority of the white Louisianians who had almost unanimously cherished General Beauregard as the Confederacy's beau sabreur endorsed, some of them openly, the communication he addressed on July 1, 1873, to his fellow citizens. Only a quarter of a century later almost no white Louisianians or white Southerners would have approved the Creole aristocrat's arguments for civil equality for the Negro.

Indeed, unless furnished with absolute proof, the sons and daughters of the men whom Beauregard had led would have denied that he had ever espoused a political coalition predicated upon the recognition of Louisiana's Negroes as fully equal citizens and a consequent union of all patriotic white and Negro citizens against the most debased of the Radical administrations in the South. For, in the intervening years, the white South had made a decision that would have more lasting consequences than any other regional option, including that of secession. The Negro must be rendered politically impotent, the decision went, for the good of all; he must also be made aware, by every possible device, of his racial inferiority and of the subservience which that inferiority ordained.

The decision was not arrived at accidentally or suddenly; nor, at the end of the post-Reconstruction deliberations, were the supporters of Jim Crow confined to the South.

Before the century's end the voices of almost all of the North's Radical Republicans had been stilled. In their stead, and in concert with the spokesmen for the unchained South, roared the voice of American imperialism, announcing the white man's manifest destiny to the barrios of the Philippines, in the market places of the Orient, across the Caribbean jungles, and above the wigwams of the western plains. This is a white man's world, the voice proclaimed. Which was what the white South had been preaching all along.

General Beauregard had not so believed or foreseen. He wanted his own warm world, his beloved Louisiana, to be governed honestly through a union of honest white and black men, each respecting the rights of the other. He was not the first hero of the Confederacy to seek a union of native whites and Negroes against political thieves, nor did the idea of fusion end with his boldly offered program. But he was foremost among Louisiana's respected leaders who broke with tradition, and he was unusual among Southerners in the extraordinary recommendations for integrated facilities to which his reasoning brought him.

In organizing and leading Louisiana's Unification Movement, which asked for complete political equality for the Negro, division of state offices between the races, and the abandonment of segregation in public places, public conveyances, and public schools, Beauregard was well aware of the criticism which his preliminary efforts had brought. In the formal, printed address to his fellow Louisianians, under the title "The Unification Question," he noted in the opening paragraph:

"I have been made the subject of ungracious and illiberal observation here and elsewhere because of my report of resolutions recommending a closer union of all the members of the permanent population of the state, to promote . . . a wise and provident legislation. The ends proposed are not only unobjectionable, but patriotic and praiseworthy.

"The complaint is of the means. Those means consist of a candid and frank acknowledgement of constitutional and legal facts which none can deny, and the conforming of our conduct to those provisions of the constitution of the state of Louisiana which are as follows:

"Art. 13. All persons shall enjoy equal rights and privileges upon any conveyance of a public character: and all places of business or of public resort, or for which a license is required by either State, parish or municipal authority, shall be deemed places of a public character, and shall be opened to the accommodation and patronage of all persons, without distinction or discrimination on account of color.

"Art. 135. All children of this state between the ages of 6 and 21 shall be admitted to the public schools or other institutions of learning, sustained or established by the State, in common, without distinction of race, color or previous condition."

Thereupon the quondam slaveowner and soldier of the Confederacy advised his fellow citizens to accept and abide by the two most objectionable and disregarded provisions of a constitution which had been created and adopted under Radical domination, in order to rid the state of those very Radical overlords.

And for what reason?

Beauregard's argument was as lucid as it was unacceptable to the majority of Louisiana's white citizens.

"My proposition is, if possible, to unite these various conditions of men, into a common effort to improve the conditions of the state; to remove, if it can be done, all questions that are special to any of these conditions, and to fix the hearts of all upon higher and more important aims.

"The strife, hostility, distrust and estrangement that has followed from such questions has placed our state under the control of the depraved, dishonest, over-reaching and corrupt. The reputation of the state has suffered, its credit blasted, its finances disordered, its honor stained, and public and private prosperity retarded under the influence of the strife and the use made of it by the artful and selfish adventurers, who have employed power to accomplish these disastrous results. In our distracted condition, after the general election of last November, we appealed in vain to Congress for relief; the Administration has, moreover, thrown its powerful influence on the side of our corrupt, usurping State government, and we can evidently hope for no assistance from our sister State. We must therefore look only to ourselves for salvation, which can only be secured by making a firm alliance with all classes of our population to rid us of these vampires who are sucking the very life blood of our people white and black."

After all, Beauregard argued, Louisiana's whites and Negroes already were on equal terms in many civil and political matters. But, throughout the years of Reconstruction, he said, the denial by the native whites of the Negroes' constitutional right to enter their children in any public school, to travel on public conveyances, and to enter public places on non-segregated bases "has been the means of arraying whites and blacks almost solidly in bitter political hostility against each other.

"It has driven the blacks into an unnatural coalition with a horde of unscrupulous adventurers, who have thus secured the political power of the commonwealth. How have they used it? To what a sad condition have they not reduced the State! It is an oft told tale which I, a son of Louisiana, holding her honor dearer than 'the ruddy drops which visit this sad heart,' have no disposition to repeat.

"I may be mistaken in supposing that a frank and cordial concession of absolute and practical civil, as well as political equality between all citizens, without discrimination on account of race or color, as proposed in this movement, would remove the last barrier which opposes the political co-operation of good men, of whatever color, for the regeneration of the state; but I am earnest in my conviction that I am not mistaken. . . .

"I am persuaded that the natural relation between the white and colored people is that of friendship. I am persuaded that their interests are identical; that their destinies, in this state where the two races are equally divided, are linked together; and that there is no prosperity for Louisiana which must not be the result of their co-operation.

"I am equally convinced that the evils anticipated by some of the practical enforcement of equal rights, are mostly imaginary, and that the relations of the races and the exercise of these rights will speedily adjust themselves to the satisfaction of all.

"I take it that nothing but malice or stupidity could find anything either in the letter or spirit of the unification resolutions which contemplates any interference or dictation in the private social relations of the people. These lie entirely outside the domain of legislation and politics. It would not be denied that, in travelling, and at places of public resort, we often share these privileges in common with thieves, prostitutes, gamblers, and others who have worse sins to answer for than the accident of color; but no one ever supposes that we thereby assented to the social equality of these people with ourselves. I therefore say that participation in these public privileges involves no question of social equality. By the enjoyment in common of such privileges, neither whites nor blacks assert, or assent to, social equality, either with each other or even between individuals of the same race.

". . . This is a full, candid, and to my mind accurate view of the situation, and I shall regulate my conduct accordingly, so as to free ourselves from 'carpet-bag' rule and the improper interference of the Federal Government in our State affairs."

Not many whites had supported General Beauregard's Unification Movement as a party which would be attractive to decent Negroes, but they came principally from the upper economic and social groups and included some of the wealthiest planters, professional and businessmen of New Orleans and south Louisiana. Historically the Louisianians of French descent had been more tolerant of the Negro and of the free men of color than were their compatriots elsewhere in the South; by 1873 they were animated by Beauregard's vision of relief from onerous taxation and conscienceless officials. But the predominantly Anglo-Saxon whites of central and northern Louisiana were all but united regardless of class in opposing the Unifiers' platform of political equality, integration in the public schools, public meeting places, public gathering places, and on public conveyances, and a fair interracial division of political offices.

The Louisiana Unification Movement died almost a-borning. The majority of the whites had decided the price Beauregard was willing to pay was too high.

Moreover, most of the Negroes of Louisiana chose to listen to Republican leaders of their own race, who not only had their own axes to grind but were logically suspicious of the overtures of the planters and merchants and professional men who had once owned them. The Negroes found it hard to believe that General Beauregard and his associates really believed in racial equality.

Another three years would elapse before the whites would win out on their own terms in Louisiana and in Mississippi, South Carolina, and Florida. Louisiana would be further despoiled. Hundreds of whites and Negroes would be killed or wounded in civil disturbances; and Beauregard's idealistic plan for solving the Southern dilemma would await, in an unrespected limbo, its eventual, lawful burial.

Yet legally sanctioned segregation and disfranchisement were not made immediately the penalties which the Negro had to pay for his ill-directed, ill-employed participation in Southern political life.

Save in extremely limited areas, notably east Tennessee, the Republican party became dormant and all but dead, after 1876, as an organized political expression at the state and local levels. But the voting Negro did not so quickly vanish, nor did certain of the other privileges which Reconstruction had afforded him. A considerable minority of enfranchised Negroes, through intimidation, persuasion, or disillusion, had aided the white Conservatives in destroying the alien incubus, even without the rewards which Beauregard wanted to offer them. Thereafter, for as long as the Bourbon oligarchies—economically impregnable, serene in their belief that they could guide or manipulate the Negro vote, and undisturbed by any fear of a social breakthrough—held political power, no Southwide effort was made to disfranchise totally the Negro. Nor was the freedman soon excluded from those areas of public co-mingling into which he had timorously advanced. Only after the Negro voter became a decisive balance of power in the intraparty struggle between Democrats who were small farmers and Democrats who held the purse strings did legal disfranchisement become the Negro's lot and Jim Crow his constant companion.

Throughout most of the South, Mississippi being the principal exception, Negroes continued to vote in appreciable numbers—or as a Southern demagogue would more correctly put it much later, "to be voted"—for more than twenty years after the end of Radical Reconstruction. The right was not always gladly accorded or wisely or honestly employed; but, as the old Abolitionist, Colonel Thomas Wentworth Higginson, explained it in 1878, after a Southern journey to discover what had happened since the debacle of the Radicals, "The Southern whites accept them precisely as Northern men in cities accept the ignorant Irish vote—not cheerfully, but with acquiescence in the inevitable, and when the strict color line is once broken, they are just as ready to conciliate the Negro as the Northern politician . . . the Irishman."

Moreover, and as strange as it may seem today, the Negro was not denied unsegregated access to most public facilities in many parts of the South— schools and churches being the consistent exceptions—for from fifteen to twenty-five years after Redemption. Even Colonel Higginson found no signs of ill-treatment of Negroes; he noted that they traveled freely on integrated trains, boats, and streetcars, and Negroes were still serving, though in greatly reduced numbers, in state legislatures, on municipal police forces, and in state militia companies. When Colonel Higginson again visited the South in 1884 he found little change in such relationships.

The Negroes' status in relation to the white society, immediately after the white Redemption, was not determined in most of the South by statute but by locally accepted usages. In Columbia, South Carolina, which had more reason than most Southern communities to be vengeful, Negroes continued to be served for several years after the end of Reconstruction in bars and at soft-drink fountains, though not frequently in restaurants. In much of the South Negroes were admitted to theaters and lectures on an unsegregated basis, as well as to more impersonal public facilities. In 1879 Sir George Campbell, an English traveler, noted a friendly association between the races and general Negro participation in political affairs. In 1885 T. M. Stewart, a Northern Negro newspaperman, who came South looking for trouble, admitted that in Virginia, where little public segregation existed until after 1900, and in North Carolina and South Carolina he met with scant discrimination. His first-class ticket was good on any coach, and he was served in unsegregated saloons and refreshment booths.

Even in Mississippi most saloons served whites and Negroes at the same bar, restaurants allowed them to dine in the same rooms, though at separate tables, and they were permitted in Jackson to use a public park, ordinarily open only to whites, for picnics and to hold dances at a hall also usually patronized only by whites.

But by 1890 the races were almost wholly segregated in most of the deep South in contrast to the considerably less rigid divisions in the upper seaboard South. Yet well after 1900 numerous Southern soda fountains dispensed pop and other soft drinks impartially to white and Negro customers, though usually employing glasses of one color for the whites and of another for the Negroes.

In three areas of possible interracial contact—educational, religious and social—segregation was all but universal during and after Reconstruction, one at the insistence of the white Southerners, the second by the choice of the Negroes as well, and the third by unspoken, common consent.

No serious attempt was made to integrate the public schools during Reconstruction save, for a very short time, in four states, and these efforts collapsed before adamant white resistance. Not the whites but the Negroes first showed their preference for separate churches; they wanted no such reminders of their former condition as the slave galleries and the pulpits from which the ante-bellum preachers had dwelt on the blessedness that came to the meek and the poor. Nor, save for the lapses of some few white Carpetbaggers and Scalawags, whose own associates frowned upon their behavior, was there any formal social co-mingling. Negroes prominent in politics did attend such functions as inauguration balls, state receptions, and the like; but only by fanciful pretense could these be considered to be social rather than political affairs. Social intimacy between the races was restricted almost entirely to the classic sexual relationship between the white man and the Negro woman.

What has been all but lost sight of in the nearly sixty years since Jim Crow clamped down is that the ordinances and statutes and court decisions which made Jim Crow the all but unchallenged arbiter of the South's social and political mores were not widely adopted until after the savage contest between the Bourbons and the independents had convinced the white adversaries themselves that the South's political salvation lay in immobilizing the black pawns. And practical politics dictated that disfranchisement should precede, or at least accompany, arbitrary segregation, since the voting Negro could have used the ballot to make clear his objection to his status.

The relevant question here is: why didn't disfranchisement and segregation by law become part of the South's way of life as soon as her white citizenry regained political mastery? To arrive at an answer, we must return to the final days of Reconstruction when two temporary barriers yet intervened. For one thing, even though the Republican North of 1876 was not the North of Thad Stevens and Charles Sumner, the South could not be sure that, should abrupt disfranchisement and widespread discrimination bob up in the wake of victory, Northern interference, with or without bayonets, would not be resumed. There was also a finer impulse. A minority of the Conservative leaders, but an important minority, felt some gratitude and an unwarranted self-confidence in their ability to continue to direct those

Negroes who had deserted Radicalism and had thrown in with their fellow Southerners under the Conservative banner. Most of those who thought this way were members of the upper class, paternalistic former slaveholders. Few of them would have gone as far as General Beauregard had proposed, but they did not intend to humiliate, bar from impersonal public accommodations, or reduce to political serfdom the repentant Negro, if for no other reason than that under Conservative guidance he could help maintain the kind of government which, so they believed, the South required.

When home-grown Radicalism, spurred by the agrarian revolt, challenged the Bourbons, the Negro became an entity to be cajoled or threatened into supporting one or the other of the warring white factions. Left to himself, the Negro would probably have found anchorage among the insurgents, as indeed for a while he did. The Bourbons could not afford to let him make so natural a selection. The resultant white ambivalence ended in the sacrifice and the removal from the political board of the too amenable pawn.

Not in concert, but through much the same reasoning, white Conservative and Populist alike eventually decided that the Negro must not be permitted ᴜ sell support first to one faction and then to another, or to tempt either, through the imperative of his numbers, to court him. A delegate to the Alabama Constitutional Convention which disfranchised the Negro stated the case boldly. "Now we are not begging for 'ballot reform' or anything of that sort," explained William A. Handley, for the record. "But we want to be relieved of purchasing the Negro to carry elections. I want cheaper votes."

Once the reaction against the Negro voter commenced there was no stopping it. On one hand the Conservatives had been badly frightened by the implications of the Negro-agrarian combination. On the other the frustrated independents blamed the unhitchable Negro and the onus of his identification with their cause for their failure in the South.

The critic remote in time and place should realize that the decision to eliminate the Negro from politics was not made by many white Southerners without considerable soul-searching. Their conclusion, that the only way to cure the all too apparent perversion of the elective process was the elimination of the Negro as a voter, was a considered one. The cynical and the sincere apologists for disfranchisement alike could remark that the Negro voter had always proved easy to purchase or coerce or mislead and had never truly been assimilated into the body politic.

Even as the divided South began thus to reason, threatening shadows were gathering again.

The Republicans swept the congressional elections of 1888. The House of Representatives approved young Henry Cabot Lodge's so-called Force

Bill. The Senate turned it down, but the raising of the civil rights issue, after a decade of Northern indifference, warned the South that the disfranchisement and subordination of the Negro must be made legally airtight.

Mississippi was the first state to hold a constitutional convention for that purpose. The conveners also had other constitutional proposals in mind, among them educational requirements for jurors; but the principal objective of the convention, which opened in August 1890, and of similar conventions which were held later in the other Southern states, was the elimination of the Negro as a voter.

The delegates of Mississippi knew better than to deny the vote to the Negro as a Negro. But the qualifications they proposed so hindered even the ablest Negro that the game did not seem worth the candle.

When the convention had finished its work it was all but impossible for a Negro to vote in Mississippi. A voter had to be a resident of the state for two years and of his district for one year. He was required to pay a poll tax of two dollars and "must be sane and not have been convicted of bribery, burglary, theft, arson, perjury, fraudery, embezzlement, murder or bigamy." He also had to "be able . . . to read any section of the state constitution; or to be able to understand the same when read to him, or give a reasonable interpretation thereof." To make doubly sure that never would Negro legislators constitute a majority of the state legislature, additional seats, out of proportion to their populations, were awarded to the predominantly white counties, and new legislative districts were created out of predominantly white sections of heavily Negro counties.

The "understanding clause" did not meet with universal white approval. Many leaders among the semi-literate or illiterate poor whites protested that this was an odious device for the disfranchisement of the common man, regardless of race. The Vicksburg *Post* spoke for them roundly: "That a lot of politicians fertile in tricks could concoct this scheme is not inconceivable; but that a man who aspires to statesmanship can cheat his conscience and impose the delusion upon his mind that such a measure can bring anything but mischief and disaster, is simply incredible." The new constitution was not submitted to the voters for approval. The convention itself simply promulgated the document, an evasion that every other Southern state which wrote new constitutions, save Alabama, would copy.

Mississippi had been second only to South Carolina in seceding. She had been the first to set up a Black Code for handling the freed Negroes, the first to employ a show of organized force—"the Mississippi Plan"—which through a combination of terrorism and persuasion had restored the white Conservatives to political power. Now she was the first of the Southern states to systematically disfranchise the Negro. South Carolina followed in 1895, Louisiana in 1898, North Carolina in 1900, Alabama in 1901, Virginia in 1901–02, and Georgia in 1908. Florida, Tennessee, Arkansas, and Texas did not adopt new constitutions as a means of disfranchising the Negro but accomplished the same ends through imposing poll taxes and requiring by statute other crippling qualifications.

Fifteen years after the adoption of the Mississippi constitution of 1890 a scholarly planter-congressman, Benjamin G. Humphreys, a man who sincerely believed that the Negro had no better friend than he, would relate the reasons, as he saw them, for disfranchisement. His article was entitled "A Negro's Chance—How the Race Problem Is Answered in the Blackest Portion of the Black Belt." Humphreys confined his observations to his "whiplash district of the Yazoo-Mississippi Delta," whose population in 1900 numbered 200,084 Negroes and only 32,090 whites. His thesis was that because of the historic nature of the Anglo-Saxon, the white minority would "boldfully assert and at least make a very desperate effort to maintain their racial supremacy."

In Mississippi the whites had assured their supremacy in "an orderly and constitutional way," Humphreys told the *Post's* readers. The convention's accomplishments were admirable "from the white man's standpoint." This was something of an understatement. By 1903 only 28 Negroes out of 21,000 of voting age were qualified to vote in Leflore County, Mississippi, and in Washington County, only 388 Negroes out of 44,000. Both counties were in Humphreys's district.

"Yet the door of hope was not closed to the Negro," Humphreys wrote, even though he could not vote. Race relationships in his district were good. ". . . Negroes not only do not desire social equality, but will not tolerate it. Whenever a white man attempts to put himself on terms of social equality with them, they immediately put themselves above him, and thenceforth entertain for him a most apparent and supreme contempt."

Save in politics, said Humphreys, opportunities for the Negro in his district abounded. He cited eight hundred Negro homeowners in Greenville, the largest town in his district. He told of successful Negro doctors, lawyers, trained nurses, brick masons, paper hangers, cotton samplers, bookstore owners, and bankers. He quoted an A. S. Caldwell, a Northern-born citizen of Memphis and a convert to the Southern white point of view: "I believe the Negro would become an industrious citizen if he owned his farm; not education but land ownership was the thing to elevate the Negro." Caldwell, reported Humphreys, had subdivided twenty thousand acres into small farm plots for sale to Negroes, and less than one quarter of them had been repossessed. "In every instance the Negro who bought the land has become a good citizen, an industrious citizen and ambitious further to better his condition."

But an unpleasant truth must be faced: "The great body of the Negroes are not thrifty, but on the contrary are wasteful, improvident, careless, lazy. That every avenue which leads to industrial success is open to the race is shown by the fact that some have attained it in all the callings. The fact that the great mass of the Negro population prefers the ease of indolence and squalor and refuses to pass through the door of hope, may discredit them, but it does not close the door."

All in all, Humphreys concluded, the Negro was prospering under the white man's government in the Yazoo-Mississippi Delta to a degree he had never before known and never could enjoy under a Negro government anywhere in the world.

So ran the kindlier Southern rationalization and defense of the elimination of the Negro as a political being. But it was not the most popular one in the South. The vindication which the mass of the Southern whites applauded most readily and emotionally was neither reasonable nor hopeful nor kind. It rested instead upon racial animosity and the assumption that the Negro was a biologically inferior human. Among its exponents none surpassed, and none save Tom Watson equaled, South Carolina's Benjamin Ryan Tillman, the irascible, hard-faced politician, who, as a militant racist and agrarian, decided for nearly twenty years the political fortunes of his state.

Perhaps Tillman's surly ruthlessness was born of family tragedy. Of his farmer father's seven sons, two were killed in the war, one died of fever, and two others were slain in personal encounters, and one killed a bystander in a gambling quarrel and went to jail for two years; Ben, who wanted desperately to fight for the Confederacy, was laid low by illness after he quit a rustic academy to enlist and remained an invalid for two years, losing his left eye. A member of South Carolina's "All-Outs" who opposed Wade Hampton's moderation, he engaged in the Hamburg and Ellenton riots of 1876 and was singularly successful in terrifying would-be Negro voters. An unsuccessful farmer, he took to politics in 1885 and almost immediately won a tremendous farm following by turning upon the lawyers and merchants of the state as betrayers of the little man and by demanding a state system of agricultural education. He was elected governor in 1890, served later in the United States Senate, and so completely dominated South Carolina that he could even replace such South Carolinians as Hampton and Samuel McGowan with his own men. Under any circumstances he would have been a fearsome opponent. He was at his best, or worst, as a professional race-baiter; and his principal achievement as governor was his political neutralization of the Negro.

For eight years "Pitchfork Ben" Tillman—in his campaign for election to the United States Senate in 1894 he had promised to "stick my pitchfork into [Grover Cleveland's] old ribs"—put in considerable time on the Chautauqua circuit, repeating over and over his conviction that the Negro was a savage, and promising that his state would again resort to fraud and shotguns if the white man's rule was challenged. The Negro, he declaimed, could never be anything but a jungle brute, a creature nearer to the monkey than to man. He defended a caste system, based on race, as the only alternative to the creation of a mulatto people. He shocked his fellow United States senators by justifying lynching as a proper punishment for rape.

"As governor of South Carolina," he said, "I proclaimed that although I had taken the oath of office to support the law and enforce it, I would lead a mob to lynch any man, black or white, who ravished a woman, black or white. This is my attitude, calmly and deliberately taken, and justified by my conscience in the sight of God."

Tillman believed—or so he said—that Radical Reconstruction had so affected the Negro that he would never recover the virtues he had acquired as a slave and that the most foolish of all Reconstruction undertakings had been the attempt to educate the Negro. The education of the inferior race, he said, created longings impossible of achievement; therefore only discontent and crime could ensue. To nullify such a reaction, the South should organize military bodies to keep the Negro in check and to prevent the appointment of Negroes to federal jobs in the South.

"We will not submit to Negro domination under any conditions you may prescribe," he told his fellow senators in 1902. "Now you have got it. The sooner you understand it fully and thoroughly, the better off this country will be."

Many Southerners would not express their feelings so immoderately; but it is certain that the essence of what Tillman told the North was, by the century's end, gospel to the white South. And the white South proceeded to "put the Negro in his place," politically, socially, economically, and psychologically.

The political and social debasement of the Southern Negro after Reconstruction was almost as much the North's doing, though by default, as it was the South's. As long as federal bayonets supported the Republican party in the South the Negro was both a ward of the government and a major bulwark of the national Republican party. When the bluecoats were removed the Negro was no longer ward or political asset. It is all but certain that by 1876 a majority of white Northerners were willing to sacrifice the Negro for the sake of national unity. Moreover, the country was convulsed by economic and political issues that had nothing to do with the role of the Negro in American life. The changed climate of public opinion was reflected in Republican political maneuvering, in a succession of Supreme Court decisions that all but completely negated Radical civil rights legislation, and in the prideful posturing of a nation self-consciously coming of age and measuring itself against older and once stronger world powers.

The Republicans' Southern strategy, as the nineteenth century waned, envisioned the wooing of the white Conservatives and the rebuilding of the party under native white Conservative leaders.

The most devious of the strategists was William E. Chandler, the co-originator of the coup which ultimately made Hayes President. Chandler, who in Reconstruction had been the national party's principal manipulator of Negro and Carpetbag legislatures, tried anything he thought might work in his efforts to split the solid South. His methods were bold, conscienceless, and all but entirely ineffective. He wrote in the Washington *National Republican* in August 1882 that the party's war cry should be "Anything to beat the Bourbons"; and to Senator James G. Blaine he explained, ". . . our straight Republican, Carpetbag-Negro government, whether fairly or unfairly, has been destroyed and cannot be revived . . . ; do not be narrow-minded, or hesitating but place yourself unmistakably on the side of progress at the South." Chandler made available to Billy Mahone, the Virginia maverick, more than two thousand federal patronage jobs and proposed to aid likewise any Southern candidates likely to divide the Southern ranks. In Virginia he backed the Repudiationists, in Tennessee the anti-Repudiationists; he aided the Greenbackers in Texas, Mississippi, South Carolina, and Alabama and opposed them in Arkansas. But nowhere did he encourage Negro Republican leadership.

Meanwhile a number of Supreme Court decisions were nullifying most of the gains made by the Negroes through federal legislation. The Sumner-inspired Civil Rights Act of March 1, 1875, enacted after its author's death and the last to be approved for three quarters of a century, had prohibited discrimination on account of race or color in "inns, public conveyances on land or water, theaters and other places of amusement" and the exclusion of Negroes from jury duty. In 1883, acting upon five cases in which Negroes had been refused equal accommodations or privileges allegedly in violation of the act of 1875, the Supreme Court held that while the Fourteenth Amendment prohibited the invasion of civil rights by the constituted states, it did not protect against the invasion of such rights by individuals, unsupported by state authority. The decision all but ended federal attempts to protect the Negro against discrimination by individual citizens. In 1896 the Court upheld a Louisiana law requiring mandatory segregated railroad facilities, declaring that as long as accommodations were equal segregation did not constitute discrimination and that the Negro was accordingly not deprived of equal protection of the law under the Fourteenth Amendment. In 1898 the Court approved Mississippi's constitutional disfranchisement of the mass of Negroes.

To the political and judicial discouragement of the Negro in his efforts to regain or secure civil equality was added a psychological barrier, inherent in the rising American spirit of nativism and imperialism and in the necessity to find for it a moral vindication.

Nativism had plagued the United States almost since its origins: nativism now compounded of anti-Catholicism, swelling as the tides of immigration brought hundreds of thousands of principally Irish and Italian Roman Catholics to the country; of the fear of foreign radicals, born long since in young America's reaction to the bloody excesses of the French Revolution; and of Anglo-Saxon pretensions to superiority over all other people of whatever nationality or color. Nativism and religious bigotry led to the wartime singling out of Jews as exploiters of the nation's peril. Social unrest and economic upheavals intensified the nativism of working-class Americans as they came up against the competition of the immigrants.

Consciously and unconsciously the North was finding that it could not at one and the same time denounce the South for discrimination against the Negro and indulge comfortably its own prejudices or defend the imperialism with which the Republican party became identified. Southerners jibed at the intellectual racism of Henry Cabot Lodge, who had sought unsuccessfully the passage of the so-called Force Bill in the Negro's behalf. In 1891 Lodge sponsored, apparently ignorant or unmindful of the contradiction, a statistical analysis of the abilities of the American population by national and racial origins. The study indicated the inferiority of every non-English population group and concluded that the new immigration from Europe gravely threatened the nation's racial integrity.

Southern spokesmen for white supremacy mocked then and many times again throughout the next several years, none more acridly than did Ben Tillman, who observed, after Republican foreign policy led to the crushing of the Filipinos: "No Republican leader, not even Governor Roosevelt, will now dare to wave the bloody shirt and preach a crusade against the South's treatment of the Negro. The North has a bloody shirt of its own. Many thousands of them have been made into shrouds for murdered Filipinos, done to death because they were fighting for liberty." When the Supreme Court in 1898 upheld the legality of constitutional disfranchisement in Mississippi, *The Nation* observed the "interesting coincidence that this important decision is rendered at a time when we are considering the idea of taking in a varied assortment of inferior races in different parts of the world . . . which, of course, could not be allowed to vote." And the Boston *Evening Transcript* commented that the Southern policy in regard to race had been adopted by "the very [Republican] party which carried the country into and through a Civil War to free the slaves."

Coercion and constitutional barriers were not the only ingredients in the Conservative formula that kept thousands of Negroes away from the polls either in the waning years of Reconstruction or afterward and induced others to vote as Democrats. Before 1876 disheartened Negro leaders voluntarily deserted the Radicals, taking with them many of the rank and file who listened to them and to such wartime Union generals as Sherman and Meade and Hancock, McClellan, Slocomb, Buell, Thomas, and others who had helped liberate them. The literate ones were reading of the degeneration of Radicalism in the liberal magazines of the North, their tune now changed, as well as in the less detached newspapers of the South. Richard Harvey Cain, Negro editor of the Charleston *Missionary Record,* spoke for many dispirited freedmen when he wrote in 1871: "When the smoke and fighting is over, the Negroes have nothing gained and the [Southern] whites have nothing left, while the jackals have all the booty." The generally better-educated Negroes of the North were scarcely less disgruntled as they saw the fruits of political mastery accrue in the North as in the South to the white mentor.

And the belief soon grew in the North that the Negro was incapable of exercising his right to full citizenship. In April 1877, less than six months after Horace Greeley's death, the *Tribune* commented that the Negroes had proved that "as a race they are idle, ignorant and vicious." Soon after Louisiana's redemption a correspondent for the New Orleans *Times-Picayune,* touring the North, would observe that "in Pittsburgh, the most solidly Republican city on the continent, resolutions favoring speedy solutions of the impending difficulties were most emphatic. If these manifestations mean anything, they mean that any further attempt to kill the goose that laid the golden egg has been abandoned . . . They require other fields for their surplus labor and capital and more and better customers for their surplus manufactures . . . Home rule in the South is considered essential to their prosperity."

Though the Republicans tried to keep the Negro vote together in the North, and largely succeeded, few important plums came the Negro's way. And the Negro found himself, by the turn of the century, in the unenviable position of not being greatly sought after by either party. The Republicans could count on the Negro vote because it then had no other place to go. The Democrats didn't need it because they had eliminated it in the only states where it could then be most effective.

From time to time the Negroes in the North did try to become politically important. They sought to pin down white candidates on their racial attitudes; some among them ran for elective office. But for the most part the Negro voter had sunk by 1900 into an apathy from which he would not be lifted for more than thirty years.

And with political apathy came resignation, for the time being, to the inferior status of which the Jim Crow laws made him ever aware. Had the separate facilities to which he was directed been equal, the segregation upon which the Southern whites insisted would not have become the symbol of that status. But nowhere did the facilities approach equality. Schools, railroad coaches, public toilets, parks—or, for the Negro, the lack of them—all proclaimed Jim Crow's underlying assumption: The Negro not only looked different. He belonged to a sub-human order.

CHAPTER 5

A Culture Distinct

For nearly fifty years before the war the South had been virtually a nation within a nation, and through four years of secession and conflict the Confederacy had functioned as a nation in being. The Reconstruction period made of the white South an all but single folk whose cultural patterns became so formulated as to endure with little change far into the twentieth century.

This Southern culture is many-faceted and sometimes contradictory. It bore and still bears, though decreasingly, the stamp of an agricultural people, gracious, unsophisticated, conservative, and pietistic, bound usually by ties of blood and by the shared ordeal of defeat, unique in the American experience. Its nigh-ineradicable hallmarks are a racially based unity, a regional conformity of thought, a sensitive and sentimental loyalty to an idealized past and a lost cause; a group willingness to condone almost any means for the accomplishment of the overriding end, which is the maintenance of the white South's re-established political and economic supremacy; and the continuance of a social order resting upon racial separateness.

The culture of the South had not always been as rigid. Before the war the South had condoned, if reluctantly, her nonconformists. A man could vote the Whig ticket in a Democratic hotbed, he could free his slaves, he could be a Unionist down to the day of Sumter—and, not infrequently, remain one throughout the struggle—and still not be set apart as an untouchable. But Reconstruction put an end to Southern tolerance of the home-grown dissenter and critic. From the consequent strait-jacketing the South suffered its most grievous and enduring trauma.

These observations may serve to introduce us to a man who could better attest than most to the intellectual peril and social punishment attendant upon cultural nonconformity in the Reconstruction period and afterward. He was pint-sized George Washington Cable, a onetime teen-age Confederate cavalryman and a gifted and courageous man of letters.

Some might have blamed Cable's free-thinking antecedents for his deviationism. True, he had been born, reared, and educated in Louisiana, and during the war the Cables had been loyal Confederates. When his sisters had refused to take the oath of loyalty after the fall of New Orleans, they and their widowed mother were sent beyond the Union lines. With them went the undersized eighteen-year-old brother, so small that he was not suspected of being almost a man grown, and so self-reliant that he had been his mother's principal support since the death of his father four years before. Enlisting forthwith in the Confederate Army, he served until the war's end in the Fourth Mississippi Cavalry, haunting, between skirmishes and battles, regimental headquarters "where men, when they did steal, stole portable volumes, not currycombs."

But the Cables were, nevertheless, open to some suspicion well before George himself began shocking everyone. His first paternal ancestor to reach America was a German named Jakob Kobell, who had left the pleasant valley of the Rhine to escape religious persecution. His grandparents, Virginia slaveowners, had freed their slaves and moved to southern Pennsylvania. His father, also George Washington Cable, was born in Virginia but spent his boyhood in Pennsylvania and had accompanied his parents in 1830 to Indiana where he married Rebecca Boardman, Indiana-born but of a New England family, a fact to which Cable's critics would slightingly refer. In *The South and American Literature, 1607–1900* Jay B. Hubbell discards the assumption so prevalent during Cable's controversial career that he had inherited Puritan traits from his mother, "as if somehow human nature in that region [New England] must be essentially different from that in the deep South." Dr. Hubbell makes the point that more than one Southern writer whom he discusses had one or both parents who were Northerners by birth and yet were not labeled Southern Yankees.

"Cable's mother was a stern and devout member of one of the Evangelical churches," Hubbell writes, "but so were the mothers of Johnston, Lanier and Mark Twain. If Cable was a 'Southern Puritan' so were Stonewall Jackson and thousands of other men in every state in the South . . . It is better to regard Cable as one of the first Southerners of his generation to return to the liberalism of Jefferson, who detested slavery as thoroughly as the little Louisianian."

Certainly young Cable had no affinity with the slave-owning aristocracy. His father was unsuccessful in business in New Orleans. For much of the Cables' married life Rebecca and her children had to stay with relatives in Indiana; and after his father's death George quit school and found work stamping boxes in the Customs Office.

Not yet twenty-one at the war's end, he went to work on a state levee-surveying project on the Atchafalaya River. There he fell seriously ill of malaria and for two years was able to work only intermittently. It was then that he began writing. To the New Orleans *Picayune* he contributed a weekly miscellany under the heading "Drop Shot" which became so successful that it was made a daily feature. In 1869 Cable joined the staff as a reporter. His journalistic career, however, was brief—he was fired from the *Picayune* for refusing to attend a theater to report on a play—and until he began to make a living from his writing he worked variously as an accountant and a correspondence clerk, meanwhile educating himself and becoming proficient in French. After mastering the language he began delving in the city's French archives and fashioning the records he unearthed into his earliest narratives.

Meanwhile Cable's developing social conscience was directing him to the inevitable schism with his fellow Southerners. Even during the war the young cavalryman, hearing that Vice-President Stephens and Governor Robert Toombs were threatening to lead Georgia out of the Confederacy, commented to his comrades that "this shows me that we are fighting to establish a scheme of government that will work our destruction as sure as we succeed. We shall go to pieces as soon as we are safe from outside enemies." Possessed of a curious detachment, the boy had been strongly anti-secessionist; but after the war he had no sense of loyalty to the Union, nor did he then believe that to fight for slavery had been unrighteous. Yet his conscience in time impelled him to conclude that the South had not had the right to secede and that slavery had been an odious institution.

Long before his literary triumphs in the 1870s he was becoming outspokenly critical of the Southern interracial patterns, protesting in letters to the New Orleans press against segregation in schools and on horsecars, and finally turning into as rankling a critic of Southern institutions and attitudes as any Northern reformer. Especially did he infuriate the proud Louisiana Creoles in his highly successful *Old Creole Days* and *The Grandissimes,* though they were widely read elsewhere in the South. The Creoles hated him almost from the beginning. And when, after his initial successes, he won national note and greatly added to his income by lecturing, singing Creole songs and reading his short stories, his inclination to question and to castigate Southern intolerance made him suspect in the South. When in the '80s his untender comments on the treatment of the Negro in the South were published in Northern magazines, the white South disowned him. George Cable was a dangerous radical, his compatriots proclaimed, an agitator for social equality—though he only asked for civil equality—a renegade who was contemptuous of his fellow Louisianians even to the point of intimating that more than a few French Louisiana families had a touch of the tar brush.

Other Southerners who could be characterized as Southern moderates, such as Henry W. Grady, could not accept his views. Cable's first public address, at the University of Mississippi in June 1882, was an augury of displeasure to come. In it he pled for a national point of view in Southern literature: "We have been already too long a unique people," he said. "Let us search provincialism out of the land . . ." Though the audience seemed to receive his comments well enough, the Reverend O. K. Marshall, who had given the commencement sermon the day before, angrily told the audience at the conclusion of the talk that Cable's views were heretical.

After 1880 Cable's concern with social reform transcended his interest in writing and, inescapably, marred his creative work. He began to strike out at any and everything he thought wrong in the South. In 1884 he exposed the convict lease system prevalent in ten Southern states, protesting that the penitentiary systems were based upon profit making alone. Convict leasing, he said, was "murder for money" and the reason for the high death rate among prisoners; he denounced the states for giving to the lessees a life-and-death authority over the convicts, most of whom were Negroes. The attack won him national recognition as a social reformer but made him no friends at home.

In 1885 he wrote for *Century Magazine* "The Freedman's Case in Equity," a protest against the Negroes' unequal treatment before the law. Though he believed that behind the angry outcry against him in the South there was "a silent South needing to be urged to speak and act," Southern condemnation appeared general. His essays thenceforth were rejected by Southern publications, and the South's lecture platforms were denied to him. So bitter and widespread and continuous was the invective that Cable finally left the South and made his home thenceforth in Northampton, Massachusetts.

But his criticisms were not made in vain. The best of his related essays were published in two volumes, *The Silent South* and *The Negro Question,* and were widely read throughout the nation and even in the South. In them Cable denounced the treatment of the Negro as a debased class, an alien menial in a nation whose traditions demanded that a Negro be permitted to be free to the same extent that a white man was. But he made clear that he was speaking of civil rather than social equality; the latter he said was "a fool's dream," and though segregation must be abolished, it would not and should not bring about social comingling. Ridiculing the thesis that the electorate could be purified by eliminating the Negro as a voter, he declared that "no people ever learned how to vote except by voting." He advocated federal aid to education, arguing that since the crime of slavery was the nation's, it was the nation's responsibility to eliminate illiteracy. As for the gradualist: "It is an insult to a forebearing God and the civilized world for us to sit in full view of moral and civil wrongs manifestly bad and curable, saying that we must expect this or that, and that, geologically considered, we are getting along quite rapidly."

Inevitably the idealistic iconoclast, the most distinguished Southern man of letters of his generation next to the poet, Sidney Lanier, was scorned in the South almost throughout his long lifetime.

But Cable earned vindication of a sort before his death in 1925 at the age of eighty-one. Among his literary contemporaries in New Orleans was gentle Grace King, seven years his junior, who likewise wrote of the New Orleans Creole, more lovingly and less penetratingly, and who had despised him as fervently as had her close friend, Charles Gayarré, the Creole historian. In her autobiography, which was prepared for publication just before her death in 1932, Miss King castigated him: "Cable proclaimed his preference for colored people over white and assumed the inevitable superiority . . . of the quadroons over the Creoles," and he had "stabbed the city in the back . . . in a dastardly way to please the Northern press." But twelve years earlier, in 1920, after meeting him for the first time when he was on a rare visit to New Orleans, she gave in an interview with the Boston *Transcript* what was undoubtedly a more honest appraisal of a fellow artist: "I understand him now. I would say he wrote too well about the Creoles. I wanted him to read something of his at a meeting of our Historical Club. Some of the members objected, but we finally made arrangements. He captured the audience. Everybody rushed up and shook hands with him. Many of us never dreamed the day would come when we would shake hands with Cable. . . . The hall was packed. When he finished everybody stood up and I never heard such applause. I am glad that at last he got that compliment from New Orleans. He deserved it, not only as a tribute to his genius, but as compensation for the way we had treated him. I am glad. He is an old man, very picturesque, very sad, with beautiful manners."

In his compulsion to protest against the South's seamier side George Washington Cable was, in his time, all but unique. True, two other Southern writers who were beloved in their homeland, Joel Chandler Harris and Lanier, also said that the South's writers should be national in their viewpoints. But the one endeared himself with his loving tales of an old Negro and a little white boy, and the writings of the other had the timeless, placeless quality of lyric poetry.

Not until well into the next century would other Southern writers come to deal realistically with the traditional South: Mary Johnston, Ellen Glasgow, and James Branch Cabell would be followed by Paul Green, Julia Peterkin, T. S. Stribling, Erskine Caldwell, Eudora Welty, Robert Penn Warren, and William Faulkner.

When they read books at all most Southerners of Cable's day and for a generation afterward preferred authors who enshrined or at least reflected the best of the Southern past, defended their traditional points of view, or engaged, with varying skill and success, in a kind of writing which can be lumped together as belonging to the local color school. To this audience Father Ryan, Alabama's poet priest, was far more welcome than was Walt Whitman. They could solace themselves unashamedly with *The Conquered Banner,* a tender requiem for the vanished Confederacy:

> *Furl that Banner, softly, slowly!*
> *Treat it gently—it is holy—*
> *For it droops above the dead.*

Touch it not—unfold it never,
Let it droop there, furled forever,
For its people's hopes are dead!

The Reconstruction and the post-Reconstruction South did not want to be reminded of the mistakes of the past or the harsher realities of the present; and the North itself was fascinated by the strange region populated by a vivid array of characters, white master and black tenant and former slave, aristocrat and mountaineer, exotic Creole and Elizabethan Anglo-Saxon, coon hunter and cavalier. A whole school of·major and minor Southern writers presented in Northern magazines and a myriad of books published in the North this Southern world and their loving defense of it. Among them were William Hande Browne, co-editor of the Richmond *Eclectic*, who wrote in 1870, "I want the new South, so far as it may be new, to be distinctly and essentially the *South* and not a bastard New England"; Albert Taylor Bledsoe, the kindly idealizer of the Southern past; English-born Francis Hodgson Burnett, one of the first Southern authors to win acceptance in Northern magazines after· the war, and an at least numerically imposing list of others, early and late; Mary Noailles Murfree, James Lane Allen, Sherwood Bonner, Richard Malcolm Johnston; and the later, and with Cable the most successful miner of the local color lode, Thomas Nelson Page; Francis O. Tichnor, Irwin Russell, Charles C. Jones, Jr., Henry Timrod, Paul Hamilton Hayne, unreconstructed intimate of the prewar literary notables of the South, friend of Longfellow and Whittier and gifted reviewer and poet, Augusta Jane Evans, Margaret Junkin Preston, the South's best woman poet of the period; William Gilmore Simms, like Hayne a tragic reminder of war's destructiveness whose prewar historical romances were as praiseworthy as any written in the United States, but who, financially ruined by the war, wrote feverishly, voluminously, and generally poorly in order to feed his family. Much of this writing was genuinely good, especially the works of the more talented members of the local color group. Some of it, as with Mark Twain and Joel Chandler Harris, held sociological undertones too subtle to distract the average reader.

In most of these assorted productions the Negro was the central character, usually as a loyal, likable foil for his master. The numerous and prolific Southern poets, short-story writers, essayists, historians, and biographers and novelists had in common a determination to resist the North's apparent inclination to remake the South in its own likeness. Save for a recognizable few, they did not produce a lasting literature. The principal reason was that most of the South's writers were primarily propagandists, and the defensive quality of their writing was debilitating.

Of the authors of the period, Joel Chandler Harris commented that they were all romancers because they did not dare to draw "an impartial picture of Southern civilization, its lights and its shadows." Another reason, inherent in a culture characterized first by self-isolation and then by defeat, was pitifully summed up in a letter which Sidney Lanier wrote to Bayard Taylor in 1875:

"I could never describe to you what a mere drought and famine my life has been, as regards that multitude of matters which I fancy one absorbs when one is in an atmosphere of art, or when one is in conversational relation with men of letters, with travelers, with persons who have either seen, or written, or done large things. Perhaps you know that with us of the younger generation in the South since the war, pretty much the whole of life has been merely not dying!"

The defensive quality of Southern life and letters derived much of its impetus from the very real injustices done to the memory and to the reputations of Southern wartime leaders, as soon as the conflict had ended, by Northern authors. Writers of Northern textbooks outdid themselves in calumniating the defeated South and in extolling Northern political and military figures whom the South had best reason to hate. In answer Southerners entered into textbook publishing themselves, the principal such venture being the University Publishing Company, located in New York, but owned by three thousand Southern stockholders. The company's authors were pre-eminent Southern scholars—such men as Basil L. Gildersleeve in Latin, Richard Malcolm Johnston in English classics, Matthew F. Maury, the renowned geographer, Charles S. Venable in arithmetic, John and Joseph LeConte in science, George Frederick Holmes in readers, spellers, and history text. The textbooks they produced needed no apology. They were admirably written and in general much superior to their Northern counterparts.

Less laudatory than the works of the South's novelists, poets, historians, and textbook writers was the over-all product of her postwar newspapers which were closer then, as now, to the white Southern masses than were the creative writers. Even by the limited standards of the day few of the fifteen hundred newspapers in the South in 1880, most of them struggling weeklies, had any real professional, financial, or political standing. There were, of course, some brilliant exceptions. Josiah Turner, editor of the Raleigh *Sentinel,* would have been a notable journalist in any age. So would have Francis W. Dawson, an Englishman but a devoted Southern Democrat, who was editor of the Charleston *News and Courier,* Henry Watterson of the Louisville *Courier-Journal,* Albert Pike of the *Memphis Appeal,* Alexander H. Stevenson of the *Atlanta Sun,* Henry W. Grady and Joel Chandler Harris of the *Atlanta Constitution,* and, curiously, Admiral Raphael Semmes, the Annapolis-trained Confederate sea raider who for a while edited the Memphis *Bulletin.* The tradition which these few set would be vigorously preserved.

The good and the poor newspapers were alike almost completely and defensively regional in outlook, though a few editors criticized some aspects of the emerging South.

The most singularly independent among the critical few was Walter Hines Page, the twenty-eight-year-old son of a North Carolina Union Whig, who in 1883 acquired control of the *State Chronicle* in Raleigh and transformed it into an unswerving voice for social and educational change and a persistent questioner of the traditional, already romanticized South. Page, who had remained loyal to the Union, even dared to oppose, with biting wit, the political dominance of the Confederate veteran, and mocked the specter of Negro rule and of religious orthodoxy. He was a bold pleader for public education, not only for the poor whites of the South but for the Negro; he enraged the Bourbon rulers of the post-Reconstruction South and on every issue stood for the common man of both races. He soon found the reaction of his enraged fellow Southerners as intolerable as had Cable; and a few years after establishing his newspaper he sold his interest in the *State Chronicle*, now anything but a financial success, and settled in New York, to spend the rest of his life in the East in newspaper and magazine work and as a book publisher. His *The Southerner*, published well after the turn of the century, was essentially a summation of his opinions of what was wrong with the South.

The Wattersons, the Turners, the Gradys, and the Pages were not typical. Most Southern newspapers of Reconstruction were little more than shrill, bombastic organs of personal opinion or grossly partisan political mouthpieces. Save for the short-lived Radical weeklies, all of them shared a passionate loyalty to the South and maintained a necessary requirement that their editors be courageous men. It was considerably less important for an editor of a Democratic newspaper during Reconstruction to be a grammarian than to be a quick and willing man with a Navy colt, a dirk, or a shotgun. Duels among editors, even within the Democratic fold, or between editors and irate citizens who had been butts of intemperate, generally libelous attacks, were frequent, and the mortality rate among newspapers and their editors was high. They dealt in fire and brimstone. Occasionally, during military Reconstruction, some editors wound up for brief spells in jail, for the Army commanders sometimes tried to intimidate the Southern newspapers, though with little success. But for the most part the federal government and even the Army were amazingly tolerant of these quill-pen warriors, most of them veterans of the Confederate Army, who were so determined to win back with verbal fire power what they had lost to superior military fire power in the war. And intemperate as they were, most of them caring less for factual reporting than for sulphurous rodomontade, they were nevertheless a tremendous force in bolstering the spirit of the resisting South of Reconstruction.

These Southern firebrands did not have the field to themselves; Republican editors appeared in the occupied South even before the war had ended, beginning publication of party newspapers almost as soon as any sizable community was captured. For a while the established newspapers of Vicksburg and of Charleston, under new management, were pro-Union. During Reconstruction an undetermined number of Republican newspapers, probably more than one hundred but most of them short-lived, were established as unabashedly party organs, directly or indirectly subsidized by the Radical state administrations and even the federal government itself.

Some of them became uncommonly prosperous through the printing of legal notices and proceedings as required by state law, through advertisements for the Loyal Leagues, and through party contributions. During the three years of his administration Rufus B. Bullock, the Carpetbag governor of Georgia, authorized $98,000 for the advertising of his proclamations. The total amount spent by the state for the same purpose from 1855 to 1860 had been $5000. Only two of these Southern Republican newspapers, the Savannah *Republican* and the Atlanta *New Era,* could be considered reputable. The rest were wholly and cynically self-seeking. Although it is difficult to determine which was the worst, a Georgia newspaper, *The American Union,* edited by Jay Clarke Swayze, probably deserves that distinction. Somehow Swayze escaped death during his stay in Georgia, but he was assassinated after moving to Kansas. Almost equally vicious was the Augusta *Loyal Georgian,* whose editor, J. E. Bryant, was a Maine man. Among Negro Republican newspapers the most incendiary was the New Orleans *Tribune,* whose editor, a Negro from Santo Domingo, advocated making Louisiana a Negro state; such other Negro publications as the *Weekly Planet* of Memphis, the *Weekly Pilot* of Nashville, and the *Missionary Record* also assiduously cultivated the field of racial discord. Although they enjoyed the protection of the Army for part of the Reconstruction period, these Carpetbag, Scalawag, and Negro newspaper editors must have had courage themselves, for they operated in hostile territory among a citizenry whose hatred was readily expressed in violence.

The loyal Southerner did not really need bard or storyteller or editor to proclaim to the world his conviction that his cause had been just, his abandoned institution of slavery conducive to domestic tranquillity, his leadership spotless, and his temporary withdrawal from the Union sanctioned by the Constitution of the United States itself. He was always doing it himself.

The South's preoccupation with self-justification probably had more to do than did any other factor in the creation of a united folk in the wake of defeat. This determination found many expressions, some of them laughable to the outsider, some noble, some inordinately romantic, and none requiring rationalism as a support. The former soldiers of the Confederacy and the Confederate dead were revered just short of beatification; and rash to the point of lunacy was the quibbler who dared point out that the fighting men of the South, being as human as Yankees, had their own full share of deserters and skulkers and poor leaders. Certain customs, items of daily fare, descriptive words and epithets acquired connotations that survive even now, and rare yet is the Southerner who does not experience a special and sectional reaction to at least some of them: *nigger lover, corn pone, Yankee, collard greens, hushpuppies, hominy grits, white supremacy, burgoo, beaten biscuits, Gettysburg, Vicksburg, Bull Run, Appomattox, uppity, spareribs, gumbo, Southern belle, Southern womanhood, Ku Klux Klan, Bonnie Blue Flag, Scalawag, Black Republican, Southern way of life, foreigner. . . .*

Deservedly Robert E. Lee became and remained long after his death the incorporation of every one of what the South believed to be the finest human qualities. Undeservedly she cloaked in mantles of glory too many lesser men who had followed him.

As early as 1866 Southerners began forming state, local, and Southwide historical societies, primarily to answer Northern versions of the causes and the campaigns of the war and to preserve also the records of individuals, companies, regiments, and armies. The most eminent among these groups was the Southern Historical Society organized in New Orleans in 1869 by General Dabney H. Maury with an imposing array of generals as cofounders—among them R. M. T. Hunter, the Confederacy's Secretary of State, Generals Beauregard and Early and Admiral Semmes—and with a former Confederate chaplain and Presbyterian minister, Benjamin M. Palmer, as its first president.

Almost every Southern community had its monument to the Confederate soldier, its chapters of United Confederate Veterans, in time its Sons and Daughters of the Confederacy. Not for more than three quarters of a century would Vicksburg celebrate the Fourth of July, for it was on that day in 1863 that the starving city on the bluffs of the Mississippi had surrendered. To the individual Yankee who settled among them as farmer, business or professional man, Southerners far more often than not were courteous, even friendly, so long as the newcomer neither preached at them, gloated over the late Northern success in arms, or challenged their mores; but for the unforgetting—a substantial minority—hatred for the genus Yankeensis, in general, was an enduring occupation. The intensity of this dislike can be gauged by the delight of some Southerners when Boston and Chicago suffered disastrous fires in the '70s. They recalled the deliberate wartime flames that had devoured their own cities and homes, and they repeated the bitter comment of Robert Toombs who said of the Chicago fire that while everything was being done to put it out, "the wind is in our favor."

Amusing now, though not then, was the rapidity with which quick-witted businessmen and manufacturers, North and South, took advantage of the near idolatry of the South for the Confederacy and its leaders and turned out a host of products, from gadgets to smoking and chewing tobaccos, clothing and manufactured items, under trade-marks remindful of the Lost Cause, its flag, and its heroes.

The compulsion to defend the Southern past took many forms. The more sentimental reminded each other that no matter how ragged or hungry was the Confederate soldier, there could be found on his person, living or dead, a toothbrush, improvised from an elm twig, and a tattered Testament. Literate Southerners comforted themselves with the couplet of a minor English poet, P. S. Worsley:

> No nation rose so white and fair
> Or fell so pure of crimes.

The South even forgave Vice-President Alexander H. Stephens who had consistently embarrassed and frequently caused considerable trouble to the Confederate government and who had sought a negotiated peace in 1864; for Stephens, after a postwar period of imprisonment, was refused the seat in the United States Senate to which he was elected and, becoming more vigorously anti-Northern than almost any Southerner, wrote his own historical vindication of the South's cause. Jefferson Davis found far more Southern supporters in later years than he had as the Confederacy's President; for his vindication was the vindication of the South. The South's philosophers of government were to argue unendingly that secession had been a constitutional right and thus could not be punished as a crime, and that since secession had been the act of states and not of persons no Confederate should have been personally accused or found guilty. Three generations of Southerners were to derive comfort from a conviction that the theory of state compact and state sovereignty justified secession, that the North bore the brunt of the war guilt, that slavery itself had not been a true cause of the war, and that the postwar Radical administrations in their treatment of the defeated states had simply prostituted the United States Constitution.

And what of the social order?

The hardships and animosities of Reconstruction contributed nothing basically new to the singular social mores which the South had known and abided by before the war; but the afflictions of a worsted region did serve further to set apart the social life of the South, even in its lightest aspects, from the North, if not from the frontier West.

A few sophisticated enclaves to the contrary—New Orleans with its Latin antecedents and propensities, Richmond, the capital of Tidewater Virginia's aristocracy, aloof Charleston, small, untypical Natchez with as many millionaires in the '40s as any eastern city, and, somewhat surprisingly, Nashville—the ante-bellum South neither possessed nor apparently envied the intellectual interests or cosmopolitan eclecticism of the eastern seaboard. Her moral, economic, and political traditions were Cavalier rather than Puritan, frontier rather than urban.

The social life of the Reconstruction South, so far as her poverty and sorrow would permit, took up where it had left off before the war. The South's adaptation of that life to the realities of the ashes and the headstones and her adherence to the ways of a happier, if nostalgically exaggerated, past give neglected testimony to a great folk courage and resilience. Too easy it is to smile at some of the more superficial aspects. To a considerable degree a people are what they imagine themselves to be and to have been. The South's aristocratic and social realities and pretensions were rooted in the land. The land produced the cavalier, the legend went, and the cavalier rode upon the land, and no matter that the colonial ancestor may have had neither blue blood nor freedom of movement. The postwar South sought refuge in the selfsame land and in a land of make-believe, which, as Mark Twain said, was fashioned more by the chivalric notions of Sir Walter Scott than by anything else. The South erected her votive shrines to what she had remembered as good; and the remembrance long survived her time of humiliation and sorrow.

Most Americans of the Reconstruction period, North and South, still lived on farms or in small towns, but above the settled horizons of the North climbed the smokestacks of industry. The North rejoiced in an industrial expansion, and her people indulged—the favored ones—in an orgy of money-making and money-spending which made of the industrialist and the capitalist a demigod to be served and envied and, wherever possible, imitated. The South had known a wealthy class before the war, though a small one, and had contained an appreciable number of well-to-do farmers and townsmen, and some Southerners managed honorably to recoup their fortunes during the Reconstruction period. But the degree to which the South industrialized during Reconstruction was insignificant, both economically and culturally; the region did not experience the cultural and religious impact made by the millions of German, Irish, Scandinavian, Latin, and Mediterranean immigrants, who brought to the North and Midwest the nation's first significant numbers of Roman Catholics and Jews, or the intellectual ferment and ethnic leavening with which these newcomers from Europe impregnated the North and the Midwest.

Instead, as the rest of the nation underwent a massive social transformation, the South, even the minor, industrial South, became in her societal behavior more Southern. Her social leadership rested upon pride of place and family and past more than upon money, though money of itself was not hurtful. Her social pursuits were centered on the home and the church and the informal gathering; in only a few of her cities did social pretensions or activities approach those of the North. Because her men largely kept to farming, their pastimes as well as their occupations remained related to the outdoors.

Some other meaningful aspects of the white Southern culture remain to be inspected. One is the role allotted to woman—the Southern Woman. Before, during, and after Reconstruction—some place her descent to earth in the time of the first World War—Southern Woman stood, willy-nilly, upon a pedestal, placed there by her menfolk who liked her thus elevated as long as there abounded the readily possessible chattels, some as light-skinned as the wives and daughters and sisters whom they so conveniently converted into disembodied, impossibly ethereal idealizations. The Southern Woman had never been such a creature; no woman could be. The prewar planter's wife might have resembled superficially a Godey's Lady's Book cutout; but more often than not she was, and had to be, a tough-fibered, capable administrator, understanding and tolerant of male weaknesses. The woman who survived war and Reconstruction was even more tough-fibered and far more a realist. Her goads and challenges were the poverty and the despair, the bruised pride and the near-unending frustrations of her men. Her coquetry, her pretenses of feminine helplessness and subservience to the male were both balm for the survivors of the war and the readiest way to win a mate from among those outnumbered survivors for whom she and her sisters competed.

It was indeed a make-believe world, but only on the surface. Beneath lay a resolution and a realism that enriched the Southern culture in a way which the South, preferring its romanticized notions, kept too long hidden.

These cultural manifestations set apart the South from the melting pot which was the rest of the United States. Yet Southernness would not have become or remained so recognizably distinct had it not been for the Negro. The presence of the Negro within the Southern society, the conditions under which he had been brought to America and employed here, the vast cultural gap between him and his master, the violence and suddenness with which his position in and his relation to the rest of the American and Southern community had been changed, and, above all, the white South's own counterrevolution against revolutionary Reconstruction, conspired to weave into the cultural design of the white South some persistent contradictions which unmistakably combine to identify the region.

These contradictions are readily perceivable; all of them can be resolved by the same human circumstance, the presence of the Negro.

Here are the contradictions and their resolutions.

Much of the South was settled as early as or earlier than the rest of the colonies; yet even today it remains the principal American frontier.

The South remains a frontier because for nearly three hundred years it geared itself to a primitively agricultural economy, resting on the backs of unskilled black men, slave and free. Its technological potential and its industrial balance were delayed until it was overtaken by the inevitable failure of a cheap-labor, one-crop economic system.

In the South, for longer than have the people of any other American region, live the nation's most homogeneous people, sharers of a common language, a common tenure, a once common occupation, and a common religious creed. Yet among these inheritors dwell also the largest unassimilated and still unassimilable racial group in the United States.

The imported and enslaved Negro perforce adopted the folkways of the homogeneous white South, but he did not share in that homogeneity because of the conditions of his presence, his cultural lag and the recognizable physical differences between master and slave.

In common with all people of predominantly agricultural background the Southerner has an abiding affection for the land, for the home place of his fathers. Yet a larger proportion of its farm workers are and traditionally have been landless; and its land has been the nation's most cruelly wasted.

Cheap labor and one-crop agriculture are wasteful. The Southern white landowner had no other course after the Civil War than to continue the old ways under a system of landless tenantry for the freed black and the submarginal white man.

The South, predominantly Protestant, can probably count more churchgoers in proportion to her population than can any other region, and organized religion plays a wholesome and unusually significant part in the Southern mores. But in most Southern churches little practical stress is placed upon Christianity as bespeaking the brotherhood of man under the fatherhood of God.

Most Christians in the South make special reservations. Fundamentalist interpretation of the Old Testament, tradition, emotion, custom, and even law combine to exclude the Negro from the Protestant Christian fellowship.

The Southerner is an individualist. Nowhere else is the citizen as likely to stand up so persistently for his personal rights, his personal honor, and his personal opinions. Yet, politically and in certain aspects of his social thinking, the Southerner is also the nation's most regimented man, a conformist who finds it inexpedient or disloyal to differ from his neighbor.

The otherwise independent-minded white Southerner is a prisoner of rigid social and political conformity because of a folk insistence upon racially-based unity.

The South is a kindly land to the stranger. Southern courtesies and Southern hospitality have been overemphasized and exaggerated, but it is likely that Southerners are more ready than are other Americans to welcome and share with the visitor whatever they have. Yet they, above all Americans, are suspicious of the stranger who challenges and criticizes their social and economic and political structures.

Southern suspicion of the critical stranger goes back at least as far as the days of the Underground Railroads through which the escaping slaves were spirited to freedom. It has encompassed in turn the Reconstruction Carpetbagger, the free-lance writer, and the sociologist for whom the Negro in the South has been an irresistible and often a remunerative magnet.

The Southerner, white and black, is proverbially gentle in manner. It has been said that until he is angered enough to kill you he will treat you politely. Yet in crimes of passion the South leads the rest of the country.

White Southern tolerance of violence is greatly caused by racial considerations, though the distorted notions of personal honor and the historic necessity for the frontiersman and the farmer and the small-town citizen to be his own policeman cannot be overlooked. Moreover, so long as the Negro, who commits most of the South's crimes, harms only other Negroes, the white Southerner remains relatively indifferent to his lawbreaking. On the other hand, the white Southerner has reacted severely when the white man has been the Negro's victim. Race has been the determining factor in crime and punishment.

The South is patriotic. For the past seventy-five years she has voluntarily responded to the calls to battle in relatively greater numbers than has any other section; and, if only because the region knows what it is to be a defeated and overrun land, her spokesmen have consistently supported measures to insure the nation's safety. Yet the Southerner is, under certain provocations, more defiant of national authority than is any other American.

The rebellious Southerner of today is a rebel only when the racial patterns he has established are threatened by federal authority. Fear of Negro domination was the chief reason for the formation of the old Ku Klux Klan immediately after the Civil War. Antagonism toward the racial policies of the Roosevelt and Truman administrations was almost the only reason for the States' rights revolt of 1948. Southern discontent today arises principally from the Supreme Court's historic school desegregation decision.

The South probably takes her politics more intensely than does any other area, yet relatively fewer of its citizens vote, and more obstacles are put in the way of their voting than anywhere else in the United States.

The otherwise political Southerner is willing to make voting difficult because, up to now, the restrictive devices kept far more Negroes from voting than whites. Similarly Southern rejection of a two-party system continues principally because of the fear that the Negro could otherwise hold the balance of political power.

In all such matters there persists a unity still so unbreached that the white

Southerner who utters aloud the private maxim of George Washington Cable is comparatively a lonely man—though not nearly as lonely as was the little Louisianian who coined that maxim for his own guidance:

"There is no room in America for a peasantry."

A people which had defended, condoned, or passively accepted the institution of slavery could not encourage a cultural convulsion that would permit the metamorphosis from slave to equal within the span of a year or ten years or even within what now approaches a full century. Before the disquieting majority be judged, study what one observer said of George Washington Cable and the people from whom he severed himself. Cable belonged, so William Malone Baskervill perceived in 1897 in his *Southern Writers,* to "the class of thoroughgoing men, actuated by thoroughgoing logic, lovers of abstract truth and perfect ideals, and it was his lot to be born among a people who by the necessities of their situation were controlled by expedience. They were compelled to adopt an illogical but practical compromise between two extremes which were logical but not practical."

CHAPTER 6

Heritage

EIGHTY years have gone by since the white Democrats of Louisiana and South Carolina traded off austere Samuel Tilden for Republican surrender of control of state, county, and community governments in those states; and it is nearly seventy years since the careful Southern legalists began fashioning the state constitutions which would insure in perpetuity, so they believed, white political rule no matter how greatly the white citizenry might be outnumbered by the challenging Negro.

Since then our nation has fought two major and two lesser wars and has become inextricably involved in a world revolution of ideology and of race. Experimental man has produced the ultimate tools for the destruction or the transformation of life on his planet. So much has almost every aspect of American life been altered that many of us, in fear or hope for tomorrow, forget today the crises of yesterday.

But the memory of Reconstruction endures meaningfully among nearly thirty million white Americans in the South and, to a considerably less extent, among the ten million Southern Negroes. The yet livid scar of Reconstruction also affects, if indirectly, one hundred and twenty million other Americans and, most certainly, many other people elsewhere who have never heard of Thaddeus Stevens of Pennsylvania or of South Carolina's Wade Hampton or of Louisiana's White Leagues. Millions of distant, dark-skinned folk have been continuously aroused against the United States by contemporary incidents within our borders which have their remote origins in Reconstruction itself.

In our day the scar's outline may have seemed to grow fainter. But with the crucial decision of the United States Supreme Court to reverse all earlier related rulings, and so make illegal the continuance of racially separate public school systems, old specters took menacing shape again, and so quickly that we know surely that they had never really vanished. The same resolutions offering resistance to national authority are being adopted today as if time since 1876 had stood still. Let the rest of the nation speak in indignation to the South for an unpunished racial murder or in protest against the denial of the ballot or in rebuke for disobedience of the Supreme Court's edict, and the voices of most of the South's politicians, much of its press, and even some among its educators and churchmen, sound the grim echoes from the unforgotten past.

Leave us alone . . . It's our problem and we know how to handle it . . . Clean up your own backyard first . . . This is a white man's country . . . Interposition . . . Nullification . . . Go to Hell . . .

Despite historical re-evaluations—and how soon or how often have the records of history altered folklore?—the cherished tales and convictions and stereotypes have persisted. *We were needlessly humiliated,* men still say in the South as if they were talking of yesterday; *Yankee retaliation after the surrender violated all civilized conduct, for never before had the foot of the ignorant slave been placed by white hands upon the necks of a defeated enemy who was also white . . . All thieving is evil but the thief who steals from the hungry and the helpless, with a policeman at his side and the government urging him on, is the worst of all thieves . . . The education of the ignorant is a worthy objective, but not a policy of education which abandons to the spoilsmen the established institutions and concentrates upon an educational revolution . . . The Southern white man who linked his fortune with the Northern interloper was a Scalawag, a predatory renegade to caste and race or a poor white hating his betters. The Northerner who came down hungrily was a graceless adventurer with all that he owned packed in a carpetbag, his single piece of luggage; and his only purpose was to enrich himself and to debase the South by forcing racial intermingling and even intermarriage . . . The Negro politician was an ignorant buffoon, a stupid tool, a defiant savage, intent only upon getting what he could, lusting for the women of his former masters and ready to sell his vote and his soul itself for anything but a Confederate dollar . . . The Yankee churchmen knew only the God of wrath and came to desecrate and to offer a spurious Christianity to the Negro and to destroy their white brothers in*

Christ . . . The Ku Klux Klan of Reconstruction and all who turned to the rifle and the faggot, the rope and the lash in the name of white supremacy were the South's saviors; heroic, consecrated men whose ghostly riding alone kept alive the hope of white survival . . .

The proportion of fact to fable varies with the purposes of the narrators and the severity of the old or new experience about which the tales revolve. The former Confederate soldier might have confided to a crony over a tall julep, seventy-five years ago, that he had had an odd sort of liking for the Yankee who settled down on the next farm to his after the war. But this he would not shout from the hustings. A minister in an Alabama church of Reconstruction might have admitted privately that the invading Yankee Methodists had a sincere if misguided sense of divine mission. He could not say this to his congregation, then or even now, without furious challenge.

A story about two young American college students who were on a bicycle tour of Ireland one summer during the troubles of the 1920s is applicable here. The unhappy island was wracked by assassinations, executions, and guerilla warfare between the Irish Republican Army and the British-directed constabulary, the Black and Tans. One day the travelers halted in a small village not far from Dublin for a mug of beer. They were soon in conversation with an old Irish woman who had recognized them as Americans and had inquired about her kinsmen in Boston. Soon she was telling tales of British perfidy and tyranny.

"And do ye know what was done to three hundred poor Irish lads only a stone's throw from this very place?" she demanded. The Americans said they did not know.

"They were burned to death at the stake, poor lads, every mother's son of them!"

"My God," answered one of the listeners, wondering how they had missed such a story in the newspapers. "And when did this awful thing take place?"

The old woman's voice quavered with rage. "Cromwell did it," she shrilled, "the dirty, murdering dog."

And that's that. The losers always remember strife and ruin and abuse far longer and more imaginatively than do the victors, whether they dwell in Ireland or India or Georgia; and eighty years do not seem so long when we consider that men presently in their prime and occupying places of political leadership in the South today were born no later than midway between the beginning of Reconstruction and now. As boys and young men they heard the patriarchal—and matriarchal—tales told and believed by teller and hearers as unchallenged proof of Yankee avarice and vengeance and Southern suffering and heroism. And no matter how filmy the stuff of which some of the tales are spun, they cannot be laughed away.

There are other reasons for the survival of Reconstruction memories. Military disaster dealt a profound psychological blow to a people who had produced and followed the nation's only warrior caste and had believed themselves militarily invincible. And in the wake of Appomattox came the enormous complications and chaos attendant upon the need to revise a slave-based agricultural economy which no longer existed as such. The freeing of the slaves had wiped out more than two billion dollars in once negotiable investments. The destruction of the South's railways and rolling stock and much of its scant industry, and the prewar neglect of its industrial potential in favor of cotton, left the South no other road to recovery than agriculture. The lack of a continuing national program to rehabilitate the former slave, and to aid the dispossessed master, the small non-slaveholding farmer, and the urban worker retarded the region's economic recovery.

The Freedmen's Bureau which sought to provide the Negro with employment and food and medical and hospital care and to resettle the wandering masses was staffed too much by ambitious political mediocrities, by incompetents, and by some thieves, and it failed to win support from the affronted whites. Instead the Bureau was added to the wrathful legend.

More important than these material stimuli to the South's long memory was the political convulsion which enfranchisement of the Negro brought about. To military chastisement and economic chaos were joined a revolutionary political realignment and an ultimatum to the South. Never before had a nation or a people been put into political irons concurrently with the unshackling of an imprisoned multitude, different in race, culturally disparate, and untrained for freedom.

Moreover, some of the aggravations that accompanied the beginning of the Reconstruction era were needlessly petty, stupid, shortsighted, or cruel. The removal of the proscribed military buttons from uniforms which were all so many had to wear . . . The seizure of Southern churches for the use of ministers of Northern denominations . . . The requirement of the loyalty oath from Southern women when they appeared at a military headquarters to seek rations or assistance. These things were remembered. Forgotten were the generosity with which Northern charitable groups soon aided destitute Southerners; the generally good relations between white federal occupation troops and the people, and the selflessness of the Yankee schoolteachers whose efforts to educate the Negroes had, in time, beneficial results. The wrath and the shame of the white Southerners were heightened by the knowledge that their fellow white men, their very brothers, were elevating the black men to political equality. The South was not so much galled by the political corruption of Reconstruction as it was by the fact of Negro participation, free of Southern direction, in the region's political life. Even had the neophyte Negro lawmakers been uniformly honest and capable, they would have been resented almost as much; for such honesty contradicted the white man's concept of the Negro in politics. What was basically intolerable was the knowledge that the white Radical Republicans in Washington and in the Southern states were principally responsible for the Negro on the bench, in the legislature, and in Washington itself, and especially so since the Southerner read into the demands for Negro suffrage and political acceptance a social meaning which was unacceptable to him.

The negation of the Radical philosophy of Negro political equality thus became and remained the first consideration of the Southern white leadership which emerged in reaction to Radical Reconstruction policies. The restoration of white domination—which had been threatened seriously in its political aspects but hardly at all in the economic or social spheres—took precedence over all else, over material needs, basic political cleavages within the white group, and even honesty in government itself.

The racial aspect of the Reconstruction struggle doomed all programs of the Radicals and left tragic legacies which have not yet been expended or likely will be in our time. The legacies are fourfold—political, cultural, economic, and moral. Before we examine them let us first review the positive accomplishments of the Reconstruction administrations and then the ancillary causes for the eventual resurgence of the white Southern Democrat.

The South in its bitterness and the North in its disinterest are alike unaware of the temporary or lasting achievements of the Reconstruction invaders. The Carpetbag administrations did assure free school systems to both races, the first to be provided not only for Negroes but for many of the whites. Their record in public school expansion was, in general, and despite accompanying corruption, better than were the performances of the Redemptionist administrations which followed Reconstruction, and, for that matter, better than the public educational achievements of the prewar South where the novel idea of free, mass education had not caught on. The Reconstruction administrations also sought, with at least temporary success, to widen the democratic base. The constitutions which they adopted provided for efficient changes in the taxing systems and the judiciary, and some of their reforms were kept intact in the constitutions of the white Redemptionists. They introduced new social services to an area chronically lacking in them. Their efforts to rebuild war-destroyed roads, schools, and public buildings were commendable.

This is not to say that on balance the good outweighed the bad. It did not; but had the constructive record been far better, Radical Reconstruction would nevertheless have failed. The refusal of the white South to accept the new status of the Negro was the principal and the only needful reason.

What were the other reasons for the failure?

High among these was the watering down of initial Radical idealism. The zealots gave way to the practical politicians and the plunderers, so that in time the nation, no less than the South, began to sicken of the looting that was as marked in the North, during the Grant administration, as it was anywhere in the Southern states. Another reason, and a telling one, was the absence of a lasting program for the material rehabilitation of the freed Negro. His benefactors were chiefly concerned with him as a political force, and eventually he found this out. Republican manipulation of the Negro voter ultimately aroused Northern sympathy for the Southerners and strengthened the resurgent Democratic party. The roughshod tactics of the Carpetbaggers made it impossible for them to enlist any appreciable support from the Southern white leadership. In time thousands of Negro voters in the South also became wary of their Republican bosses; and, because of their disillusion or through Democratic coercion and bribery, they entered the party of their former masters. But all of these reasons together were not as responsible for the doom of Reconstruction as was the racially motivated unity of the white Southerner.

What is now set down here about the cultural, political, economic, and moral legacies of Reconstruction is, of course, a general summation and one not uniformly applicable.

More often than not the middle-aged and older Southerner—the son or grandson of Confederate and Redeemer—is aggressively regional-minded about almost everything. He looks upon himself as a citizen of a nation within a nation and acts accordingly. His near single-minded concentration upon his problems and his biases cannot be ascribed solely to Reconstruction, but the period provided its most durable motivation. He has inherited and retained his Reconstruction forebears' suspicion of the critical stranger, the inquisitive writer, the agent of a central government, and the visiting student of his affairs. He is distrustful of the younger generation's talk of "moderation" of his insistence upon racial separateness. His solidarity is at the same time healthy and disruptive. In his self-conscious homogeneity he gives his strongest loyalties to the family, the clan, the community, and the region; and in a day of centralization of regulatory functions and of metropolitan anonymity these localized and individualistic concerns often make for a needed balance. When he dwells upon his past, which is rather often, he prefers folklore to fact if fact is unpalatable; and when reason goes against his convictions he is likely to discard reason. In his loyalties and hatreds he is an extremist. He is acutely sensitive to criticism even while he denies that he is even attentive to it; and he is convinced, and with considerable reason, that his region is misunderstood, his problems minimized, and his good intent doubted elsewhere. His homeland has produced more than its share of creative folk, but few have escaped the confines of regionalism. He has been diverted by his racial concerns from broader and more purposeful considerations. He suffers still from the intellectual impoverishment experienced during Reconstruction because of necessary pre-occupation with political and economic survival.

Even though his region peculiarly reflects a political genius, his political legacy has not enriched him. Save for the relatively brief period of Populist-Bourbon conflict over yet unresolved issues, his politics mirror primarily the factionalism inevitable in a one-party society, the racial compartmentalization within which his leaders work, and a unity based on race, without reference to economic goals and needs.

Yet social consciousness, which survives today, was characteristic of most of the new breed of demagogues of the post-Reconstruction period. They were aware of the plain people and of the need for social reform. But they struck brutally at the Negro, either from actual distaste or for fear of being tarred as "nigger lovers" and disrupters of white unity. Of all the notable Southern demagogues only Huey P. Long of Louisiana did not make the Negro a whipping boy. So the Southerner continues to insist upon one-party conformity—at least on state and local levels—for the very logical reason that should the Southern whites be divided the Negro could hold the balance of power within the region just as he does in a half dozen or more Northern states. The white South regained political control during Reconstruction in great part through bloodshed and corruption, and it has remained relatively indifferent to corruption and inefficiency in its political life so long as its white Democratic foundations are not threatened.

The economic impact of Reconstruction has also persisted. Since the North devised no alternate program, the Southerner of Reconstruction had no other choice at Reconstruction's outset than to make the new relationship between freed black worker and impoverished landowner as nearly like the old system as possible. He usually wanted it that way anyhow, if only because of a preference for the familiar. In his traditional indifference to other commercial pursuits than the raising of cotton, tobacco, rice, and sugar, he permitted his forests to be destroyed and much of his other natural resources appropriated by the Northern financier and speculator. Because of his political peonage and the long national dominance of the Republican party he could do nothing against the high tariffs which further disadvantaged him. He accepted and even encouraged the idea that the lower the wage scale the better, primarily because he was unwilling for the Negro to receive in other competitive pursuits the wages that he was both reluctant and unable to pay him in the cotton field. The plantation system and the competitive presence of the landless white and the Negro discouraged the immigrant who could have brought new talents and determination. Post-Reconstruction's small farm owner and poor white submitted to economic exploitation by the bankers, the lawyers, and the generals, the planter aristocracy, partly because these had been their wartime leaders and mostly because, before and after the Populist lapse, they became convinced again that salvation lay in racial solidarity.

How long will the memory of the Reconstruction period affect the South and the nation?

There can be no certain answer. The South is reacting in predictable fashion to old and new racial pressures. The doctrine of nullification has been advanced as fervently as it was ever propounded by John C. Calhoun. Today the Southern moderate is as suspect as were his Reconstruction prototypes. Today a more determined Negro is again faced by a nearly unified white South no less determined than in 1868 to circumvent the intent of the federal government. Today the singing of "Dixie," the waving of a Confederate flag, and the stump orator's passionate appeal to the past are as sure fire as in the 1870s.

And the end is not in sight.

Bibliography

Andrews, Sidney: *The South Since the War, 1866.*

Aptheker, Herbert: *Negro Slave Revolts in the United States.* 1939.

Barnard, Harry: *Rutherford B. Hayes and His America.* 1954.

Beale, Howard K.: *On Rewriting Reconstruction History.* 1940.

Beale, Howard K.: *The Critical Year: A Study of Andrew Johnson and Re-construction.* 1930.

Beard, Odum Howard W.: *The Way of the South.* 1947.

Blake, Nelson M.: *William Mahone of Virginia, Soldier and Political Insurgent.* 1935.

Bond, Horace M.: *Negro Education in the South.* 1939.

Bowers, Claude G.: *The Tragic Era.* 1929.

Bradford, Gamaliel: *Confederate Portraits.* 1914.

Buck, Paul H.: *The Road to Reunion, 1865–1900.* 1937.

Buck, Solon J.: *The Agrarian Crusade: A Chronicle of the Farmer in Politics.* 1921.

Carter, Hodding: *Lower Mississippi.* 1942.

Cash, W. J.: *The Mind of the South.* 1941.

Cate, Wirt Armistead: *Lucius Q. C. Lamar.* 1935.

Chandler, Julian A. C.: *The South in the Building of the Nation.* (13 vols.) 1909–13.

Channing, Edward: *History of the United States.*

Chesnut, Mary B.: *Diary from Dixie.* 1929.

Clayton, Powell: *The Aftermath of the Civil War in Arkansas.* 1915.

Cohn, David L.: *The Life and Times of King Cotton.* 1956.

Coulter, E. Merton: *Civil War and Readjustment in Kentucky.* 1926.

Coulter, E. Merton: *Parson Brownlow, Fighting Parson of the Southern Highlands.* 1937.

Coulter, E. Merton: *The South During Reconstruction, 1865–1877.* 1947.

Craven, Avery O.: *The Growth of Southern Nationalism, 1848–1861.* 1953.

Davidson, Donald: *The Tennessee.* Vol. 2. 1948.

Dorris, Jonathan Truman: *Pardon and Amnesty under Lincoln and Johnson.* 1953.

Dorris, Jonathan Truman: *Pardon Seekers and Brokers: A Sequel of Appomattox.*

Du Bois, W. E. B.: *Black Reconstruction.* 1934.

Dunning, William A.: *Reconstruction, Political and Economic.* 1907.

Eckenrode, Hamilton J.: *Rutherford B. Hayes, Statesman of Reunion.* 1930.

Eckenrode, Hamilton J., and Conrad, Bryan: *James Longstreet, Lee's War Horse.* 1936.

Farish, Hunter D.: *The Circuit Rider Dismounts: A Social History of Southern Methodism, 1865–1900.* 1938.

Fleming, Walter L.: *Civil War and Reconstruction in Alabama.* 1905.

Fleming, Walter L.: *The Sequel of Appomattox.* 1919.

Fletcher, John Gould: *Arkansas.* 1947.

Franklin, John Hope: *From Slavery to Freedom.* 1947.

Franklin, John Hope: *The Militant South, 1800–1861.* 1956.

Frazier, E. Franklin: *The Negro in the United States.* 1949.

Furnas, J. C.: *Goodbye to Uncle Tom.* 1956.

Garner, James W.: *Reconstruction in Mississippi.* 1901.

Going, Allen J.: *The South and the Blair Education Bill.* The Mississippi Valley Historical Review. September, 1957.

Goldstein, Naomi Friedman: *The Roots of Prejudice Against the Negro in the United States.* 1948.

Gonzales, John Edwin: *William Pitt Kellogg, Reconstruction Governor of Louisiana.* The Louisiana Historical Quarterly. April, 1946.

Hart, Albert Bushnell: *The Southern South.* 1910.

Henry, Robert S.: *The Story of Reconstruction.* 1938.

Hesseltine, William B.: *Civil War Prisons.* 1930.

Hesseltine, William B.: *History of the South.* 1936.

Hesseltine, William B.: *The Propaganda Literature of Confederate Prisons.* The Journal of Southern History. February, 1935.

Hesseltine, William B.: *Ulysses S. Grant, Politician.* 1935.

Hicks, John D.: *The Populist Revolt.* 1931.

Higham, John: *Strangers in the Land.* 1955.

Holzman, Robert S.: *Stormy Ben Butler.* 1954.

Horn, Stanley F.: *The Invisible Empire: The Story of the Ku Klux Klan, 1866–1871.* 1939.

Hubbell, Jay B.: *The South and American Literature, 1607–1900.* 1954.

Hundley, Daniel R.: *Social Relations in Our Southern States.* 1860.

Hyman, Harold Melvin: *Era of the Oath.* 1954.

Jarrell, H. M.: *Wade Hampton and the Negro.* 1949.

Johnson, Allen, and Malone, Dumas (editors): *Dictionary of American Biography.* 1935.

Johnson, Gerald W.: *American Heroes and Hero Worship.* 1941.

Johnson, Manie White: *The Colfax Riot of April, 1873.* The Louisiana Historical Quarterly. July, 1930.

Kennedy, John F.: *Profiles in Courage.* 1956.

Knight, Edgar W.: *Public Education in the South.* 1922.

Leach, Marguerite T.: *The Aftermath of Reconstruction in Louisiana.* The Louisiana Historical Quarterly. July, 1949.

Loth, D. G.: *Public Plunder.* 1938.

Lynch, D. T.: *The Wild Seventies.* 1941.

McDaniel, Hilda Mulvey: *Francis Tillou Nicholls and The End of Reconstruction.* The Louisiana Historical Quarterly. April, 1949.

Milton, George F.: *The Age of Hate: Andrew Johnson and the Radicals.* 1930.

Minutes of the Holston Conference of the Methodist Church, 1863–1880.

Moore, A. B.: *Railroad Building in Alabama During the Reconstruction Period.* The Journal of Southern History. November, 1935.

Morison, Samuel Eliot, and Commanger, Henry Steele: *The Growth of the American Republic.* 1942.

Morris, Richard B.: *Encyclopedia of American History.* 1953.

Morrow, Ralph E.: *Northern Methodism in the South During Reconstruction.* The Mississippi Valley Historical Review. September, 1954.

Nevins, Allan: *The Emergence of Modern America, 1865–1878.* 1927.

Nixon, Raymond B.: *Henry W. Grady, Spokesman of the New South.* 1943.

Nordhoff, Charles: *The Cotton States in 1875.* 1876.

Odum, Howard W.: *An American Epoch.* 1930.

Otken, Charles H.: *The Ills of the South.* 1894.

Owsley, Frank L.: *Plain Folk of the Old South.* 1949.

Patton, James W.: *Unionism and Reconstruction in Tennessee, 1860–1869.* 1934.

Pearson, Charles C.: *The Readjuster Movement in Virginia.* 1917.

Percy, William Alexander: *Lanterns on the Levee.* 1941.

Phillips, Ulrich B.: *American Negro Slavery.* 1929.

Pike, James S.: *The Prostrate State: South Carolina under Negro Government* (new ed.). 1935.

Pressly, Thomas J.: *Americans Interpret Their Civil War.* 1954.

Randall, James G.: *The Civil War and Reconstruction.*

Ravenel, Henry William: *The Private Journal of Henry William Ravenel, 1859–1887.* Edited by Professor Arney Robinson Childs. 1947.

Reid, Whitelaw: *After the War—A Southern Tour.* 1866.

Rust, W. A., Jr.: *The Influence of the Methodist Church upon Reconstruction.* Susquehanna University Studies, I. 1937.

Rust, W. A., Jr.: *Registration and Disfranchisement under Radical Reconstruction.* The Mississippi Valley Historical Review. August, 1934.

Sandburg, Carl: *Abraham Lincoln: The War Years,* Vol. 4. 1939.

Schurz, Carl: *Reminiscences.* 1907–08.

Senlon, Paul E.: *The Notorious Swepson-Littlefield Fraud.* Florida Historical Quarterly. April, 1954.

Simkins, Francis Butler: *Ben Tillman's View of the Negro.* The Journal of Southern History. May, 1937.

Simkins, Francis Butler: *New Viewpoints of Southern Reconstruction.* The Journal of Southern History. February, 1939.

Simkins, Francis Butler: *The South Old and New.* 1947.

Simkins, Francis Butler: *The Tillman Movement in South Carolina.* 1926.

Simkins, Francis Butler, and Woody, Robert H.: *South Carolina During Reconstruction.* 1932.

Skipper, Ottis C.: *De Bow's Review After the Civil War.* The Louisiana Historical Quarterly. April, 1956.

Stokes, Thomas L.: *The Savannah.* 1951.

Stryker. Lloyd P.: *Andrew Johnson, A Study in Courage.* 1929.

Suchon. Walter J., Jr.: *The Dubious Origin of the Fourteenth Amendment.* Tulane Law Review. December, 1953.

Swint, H. L.: *The Northern Teachers in the South.* 1941.

Taylor, Lieutenant General Richard: *Destruction and Reconstruction.* 1877.

Thomas, David Y.: *Arkansas in War and Reconstruction.* 1926.

Thompson, C. Mildred: *Reconstruction in Georgia, 1865–1872.* 1915.

Thorp, Willard: *A Southern Reader.* 1955.

Vestler, C. M.: *American Radicalism.* 1946.

Wallace, D. D.: *The Question of the Withdrawal of the Democratic Presidential Electors in South Carolina in 1876.* The Journal of Southern History. August, 1942.

Warmoth, Henry C.: *War, Politics and Reconstruction: Stormy Days in Louisiana.* 1930.

Weatherford, W. D.: *American Churches and the Negro.* 1957.

Wecter, Dixon: *When Johnny Comes Marching Home.* 1944.

Wiley, Bell Irwin: *The Life of Johnny Reb.* 1941.

Wiley, Bell Irwin: *Vicissitudes of Early Reconstruction Farming in the Lower Mississippi Valley.* The Journal of Southern History. November, 1937.

Williams, T. Harry: *An Analysis of Some Reconstruction Attitudes.* The Journal of Southern History. November, 1946.

Wilson, Woodrow: *History of the American People.* 1901.

Wish, Harvey: *The Slave Insurrection Panic of 1856.* The Journal of Southern History. May, 1939.

Woodward, C. Vann: *Origins of the New South, 1877–1913.* 1951.

Woodward, C. Vann: *Reunion and Reaction.*

Woodward, C. Vann: *The Irony of Southern History.* The Journal of Southern History. February, 1953.

Woodward, C. Vann: *The Strange Career of Jim Crow.* 1955.

Woodward, C. Vann: *Tom Watson, Agrarian Rebel.* 1938.

Woodward, C. Vann: *Tom Watson and the Negro in Agrarian Politics.* The Journal of Southern History. February, 1935.

Index